London

With Day Trips to Bath, Brighton, Cambridge, Oxford, Windsor, and Other Popular Destinations

ECONOGUIDE.COM | 2002

Corey Sandler

Contemporary Books

Chicago   New York   San Francisco   Lisbon   London   Madrid   Mexico City
Milan   New Delhi   San Juan   Seoul   Singapore   Sydney   Toronto

Contemporary Books

A Division of The **McGraw-Hill** *Companies*

1 2 3 4 5 6 7 8 9 0   LBM/LBM   0 9 8 7 6 5 4 3 2 1

ISBN 0-8092-2625-1
ISSN 1523-5963

This book was set in Stone Serif by Word Association, Inc.
Printed and bound by Lake Book Manufacturing

Cover photograph copyright © Corbis/DigitalStock

Econoguide is a registered trademark of Word Association, Inc.

McGraw-Hill books are available at special quantity discounts to use as premiums and sales promotions, or for use in corporate training programs. For more information, please write to the Director of Special Sales, Professional Publishing, McGraw-Hill, Two Penn Plaza, New York, NY 10121-2298. Or contact your local bookstore.

This book is printed on acid-free paper.

Contents

Acknowledgments

This book is dedicated to my parents Herbert and Arlene Sandler, the original non-accidental tourists.

Dozens of hardworking and creative people helped move my words from the keyboard to the place where you now read this book.

Among the many to thank are Adam Miller and Julia Anderson of Contemporary Books.

Here at Word Association, Andrea Boucher polished my words with skill and good humor. As always, thanks to Janice Keefe for running the office and the author.

And thanks to you for buying this book. We all hope you find it of value; let us know how we can improve the book in future editions.

If you send a letter, please enclose a stamped envelope if you'd like a reply; no phone calls, please.

Corey Sandler
Econoguide Travel Books
P.O. Box 2779
Nantucket, MA 02584

To send electronic mail, use the following address:
csandler@econoguide.com.

You can also consult our Web page:
🖳 **www.econoguide.com.**

I hope you'll also consider the other books in the *Econoguide* series. You can find them at bookstores, or ask your bookseller to order them. All are by Corey Sandler, and are published by Contemporary Books.

Econoguide Walt Disney World Resort, Universal Orlando
Econoguide Disneyland Resort, Universal Studios Hollywood
Econoguide Las Vegas

Econoguide Miami
Econoguide Washington, D.C., Williamsburg
Econoguide Pacific Northwest
Econoguide Cruises
Econoguide Canada
Econoguide Paris
Golf U.S.A.

Introduction

Welcome to the 2002 edition of *Econoguide London*.

One of the wonders of London is the fact that it is at the same time a place where time seems never to change and a place that lives on the cutting edge of tomorrow's culture and technology.

London is all but guaranteed to please. There are the delights of the big city: some of the world's most best museums, including the incomparable British Museum, the National Gallery, and the Tate Gallery, as well as smaller gems such as the Wallace Collection and Sir John Soane's Museum; the thriving West End theaters; the shops of Oxford Street, Regent Street, Piccadilly, and Brompton Road; the still-vibrant historical echoes of the Tower of London, the Houses of Parliament, and Westminster Abbey; and the unrivaled riches of the House of Windsor at Buckingham Palace.

But there are also myriad smaller pleasures such as the greens of Hyde Park, Regent's Park, and dozens of smaller public areas, and the joy of walking the fascinating streets around Covent Garden, Trafalgar Square, and Bloomsbury.

And many visitors to London also take advantage of the excellent railroad system of Great Britain to venture for day trips to wonderful places such as Bath, Brighton, Cambridge, Hampton Court, Oxford, Stonehenge, and Windsor.

There are two types of visitors to London: those who love her and can't wait to return, and those who are about to fall in love.

This book, then, is a labor of love, for I am one of those who include London high up on their list of favorite places to visit. When I return from a trip, I always put the leftover pounds and pence in the folder with my passport because I know I'll be heading back as soon as I can.

The British Experience

For many Americans, a trip to London is a relatively painless introduction to European travel because they don't have to learn a foreign language or undergo severe culture shock.

Well, that's more or less true.

As George Bernard Shaw observed, "England and America are two countries separated by the same language."

You'll know this when the menu offers Spotted Dick and aubergine, or when you order chips and get fries, or when you are offered biscuits and sweets for afters. You'll also know this when you walk through the subway to get to the Underground.

And then there are the sights. You'll be absolutely sure you're not in Kansas anymore within a few moments after you enter Buckingham Palace, Windsor Castle, or another of the modest pieds-à-terre of the British royalty.

Think of it this way: if a trip to Great Britain were no different from a tour to the Paramus Mall, there would not be much reason to cross the pond, would there?

Happily, London is very different. This book explores hundreds of familiar and unusual places to visit in London and in the surrounding area.

Much of the news about the United Kingdom in 2001 centered around a heartbreaking and somewhat frightening disease that spread through farms across the country and in parts of Europe. A few hundred cases of hoof-and-mouth disease among cattle and fears of a broader epidemic led to closures of hiking trails, parks, and zoos and the slaughter of millions of animals. There was no evidence that the disease could or would spread to humans. By mid-2001, the disease seemed to have been stopped in its tracks.

About *Econoguide* Travel Books

What do we mean by an *Econoguide?* Let's start with what it is not: this is not a cheapskate's guide to travel in London on $10 a day. Instead, our goal in the *Econoguide* series is to help you get the most for your money and make the best use of your time.

Another feature of the book is the exclusive section of special offers from travel agencies and tour packagers to London. A savvy consumer can easily save hundreds of dollars on a trip by using some of the coupons we publish.

An important note: the author and publisher of this book have no connection with the companies making special offers and have no financial interest in any of the discount coupons published within the book.

Our profit comes from you, the readers of this book, and it is you we hope to serve as best we can.

About the Author

Corey Sandler is a former newsman and editor for the Associated Press, Gannett Newspapers, IDG, and Ziff-Davis Publishing. He has written more than 160 books on travel, video games, and computers; his titles have been translated into French, Spanish, German, Italian, Portuguese, Polish, and Chinese. When he's not traveling, he lives with his wife and two children on Nantucket island, thirty miles off the coast of Massachusetts.

Part I
Travel to London

Chapter 1
Getting to London

Let's get something very important out of the way first: you can't drive to the United Kingdom.

A few luxury cruise ships still cross the pond a few dozen times a year. And you can take a train underneath the English Channel from France or a ferry from Ireland, Spain, Belgium, Holland, France, Germany, or Scandinavia.

But for the vast majority of visitors heading to the United Kingdom, the trip begins with a venture up into the somewhat friendly skies.

We'll explore an *Econoguide* view of air travel in this chapter; in the next chapter we'll move on to Chunnel and ferry adventures.

About *Econoguide* Travel

Don't call me cheap. Call me long distance.

In most years my family can take two or three lengthy vacations for the same amount of money most others spend on a single trip.

You can, of course, pay full price for travel or even more than full price. And you have the constitutional right to waste hours of precious vacation time waiting in line to ride a slow chairlift to a boring ski trail with too many skiers and too little snow.

Me, I prefer to make the very most of my time and money. I wait for airline fare wars, I rent hotel rooms at off-peak rates, and I clip coupons like the ones you'll find in this book.

Let me lay out the *Econoguide* Rules of Travel:

1. Plan your vacations carefully, but remain flexible on your dates of travel to obtain the best deals.

2. Research off-peak travel periods, and compare them to weather and snow conditions. Look for a golden coincidence of good prices and good conditions.

3. Learn how to ask for and receive the best prices.

About Airlines

Let's get real: do you prefer one airline over another because it offers a better quality sandwich-in-a-bag, plumper pillows, or three inches of extra legroom?

Central London

The way I figure it, one major airline is pretty much like any other. Sure, one company may offer a larger plastic bag of peanuts while the other promises its flight attendants have more accommodating smiles. But I'm much more interested in other things:

1. safety
2. the most convenient schedule
3. the lowest price

Sometimes I'm willing to trade price for convenience; I'll never risk my neck for a few dollars.

But that doesn't mean I don't try my hardest to get the very best price on every airline ticket. I watch the newspapers for seasonal sales and price wars, clip coupons from the usual and not-so-usual sources, consult the burgeoning world of Internet travel agencies, and happily play one airline against the other.

Alice in Airlineland

There are three golden rules to saving hundreds of dollars on travel: be flexible, be flexible, and be flexible.

• Be flexible about when you choose to travel. Go to London during the off-season or low-season when airfares, hotel rooms, and attractions offer substantial discounts.

• Be flexible about the day of the week you travel. You can often save hundreds of dollars by changing your departure date one or two days. Ask your travel agent or airline reservationist for current fare rules and restrictions.

The lightest air travel days are generally midweek, Saturday afternoons, and Sunday mornings. The busiest days are Sunday evenings, Monday mornings, and Fridays.

In general, you will receive the lowest possible fare if you include a Saturday in your trip, buying what is called an "excursion fare." Airlines use this as a way to exclude business travelers from the cheapest fares, assuming they will want to be home by Friday night.

• Be flexible on the time of day you choose to depart. There is generally lower demand—and therefore lower prices—for flights that leave in the middle of the day or very late at night.

• Be flexible on the route you will take or your willingness to put up with a change of plane or stopover. Once again, you are putting the law of supply and demand in your favor. A direct flight from New York to London for a family of four may cost hundreds of dollars more than a flight from New York that includes a change of planes in an American or European airport.

• Don't overlook flying out of a different airport, either. For example, metropolitan New Yorkers can take international flights from Kennedy or Newark airports, in addition to the busy LaGuardia. New Englanders can check fares from Montreal as well Boston.

Look for airports that are served by low-cost or aggressive marketers like Virgin Atlantic. You don't have to fly that airline, either; most carriers are forced to match the lowest rates of their competitors.

• Plan way ahead of time and purchase the most deeply discounted advance tickets, which are usually noncancelable. Most carriers limit the number of discount tickets on any particular flight; although there may be plenty of seats left on the day you want to travel, they may be offered at higher rates.

In a significant change in recent years, most airlines have changed "nonrefundable" fares to "noncancelable." What this means is that if you are forced to cancel or change your trip, your tickets retain their value and can be applied against another trip, usually for a fee of about $75 to $100 per ticket.

• Conversely, you can choose to take a big chance and wait for the last possible moment, keeping in contact with charter tour operators and accepting a bargain price on a "leftover" seat and hotel reservation. You may find that some airlines will reduce the prices on leftover seats within a few weeks of departure date; don't be afraid to check regularly with the airline, or ask your travel agent to do it for you. In fact, some travel agencies have automated computer programs that keep a constant electronic eagle eye on available seats and fares.

• Take advantage of special discount programs such as senior citizens' clubs, military discounts, or offerings from organizations to which you may belong. If you are in the over-sixty category, you may not even have to belong to a group such as AARP; simply ask the airline reservationist if there is a discount available. You may have to prove your age when you pick up your ticket.

• The day of the week you buy your tickets may also result in a price difference. Airlines often test out higher fares over the relatively quiet weekends. They're looking to see if their competitors will match their higher rates; if the other carriers don't bite, the fares often float back down by Monday morning. Shop during the week.

Other Money-Saving Strategies

Airlines are forever weeping and gnashing their teeth about huge losses due to cutthroat competition. And then they regularly turn around and drop their prices radically with major sales.

I don't waste time worrying about the bottom line of the airlines; it's my own wallet I want to keep full. Therefore, the savvy traveler keeps an eye out for airline fare wars all the time. Read the ads in newspapers and keep an ear open to news broadcasts that often cover the outbreak of price drops. If you have a good relationship with a travel agent, you can ask to be notified of any fare sales.

The most common times for airfare wars are in the weeks leading up to the quietest seasons for carriers, including the period from mid-May to mid-June (except the Memorial Day weekend), between Labor Day and Thanksgiving, and again in the winter, with the exception of Christmas, New Year's, and President's Day holiday periods.

Put another way: the busiest times for travel to London are the summer months of July and August, and the Christmas to New Year's holiday periods. You'll find much better prices at other times, especially in the late spring.

Study the fine print on discount coupons distributed directly by the airlines or through third parties such as supermarkets, catalog companies, and direct marketers. In my experience, these coupons are often less valuable than they seem. Read the fine print carefully, and be sure to ask the reservationist if the price quoted with the coupon is higher than another fare for which you qualify.

Consider doing business with discounters, known in the industry as "consolidators" or, less flatteringly, as "bucket shops." Look for ads in the classified sections of many Sunday newspaper travel sections. These companies buy the airlines' slow-to-sell tickets in volume and resell them to consumers at rock-bottom prices.

Look for ads for ticket brokers and bucket shops online and in the classifieds in *USA Today* and the "Mart" section of *The Wall Street Journal*.

Some travel agencies can also offer you consolidator tickets. Just be sure to weigh the savings on the ticket price against any restrictions attached to the tickets: they may not be changeable, and they usually do not accrue frequent-flyer mileage, for example.

Don't be afraid to ask for a refund on previously purchased tickets if fares go down for the period of your travel. The airline may refund the difference, or you may be able to reticket your itinerary at the new fare, paying a $75 or $100 penalty for cashing in the old tickets. Be persistent: if the difference in fare is significant, it may be worth making a visit to the airport to meet with a supervisor at the ticket counter.

Overbooking

Overbooking is a polite industry term that refers to the legal practice of selling more than an airline can deliver. It all stems, alas, from the unfortunate habit of many travelers who neglect to cancel flight reservations that will not be used. Airlines study the patterns on various flights and city pairs and apply a formula that allows them to sell more tickets than there are seats, in the expectation that a certain percentage will not show up at the airport.

But what happens if all passengers holding reservations show up? Obviously, there will be more passengers than seats, and some will be left behind.

The involuntary bump list will begin with the names of passengers who are late to check in. Airlines must ask for volunteers before bumping any passengers who have followed the rules on check-in.

If no one is willing to give up his seat just for the fun of it, the airline will offer some sort of compensation—either a free ticket or cash, or both. It is up to the passenger and the airline to make a deal.

You are also not eligible for compensation if the airline substitutes a smaller aircraft for operational or safety reasons, or if the flight involves an aircraft with sixty seats or less.

How to Get Bumped

Why in the world would you *want* to be bumped? Well, perhaps you'd like to look at missing your plane as an opportunity to earn a little money for your time instead of as an annoyance. Is a two-hour delay worth $100 an hour? How about $800 for a family of four to wait a few hours on the way home— that should pay for a week's hotel on your next trip.

If you're not in a rush to get to London—or to get home—you might want to volunteer to be bumped. I wouldn't recommend this on the busiest travel days of the year, or if you are booked on the last flight of the day, unless you are also looking forward to a free night in an airport motel. And if you arrive late at your hotel at either end, you may have to pay for the night's rental anyway; be sure to call and inform the hotel of any change in schedule.

My very best haul: on a flight home from London, my family of four received a free night's stay in a luxury hotel, $1,000 each in tickets, and an upgrade on our flight home the next day.

Bad Weather, Bad Planes, Strikes, and Other Headaches

You don't want pilots to fly into weather they consider unsafe, of course. You also wouldn't want them to take up a plane with a mechanical problem. No matter how you feel about unions, you probably don't want to cross a picket line to board a plane piloted by strikebreakers. And so, you should accept an airline's cancellation of a flight for any of these legitimate reasons.

Here's the bad news, though: if a flight is canceled for an "act of God" or a labor dispute, the airline is not required to do anything for you except refund your money. In practice, carriers will usually make an effort to find another way to deliver you to your destination more or less on time. This could mean rebooking on another flight on the same airline or on a different carrier. It could mean a delay of a day or more in the worst situations, such as a major snowstorm.

Here is a summary of your rather limited rights as an air passenger:

• An airline is required to compensate you above the cost of your ticket only if you are bumped from an oversold flight against your will.

• If you volunteer to be bumped, you can negotiate for the best deal with the ticket agent or a supervisor; generally you can expect to be offered a free round-trip ticket on the airline for your inconvenience.

• If your scheduled flight is unable to deliver you directly to the destination on your ticket, and alternate transportation such as a bus or limousine is provided, the airline is required to pay you twice the amount of your one-way fare if your arrival will be more than two hours later than the time the original ticket promised.

• If you purchased your ticket with a credit card, the airline must credit your account within seven days of receiving an application for a refund.

All that said, you may be able to convince an agent or a supervisor to go beyond the letter of the law. I've found the best strategy is to politely but firmly stand your ground. Ask the ticket clerk for another flight, for a free night in a hotel and a flight in the morning, or for any other reasonable accommodation. Don't take no for an answer, but remain polite and ask for a supervisor if necessary. Sooner or later, they'll do something to get you out of the way.

And then there are labor problems such as those that have faced several major airlines in recent years. Your best defense against a strike is to anticipate it before it happens; keep your ears open for labor problems before you make a reservation. Then keep in touch with your travel agent or the airline in the days leading up to strike deadlines. It is often easier to make alternate plans or seek a refund in the days immediately before a strike; wait until the last minute and you're going to be joining a very long and upset line.

If a strike occurs, an airline will attempt to rebook you on another airline if possible; if you buy your own ticket on another carrier you are unlikely to be reimbursed. If your flight is canceled, you will certainly be able to claim a full refund of your fare or obtain a voucher in its value without any penalties.

Airline Safety

There are no guarantees in life, but in general flying on an airplane is considerably safer than driving to the airport. All of the major air carriers have very good safety records; some are better than others. I pay attention to news reports about FAA inspections and rulings and make adjustments. And though I love to squeeze George Washington until he yelps, I avoid start-up and super-cut-rate airlines because I have my doubts about how much money they can afford to devote to maintenance.

Among major airlines, the fatal accident rate during the last twenty-five years stands somewhere between 0.3 and 0.7 incidents per million flights. Not included are small commuter airlines, except for those affiliated with major carriers.

The very low numbers, experts say, make them poor predictors of future incidents. Instead, you should pay more attention to reports of FAA or NTSB rulings on maintenance and training problems.

About Travel Agencies

Here's my advice about travel agents: get a good one, or go it alone. Good agents are those who remember whom they work for: you. Of course, there is a built-in conflict of interest here, because the agent is in most cases paid by someone else.

Agents receive a commission on airline tickets, hotel reservations, car rentals, and many other services they sell you. The more they sell (or the higher the price), the more they earn.

I would recommend you start the planning for any trip by calling the airlines and a few hotels and finding the best package you can put together for yourself. Then call your travel agent and ask him to do better.

If your agent contributes knowledge or experience, comes up with dollar-saving alternatives to your own package or offers some other kind of convenience, then go ahead and book through the agency. If, as I often find, you know a lot more about your destination and are willing to spend a lot more time to save money than will the agent, do it yourself.

A number of large agencies offer rebates of part of their commissions to travelers. Some of these companies cater only to frequent flyers who will bring in a lot of business; other rebate agencies offer only limited services to clients.

You can find discount travel agencies through many major credit card companies (Citibank and American Express among them) or through associations and clubs. Some warehouse shopping clubs have rebate travel agencies.

And if you establish a regular relationship with your travel agency and bring them enough business to make them glad to hear from you, don't be afraid to ask them for a discount equal to a few percentage points.

One other important new tool for travelers is the Internet. Here you'll find computerized travel agencies that offer airline, hotel, car, cruise, and package reservations. You won't receive personalized assistance, but you will be able to check as many prices and various itinerary routings as you'd like without apology. Several of the services feature special deals, including companion fares and rebates you won't find offered elsewhere.

Tour Packages and Charter Flights

Tour packages and flights sold by tour operators or travel agents may look similar, but the tickets may come with significantly different rights.

It all depends whether the flight is a scheduled or nonscheduled flight. A "scheduled flight" is one that is listed in the *Official Airline Guide* and available to the general public through a travel agent or from the airline. This doesn't mean that a scheduled flight will necessarily be on a major carrier or that you will be flying on a 747 jumbo jet; it could just as easily be the propeller-driven pride of Hayseed Airlines. In any case, though, a scheduled flight does have to meet stringent federal government certification requirements.

A "nonscheduled flight" is also known as a "charter flight." The term is sometimes also applied to a package that includes a nonscheduled flight, hotel accommodations, ground transportation, and other elements. Charter flights are generally a creation of a tour operator who purchases all of the seats on a specific flight to a specific destination or who will rent an airplane and crew from an air carrier.

Charter flights and charter tours are regulated by the federal government, but your rights as a consumer are much more limited than those afforded to scheduled flight customers.

You wouldn't buy a hamburger without knowing the price and specifications (two all-beef patties on a sesame seed bun, etc.). Why, then, would you spend hundreds or even thousands of dollars on a tour and not understand the contract that underlies the transaction?

Before you pay for a charter flight or a tour package, review the contract that spells out your rights. This contract is sometimes referred to as the "Operator Participant Contract" or the "Terms and Conditions." Look for this contract in the booklet or brochure that describes the packages; ask for it if one is not offered.

Remember that the contract is designed mostly to benefit the tour operator, and each contract may be different from others you may have agreed to in the past. The basic rule here is: if you don't understand it, don't sign it.

How to Book a Package or Charter Flight

If possible, use a travel agent—preferably one you know and trust from prior experience. In general, the tour operator pays the travel agent's commission. Some tour packages, however, are available only from the operator who organized the tour; in certain cases, you may be able to negotiate a better price by dealing directly with the operator, although you are giving up one layer of protection for your rights.

Pay for your ticket with a credit card; this is a cardinal rule for almost any situation in which you are prepaying for a service or product.

Realize that charter airlines don't have large fleets of planes available to substitute in the event of a mechanical problem or an extensive weather delay. They may not be able to arrange for a substitute plane from another carrier.

If you are still willing to try a charter after all of these warnings, make one more check of the bottom line before you sign the contract. First of all, is the air travel significantly less expensive than the lowest nonrefundable fare from a scheduled carrier? (Remember that you are, in effect, buying a nonrefundable fare with most charter flight contracts.)

Second, have you included taxes, service charges, baggage transfer fees, or other charges the tour operator may put into the contract? Are the savings significantly more than the 10 percent the charter operator may (typically) boost the price without your permission? Do savings cost you time? What is that worth?

Finally, don't purchase a complete package until you have compared it to the a la carte cost of such a trip. Call the hotels offered by the tour operator, or similar ones in the same area, and ask them a simple question: "What is your best price for a room?" Be sure to mention any discount programs that are applicable, including AAA or other organizations. Do the same for car rental agencies, and place a call to any attractions you plan to visit to get current prices.

Travel Insurance

The idea of falling ill or suffering an injury while hundreds or thousands of miles away from home and your family doctor can be a terrifying thought.

But before you sign on the bottom line for an accident and sickness insurance policy, be sure to consult with your own insurance agent or your company's personnel office to see how far your personal medical insurance policy will reach. Does the policy cover vacation trips and exclude business travel? Are all international locations excluded? Can you purchase a "rider," or extension, to your personal policy to cover travel?

The only reason to purchase an Accident and Sickness policy is to fill in any gaps in the coverage you already have. If you don't have health insurance of any kind, a travel policy is certainly valuable, but you might want to consider whether you should spend the money on a year-round policy instead of taking a vacation in the first place.

Also be aware that nearly every kind of health insurance has an exclusionary period for preexisting conditions. If you are sick before you set out on a trip, you may find that the policy will not pay for treating the problem.

If any significant portion of your trip is nonrefundable, consider buying cancellation insurance from a travel agency, from a tour operator, or directly from an insurance company (ask your insurance agent for advice).

The policies are intended to reimburse you for any lost deposits or prepayments if you must cancel a trip because you or certain members of your family become ill. Take care not to purchase more coverage than you need; if your tour package costs $5,000 but you would lose only $1,000 in the event of a cancellation, then the amount of insurance required is just $1,000.

Some policies will cover you for health and accident benefits while on vacation, but your existing health policy will probably handle such an emergency as well. In any case, travel insurance policies usually exclude any preexisting conditions.

Air Carriers to London

You can pretty much take your pick of carriers for a flight across the Atlantic to London.

• **The Majors.** British Airways, the largest carrier in the United Kingdom, is met with spirited competition by upstart Virgin Air. American carriers include American Airlines, Continental, Delta, Northwest, and United. This group of British and American carriers track each others' fares pretty closely. When one puts on a sale, the others are all but certain to follow; when one raises prices, nearly all fares miraculously rise, at least until one carrier attempts to gain a momentary advantage by undercutting the others.

• **The Respected Minors.** You'll also find quite a few respectable international carriers—large and small—that make stops in London to or from their home bases. Here you'll find well-known airlines Air France and KLM, as well as flag carriers such as Aer Lingus, Air India, El Al, Icelandair, Saudi Arabian, and others. You may find some bargains on these airlines, although their small size increases the risk of delay or cancellation of flights.

• **Charter Operators.** Charter airlines may work exclusively with tour packagers, or a packager may rent the equipment and crew of a scheduled airline. Either way, the operator has to follow the same stringent set of safety and maintenance rules. However, in some cases the equipment used by a scheduled carrier may be younger and presumably in somewhat better condition than that used by a charter.

• **Consolidator Tickets.** Consolidator tickets are a midway step between buying a ticket from a scheduled airline or from a charter operator, and in some cases they are the route to a very good deal. Consolidators purchase blocks of tickets from major scheduled airlines at deep discounts and then resell them to consumers. You'll fly the same planes as regular customers, eat the same wonderful food, and arrive at the same time as your seatmates who paid full freight. The disadvantages of consolidator tickets include the fact that they are usually nonrefundable and you may not be able to get exactly the flights you want. You should, though, be given the same rights as other passengers in the event of cancellation of a flight once a trip is underway. Be sure to deal with a reputable travel agent for such tickets.

London-Area Airports

London-area airports include Heathrow, Gatwick, Stansted, and Luton. Heathrow is the closest to downtown, with Gatwick just a bit farther out. A fifth airport, London City, is very close—in the Docklands area of London—but used mostly for commuter and small charter lines.

Heathrow Airport (Airport Code: LHR)

Heathrow is the world's busiest international airport, located about fifteen miles (twenty-four kilometers) west of central London. For information, call ☎ (020) 8759-4321 or consult 🖳 www.baa.co.uk/main/airports/heathrow.

Heathrow Terminals

Heathrow has four terminals, with a fifth planned.

Terminals 1, 2, and 3 are nearby to each other at the center of the airport grounds, while terminal 4 is to itself on the south side. You can walk between terminals 1 and 2; shuttle buses connect the others.

Terminal 1. British Airways domestic flights, plus European destinations *other* than Amsterdam, Athens, Moscow or Paris. Air France to Nice. British Midland, except to Germany. Aer Lingus, Icelandair, South African Airways, and Virgin Express.

Terminal 2. Most European flights by foreign carriers, including Air France, Alitalia, Austrian Airlines, British Midland (Germany only), Ethiopian Airlines, Iberia, Lufthansa, and TAP Air Portugal.

The London Underground and the Heathrow Express serve Heathrow Airport
Photo by Corey Sandler

Terminal 3. Air Canada, Air New Zealand, All Nippon, American Airlines, British Airways to Lagos and Miami Cathay Pacific, Gulf Air, Japan Airlines, Malaysia Airlines, Royal Brunei, SAS, Thai Airways International, United Airlines, United Arab Emirates, and Virgin Atlantic.

Terminal 4. British Airways to Amsterdam, Athens, Moscow, and Paris, plus intercontinental flights (except for Lagos and Miami), Air Malta, British Mediterranean, Kenya Airways, KLM, Qantas, and Sri Lanka.

Getting to Heathrow

By Train. The Heathrow Express railway line between London's Paddington station and Heathrow began service in the summer of 1998, cutting the rail trip to about fifteen minutes. Paddington is served by no less than four Tube lines with connections to the others. Coach tickets are £12 one-way, and £22 for a roundtrip ("return") ticket; children younger than three ride free. First class tickets are £20 one-way.

Unless you're in a terrific rush, get your tickets from a counter near the trains; there's a £2 penalty for buying your tickets onboard. You can also purchase tickets online or over the phone at a discount. For information, call ☎ (0845) 600-1515 or consult 🖳 www.heathrowexpress.co.uk.

Some twenty-seven airlines, including most major carriers, have opened check-in facilities at Paddington, allowing travelers to dispose of their luggage without having to drag suitcases into the airport. Passengers can check in at any time on the day of their flight, up to two hours prior to departure time.

By Underground. The Underground's Piccadilly line runs from a shared station for terminals 1, 2, and 3, and from a separate station beneath Heathrow's terminal 4, on a regular schedule. The trip takes about forty to sixty minutes. All of Heathrow's terminals are interlinked, but it is as much as a fifteen-minute hike from some baggage-claim areas to the Underground station. The adult one-way base-rate fare to central London in 2001 was £3.60. Important stops on the Piccadilly line include South Kensington, Piccadilly Circus, Leicester Square, Bloomsbury, and King's Cross–St. Pancras stations.

Trains run from London beginning about 5:30 A.M. daily and 7:30 A.M. on Sunday, running until about midnight daily and 11:30 P.M. Sunday. From Heathrow, trains begin just after 5 A.M. daily and 6 A.M. Sunday, running until about 11 P.M. from terminals 1–3 and just short of midnight from terminal 4. For information, call **London Travel Information** at ☎ (020) 7222-1234 or consult 💻 www.thetube.com.

Once the London Underground closes, the N97 night bus connects Heathrow to central London with departures every thirty minutes.

Railair Link bus connects Heathrow Airport to British Rail stations at Feltham, Reading, Woking, and Watford Junction. For information, call ☎ (020) 7222-1234.

The **Reading Railair** connects the South West, the West Country, South Wales, and the West Midlands to Heathrow. Express coaches depart Reading station every thirty minutes for the forty-five-minute journey to Heathrow. For information, call ☎ (0345) 000125.

Woking Railair runs from the Woking rail station to Heathrow Airport, a thirty-minute link to rail service from areas including Basingstoke, Bournemouth, Guildford, Portsmouth, Southampton, and Winchester. For information, call ☎ (0870) 574-7777 or consult 💻 www.gobycoach.com.

Watford Railair operates between Watford Junction station and all terminals at Heathrow Airport, in conjunction with Virgin Trains services from the northwest.

The **Jetlink 747** bus connects with the Watford Junction station for trains to the Midlands, northwest, and Scotland. Jetlink 747 makes stops for pickup and drop-off at Luton station, Luton Airport, and Stevenage. For information, call ☎ (020) 8668-7261.

By Bus. The **Airbus** service takes about an hour to central London from terminals 1, 2, and 3; add twenty or so minutes from terminal 4. Taking the Airbus is easier than wrestling luggage into and out of the Underground and offers a better view of downtown. Two Airbus routes pick up from all four terminals to central London, stopping at many hotels en route.

Airbus runs every thirty minutes from 6 A.M. to 10 P.M. to and from Notting Hill Gate, Paddington station, Bayswater, Marble Arch, Euston station, and Russell Square. Some buses continue to King's Cross station.

For information on Airbus services, phone ☎ (020) 7222-1234, ☎ (020) 8400-6690, or ☎ (020) 8400-6656. Adult tickets are about £7 one-way and £10 round-trip; tickets for children are half-price. Discounted tickets may be available through U.S. travel agents.

Airbus also runs Airbus Direct service directly to and from some of the larger hotels in central London. Departures are every fifteen minutes from 5 A.M.

and every twenty minutes from 1 P.M. to 9 P.M. For information about Airbus Direct, call ☎ (020) 8400-6655; to make reservations, call ☎ (0800) 247287.

Other destinations in the London area are served by local buses to and from Heathrow's central bus station. For information, call ☎ (0990) 747-777.

Golden Tours operates a twenty-four-hour airport car service from Heathrow Airport to hotels in London. For information in the United States, call ☎ (800) 456-6303; in the United Kingdom, call ☎ (020) 8743-3300. You can also consult 🖳 www.goldentours.co.uk.

By Taxi. A cab to central London costs about £30 to £40 and takes about thirty to sixty minutes, depending on the time of day. For information, call ☎ (020) 8745-5893. You can also arrange for a car service in advance for about the same price; a driver will meet you at the baggage claim.

By Car. Off M4, just within the perimeter of the M25.

Heathrow Airport Hotels

Hotels near the airport, most of them offering courtesy bus or car service to Heathrow, include:

Le Meridien Excelsior. ☎ (020) 8759-6611 or ☎ (0870) 400-8899. 🖳 www.lemeridien-heathrow.com.
Forte Crest Heathrow. ☎ (0870) 400-8595.
Forte Posthouse. ☎ (020) 8759-2113 or ☎ (0870) 400-9040.
Heathrow Park. ☎ (020) 8759-2400.
Hilton London Heathrow Airport. ☎ (020) 8759-7755. 🖳 www.hilton.com.
Radisson Edwardian Plaza. ☎ (020) 8759-6311. 🖳 www.radisson.com.
Renaissance London Heathrow. ☎ (020) 8897-6363. 🖳 www.renaissancehotels.com.
Sheraton Heathrow Hotel London. ☎ (020) 8759-2424. 🖳 www.sheraton.com.
Sheraton Skyline. ☎ (020) 8759-2535. 🖳 www.sheraton.com.

Heathrow Airport Rental Car Companies

Alamo. ☎ (020) 8750-2800. 🖳 www.alamo.com.
Avis. ☎ (020) 8899-1000. 🖳 www.avis.com.
Budget. ☎ (0144) 227-6000. 🖳 www.budgetrentacar.com.
Europcar. ☎ (020) 8897-0811 or terminals 1, 2, and 3, call ☎ (020) 8897-0811. 🖳 www.europcar.com.
Hertz. ☎ (020) 8897-2072 or ☎ (020) 8897-2072. 🖳 www.hertz.com.
Kenning. ☎ (020) 8890-1167 or ☎ (020) 8890-1167.
Thrifty. ☎ (020) 8897-6261 or ☎ (020) 8897-2519. 🖳 www.thrifty.com.

Gatwick Airport (Airport Code: LGW)

Gatwick is located about twenty-eight miles (forty-six kilometers) south of London, on the Surrey-Sussex border. Gatwick is the busiest single runway airport in the world, the second busiest airport in the United Kingdom, and the sixth busiest international airport in the world.

For information, call ☎ (01293) 535353 or consult 🖳 www.baa.co.uk/main/airports/gatwick.

Gatwick Terminals

Gatwick has two main terminals for international flights. The hometown British Airways uses the north terminal, along with Delta Airlines. Continental

Airlines is the largest American carrier serving Gatwick through the south terminal. A free monorail service links the north and south terminals.

Getting to Gatwick

By Train. The **Gatwick Express** runs nonstop to and from the airport to Victoria station in central London in about thirty minutes. The trains run twenty-four hours a day, every fifteen minutes from 5:30 A.M. to 8 P.M., and every half hour or hour during the night. In 2001 Standard-class tickets cost £10.50 one-way and £20 round-trip. The Gatwick railway station is part of the south terminal. For information, call ☎ (0870) 530-1530 or consult 🖳 www.gat wickexpress.co.uk.

Another train service is offered from Victoria station by **Network South Central**; this train makes a few stops along the way and is slower; you'll save a bit, though, with tickets priced at £3.90 to £4.70.

Yet another service is offered by **Thameslink**, from Gatwick to King's Cross via City Thameslink, Blackfriars, and London Bridge. Fares in 2001 were £9.80. For information call ☎ (020) 7620-6333 or consult 🖳 www.thameslink.co.uk.

For general information about rail service, call ☎ (0345) 484950.

Passengers on American Airlines, British Airways, Delta, and some other carriers have been able to check in at Victoria station in recent years; be sure to confirm this arrangement with your airline before you begin your voyage. Trains arrive at a station near the south terminal; an automated shuttle transports passengers to the north terminal.

By Bus. Flightline 777 runs from the airport to Victoria coach station daily from 5:20 A.M. to 10 P.M. The trip takes just over an hour when traffic is light, longer at other times. Tickets cost £7.50 one-way and £11 for round-trip. For information, call ☎ (0990) 747777.

Speedlink connects to Heathrow Airport. ☎ (0870) 574-7777.

Jetlink serves Brighton, East Anglia, Milton Keynes, and Northampton. ☎ (0870) 747777.

Airbus A5 to London Victoria. ☎ (0870) 575-7747,

Flightlink. Midlands destinations. ☎ (0870) 575-7747.

The Oxford Express. Oxford. ☎ (0186) 578-5400.

National Express. Nationwide services. ☎ (0870) 580-8080.

For general information on bus services, you can also consult 🖳 www.goby coach.com.

Hotelink offers minibus service from most central London hotels on demand, for a fare of £16. For information, call ☎ (01293) 532244.

Golden Tours operates a twenty-four-hour airport shuttle service from Gatwick Airport to hotels in London. For information in the United States, call ☎ (800) 456-6303. There is a bus and coach information desk in the arrivals concourse of both terminals.

By Car. The M23 runs from Gatwick to central London. At busy times of the day, the trip can take as long as two hours.

By Taxi. Expect a fare of about £55 and a trip of one hour at quiet times and as long as two hours in rush hour.

Hotels Near Gatwick

Forte Le Meridien London/Gatwick. (North terminal.) ☎ (01293) 567070. ▣ www.lemeridien-hotels.com.
Hilton. (South terminal.) ☎ (01293) 518080. ▣ www.hilton.com.
Jarvis International Hotel at Gatwick. ☎ (01293) 561186.
Forte Posthouse. ☎ (0870) 400-9030.

Rental Car Companies at Gatwick

Alamo/Eurodollar/National. ☎ (01273) 223300 or ☎ (01293) 567790.
Avis. ☎ (01293) 529721.
Budget. ☎ (0800) 626063.
Europcar. ☎ (01293) 531062.
Hertz. ☎ (01293) 530555.
Whitgift. ☎ (01293) 560060.

London City Airport (Airport Code: LCY)

London City Airport is located about six miles (ten kilometers) east of the City of London. For information, call ☎ (0207) 646-0088 or consult ▣ www.london cityairport.com.

London City Airport caters to business travelers from the Docklands area of London. The premium is on quick access to London and quick arrivals and departures from planes.

Getting to London City Airport

By Bus. The **Red Route** bus runs every ten to twenty minutes from the airport to the Liverpool Street station, a twenty-five-minute trip. The fare is £6. You can connect to the Underground at Liverpool Street. For information, call ☎ (020) 7646-0088.

The **Jubilee Line** of the Underground runs to Canary Wharf, connecting to London Bridge station and Waterloo station.

The **LCA 1** bus runs frequently to Canary Wharf in Docklands, an eight-minute trip, for a £3 fare. At Canary Wharf you can connect to the Docklands Light Railway that runs to the City of London. For information, call London Travel Information at ☎ (020) 7222-1234.

By Taxi. A taxi from downtown to the City of London costs about £18.

By Train. The Silvertown British Rail station on the North London Line is a short walk from the airport. Trains from there serve North and West London. For information on British Rail Network Southeast, call ☎ (0345) 484950.

Stansted Airport (Airport Code: STN)

Stansted is about thirty-four miles (fifty-five kilometers) northeast of London. The airport's modern terminal is an architectural wonder. For information, call ☎ (01279) 680500 or consult ▣ www.baa.co.uk/main/airports/stansted.

Getting to Stansted

By Train. Stansted Express train runs from the airport to Liverpool Street station every thirty minutes from 6 A.M. to 11:59 P.M. daily. In 2001 the fare for the forty-minute ride was £13, or £21 for a round-trip ticket. The train also stops at Tottenham Hale where connections can be made to the Underground's Victoria line. For information, call ☎ (0345) 484950 or consult 💻 www.stansted express.com.

By Bus. Airbus A6/A7 connects London Stansted with Stratford, Hendon, and Victoria coach station in Central London. ☎ (0870) 574-7777.

Jetlink 757. London Stansted to Cambridge and Oxford every two hours. ☎ (0870) 574-7777.

Jetlink 737. London Stansted to Ipswich, Braintree, and Heathrow Airport every two hours. ☎ (0870) 574-7777.

Jetlink 797. Cambridge, Stansted, Heathrow, and Gatwick every two hours. ☎ (0870) 574-7777.

Flightline 777 provides hourly service from Victoria station from 8 A.M. to 6 P.M., with additional coaches at 8 and 10 P.M. The trip, which takes about an hour and a half, costs £8. For information, call ☎ (0990) 747777.

By Taxi. The fare to central London is about £50 and takes about seventy-five minutes.

Luton Airport (Airport Code: LTN)

Luton is located about thirty-two miles (fifty-one kilometers) northwest of central London. For information, call ☎ (01582) 405100 or consult 💻 www.lon don-luton.com.

Luton was originally a base for charter flights but has expanded in recent years with the growth of low-cost carriers to domestic and European destinations.

Carriers from Luton include Airtours International, Air 2000, Air Europa, Air Mediterranee, British Midland, British Regional Airways, Brittannia, Caledonian Airways, easyJet, Eurocypria, European Air Express, Futura, Iberworld, Jersey European Airways, Manx, Monarch, Monarch Crown Service, Pegasus, Ryanair, Sata Air, and Scot Airways.

Getting to Luton

By Train. The Luton Airport Parkway Station is just minutes from the airport, connected by a free shuttle bus. **Thameslink** sends several trains per hour from Luton to central London stations, including to North London, Central London, the City, and Brighton, plus Midland Mainline services to East Midlands and Yorkshire. A return between the airport and the City Thameslink terminal is £16.80. For information, call ☎ (0207) 6206333 or consult 💻 www.thameslink.co.uk.

The **Luton Flyer** connects to London's King's Cross station, a trip of about an hour. The **Railair Coach Link** meets the trains for connections to the airport. The fare is about £9.60. For information, call ☎ (0345) 484950.

By Bus. Greenline 757 connects from Luton to London city center every thirty minutes from 8 A.M. to midnight for a fare of £5, when flying Easy Jet and £12 when flying other airlines. For information, call ☎ (0870) 608-7261.

By Taxi. The fare to central London is about £35.

Hotels Near Luton

Ibis. (At the airport.) ☎ (01582) 424488.
Chiltern. ☎ (01582) 575911.
Forte Gateway Hotel. ☎ (01582) 575955.
Hertfordshire Moat House. ☎ (01582) 449988.
Thistle Luton. ☎ (01582) 734199. 🖳 www.thistlehotels.com/thistle_luton.

Rental Car Companies at Luton

Avis. ☎ (01582) 36537. 🖳 www.avis.com.
Eurodollar. ☎ (01582) 411435.
Europcar. ☎ (01582) 413438.
National Car Rental at Luton Airport ☎ (01582) 486414.

Connections from Airport to Airport

Heathrow to Gatwick

Gatwick Airport is about an hour away from Heathrow by scheduled bus.

By Bus. Speedlink runs from terminals 1, 3, and 4 every fifteen to thirty minutes from 5:30 A.M. to 10:30 P.M. for £17. For information, call ☎ (01293) 502001.

Jetlink runs every thirty minutes from the Central bus station and terminal 4 for a fare of £12. For information, call ☎ (0870) 608-7261 or consult 🖳 www.airlinks.co.uk.

By Taxi. About £80.

Heathrow to Stansted

Stansted Airport is about two and a half hours away from Heathrow Airport by scheduled bus.

By Bus. Jetlink runs every two hours from 7:30 A.M. to 1:30 A.M., every four hours from 5:30 P.M. to 1:30 A.M. £14 fare. For information, call ☎ (0870) 608-7261.

Cambridge Coach Services runs every two hours from 7 A.M. to 1 A.M. £11 fare. For information, call ☎ (01223) 423900 or consult 🖳 www.cambridge coaches.co.uk.

By Taxi. About £120.

Heathrow to London City Airport

By Taxi. About £50.

Heathrow to Luton Airport

By Bus. Jetlink runs hourly from 7 A.M. to 10 P.M., except 9 P.M. £9 fare. For information, call ☎ (020) 8668-7261.

Cambridge Coach Services runs every two hours from 8 A.M. to midnight. £9 fare. For information, call ☎ (01223) 236333.

By Taxi. About £75.

Gatwick to Stansted

By Bus. Jetlink operates every two hours from 6 A.M. until 12 A.M., to Stansted via Heathrow; the trip takes about three hours and the fare is £16 one-way and £24 round-trip. For information, call ☎ (0870) 608-7261.

Cambridge Coach Services runs the same route from 6 A.M. to midnight for the same fare. For information, call ☎ (01223) 423900.

By Taxi. About £85.

Gatwick to Luton

By Train. The **Thameslink** train runs direct to Luton station every thirty minutes; a shuttle bus connects from the station to Luton Airport every fifteen minutes. The fare is £16.30 before 9:30 A.M. and £13.90 for the rest of the day.

By Bus. Jetlink buses run every two hours from 7 A.M. until 11 P.M. The trip takes three hours. Tickets are £14 one-way, £20 round-trip. For information, call ☎ (0870) 608-7261.

Cambridge Coach Services runs every two hours from 7 A.M. to 11 P.M., with a two-hour bus journey. Tickets are £12 one-way, £21 round-trip. For information, call ☎ (01223) 423900.

By Taxi. About £85.

Chapter 2

Getting About in the United Kingdom: Intercity Trains, Cars, Buses, and Boats

London is one of the oldest major cities on the planet, and yet it also has one of the most comprehensive and easy-to-use transportation systems anywhere. There is hardly a place in the city that is not within easy reach of an Underground station, a railroad station, or a bus route. And the system fans out from the capital city to nearly everywhere in the country.

When I travel to England, the second most important documents in my case after my passport are my London Transport travelcard and a BritRail pass.

Yes, you can also rent a car or hire a car and driver, for some added flexibility . . . and complexity.

In this chapter we'll explore intercity travel by train, car, and bus. A bit later, in Chapter 6, we'll take you underground to explain train service within London itself.

Railroad Travel

Here's a point of perspective: Great Britain, once one of the most powerful imperial nations on earth, is only slightly larger than the states of Michigan or Oregon, just a bit smaller than the combined square mileage of New York and Pennsylvania.

England and Scotland are cobwebbed with railroad tracks and served by a superb collection of rail lines; that seems only appropriate for the place where railroads were invented.

The trains are mostly clean, quick, and, except for rush hour and holiday weekends, very comfortable. Tourist travelers will find very attractive rates on individual tickets as well as through the use of BritRail passes.

Rail Information

Quite possibly the worst place to obtain information about routes and fares is at one of the major train stations. You'll find yourself in a line of travelers anxiously glancing at their watches and grumbling about the dumb Yank ahead of them who doesn't understand the difference between a cheap day-return, a supersaver return, a one-way standard, or an out-and-return first-class ticket. Or you'll find yourself behind a squad of German backpackers, each of them using a phrase book to ask the same question in different ways.

Your best bet for information and fares on any of the national railways in the United Kingdom is to call ☎ (0345) 484950. Believe it or not, you'll find a real live person at the other end of the phone, with schedules and ticket prices from anywhere to anywhere. In fact, if you get to the train station and see a line at the ticket booth, you might do better to step into a phone booth and call that number.

The phone service can direct you to the reservations line for most of the train services, and you can use a credit card to purchase a ticket to be sent to you or held at a "will call" window at train stations.

You can also obtain information from a British Tourist Authority (BTA) office in the United Kingdom, or from BritRail's offices in the United States.

If you need to purchase a ticket on the day of travel, most major train stations in London have automated ticket machines that accept currency or a credit card. You'll have to know what to ask for, though.

You may also want to consult 🖳 www.thetrainline.com, a commercial site that sells tickets on most train services in the United Kingdom. As we went to press, the service was unable to ship tickets outside of the United Kingdom, although that may change. In the meantime, it is an excellent way to check schedules and compare fares across various train companies and times of day.

Discount Rail Tickets

The most expensive train trip you can buy is a pair of one-way tickets for travel during the morning rush hour. To save a significant amount on tickets, adjust your travel to use a discount program. They include:

Off-Peak Tickets. Most rail services offer lower-priced tickets for travel after 9:30 A.M. weekdays and on weekends and bank holidays.

Cheap Day Tickets. The least expensive tickets, either one-way or round-trip, are available for off-peak travel to many destinations.

If you are going to be spending an extended period of time in the United Kingdom, consider purchasing a **Network Card** available through most railway services. This card, sold for about £20 and valid for a year, offers deeper discounts on off-peak travel for the owner and as many as three adults traveling with him or her; accompanying children ages five to fifteen years are charged a flat fee of £1 each for tickets.

The Network Card also allows an upgrade to first class on certain trains for a fee of £3.

Buying Rail Passes

Many travelers prefer to purchase their tickets before they leave their homes; this is certainly the most convenient way to travel. In some cases it may save money to purchase passes; in other instances you may find it less expensive to purchase individual round-trip tickets for use during off-peak travel times.

BritRail tickets can be purchased from most travel agencies, or through Rail Europe. Tickets can be purchased by calling ☎ (888) 274-8724 or by consulting 🖳 www.raileurope.com.

You can also purchase tickets in person in New York City from BritRail's British Travel Shop, at 551 Fifth Avenue.

Rail passes include:

BritRail Southeast Pass. Unlimited rail travel in an area around London, including Windsor, Oxford, Salisbury, Southampton, Portsmouth, Brighton, Dover, Canterbury, and Cambridge. It does not include Bath or other connections through Reading.

This is one of the best deals for many travelers; you could purchase a cheap day-return ticket to add Bath and cover all of the day trips listed in this book.

Prices listed are in dollars and were in effect in mid-2001. Children can purchase discounted tickets if they are five to fifteen years old.

	Adult First Class	Adult Second Class	Child First Class	Child Second Class
3 days out of 8	$106	$73	$31	$21
4 days out of 8	$142	$106	$31	$21
7 days out of 15	$189	$142	$31	$21

BritRail Classic Pass. Unlimited rail travel in England, Scotland, and Wales. Available for eight, fifteen, or twenty-two days, or one month. One day of travel on the ticket can be used on the Heathrow Express or Gatwick Express train services to London, or return.

Prices listed are in dollars and were in effect in mid-2001. Note that many local trains offer only standard-class accommodations, and the first-class pass price takes this into account. In 2001 BritRail continued its plan of offering a free child (five to fifteen) ticket with each paid adult pass. Senior tickets are sold to travelers sixty years and older. A youth ticket is for passengers younger than the age of twenty-six.

	Adult First Class	Adult Second Class	Senior First Class	Youth Second Class
8 days	$399	$265	$339	$215
15 days	$599	$399	$509	$279
22 days	$759	$499	$639	$355
1 month	$899	$599	$759	$419

BritRail Flexipass. Rail travel in England, Scotland, and Wales for four, eight, and fifteen days out of one month. During your trip, one day of travel can be applied toward a ticket on the Heathrow Express or Gatwick Express from the airport to downtown London.

Prices listed are in dollars and were in effect in mid-2001. Senior tickets are sold to travelers sixty years and older. A youth ticket is for passengers younger than the age of twenty-six. In 2001 BritRail continued its plan of offering a free child's ticket with each paid adult pass.

	Adult First Class	Adult Second Class	Senior First Class	Youth Second Class
4 days in 2 months	$349	$235	$299	$185
8 days in 2 months	$509	$339	$435	$239
15 days in 2 months	$769	$515	$655	$359

BritRail Party Pass. For parties of three or four adult passengers traveling together, BritRail offers a discount of 50 percent on the third and fourth persons' passes; this amounts to a 33 percent reduction on the total cost of four passes. The Party Pass applies to first- and second-class Classic and Flexipass tickets. All passengers must travel together to qualify. One child between the ages of five and fifteen travels free with each adult or senior pass. Prices are per group.

	Parties of 3 Adults First Class (Per Group)	Parties of 4 Adults First Class (Per Group)
8 consecutive days	$997	$1,197
15 consecutive days	$1,497	$1,797
22 consecutive days	$1,897	$2,277
1 month unlimited	$2,247	$2,697

BritRail Senior Party Pass. Available for travelers age sixty and older. One child between the ages of five and fifteen travels free with each adult or senior pass. Prices are per group.

	Parties of 3 Seniors First Class	Parties of 4 Seniors First Class
8 consecutive days	$847	$1,017
15 consecutive days	$1,272	$1,527
22 consecutive days	$1,597	$1,917
1 month	$1,897	$2,277

BritRail Flexi Party Pass. One child between the ages of five and fifteen travels free with each adult or senior pass.

	Parties of 3 Adults First Class	Parties of 4 Adults First Class
4 days in 2 months	$872	$1,047
8 days in 2 months	$1,272	$1,527
15 days in 2 months	$1,922	$2,307

BritRail + Ireland. Unlimited rail travel in England, Scotland, Wales, Northern Ireland, and Ireland. Also includes round-trip Stena Line service between Holyhead and Dun Laoghaire or Dublin, Fishguard, and Rollsare, or Stranraer and Belfast via ship, HSS, or Stena Lynx Catamaran. One day of travel on the ticket can be used on the Heathrow Express or the Gatwick Express between the airport and London or return.

Prices listed are in dollars and were in effect in mid-2001. One child between the ages of five and fifteen travels free with each adult or senior pass.

	Adult First Class	Adult Second Class
5 days in 1 month	$529	$399
10 days in 1 month	$749	$569

Train Information on the Web

The Trainline. An on-line booking system for trains in the United Kingdom. 🖳 www.thetrainline.com.

Timetables On-Line. An on-line timetable system for most train service in the United Kingdom. 🖳 www.rail.co.uk/ukrail/planner/planner.htm.

Central Trains. A network of trains in central England, with Birmingham as a hub. 🖳 www.centraltrains.co.uk/Map/default.asp.

Great North Eastern Railroad. High-speed rail service between London and Edinburgh and other routes. 🖳 www.gner.co.uk.

Great Eastern Railroad. Commuter and short-distance service from London to the Essex coast. 🖳 www.ger.co.uk/html/ggf.html.

Great Western Trains. Service from London to the west, and southern Wales. 🖳 www.great-western-trains.co.uk.

North Western Trains. Service to Northwest England and Wales. 🖳 www.firstnorthwestern.co.uk/home.html.

Northern Spirit. Service in northern England. 🖳 www.northernspirit.co.uk.

ScotRail. Service from London to Scotland, and service within Scotland. 🖳 www.scotrail.co.uk.

Thames Trains. London to Oxford, Stratford-upon-Avon, Windsor, and other areas. 🖳 www.thamestrains.co.uk.

Virgin Trains. London to Birmingham, Glasgow, and other areas. 🖳 www.virgintrains.co.uk.

London's Railway Terminals

London Charing Cross. Service to southeast England, including ferry terminals at Folkestone, Ramsgate, and Dover for Stena Sealink and Hoverspeed services. Charing Cross is accessible by the Northern line and Bakerloo line. The District line and Circle line are a few minutes away at Embankment Tube.

London Euston. Service to Manchester, Liverpool, North Wales, west Midlands, northwest England, and Scotland. Also the terminal for Stena line ship and ferry service to Belfast out of Stranraer, and to Dublin out of Holyhead. Euston is accessible by Underground on the Northern or the Victoria lines.

Note that Euston, King's Cross, and Saint Pancras stations are close to each other in central London, while Waterloo lies on the south bank of the Thames.

London King's Cross. Service to Cambridge, Yorkshire, Newcastle, northeast England, and Scotland. King's Cross is served by the Metropolitan, Circle,

Hammersmith and City, Northern, Piccadilly, and Victoria lines. The adjacent King's Cross Thameslink station serves Gatwick Airport and Luton station.

London Liverpool Street. Service to Stansted Airport, East Anglia, Norwich and Harwich ferry terminal. Sea-rail terminal to the Netherlands, northern Germany, and Scandinavia from Harwich to the Hook of Holland. Liverpool Street Station is accessible by Underground on the Metropolitan line, Circle line, Hammersmith and City line, and Central line.

An express bus service runs from the train station to London City Airport.

London Paddington. Service to Reading, West England, Bristol, Wales, and southwest England. Also the terminal for the Heathrow Express, and trains to Ireland via Stena Sealink through Fishguard and Rosslare. Paddington is accessible by Underground on the District line (Edgware Road branch), Circle line, Metropolitan line, and Bakerloo line.

London Saint Pancras. Service to East Midlands and Sheffield. When renovations are completed, the station will serve as the base for connecting service via Eurostar to France and Belgium.

London Victoria. Service to Gatwick Airport, Brighton, and the south coast. Trains also connect to ferries and boats to Belgium and France. The station itself is a bustling urban space with shops, restaurants, and many trains. Victoria is accessible by Underground on the District line, Circle line, and Victoria line. The railway station is close to Victoria coach station, from where coach services radiate all over Britain.

London Waterloo. Serving the Eurostar high-speed train to Lille, Paris, Brussels, and elsewhere in Europe via the Channel Tunnel. Also service to southeast England. The spectacular Waterloo International Terminal is worth a peek even if you're not heading under the Channel. Plans call for the eventual transfer of Eurostar trains to the Saint Pancras station.

Located across the Thames from Westminster, Waterloo can be reached by Underground on the Northern, Bakerloo, and the Waterloo and City lines. The extension of the Jubilee line includes a stop at Waterloo with connections to the West End and the Canary Wharf financial district.

For train times and fares on domestic trains, call ☎ (0845) 748-4950 or ☎ (0133) 238-7601. To book rail tickets, call ☎ (0141) 332-9811, ☎ (0207) 928-5151, or ☎ (0191) 261-1234. For information on Eurostar service, call ☎ (0990) 186186 or consult 🖳 www.eurostar.com.

StationLink Bus Service

In addition to Underground connections and local bus services, London Transport runs the hourly StationLink bus service linking Paddington, Marylebone, Euston, King's Cross, Liverpool Street, Fenchurch Street, London Bridge, Waterloo, and Victoria mainline rail stations. The bus also connects to Airbus A1 at Victoria coach station and Airbus A2 at Euston for Heathrow Airport.

StationLink bus SL1 runs clockwise (the order of the stations listed above), while SL2 runs counterclockwise to the same stations.

Information on bus service is available by calling ☎ (020) 7222-1234.

The Chunnel and Eurostar Rail Service

The centuries-old dream of linking the United Kingdom to Europe by a tunnel under the Channel finally was realized in 1994, and today thousands zip back and forth between London and Paris each day.

The sleek, quarter-mile-long Eurostar trains reach speeds of as much as 186 miles per hour on the French side of the Channel. Travel on the British side is often much less—about 50 to 70 miles per hour.

A trip from London Waterloo to Paris's downtown Gare du Nord takes about three hours, which can be faster than a trip by airplane when you include travel to and from the airport. On the French side, a high-speed line branches off at Lille to connect to Brussels, reducing times on the London-Brussels route to two hours and forty-five minutes.

In my experience, the three-hour promise is a bit on the optimistic side. Although some trains apparently do arrive on time, I'd suggest you figure on a half-hour cushion in either direction to allow for delays.

In recent years Eurostar trains made seventeen departures each day from London Waterloo International to Paris and eight to Brussels, with additional service on the weekend. Direct connections from London to Disneyland Paris (a trip of three hours) are also available.

Additional service is available from Ashford International in the southeast of England, with journey times of two hours to Paris and one hour to Lille.

There are 770 passenger seats (560 standard and 210 first class) on each eighteen-coach Eurostar, equivalent to two Boeing 747s. Operated jointly by Eurostar (U.K.) Limited, the French Railways (SNCF), and Belgium Railways (SNCB), Eurostar has several dozen departures each day to Paris, Brussels, Lille, Calais, and Disneyland Paris. Passengers can connect to about 150,000 miles of rail track throughout continental Europe and beyond.

Packages are also available, including train service from London to Disneyland Paris; it is possible to leave London about 9:30 A.M. and ride direct to Disneyland and spend about four hours at the park, returning that evening about 9:30 P.M. The terminal at Disneyland is just outside the gates to the park.

Eurostar also offers ski-train service to Bourg Saint Maurice and Moutiers in the French Alps during the winter season.

Chunnel Terminals

Adjacent to Waterloo mainline station, the **Waterloo International Terminal** features a tapering glass and stainless-steel roof supported by thirty-seven bowstring arches.

The ticket desk at the international terminal sells tickets for Eurostar and onward connections within Europe as well as Metro (Paris and Brussels) tickets, Disneyland Paris park passes, and some Paris museum passes.

The **Ashford International** station is just west of the entrance to the Channel Tunnel, allowing passengers from the southeast of England to cross to the Continent without having to pass through London.

Waterloo Station

The Channel Tunnel Rail Link

The slowest portion of the trip from London to Paris and elsewhere on the Continent is the trip from London to the Channel. The current journey from the Waterloo international terminal is made on old railway lines through Kent.

However, sometime around the year 2003, Eurostar trains are expected to switch to the Channel Tunnel Rail Link, a new high-speed line that will run for sixty-eight miles between London's Saint Pancras station and the Channel Tunnel. It will be Britain's first new major railway in more than a century.

The Channel Tunnel Rail Link's London terminus will be at Saint Pancras station, which will be substantially expanded—retaining its familiar Victorian structure—to take the long Eurostar trains. Saint Pancras international will offer easy interchange between Eurostar and existing mainline rail services, as well as local services.

London's first international station at Waterloo will remain as an alternative focus for international travel, with convenient rail links to the south and south-west of the country. Two new international stations are also planned at Stratford in east London and Ebbsfleet in Kent.

The new track will allow twice the number of Eurostar trains to run between Paris and Brussels, as the new railway will be able to carry up to eight Eurostars per hour each way.

Eurostar Tickets

One-way Eurostar ticket prices from London to Paris in mid-2001 ranged from about $139 for an adult second-class ticket to $369 for a first-premium seat.

Prices listed here are in dollars, as offered by Rail Europe. That organization sells tickets through its website at 🖳 www.raileurope.com, by phone at ☎ (877) 456-7245 or ☎ (877) 438-7245, and through travel agencies.

Eurostar Tickets. One-way fares in mid-2001 from London to Paris, Disneyland Paris, or Brussels.

	First Class	Second Class
First Premium	$369	NA
Full Fare	$279	$199
Leisure	$219	$139
Senior	$189	$NA
Youth	$165	$79
Passholder	$155	$75
Child	$109	$69

Senior fares are available to travelers age sixty and older. Youth fares are valid for those younger than twenty-six. Child fares are valid for those ages four to eleven.

The passholder rate offers a discount to holders of a valid BritRail Pass.

First-premium tickets include reclining seats, taxi transfer upon arrival in Paris or London, access to the Eurostar lounge and check-in facilities, and a meal. Round-trip tickets are interchangeable for air travel on British Midland.

Full-fare tickets include reclining seats and a meal. Leisure fares apply to nonrefundable advance purchase tickets.

Eurostar tickets are available from most travel agents in the United States and Canada, and from Rail Europe. In London tickets are sold at rail stations, travel agents, and at Eurostar offices at Waterloo international terminal, Ashford International terminal, and at offices at 102–104 Victoria Street, London, SW1. For information, call ☎ (0990) 186186 or consult 🖳 www.eurostar.com.

Eurostar periodically offers special fares, and there are also lower-priced leisure and excursion tickets that generally require a Saturday night stay or three days away.

Leisure Round-Trip Tickets. Itineraries require a two-night overnight stay and purchase of tickets in each direction. One-way prices listed were in effect in mid-2001.

	Adult First Class	Adult Second Class	Youth First Class	Youth Second Class
Round-Trip	$124	$79	$109	$69

Le Shuttle

Le Shuttle operates a twenty-four-hour-a-day train service to transport cars, buses, and bicycles between England's Folkestone and France's Calais terminals. Advance reservations are recommended, although it is also possible to show up and go on a standby list for the next available departure.

Special trains that carry cars and buses leave as often as four times an hour for a thirty-five-minute trip beneath the Channel. For information or reservations call ☎ (0990) 353535 or consult 🖳 www.eurotunnel.com.

Hertz car rental offers a special service known as **Le Swap** that allows renters to use a right-hand-drive vehicle in the United Kingdom and then swap it on arrival in Calais for a left-hand-drive model for use on the Continent—with no extra paperwork. For information, call ☎ (087) 0848-4848.

Ferry Lines from England to Europe, Ireland, and Scotland

Brittany Ferries. Plymouth to Roscoff; Poole to Cherbourg; Poole to Saint Malo; Portsmouth to Caen; Portsmouth to Saint Malo. ☎ (0870) 536-0360. ■ www.brittany-ferries.com.

Condor Ferries. Poole-Guernsey-Jersey; Poole–Jersey–Saint Malo. ☎ (0120) 220-7215. ■ www.condorferries.co.uk.

Cunard Line. Southampton to New York. ☎ (0170) 363-4166. U.S. representative: ☎ (800) 528-6273. ■ www.cunardline.com.

Fjord Line. Newcastle to Stavanger, Haugesund, and Bergen. ☎ (0191) 296-1313. ■ www.fjordline.no.

Hoverspeed. Dover to Calais; Folkestone to Boulogne. ☎ (0870) 240-8070. ■ www.hoverspeed.co.uk.

Hovertravel. Portsmouth to Ryde, Isle of Wight. ☎ (0198) 381-1000. ■ www.hovertravel.co.uk.

Irish Ferries U.K. Holyhead to Dublin; Pembroke to Rosslare. ☎ (0870) 517-1717. ■ www.irishferries.ie.

Isle of Man Steam Packet Company. Belfast to Douglas; Dublin to Douglas; Fleetwood to Douglas; Heysham to Douglas; Liverpool to Douglas; Liverpool to Dublin. ☎ (0162) 466-1661.

Isle of Sark Shipping Company. Guernsey to Sark. ☎ (0148) 172-4059. ■ www.sarkshipping.guernsey.net.

Isles of Scilly Steamship Company. Penzance to Saint Mary's (Isles of Scilly). ☎ (0173) 636-2009. ■ www.compulink.co.uk/~issco or ■ www.islesofscilly-travel.co.uk/main.htm.

John O'Groats Ferries. John O'Groats to Burwick, Orkney. ☎ (0195) 561-1353. ■ www.jogferry.co.uk.

Lundy Company. Bideford to Lundy; Clovelly to Lundy; Ilfracombe to Lundy. ☎ (0123) 747-0422. ■ www.lundyisland.co.uk.

Norse Irish Ferries. Liverpool to Belfast, and Liverpool to Dublin. ☎ (0123) 277-9090. ■ www.norsemerchant.com.

Orkney Ferries. Inter-Orkney Islands. ☎ (0185) 687-2044. ■ www.orkneyferries.orknet.co.uk.

P&O European Ferries. Dover to Calais; Portsmouth to Bilbao; Portsmouth to Cherbourg; Portsmouth to LeHavre. ☎ (0130) 486-4003. ■ www.poef.com.

P&O North Sea Ferries. Hull to Rotterdam; Hull to Zeebrugge. ☎ (0148) 237-7177. ■ www.ponsf.com.

P&O Scottish Ferries. Aberdeen to Lerwick; Aberdeen to Stromness; Scrabster to Stromness; Stromness to Lerwick. ☎ (0122) 458-9111. ■ www.poscottishferries.co.uk.

Red Funnel Ferries. Southampton to East Cowes, Isle of Wight; Southampton to West Cowes. ☎ (0170) 333-4010. ■ www.redfunnel.co.uk.

Scandinavian Seaways. Harwich to Gothenburg; Harwich to Hamburg; Harwich to Esbjerg; Newcastle to Gothenburg; Newcastle to Hamburg. U.S. representative: ☎ (800) 533-3755. ■ www.scansea.com.

SeaCat Scotland. Stanraer to Belfast. ☎ (0870) 552-3523. ■ www.steampacket.com.

Seafrance. Dover to Calais. ☎ (0130) 421-2696. ■ www.seafrance.co.uk.

Shetland Islands Council. Inter-islands. ☎ (0185) 672-2259. ☎ (0159) 574-4550. ■ www.shetland.gov.uk/ferryinfo/ferry.htm.

Smyril Line. (Affiliated with P&O Scottish Ferries.) Bergen to Lerwick to Tórshavn (Faroe Island). ☎ (0122) 458-9111. 🖳 www.smyril-line.com.

Stena Line. Dover to Calais; Fishguard to Rosslare; Harwich to Hook of Holland; Holyhead to Dublin; Holyhead to Dun Laoghaire; Newhaven to Dieppe; Stanraer to Belfast. U.S. representative: ☎ (800) 677-8585. 🖳 www.stenaline.com or 🖳 www.rail europe.com.

Swansea Cork Ferries. Swansea to Cork. ☎ (0179) 245-6116. 🖳 www.swansea-cork.ie/cs/scf.

Wightlink. Lymington to Yarmouth; Portsmouth to Fishbourne; Portsmouth to Ryde. ☎ (0170) 581-2011. 🖳 www.wightlink.co.uk.

The United Kingdom by Car

I'll assume it will come as no surprise to you that they drive on the left side of the road in London and the rest of the United Kingdom. The good news is that for most of us, it's not that difficult to force yourself to remember to drive on the left side of the road when you're on a straight road; the difficulty comes when you come to a rotary (one of the famed English "circuses") or when you have to merge onto a fast-moving expressway, or worst of all, when you suddenly spot an oncoming car on a two-lane road and your brain at first thinks you are headed for a head-on collision.

You'll also likely find it difficult to maneuver on narrow city streets sitting on the "wrong" side.

And then, you'll find that many rental cars have a manual transmission, and even stranger, a stick shift at your left hand.

And then there is London itself, an ancient city that grew topsy-turvy along the outlines of Roman cart paths and medieval turnpikes. There are very few straight roads and even the major thoroughfares in the city are very narrow.

Finally, once you get where you're going, where do you park your car? There are some—expensive—parking garages in parts of the city. The relatively few on-street parking spaces are usually controlled by meters or require the use of timed and dated tickets you must purchase from a "Pay and Display" machine; officers check for current tickets on windshields.

In some neighborhoods, parking is limited to residents who have permits. A single yellow line means that parking is limited; look for a nearby sign. You cannot park on a double yellow line and are not supposed to stop at a space with double red lines.

If you overstay your welcome and are lucky, you'll find a ticket that demands payment of a stiff fine. Less wonderful is to find a "boot" or "clamp" attached to one of the wheels of your car, immobilizing it until you summon the police and pay a fine. In the worst case, cars may be towed away to a police impound lot.

Then consider the fact that London is extremely well served by the Underground and bus services, and the rest of the United Kingdom has a superb network of rail lines.

So, should you consider renting a car in the United Kingdom? Maybe. I would certainly advise against having a car in central London; you'll spend more money on the rental and parking fees and waste more time in traffic than you could possibly spend using mass transit or even taxis. And there is little reason to drive a car between London and the center of most other cities; this is where the rail service shines.

I would recommend renting a car to explore the countryside at relatively slow speed and low stress. Then again, you could hire a car and driver and let the driver worry about right-hand turns from the left lane across traffic.

If you do choose to drive, here are some essentials about driving in the United Kingdom:

- **Driver's License.** A valid driver's license from your home state will be recognized for driving in the United Kingdom for a period of up to twelve months. An International Driving Permit, available through some state-side agencies such as AAA, is not required.
- **Auto Insurance.** Check with your insurance agent to determine whether you have proper coverage for driving in a foreign country. Check also with your credit card company to see if auto insurance policies available to cardholders are valid abroad. You can purchase day-to-day insurance coverage through a car rental agency, albeit at a very high cost.
- **Speed Limits.** Speed limits are generally thirty miles per hour in urban areas, sixty miles per hour on roads away from built-up areas, and seventy miles per hour on motorways.
- **Parking.** Parking is generally restricted during ordinary business hours of about 8 A.M. to 6:30 P.M. weekdays and 8 A.M. to 1:30 P.M. Saturdays. Look for information on streetlight posts.
- **Towing and Road Assistance.** For roadside assistance, call: AA at ☎ (0800) 887766, RAC at ☎ (0800) 828282, or National Breakdown at ☎ (0800) 400600. Your home auto club may have a reciprocal arrangement with the AA or RAC groups; check before you leave.
- **Gasoline.** They call gasoline *petrol*, and it is sold by the liter; one U.S. gallon is equal to a bit under four liters. Gas prices in the United Kingdom and throughout Europe also bear the equivalent of several dollars per gallon in taxes.

Road Rules

Driving in the United Kingdom is just like back home . . . except that every-one is on the wrong side of the road. That's not a minor thing, either. It's easy enough on a divided superhighway, but just wait till you crest a hill on a two-lane back road to find an oncoming *lorrie* (a truck back home) in what your mind tells you is *your* lane.

Most traffic signs follow international standards. Drivers and front-seat passengers are required to wear seatbelts; if belts are installed for the rear seats, passengers there must also wear them. Unless signs indicate otherwise, speed limits are 30 miles per hour in built-up areas, 60 miles per hour on single car-riageways, and 70 miles per hour on motorways and dual carriageways.

You'll appreciate the relative bargain back home when you fill your car's tank with petrol. In mid-2001, prices reached about £0.60 per liter, which is equivalent to nearly $5 per gallon.

Hitting the Roads

Major roads are usually assigned a number, or a letter and number combination. The M3, for example, is a high-speed motorway or freeway. One step below is an A road like the A200, which may be considered a *dual carriageway* (a road that has a barrier between oncoming lanes) or may be a normal road. Smaller roads, mostly in rural areas, are called B roads.

London has two main roads that circle the metropolitan areas; they're known as *ring roads*.

The inner ring is made up of the North and South Circular Roads. The North Circular is the A406, and the South Circular the A205. The North Circular is the segment of the road north of the River Thames; the South Circular is south of the river.

The M25 motorway circles London farther out; it is beyond the edge of the urban area. During morning and afternoon rush hours, and for much of the rest of the day, it is very crowded.

Roadways Out of London

Oxford, Stratford-upon-Avon. Northwest on the M40.
Reading, Bath, Bristol, and Wales. West on the M4.
Southampton and Southwest England. Southwest on the M3.
Portsmouth. Southwest on the A3.
Brighton. South on the M23 and A23.
Canterbury. Southeast on the M2 and A2.
Cambridge. North on the M11 or A10.
North of England. North on the M1 or A1.

Long-Distance Bus Services

First of all, they call buses *coaches* in the United Kingdom, and second, the quality of most intercity buses is notably higher than you may be used to in the United States.

The largest coach company is **National Express**, serving most of the country. Tickets are available at stations, many travel agencies, and by credit card by calling ☎ (020) 7730-3499 or consulting 🖳 www.gobycoach.com.

For about £12 foreign visitors can purchase a **BritExpress Card** that gives a 30 percent discount on tickets purchased within thirty days of first use, or a **Tourist Trail Pass** that permits unlimited travel for five days to a month. For more information, call National Express at ☎ (0870) 580-8080.

For even more savings, you might want to consider buying an **Explorer Pass**, which offers overseas visitors unlimited travel on all National Express and Scottish Citylink buses in England, Scotland, and Wales. The passes are available in various lengths of time. For information, call British Travel International in the United States at ☎ (540) 298-2232.

In London, the Victoria coach station at 164 Buckingham Palace Road is the main terminal for service to and from all parts of the United Kingdom and Continental Europe. For information and credit card booking, call ☎ (020) 7730-3499.

Day-Trip Bus Journeys from London

Destination	Mileage	Approx. Time
Bath	118	3:05
Birmingham	110	2:20
Brighton	51	1:45
Cambridge	61	1:45
Canterbury	56	1:45
Oxford	57	1:40
Stratford-upon-Avon	92	2:45

Chapter 3
Things to Know Before You Go

Arriving in the United Kingdom

All visitors must have a valid passport to enter the United Kingdom. (You'll also have to produce the passport at airline counters in the United States before you board a jet bound for most international destinations.)

American and Canadian citizens do not require a visa to enter the United Kingdom; if you are traveling from another nation, contact the British Embassy or Consulate in your own country for information.

Customs and Duties

At most major points of entry you'll find red and green channels. Use the green line if you are not carrying anything over the customs allowances; use the red line if you have goods to declare or are unsure about import restrictions.

Visitors from member nations of the European Community (including Austria, Belgium, Denmark, Finland, France, Germany, Greece, Italy, Luxembourg, Portugal, Spain excluding the Canary Islands, Sweden, the Netherlands, the Republic of Ireland, and the United Kingdom excluding the Channel Islands) can pass freely through a separate E.C. exit.

All travelers are still subject to selected inspections for drugs, weapons, indecent material, and threats to health and the environment.

You may bring in and take out banknotes, traveler's checks, and letters of credit in any currency and up to any amount.

Duty- and tax-free allowances for products brought into the United Kingdom (subject to change) are:

Tobacco products. Two hundred cigarettes, one hundred cigarillos, fifty cigars, or 250 grams of tobacco

Alcohol. 2 liters of still table wine, plus 1 liter of liquor or 2 liters of fortified or sparkling wine

Perfume. 60cc (2 fl. oz.)

Toilet water. 250cc (9 fl. oz.)

Other goods (including gifts, souvenirs, cider, and beer). £71 worth for passengers arriving from E.C. countries, £136 worth for passengers arriving from outside the European Community.

Air-Passenger Duty Tax

A fee of £5 for destinations within the European Community and £10 for other airports is included in airline ticket charges.

Traveling with Pets

Britons take their pets (and their livestock) very seriously and impose strict quarantine regulations on all animals brought into the country.

All pets entering the United Kingdom must have a current license and must be placed in an approved quarantine location for six months. Pet birds may be brought into the country under a different set of regulations.

Authorities warn that any illegally imported animal is likely to be destroyed. For further information, contact:

Ministry of Agriculture, Fisheries, and Food
Government Buildings (Toby Jug Site)
Hook Rise South, Tolworth, Surbiton
Surrey KT6 7NF
England

Financial Matters

The British Monetary System

British money is based on the pound. Like any foreign currency, its value in relation to money from other countries will fluctuate over time.

In mid-2001 the British pound was worth about $1.40 in U.S. currency. In other words, it would cost that much in U.S. dollars to buy a pound. To convert a price stated in pounds to dollars, multiply the price in pounds times the exchange rate; a dress priced at £100 pounds would cost about $140 in American dollars. To go from dollars to pounds, divide the amount of dollars by the exchange rate; in other words $280 in your wallet is worth £200 pounds ($280/1.40 = £200).

(For Canadian travelers, the British pound was worth about $2.13; $426 in Canadian dollars was worth about £200 in mid-2001.)

Each pound is divided into 100 pence; you'll find 1p, 2p, 5p, 10p, 20p, 50p, and £1 coins. Banknotes are issued in £5, £10, £20, and £50 denominations. (In Scotland, £1 notes are also in circulation.)

Paying Your Bills

In general, the best way to pay your bills is to use a credit card. Not only will you receive the benefit of a fair exchange rate for your dollars, but you will also have the safety net of the credit card company in case you need to dispute any charges and you will not have to carry around cash.

Credit cards are widely accepted in the United Kingdom. Retailers are permitted to charge more for goods and services bought by credit card, although this practice is relatively rare.

Before you travel, find out how much of a surcharge your credit card company places on international exchange transactions, usually in the range of 1 to

3 percent. Credit cards are still the best way to pay for purchases, but some cards offer a better deal than others.

You can also use traveler's checks. American Express, Barclays, and some other providers sell checks denominated in pounds through major banks and AAA agencies in the United States. If you bring checks denominated in U.S. dollars, you'll have to trade them in for pounds at a foreign exchange bureau or a bank in the United Kingdom, paying a fee and receiving a retail and less-advantageous exchange rate.

Banks are usually open weekdays from 9:30 A.M. to 3:30 P.M., with many banks open for additional hours and Saturday mornings. All banks are closed on Sunday and public holidays.

ATMs are widely available, and most work with American banking syndicates; be sure to check with your home bank to find out service fees for withdrawals.

Foreign exchange bureaus (sometimes referred to by the French or Italian terms *Bureau de Change* or *Cambio*) are common in airports and in most cities in the United Kingdom and elsewhere in Europe. They are convenient, quick, and expensive. Most offer disadvantageous exchange rates, however, and some even tack on a service charge.

Lost Credit Cards

If your credit card is lost or stolen, you must contact the card issuer to protect yourself against unauthorized charges. Here are British contact numbers for several cards:

American Express. ☎ (0127) 369-6933.
Master Card. ☎ (0800) 964-767.
Visa. ☎ (0160) 423-0230.

If you are unable to notify the credit card company through its British office, you should call the United States for that purpose. Some companies will accept collect calls from overseas. You might enlist a friend or relative to make notification for you.

Keep a record of all your calls and obtain a confirmation code or the name of the person you spoke with to protect yourself against issues when you return home.

Enter the euro. Eleven European nations began a new era of financial unity in 1999 with the birth of a new monetary unit, the euro. The result is an economic giant of 290 million people stretching from the Arctic Circle to the shores of the Mediterranean.

The members of the club are Germany, France, Italy, Spain, the Netherlands, Belgium, Austria, Portugal, Finland, Ireland and Luxembourg.

Not included are Britain, Denmark, and Sweden, where the government and citizens balked at giving up independence in financial affairs. Greece wanted to be a member of the group, but was unable to get its economy in proper shape in time to join.

Beginning January 1, 2002 euro banknotes and coins will go into circulation, marked with the € symbol. After March 1, the euro will be the only legal tender in participating nations.

Old coins can be exchanged at designated banks and offices for a three-year period, and banknotes for ten years after the changeover.

In mid-2001 the euro had fallen back from near-parity with the dollar to be worth about $1.16.

And here's a tip: make two copies of all your credit card account numbers and telephone contact numbers. Keep one copy at home or with trusted friends or relatives so they can make notification on your behalf, and keep the other copy with you on your trip. If you're worried about the list itself being stolen and used by a thief, consider using a simple code to scramble some of the numbers. For example, reverse the order of the last three numbers of all the cards; that should be enough to confuse most ordinary thieves.

Shopping

Most retail shops in central London and other major cities are open from about 9 A.M. to 5:30 P.M. daily; larger shops are open on Sunday as well. In London, shops in Knightsbridge and Kensington High Street are generally open until about 7 P.M. on Wednesday; in the West End, shops generally stay open until 7 P.M. on Thursday.

You'll find some stores in tourist areas open a bit later in the night. The urban blight of superstores has begun to arrive in the suburbs, and many of these retail operations have extended hours.

On the other hand, in small towns many shops will still close for a lunch break in the middle of the day.

Value-Added Tax

Nearly every product sold in the United Kingdom includes a value-added tax (VAT) of 17.5 percent as part of its price; the tax is also applied to services such as hotels, restaurants, and auto rentals. Visitors from the United States and other non–European Community countries can obtain a refund of a large portion of VAT for goods purchased for export and taken out of the European Community within three months of purchase.

To claim a refund, you can obtain a VAT 407 Refund Form from the store where you make a purchase and have it stamped by the VAT office at an airport or port; you may have to show the items to the officials, so don't pack them too deeply in your luggage. Once the form has been approved, mail it back to the place where you made your purchase to request your refund.

Many shops will arrange for the refund of VAT paid on items above a minimum level, sometimes assessing a service charge for their trouble.

Note that although VAT is also charged on services, including hotels, restaurants, and auto rental, refunds of VAT on services are not available.

Telephones: Cracking the Code

British style for indicating telephone numbers is different from that of the United States, and to make things even more difficult, it is not consistent from place to place within Britain.

In this book, we have chosen to present seven- or eight-digit phone numbers in the American style, like this: ☎ (CITY CODE) XXXX-XXXX.

Some phone numbers, including certain national codes or toll-free codes, use a four- or five-digit area code and a six-digit number. They appear like this: ☎ (CITY CODE) XXXXXX.

The Big Number

OK, just when you thought maybe you were beginning to sort of, kind of, maybe understand the telephone system in the United Kingdom, here comes the Big Number. That's the name given to a massive changeover of telephone numbers across much of the United Kingdom, which began in 1999 and continues through 2001.

Six geographic areas were assigned new area codes: London (020), Portsmouth/Southampton (023), Cardiff (029), Coventry (024), and Northern Ireland (028). All six areas will have a three-digit code followed by an eight-digit number. For the time being, other areas will stay within an (010) code.

Before this changeover, London had been within two codes, 0171 for central London and 0181 for outlying areas.

Here's the way the Big Number change works in London:

Area Code: Changed from (0171) or (0181) to (020).

Local Number: Create the new eight-digit number by adding 7 or 8 to the front of the existing local number. Here's an example:

Old Number	New Number
(0171) XXX-XXXX	(020) 7XXX-XXXX
(0181) XXX-XXXX	(020) 8XXX-XXXX

As part of the change, a new series of area codes was also added. The "family" system is intended to help users know what kind of number they are calling. The codes are:

00 International codes
01 Existing area codes
02 New area codes
03 Reserved
04 Reserved
05 Reserved
06 Reserved
07 Mobiles, pagers, personal numbers
08 Freephone and special rate services
09 Premium rate services

Emergency. For police, fire, or ambulance, call ☎ 999 or ☎ 112. No coin or card is necessary to call police, fire service, or ambulance service from any telephone or public call box.

Telephone Operator. For help connecting to a number, dial ☎ 100; to reach the international operator, call ☎ 155.

Directory Inquiries. Dial ☎ 142 for London and ☎ 192 elsewhere.

International Calls. If you plan to call the United States from the United Kingdom, sign up for an international telephone credit card before you leave home. All of the major carriers including MCI, Sprint, AT&T, and smaller companies offer cards that allow you to tap into their networks using a toll-free number. Such services are much less expensive than using one of the British pay telephones. And the *most* expensive way to call is to dial directly from your hotel room.

Street phones in London

Many public phones accept coins; some also work with pre-paid phonecards or credit cards. Increasingly, some phones will only accept cards or connect to computerized calling card networks. Phonecards with values from £2 to £20 are sold at post offices and some shops.

Calling the United Kingdom from the United States. You'll need to access the international phone system and add a country code to phone numbers. Begin with 011 to signify an international call. Add the country code of 44 for the United Kingdom. Then drop the 0 before the city code, what we would call the area code.

Here's are two examples:

To call ☎ (020) 7222-1234 in London from the United States call ☎ 011-44-20-7222-1234.

To call ☎ (01273) 292599 in Brighton from the United States call ☎ 011-44-273-292-599.

Electrical Voltage

In the United Kingdom, electrical mains provide current at 240 volts AC, 50 Hz. Plugs are also shaped differently from those in the United States and Canada.

Some devices from the United States are able to automatically convert the power but require a plug adapter; be sure to check the instruction manual for any device before you connect to 240 volts in this manner.

The other way to connect is to use a converter that steps down 240 volts to a level near 110 volts; the converter must also have the proper adapter to allow it to plug into the main.

Before leaving home, a visit to a Radio Shack or other well-stocked electronics store would be helpful.

Videotapes and Televisions

The British television system uses a different (and slightly higher resolution) standard known as PAL for its broadcast signal. The television set in your hotel or flat will work the same as at home. However VCR and video camera owners are in a different situation.

1. Don't purchase a PAL videotape in Britain and expect to be able to play it on your home VCR. You may find videotapes made for the U.S. market; they will be marked as working with the American NTSC standard.

2. Don't expect to be able to play a videotape you brought from home, or made in a portable video camera, on a British PAL standard television.

There are devices that allow you to play one type of tape on another type of device or make a converted tape. Service bureaus can perform the work for you if you come home with an irreplaceable tape of the wrong type.

Pubs

The ubiquitous British pub is generally open from about 11 A.M. to 11 P.M. Monday to Saturday, and from noon to 10:30 P.M. on Sunday.

You must be at least eighteen years old to buy and consume alcohol in a bar in England; in Scotland sixteen and seventeen year olds can buy and consume mild alcoholic drinks.

In England, Scotland, and Wales children younger than fourteen accompanied by an adult are allowed into certain sections of pubs that hold a children's certificate.

Tipping

Tipping protocol in the United Kingdom is similar to that of the United States. Check your hotel and restaurant bills, though, to see if a service charge has already been added.

Hotels. Some establishments will add a service charge of 10 to 15 percent.

Porters. £1 per piece of luggage.

A typical London pub

Restaurants. If a service charge is not included, it is customary to leave a tip of 10 to 15 percent of the bill.

Taxis. 10 to 15 percent of the fare.

Print Media, TV, and Radio

Newspapers

London is the home of one of the most dog-eat-dog media markets in the world; some of the most famous newspaper battles of all time took place among the publishers along Fleet Street in central London.

The newspapers have all departed for the outlying districts now, but they still compete for readers every day in the Underground and street-corner kiosks; they're joined now by brash competition among independent television and radio stations. Most of the newspapers consider themselves national in scope.

The grande dame of newspapers is still the *Times of London*, although it has come down from its lofty perch in recent years under the ownership of global media magnate Rupert Murdoch. You can read an electronic version of the paper over the Internet at 💻 www.the-times.co.uk.

The Sunday edition is available at 💻 www.sunday-times.co.uk.

The *Financial Times* concentrates on business and economic stories, with a strong international news section. It is available on-line at 💻 www.ft.com.

The *Guardian* is slightly left of center. It is offered on the Internet at 💻 www.guardian.co.uk.

On Sunday, the same publisher offers the *Observer*, available on-line at 💻 www.observer.co.uk.

Right of center is the *Daily Telegraph*. It can be consulted on-line at 💻 www.telegraph.co.uk.

More or less up the middle is the *Independent*. Its online pages are at 💻 www.independent.co.uk.

The *Evening Standard* is the only remaining afternoon daily newspaper; unlike most of the other papers, its focus is mostly on London. It is available on-line at 💻 www.thisislondon.co.uk.

An important source of information about entertainment options of almost any description is *Time Out*, sold at most newsstands. An electronic version, worth consulting before you head for the United Kingdom, is available at 💻 www.timeout.com.

Television

When television first came to the United Kingdom, it was entirely under the sober control of the British Broadcasting Corporation (BBC), which presented a mix of news, classical music, and strange British sitcoms on a commercial-free network.

The "Beeb" is still on the air, with its flagship news presented each night at 9 P.M. It has been joined by BBC2, with an emphasis on documentaries and cultural presentations.

Channel 3 is ITV, a bit looser than BBC and it includes commercials; its evening news is offered at 10 P.M. Channels 4 and 5 are also commercial operations, offering a mix of British sitcoms, movies, and American shows.

Many hotels and apartments will also offer cable or satellite channels, among them several "Sky" channels that provide news, sports, and movies, as well as American offerings.

Radio

Here's a selection of some of the more interesting of London's radio stations:

1035 Ritz. MW 1035 kHz. Music and talk. 🖳 www.ritz1035.com.

BBC Radio 1. FM 98.8 MHz. Pop and rock. 🖳 ww.bbc.co.uk/radio1.

BBC Radio 2. FM 89.1 MHz. Talk, drama, and music. 🖳 www.bbc.co.uk/radio2.

BBC Radio 3. FM 91.3 MHz. Classical music and jazz. 🖳 www.bbc.co.uk/radio3.

BBC Radio 4. FM 93.5 MHz and AM 720 kHz. Talk and documentary. 🖳 www.bbc.co.uk/radio4.

BBC London Live. FM 94.9 MHz and MW 693 kHz. News and sports. 🖳 www.bbc.co.uk/londonlive.

BBC Radio 5. AM 909 kHz. Sports, news, and talk. 🖳 www.bbc.co.uk/fivelive.

Capital FM. FM 95.8 MHz. Pop music. 🖳 www.capitalfm.com.

Capital Gold. MW 1548 kHz. Golden oldies. 🖳 www.capitalgold.com.

Choice FM. FM 96.9 MHz. Dance, reggae, and soul. 🖳 www.choice969fm.co.uk.

Classic FM. FM 100.9 MHz. Classical music. 🖳 classicfm.com.

Heart FM. FM 106.2 MHz. Pop music. 🖳 www.heart1062.co.uk.

Jazz FM. FM 102.2 MHz. Jazz. 🖳 www.jazzfm.com.

Kiss FM. FM 100.0 MHz. Mainstream rock, originally a pirate station before corporate types took over. 🖳 www.kissonline.co.uk.

Liberty. AM 963 and 972 kHz. Music and talk. 🖳 www.libertyradio.co.uk.

London Greek Radio. FM 103.3 MHz. Ethnic.

Magic FM. FM 105.4 MHz. Easy listening.

News Direct. FM 97.3. News, talk, and weather. 🖳 www.newsdirect.co.uk.

Sunrise. MW 1458 kHz. Asian.

Talk Sport. MW 1089 kHz. 🖳 www.talksport.net.

Virgin Radio. FM 105.8 MHz, MW 1197 kHz. Rock music. 🖳 www.virginradio.co.uk.

Xfm. FM 104.9 MHz. Alternative new music. 🖳 www.xfm.co.uk.

Post Offices

In most city locations, post offices are open weekdays from 9 A.M. to 5:30 P.M., and from 9 A.M. to 12:30 P.M. on Saturdays.

Stamps are available at post offices and most newsagents. Post offices are open 9 A.M. to 5:30 P.M. weekdays, and 9 A.M. to 12:30 P.M. on Saturdays.

Airmail postage for postcards is 36p to countries in the Europe, and 45p to other destinations including the United States.

Airmail postage for letters is 36p within the European Community. The United States is in zone 1, which is charged at 45p for a super-light ten-gram letter, 65p for a twenty-gram letter, and £1.35 for 60 grams, which is about an ounce. (A considerably slower surface-mail service is also available, charged at 58p for a sixty-gram letter.)

Note that the Royal Mail has applied for a rate increase that if approved would boost prices by at least 1p in late 2001.

Medical Matters

Tourists who become ill or are injured while in Britain are eligible for free emergency treatment through the National Health Service at accident and emergency departments of hospitals.

In general, tourists and visitors from the United States must pay for nonemergency medical treatment in hospitals and for services in doctors' offices; some countries that have national medical systems have reciprocal arrangements with Great Britain that allow for free or reduced-cost care. They include members of the European Community and Australia, Hong Kong, New Zealand, Russia, Norway, Sweden, Finland, and Iceland.

To find the nearest hospital or doctor, call the telephone operator by dialing ☎ 100. For emergencies, dial ☎ 999 or ☎ 112 and ask for the ambulance service.

Check with your insurance agent to be sure you have appropriate coverage for medical emergencies while you are traveling. Some policies include payment for emergency air travel from a foreign country to your home.

Accident and Sickness Insurance

The idea of falling ill or suffering an injury while hundreds or thousands of miles away from your home and family doctor can be a terrifying thought. But before you sign on the bottom line for an accident and sickness insurance policy, be sure to consult with your own insurance agent or your company's personnel office to see how far your personal medical insurance policy will reach. Does the policy cover vacation trips and exclude business travel? Are all international locations excluded? Can you purchase a "rider," or extension, to your personal policy to cover travel?

The only reason to purchase an accident and sickness policy is to fill in any gaps in the coverage you already have. If you don't have health insurance of any kind, a travel policy is certainly valuable, but you might want to consider whether you should spend the money on a year-round policy instead of taking a vacation in the first place.

Also be aware that nearly every kind of health insurance has an exclusionary period for preexisting conditions. If you are sick before you set out on a trip, you may find that the policy will not pay for treating the problem.

British Travel Information

For the official word on travel to England and other parts of the United Kingdom, there's a wealth of information available from tourist boards.

The British Tourist Authority offers a comprehensive set of Internet Web pages for travelers to Britain, at ▆ www.visitbritain.com.

You can contact the British Tourist Authority (BTA) at one of the following addresses for the latest brochures:

British Tourist Authority
551 Fifth Avenue, Suite 701
New York, NY 10176
☎ (800) 462-2748

British Tourist Authority
625 North Michigan Avenue, Suite 1510
Chicago, IL 60611

Northern Ireland Tourist Board
551 Fifth Avenue, seventh floor
New York, NY 10176
☎ (800) 326-0036

London Pass

One way to cut the price on many attractions in London is to purchase the **London Pass.** Available in one-, two-, three-, and six-day time periods for individuals or families, it offers free admission to more than sixty attractions, tours, and historic sites. Passes purchased outside of England also include a London Visitor Travelcard, valid on the Underground in zones 1–6, on London buses, and on the river Thames from Embankment to Greenwich. You can also get a free tour with London Pride open-topped sightseeing buses.

Participating attractions and sites include: Alexander Fleming Laboratory Museum; Bank of England Museum; Bankside Gallery; Banqueting House; Battersea Park Children's Zoo; HMS *Belfast*; British Museum; Catamaran Cruisers; Cathedral and Abbey Church of Saint Alban; Chislehurst Caves; Chiswick House; Couper Collection; *Cutty Sark*; Dail Universe; Dulwich Picture Gallery; Eltham Palace; Estorick Collection of Modern Italian Art; Fan Museum; Florence Nightingale Museum, and the Guards Museum.

Also, Hampton Court Palace; Institute of Contemporary Arts; Jewel Tower; Jewish Museum (Camden); Jewish Museum (Finchley); Kensington Palace; Kenwood House; Kew Bridge Steam Museum; London Aquarium; London Bicycle Tour; London Brass Rubbing Centre; London Canal Museum; London Dungeon; London Pride Sightseeing Tour; London's Transport Museum; London Zoo; Marble Hill House, and Museum of Fulham Palace.

And, Old Operating Theatre, Museum and Herb Garret; Pollock's Toy Museum. Queen Elizabeth's Hunting Lodge; Royal Air Force Museum; Royal Botanic Gardens (Kew); Royal Mews; Saatchi Gallery; Saint Paul's Cathedral; Shree Swaminarayan Mandir; Southside House; Southwark Cathedral; Stepping Out Walks; Tate Britain; Thames Barrier Visitors Centre; Tower of London; Verulamium Museum; Westminster Abbey Chapter House; The Wetland Centre; Wimbledon Lawn Tennis Museum; Windsor Castle.

On-line prices in mid-2001 were:

	1-Day	2-Day	3-Day	6-Day
Adult	£22	£39	£49	£79
Child (5–15)	£14	£24	£30	£42

The pass is available online through ▣ www.londonpass.com and through some travel agencies in the United States.

It can also be purchased in London at the British Visitor Centre at 1 Regent Street, or at some twenty Exchange International stores throughout London. It is also available at the London Transport Information Centre at Heathrow and the London Tourist Information Centre at Heathrow Terminals 1, 2, and 3.

The only way to obtain the pass with the London Visitor Travelcard is to order it from outside Great Britain.

In recent years, similar products have been called the GoSee Card and the London White Card. Both have been discontinued.

Chapter 4
A Place to Lay Your Head

Hotels in London

London is well stocked with hotels of most every description.

There are classic luxury hostelries like the Ritz, Claridge's, the Dorchester, the Waldorf, and the Langham Hilton where you'll find legions of bellmen, doormen, and concierges, as well as opulent lobbies, restaurants, and public rooms.

You'll also find some smaller gems such as the Halcyon, Blakes, and Brown's. When I stayed at Brown's, I was met at the door by an assistant manager and escorted to a desk in her office where I was presented with my check-in documents—already prepared—and an invitation to high tea.

Luxury and personal attention, though, come at a high price: the top rank of London hotels typically start their rate cards at about £200 per night (about $288) for a basic room. You'll generally find the highest rates in central locations such as Piccadilly, Mayfair, and sections of Brompton.

At the other end of the price spectrum, you can find hotels in outlying districts like Paddington, Kensington, Notting Hill, Westminster, and elsewhere. Here, room rates usually start at about £50 to £70 per night (about $72 to $101) in small hotels.

In general, hotel rooms in London—even at the luxury level—are small. Parents traveling with children may not be able to squeeze the youngsters into the same room; to compound the problem, connecting rooms are relatively scarce in older hotels. Some of the newer hotels offer somewhat larger rooms.

Be sure to discuss your specific needs with your travel agent or with the hotel directly before you make your plans.

You'll find a listing of nearly 250 hotels in London in the appendix of this book. You'll also find the names of dozens of hotel booking companies and travel agencies specializing in London.

If you have access to the Internet, use a browser to search for direct offers from many London hotels and apartments.

And be sure to check out the section of discount coupons and special offers at the back of this book.

Apartments and Bed-and-Breakfasts

If you are going to visit London for more than a few days, I would highly recommend you consider renting an apartment or staying at a bed-and-breakfast. For many travelers, either option will give you a bit (or a lot) more room at a comparable price to a hotel or at a savings.

Most apartments come with a kitchen. Some visitors may choose to save hundreds of dollars on a trip by cooking meals in their apartment; others can still enjoy the convenience of breakfasts and snacks at "home" before setting out for a day in London.

You'll find a large selection of apartments throughout London; the lowest rates are generally found in the outlying districts, but some bargains can be had in buildings in Kensington and Bloomsbury, for example. Typical weekly rents range from about £400 to £1,000 for two- or three-bedroom flats with kitchens.

In recent years, I have rented a two-bedroom flat off Tottenham Court Road for about £150 per night.

Bed-and-breakfasts, as the name implies, generally offer a communal morning meal as part of the package. Rooms may be smaller or larger than those in hotels, and some B&Bs offer shared bathrooms.

Hotel Ratings

The English Tourist Board rates participating hotels and guest houses throughout England; a similar system is in place in Scotland, Wales, and Northern Ireland. Ratings range from a basic 1 Crown to a highest mark of 5 Crowns. Look for the Crown rating at establishments.

Part II
Getting Around London

Chapter 5
Understanding London's Geography

The largest city in Europe, Greater London sprawls out in all directions, encompassing more than six hundred square miles and nearly seven million people.

The heart of London, as it has been for two thousand years, lies along the northern shore of the River Thames as it wanders in an upside-down U on its way to the sea.

In this book, we explore London, neighborhood by neighborhood. That's one way to do the big city. Another way is to pick and choose your destinations: visit one of the fabulous museums or galleries and then explore the surrounding neighborhood.

The beauty of the big city is that no two points in Greater London are more than about an hour apart by Underground, bus, or taxi.

Here is the way we carve up London for the purposes of this book:

• **Whitehall and Westminster.** Chapter 10, pages 79–92. The seat of government of the United Kingdom, Whitehall and Westminster include the **Houses of Parliament** and the prime minister's residence at **Downing Street**. In the sub-basements, Winston Churchill directed the war effort from the **Cabinet War Rooms**. And keeping watch on the reins of power is one of the enduring symbols of London and England: **Big Ben**.

Westminster is also the home of some of the most important churches in England, including **Westminster Abbey**. And then there are the national treasures of the **Tate Gallery**.

• **Piccadilly and Saint James.** Chapter 11, pages 93–106. Piccadilly is the Times Square of London, the commercial heart of the city, and an icon of its vibrancy—in neon.

And **Saint James's Park**, just a few blocks south, could not be more different. Here you'll find the stiffest upper lips of England: **Buckingham Palace**, **Saint James's Palace**, and the formal processionals of the **Mall** and **Birdcage Walk**.

• **Trafalgar Square, Soho, Leicester Square, and the West End**. Chapter 12, pages 107–114. Take a walk on the somewhat wild side of London, home of the lively shops and restaurants of Soho, **Carnaby Street**, and **Chinatown**. And then enter into London's West End, its thriving theater district off Shaftesbury Avenue and Leicester Square. (We cover the **West End Theater District** in more depth in Chapter 24, pages 229–238.)

And for a bit of classical culture, the area also includes the **National Gallery** and the **National Portrait Gallery** and the church of **Saint Martin-in-the-Fields,** which doubles as a renowned live-music concert venue.

• **Covent Garden and the Strand.** Chapter 13, pages 115–122. Covent Garden has been one of the capital's best places to hang out since the 1630s when Inigo Jones designed the **Piazza** as the city's first square. Today, the Piazza and the surrounding Victorian-era warehouses and shops have been given new life as home to trendy shops, fascinating open-stall markets, and public spaces for music, entertainment, and casual dining. The former wholesale market at Covent Garden has been covered over with glass and steel arches to make it an attractive indoor-outdoor setting.

Children of all ages will enjoy a visit to the **London Transport Museum** at Covent Garden, where there's an opportunity to climb all over a collection of old buses and underground trains. And then there is the small but exceedingly rich collection of art at the **Courtauld Institute Galleries.**

• **Holborn and the Inns of Court.** Chapter 14, pages 123–126. Holborn and the Inns of Court are very British, very formal, and very interesting. Here you'll find bewigged barristers scurrying back and forth between their posh offices in and around the Inns of Court and the **Royal Courts of Justice.**

Other highlights include the eclectic collection of **Sir John Soane's Museum** crammed into an exotic nineteenth-century gallery.

• **The City, Smithfield, and Spitalfields.** Chapter 15, pages 127–147. The City, built on the site of the original Roman settlement of Londinium, is the financial center of England. Roman carts and amphitheaters are replaced by Rolls-Royces and glass and chrome skyscrapers.

But old London is still present in the fabulous collection of the **Museum of London,** which reaches back to Roman times and beyond. You can walk the bloodied yards and spires of the **Tower of London.** And there is the unusual tour of the **Tower Bridge,** where you can cross over the River Thames on the high catwalk and then explore the foundations and Victorian steam-lifting mechanism of the landmark.

And finally, the City includes **St. Paul's Cathedral,** which rose from the ashes of the Great Fire of 1666.

• **Greenwich.** Chapter 16, page 149–160. Greenwich is all about time: the home of the **Old Royal Observatory** where millions of visitors have stood with their feet on either side of the prime meridian; the **National Maritime Museum,** which holds a priceless collection of artifacts and artwork that tells the story of Great Britain's seafaring past; the well-preserved *Cutty Sark,* one of the last of the great clipper ships; and the **Queen's House,** a quietly elegant royal party house on the Thames.

• **Southwark, Bankside, and the London Bridge Area.** Chapter 17, pages 161–174. The other side of the river from London was the wild side in the sixteenth century, a place of bear pits, houses of ill repute, and William Shakespeare's **Globe Theatre**. Not coincidentally, it was also home to the **Clink**, the prison that gave birth to the nickname for jails for centuries to come.

Also notable are **Southwark Cathedral** and a collection of small but interesting museums, including the **Bankside Gallery**, the **Bramah Tea & Coffee Museum**, and the **Design Museum**.

• **South Bank**. Chapter 18, pages 175–182. Across the river from Saint James's Park, Whitehall, the Houses of Parliament, and Covent Garden, the South Bank is home to a trio of notable museums: the **Imperial War Museum**, the **Museum of the Moving Image**, and the **London Aquarium**.

And the South Bank's relative obscurity has been all but erased with the arrival of the impossible-to-overlook **London Eye**, a four-hundred-foot-high modern ferris wheel that circles high above the Thames. It became an instant hit with tourists and locals after its opening in early 2000.

• **Bloomsbury and Fitzrovia**. Chapter 19, pages 183–190. The literary soul of modern London, this was the home of current-era writers from Virginia Woolf and other members of the Bloomsbury Group, to poet Dylan Thomas, and in the nineteenth century, Charles Dickens.

One of the reasons they gathered there was the presence of the fabulous **British Museum** and the **British Library**. The museum includes some of our planet's most extraordinary artifacts, including the Rosetta Stone, the Elgin Marbles from the Parthenon, and an amazing collection of mummies, sarcophagi, and statuary. The British Library, with its own treasure of books and recordings, moved to a spectacular new home at Saint Pancras in 1997.

• **Regent's Park, Camden**. Chapter 20, pages 191–200. Regent's Park is a grand preserve, encompassing the historic **London Zoo** and a scenic portion of the **Regent's Canal**.

At its south end are some splendid homes and churches, as well as the tourist magnet of **Madame Tussaud's** waxworks and a museum on Baker Street that memorializes detective Sherlock Holmes at the address where he would have lived if he were other than a fictional character.

You'll also find the splendid **Wallace Collection**, home of European masterpieces you'll recognize without any training in art history.

• **South Kensington, Kensington, Knightsbridge, and Notting Hill**. Chapter 21, pages 201–210. The riches of Kensington and South Kensington alone would be the jewels of many a nation. Museums and galleries include the incomparable **Natural History Museum, Science Museum**, and **Victoria and Albert Museum**. The sumptuous **Brompton Oratory** is a treasure of ecclesiastic and musical worlds; the **Royal Albert Hall** is home to classical concerts, including the famed BBC Proms conducted each summer.

There's also the **Kensington Palace**, created by William and Mary as a country home, and much later the bachelor quarters for Princess Diana. **Hyde Park**, including its famed **Speakers' Corner** and **Marble Arch**, is nearby.

World-class shopping in Kensington includes the busy **Harrods Department Store**; much funkier shops are along Portobello Road, the Queensway, and in the transplanted Third World of the Notting Hill district.

• **Chelsea**. Chapter 22, pages 211–213. A picturesque village of Tudor homes and gardens along the Thames, Chelsea is just minutes away from Kensington and the heart of London. The notable **National Army Museum** also is in the district.

Then we delve into London's West End Theater District. And later in this book, we'll explore some wondrous day trips from London, including **Hampton Court, Windsor Castle, Bath, Brighton, Cambridge, Oxford**, and much more.

You'll find in this book local maps for each of the neighborhoods of London. There are three other resources I would recommend you add to your back pocket or purse.

First, pick up a free copy of the *Central London Bus Guide*, available in many Underground stations and at London Transport tourist offices. This map includes all bus routes as well as major tourist destinations in London; the well-designed map also shows Underground and rail stations.

Next, stop by the half-price ticket booth at Leicester Square for a copy of *The Official London Theatre Guide*; copies are usually found on the backside of the theater-listing boards that flank the booth. The guide includes current listings for all major theater productions as well as a good map of "Theatreland" that marks the locations of nearly fifty theaters.

And finally, if you really want the inside skinny on London street by street, purchase a copy of *London A–Z* from a bookstore or newsstand. This is a book of maps with an index that covers all of London in tremendous detail.

Chapter 6
London Underground, Inner-City Buses, and Taxis

London Underground

The London Underground is the world's oldest and largest metropolitan railway system. Most everyone calls it the "Tube," but you can call it the Underground or the London Transport; just don't call it a "subway." In England, a subway is a pedestrian tunnel under a road.

Whatever you call it, you can get from just about anywhere in London to anywhere else with relative speed and comfort at a reasonable price; add in the London Transport bus system and the city is literally at your feet or above your head.

The Underground is made up of twelve railway lines; most were originally competing private companies, but over the years they have been integrated into a single system with free transfers. Most of the track lies on the north side of the River Thames, although several lines go under the river where they meet up with railroad and bus connections.

The Underground stretches nearly 250 miles, including the Jubilee Line extension of 1999. A bit less than half of the track is in tunnels, including 20 miles in relatively shallow cut-and-cover tunnels such as those on the District and Circle lines, and 86 miles in deep-level Tube tunnels such as on the Northern and Central lines.

The maximum depth below ground level is on the Northern line, at Holly Bush Hill, Hampstead, at 221 feet; the maximum depth below mean sea level is also on the Northern line, just south of Waterloo station, at seventy feet. The greatest height above ground level is yet again on the Northern Line, at Dollis Brook viaduct, which carries the line sixty feet over Dollis Road, Mill Hill.

London Travel Information

Most lines operate from about 5:30 A.M. to 12:45 A.M. weekdays, from 6 A.M. to 12:45 A.M. Saturday, and 7:30 A.M. to 12:45 A.M. Sunday. Each station has a sign indicating the last train of the day. During rush hour, trains may be two

51

minutes apart; late at night, they may arrive at fifteen-minute intervals. Some stations close earlier in the evening, and a few are not open on weekends.

Information and route planning for London Underground, buses, night buses, and the Docklands Light Railway is available twenty-four hours a day by calling ☎ (020) 7222-1234; for information about current transport conditions, call ☎ (020) 7222-1200. The Docklands Travel Hot Line provides information on all buses and trains in the Docklands area at ☎ (020) 7918-4000.

London Transport is on the Web with fare information and an interactive map. Consult 🖳 www.thetube.com or 🖳 www.londontransport.co.uk.

In London you can also visit one of the London Transport Travel Centres for travel advice, maps, timetables, travelcards, bus passes, and reservations for certain attractions. The centers are at Euston and Victoria rail stations, plus Underground stations at King's Cross, Liverpool Street, Oxford Circus, Piccadilly Circus, Saint James's Park, and Heathrow terminals 1, 2, and 3.

The Jubilee Line and Docklands Light Railway Extensions

As part of the millennium celebration in Greenwich, the Jubilee underground line was extended south and east from Westminster to link central London with Waterloo, the South Bank, Greenwich, and Stratford in east London. New stops include North Greenwich and Canary Wharf for Docklands.

At the same time, the Docklands Light Railway was extended from Island Gardens under the Thames to Cutty Sark in Greenwich and beyond to Elverson Road, Deptford, Creek, and Lewisham.

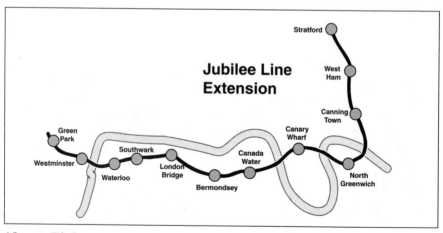

About Tickets

There are six zones in concentric circles from the heart of London to the outlying areas. The price of a ticket depends on which zone you travel within, or which zones you cross. Nearly all of the London museums, theaters, and attractions in this book lie within zone 1.

Most London Transport tickets can also be used on buses and National Railway trains within the same zones on the tickets. (The bus zone map is slightly different in outlying areas from that of the Underground.)

The simplest way to travel is to buy an individual ticket each time you show up at the station; there's a ticket machine and ticket window at most stops. That's not the most efficient way to spend your time and money, though; there is a wide range of multitrip or multiday tickets available in London or in advance from travel agencies in the United States, Canada, and other countries.

Up to two accompanied children younger than five can travel free on buses; all children younger than five travel free on the Underground.

Which Zone?

Here are some of the most popular Underground and Docklands Light Railway (DLR) stations in London with their zones listed:

Underground Station	Zone		
Canary Wharf DLR	2	London Bridge	1
Covent Garden	1	London City Airport BritRail	3
Elephant and Castle	1 and 2	Paddington	1
Greenwich BritRail	3	Piccadilly Circus	1
Heathrow Airport	6	South Kensington/Kensington	1
Island Gardens DLR	2	Tower Hill	1
Kew Gardens	3	Waterloo	1
Leicester Square	1		

Using Tickets

At most stations there is an automatic ticket gate; insert your ticket into the slot and retrieve it from the slot on the other side of the gate as it opens. Reverse the process at your destination. If you are using a multitrip or multi-day ticket, the turnstile will return your ticket; if the value on a one-trip ticket has been used up, the machine will keep the ticket.

At most larger stations, including the terminal at Heathrow Airport, you'll find a wide gate for persons traveling with luggage. Otherwise look for an attendant to help with luggage or wheelchairs. (Note that many Tube stations have stairs or escalators, posing some problems for travelers who have disabilities.)

Prices for London Transport trains and buses listed here were in effect in mid-2001, and are subject to change.

Single Tickets

(Good for one trip, limited to the zones purchased.)

	Adult	Child (5–15 years)
One Zone		
Within Zone 1	£1.50	£0.60
Within Zones 2–6	£0.90	£0.40
Two Zones		
Zone 1–2	£1.90	£0.80
Other Pairs	£1.20	£0.60
Three Zones		
Between Zones 1–3	£2.20	£1.00
Other Zones	£1.60	£0.80
Four Zones		
Between Zones 1–4	£2.70	£1.20
Other Zones	£2.00	£1.00

Five Zones

Zones 1–5	£3.30	£1.40
Zones 2–6	£2.20	£1.10
All Zones (1–6, including Heathrow Airport)		
	£3.60	£1.50

One-Day Travelcard

The one-day travelcard allows you unlimited travel on the Tube, buses, the Docklands Light Railway, and railroad lines within the specified zones on a single day. It is not valid in the morning rush hour, though; the cards can be used after 9:30 A.M. during the week and all day on weekends and public holidays. The card is not valid on Airbus, night buses, and other special services. Also available is a discounted two-day weekend travelcard.

An all-zone pass can also be purchased as a one-day road extension to a weekly travelcard to permit visits by rail to outlying London areas, including Hampton Court.

ONE-DAY TRAVELCARD

	Adult	Child (5–15 years)
Zones 1–2	£4.00	£2.00
Zones 1–4	£4.30	£2.00
All Zones (1–6)	£4.90	£2.00

LT Card

The one-day LT card has no restrictions on the Underground, buses, and the Docklands Light Railway. It is not valid on Airbus, night buses, or other special services or for travel to stations north of Queen's Park on the Bakerloo line.

LT CARD

	Adult	Child (5–15 years)
Zones 1, 2	£5.10	£2.50
Zones 1–4	£6.20	£3.00
All Zones (1–6)	£7.70	£3.30

Weekly or Monthly Travelcard

The best deal on transport is a weekly or monthly pass, sold in London at ticket counters at most major stations, at London Transport offices, and at some newsagents. The first time you purchase a card you'll need to obtain a free photocard and attach to it a passport-sized photograph; you'll need to be able to produce the photocard and the travelcard at stations.

A travelcard is not valid on Airbus or other special services.

WEEKLY TRAVELCARD

	Adult	Child (5–15 years)
Zone 1	£15.90	£6.60
Zones 1, 2	£18.90	£7.70
Zones 1–3	£22.40	£10.30
Zones 1–4	£27.60	£12.80
Zones 1–5	£33.30	£14.10
All Zones (1–6)	£36.40	£15.40

MONTHLY TRAVELCARD

	Adult	Child (5–15 years)
Zone 1	£61.10	£25.40
Zones 1, 2	£72.60	£29.60
Zones 1–3	£86.10	£39.60
Zones 1–4	£106.00	£49.20
Zones 1–5	£127.00	£54.20
All Zones (1–6)	£139.80	£59.20

Tickets for other zones and combinations of zones are available.

Family Travelcard

A family travelcard is a discounted pass for groups of up to two adults, traveling with at least one and up to four children. Members of the party do not need to be related, but they must travel together at all times. Travel is permitted after 9:30 A.M. weekdays and at any time on weekends and public holidays. The pass is valid for unlimited trips on one day on the Underground, the Docklands Light Railway, rail services within the zone you purchase, and the Airbus and London Transport buses other than night buses.

Adult tickets are twenty percent cheaper than normal travelcard prices for adults; children are each charged a flat fare of 60p. The pass is available in the usual zone combinations. It is not valid on night buses.

FAMILY TRAVELCARD

	Adult	Child (5–15 years)
Zones 1–2	£2.60	£0.80
Zones 1–4	£2.80	£0.80
All Zones (1–6)	£3.20	£0.80

Weekend Travelcard

The weekend travelcard is valid for the two days of the weekend, or for travel on any two consecutive days during public holidays. Available in the usual zone combinations, it is not valid on night buses.

WEEKEND TRAVELCARD

	Adult	Child (5–15 years)
Zones 1–2	£6.00	£3.00
All Zones (1–6)	£7.30	£3.00

London Visitor Travelcard

One more option for tourists is to purchase a London Transport pass through a travel agency before departure. The pass has some advantages—it does not require a photo and it has no restrictions on the times it can be used. It is also available for three, four, or seven consecutive days in an all-zone version usable in all six zones on the Underground, Docklands Light Railway, railroads in the London area, and buses; it cannot be used on Airbus service from Heathrow. A central zone–only pass is also sold.

The cards are sold from U.S. travel agencies and bureaus and are priced in dollars; they are not available in the United Kingdom. Based on exchange rates at the time this book went to press, the visitor travelcard is slightly more expensive than its equivalent—an all-zone travelcard—purchased in London, and most travelers will not need to visit the outlying zones on a daily basis. Compared to a one- or two-zone travelcard, it is considerably more expensive.

Visitor Travelcards are available in most major countries around the world. In the United States, agents include:

Rail Europe. Westchester, New York ☎ (888) 274-8724. 🖳 www.raileurope.com.

Rail Europe (Canada). Mississauga, Ontario. ☎ (905) 602-4195. 🖳 www.raileurope .com.

DER Travel Services. Rosemont, Illinois. ☎ (800) 782-2424. 🖳 www.dertravel.com.

Europe Express. Bothell, Washington. ☎ (800) 927-3876. 🖳 www.europeexpress. com.

Note that prices may fluctuate depending on changes in exchange rates.

LONDON VISITOR TRAVELCARD (Central Zone)

	Adult	Child (5–15 years)
3 Days	$20	$9
4 Days	$25	$10
7 Days	$30	$13

LONDON VISITOR TRAVELCARD (All Zones)

	Adult	Child (5–15 years)
3 Days	$29	$13
4 Days	$39	$16
7 Days	$58	$25

Carnets

A *carnet* is a book of ten single tickets for travel on the Underground in zone 1 only, sold for £11.50, a savings of £4 on the price of individual tickets. Books for children are also available for £5. A carnet can be shared among more than one person. Each ticket must be validated by passing it through the ticket gate at the start of the journey.

Docklands Light Railway

The Docklands Light Railway (DLR) opened in 1987 as part of the redevelopment of the old Docks area of east London. It has city terminals at Bank Tube station and Tower Gateway DLR, adjacent to Tower Hill Tube station.

One line runs from the east to Island Gardens in the Docklands via Canary Wharf; from there you can walk under the Thames to Greenwich through an old pedestrian tunnel. A second line runs to Beckton via Prince Regent for the London City Airport. A third line runs from Stratford to Canary Wharf.

DLR tickets are also valid on the Underground system and there is free transfer between the systems; some of the DLR lies within zone 2, though, and you must have the appropriate fare.

Trains run weekdays from 5:30 A.M. to 12:30 A.M., Saturday from 6 A.M. to 12.30 A.M., and Sunday from 7:30 A.M. to 11:30 P.M.

For information, call ☎ (020) 7918-4000.

Railway Services Within London

Most railway lines terminate at a main station such as Waterloo or Victoria, where you'll likely have to transfer to the Underground to reach central London. An exception is the Thameslink service, which runs from the south of

Docklands Light Railway

England via Gatwick Airport to the heart of the City of London, continuing to the north via King's Cross to Luton (for Luton Airport).

Another useful inner-city railway is the North London line, which runs across inner north London with a stop at Silvertown, which is a few minutes' walk from London City Airport.

Central London Bus Service

There are nearly 150 daytime bus routes in central London and dozens more in outlying areas. Copies of the *Central London Bus Guide* are available at most Underground stations and at London Transport Travel Centres. You can also call a twenty-four-hour travel information line at ☎ (020) 7222-1234 for advice, or consult 💻 www.londontransport.co.uk/buses/index.shtml.

Bus stops are marked with the London Transport symbol; at the stop you'll find a local map and list of major stops for each bus. Most bus lines come together at one or another major transfer points within the city, including Trafalgar Square, Oxford Road, and Piccadilly Circus.

London Transport travelcards are valid on buses; just show the pass to the driver or the conductor.

The famous red double-decker London buses—they're known as "Routemasters" among those who keep track of model types—are still used in central London and some outlying districts. Many of the buses are old, dating from the 1950s, and are rapidly being replaced by more modern, single-level transports. Grab a ride on one of the double-deckers if you can, and head for the upper level for an extraordinary view of places such as Piccadilly Circus.

London's bus services are run by a number of private companies, and many of the lines have forgone the traditional red in favor of other colors. The fare structure and ticketing system is common across the entire network, though; in addition to cash, travelers can also use a travelcard.

In mid-2001 any bus into, from, or within and across London central Zone 1 cost £1. Buses that travel within outer London cost 70p. Child fares in all zones were 40p. In the late evening, Night Bus fares were £1.50 within Zone 1 and £1 in outer London.

Major routes may run as often as every two to three minutes, while less frequent routes may operate every twenty minutes. During rush hours, it is not uncommon to see three or four buses running bumper-to-bumper through traffic. The most heavily used routes operate until about midnight.

Bus service is reduced during late evening through early morning. Special night bus routes, marked with "N" numbers, fan out to most areas of the central city with a hub-and-spoke system through Trafalgar Square at an interval of about thirty minutes. Note that some Underground passes are not valid on night buses.

A stop marked with a red symbol on a white background is a compulsory stop. A stop with a white symbol on a red background indicates a *request stop*, meaning that buses must be signaled.

Bus information is available by calling ☎ (020) 7222-1234.

London Taxis

The famous London cabs—large, polished, black taxis, with attentive and all-knowing drivers—still exist. Alas, some are now painted pink or orange and carry garish ads for clothing, Web pages, or airlines. The drivers still have to know London inside and out, passing a tough government exam known as "The Knowledge."

The cabs charge fares that are based on a mileage meter; fares are higher after midnight and on weekends. Drivers expect a tip of 10 to 15 percent. Cabs are allowed to respond to persons who hail them on the street; look for an orange light on the roof in the middle of the front windshield for indication of an available cab.

You'll also find minicabs, unlicensed vehicles that are prohibited from picking up customers in the street. To engage one of them, you'll have to call them in advance. Minicab operators have fixed rates for most destinations; be sure to ask the price before you start your trip. In general, minicab rates are lower than those of black cabs.

Black Cab Companies

Capital Taxis. ☎ (020) 7633-9733
Computer Cabs. ☎ (020) 7286-0286
Datacab. ☎ (020) 8964-2123
Dial-a-Cab. ☎ (020) 7253-5000
Radio Taxis. ☎ (020) 7272-0272

Chapter 7
London by River

The Thames Highway

The River Thames was the raison d'etre of the original London settlement and later the reason for the growth of the city as a world center for trading and finance. For a sense of history and an intriguing and sometimes beautiful view of London, consider a tour by river.

For information on many riverboat operators, call the London Tourist Board Riverboat Information Telephone at ☎ (0906) 850-5471.

Circular Cruise. Circular Cruises. Westminster Pier, SW1. Underground: Westminster. Operates daily 11 A.M. to 6:30 P.M. every thirty minutes. Telephone: ☎ (020) 7936-2033. One-hour circular cruise from Lambeth Palace to Saint Katharine Docks.

To Greenwich. Catamaran Cruises. Charing Cross Pier, WC2. Underground: Embankment. Operates daily 10 A.M. to 4 P.M. every thirty minutes. ☎ (020) 7839-3572 or, for reservations, ☎ (020) 7925-2215.

Westminster to Greenwich Passenger Boat Services. Westminster Pier, SW1. Underground: Westminster. Operates daily 10 A.M. to 5 A.M. every thirty minutes. ☎ (020) 7930-4097.

To Hampton Court via Kew Gardens. Westminster Passenger Service Association (Upriver). Westminster Pier, SW1. Underground: Westminster. Operates daily 10:30 A.M., 11:15 A.M., and noon. ☎ (020) 7930-2062.

To Kew Gardens. Westminster Passenger Service Association (Upriver). Westminster Pier, SW1. Underground: Westminster. Operates daily 10:15 A.M., 10:30 A.M., 11 A.M., 11:15 A.M., noon, 2 P.M., and 2:30 P.M. ☎ (020) 7930-2062.

To Thames Flood Barrier. Thames Cruises. Westminster Pier, SW1. Underground: Westminster. Operates daily 11:15 A.M., 12:15 P.M., 1:45 P.M., 2:45 P.M. ☎ (020) 7930-3373.

To Tower of London. Catamaran Cruises. Charing Cross Pier, WC2. Underground: Embankment. Operates daily 10:30 A.M. to 4 P.M. every thirty minutes. ☎ (020) 7839-3572.

City Cruises. Westminster Pier, SW1. Underground: Westminster. Operates daily 10:20 A.M. to 6 P.M. (and until 9 P.M. June through August) every twenty minutes. ☎ (020) 7930-9033.

To Westminster. City Cruises. Tower Pier, EC3. Underground: Tower Hill. Operates daily 11 A.M. to 6 P.M. (and until 9:30 P.M. June through August) every thirty minutes. ☎ (020) 7488-0344.

Canal Boat Trips to London Zoo and Camden Lock Market. London Waterbus Company. Camden Lock to Little Venice along the Regent's Canal, with a stop at the London Zoo. The company operates three converted traditional narrowboats—*Milton, Perseus,* and *Gardenia*—and one purpose-built tour boat.

Regent's Canal was opened in 1820 to link the Grant Union Canal with the London Docks. Today it is used for enjoyable boat trips between Little Venice, London Zoo, and Camden Lock, where there is a crafts market.

The leisurely ride from Little Camden Lock to Little Venice takes about fifty minutes, about thirty-five minutes from Little Venice to the London Zoo, and fifteen minutes from Camden Lock to the zoo. In the summer, boats leave hourly. In the winter, from November 1 through the end of March, boats operate ninety minutes apart on weekends only.

Round-trip fares from Little Venice to Camden Lock are £5.50 for adults, and £3.50 for children; from Little Venice to the zoo, round-trip tickets cost £3.40 and £2.30. Tickets are sold onboard the boat, and one-way fares are also sold.

For information, call ☎ (020) 7482-2550.

The Waterbus Company also runs special day trips in the summer to Limehouse, Three Mills, and Brentford. Warwick Avenue or Camden Lock, off Chalk Farm Road, NW1. Underground: Camden Town. Trips from both locks daily 10 A.M. to 5 P.M. every hour. No reservation necessary. ☎ (020) 7482-2550.

Part III
Econoguide Must-Sees

Chapter 8
London *Econoguide* Must-Sees

Museums and Galleries

WOW British Library. Chapter 19: Bloomsbury and Fitzrovia

WOW British Museum. Chapter 19: Bloomsbury and Fitzrovia

WOW Courtauld Gallery. Chapter 13: Covent Garden and the Strand

WOW Dulwich Picture Gallery. Chapter 17: Southwark, Bankside, and the London Bridge Area

WOW Imperial War Museum. Chapter 18: South Bank

WOW London Transport Museum. Chapter 13: Covent Garden and the Strand

WOW Museum of London. Chapter 15: The City, Smithfield, and Spitalfields

WOW National Gallery. Chapter 12: Trafalgar Square, Soho, Leicester Square, and the West End

WOW National Maritime Museum. Chapter 16: Greenwich

WOW National Portrait Gallery. Chapter 12: Trafalgar Square, Soho, Leicester Square, and the West End

WOW Natural History Museum. Chapter 21: South Kensington, Kensington, Knightsbridge, and Notting Hill

WOW Queen's House. Chapter 16: Greenwich

WOW Old Royal Observatory. Chapter 16: Greenwich

WOW Sir John Soane's Museum. Chapter 14: Holborn and the Inns of Court

WOW Science Museum. Chapter 21: South Kensington, Kensington, Knightsbridge, and Notting Hill

WOW Tate Britain. Chapter 10: Whitehall and Westminster

WOW Tate Modern. Chapter 17: Southwark, Bankside, and the London Bridge Area

WOW Victoria and Albert Museum. Chapter 21: South Kensington, Kensington, Knightsbridge, and Notting Hill

WOW Wallace Collection. Chapter 20: Regent's Park, Camden

Castles, Palaces, and Cathedrals

WOW Buckingham Palace. Chapter 11: Piccadilly and Saint James

WOW Kensington Palace State Apartments. Chapter 21: South Kensington, Kensington, Knightsbridge, and Notting Hill

WOW Saint Paul's Cathedral. Chapter 15: The City, Smithfield, and Spitalfields

WOW Southwark Cathedral. Chapter 17: Southwark, Bankside, and the London Bridge Area

WOW Tower of London. Chapter 15: The City, Smithfield, and Spitalfields

WOW Westminster Abbey. Chapter 10: Whitehall and Westminster

Monuments and Government Buildings

WOW Houses of Parliament. Chapter 10: Whitehall and Westminster

WOW Trafalgar Square. Chapter 12: Trafalgar Square, Soho, Leicester Square, and the West End

Attractions

WOW Cabinet War Rooms. Chapter 10: Whitehall and Westminster

WOW Covent Garden. Chapter 13: Covent Garden and the Strand

WOW London Aquarium. Chapter 18: South Bank

WOW London Dungeon. Chapter 17: Southwark, Bankside, and the London Bridge Area

WOW London Zoo. Chapter 20: Regent's Park, Camden

WOW Madame Tussaud's and London Planetarium. Chapter 20: Regent's Park, Camden

WOW Piccadilly Circus. Chapter 11: Piccadilly and Saint James

WOW Shakespeare's Globe Theatre. Chapter 17: Southwark, Bankside, and the London Bridge Area

WOW Soho. Chapter 12: Trafalgar Square, Soho, Leicester Square, and the West End

WOW Tower Bridge. Chapter 15: The City, Smithfield, and Spitalfields

Day Trips Out of London

WOW Ashmolean Museum of Art and Archaeology. Chapter 31: More Day Trips West: Oxford and Windsor

WOW Disneyland Paris. Chapter 33: Disneyland Paris

WOW Hampton Court Palace. Chapter 29: Day Trips South

WOW Oxford. Chapter 31: More Day Trips West

WOW Roman Baths Museum. Chapter 30: Day Trips West

WOW Royal Pavilion. Chapter 29: Day Trips South

WOW Stonehenge. Chapter 30: Day Trips West

WOW Windsor Castle. Chapter 31: More Day Trips West

> **Price Bands**
> ❀ Free
> ❶ £1–£3
> ❷ £3–£5
> ❸ £5–£7
> ❹ £7–£10
> ❺ £10–£15
> ❻ £15 and up
> Admission indicates prices for A: adult; C: child; and F: family ticket.

Index of Major Attractions

Attractions	Chapter	Phone	Admission	
HMS *Belfast*	Chapter 17: Southwark, Bankside, and the London Bridge Area	☎ (020) 7940-6300	A ❷ C ❶ F ❺	
WOW Cabinet War Rooms	Chapter 10: Whitehall and Westminster	☎ (020) 7930-6961	A ❷ C ❶ F ❺	
Chessington World of Adventures (Mar–Nov)	Chapter 29: Day Trips South	☎ (0137) 272-7227	A ❻ C ❺	
WOW Covent Garden	Chapter 13: Covent Garden and the Strand		❀	

Attractions	Chapter	Phone	Admission
Legoland Windsor	Chapter 31: More Day Trips West	☎ (0990) 040404	A ❻ C ❺
WOW London Aquarium	Chapter 18: South Bank	☎ (020) 7967-8000	A ❹ C ❷
London Planetarium (Madame Tussaud's)	Chapter 20: Regent's Park, Camden	☎ (020) 7935-6861	A ❸ C ❷
WOW London Zoo	Chapter 20: Regent's Park, Camden	☎ (020) 7722-3333	A ❹ C ❸ F ❻
WOW Madame Tussaud's	Chapter 20: Regent's Park, Camden	☎ (020) 7935-6861	A ❹ C ❸
Madame Tussaud's/ London Planetarium combo ticket	Chapter 20: Regent's Park, Camden	☎ (020) 7935-6861	A ❺ C ❹
Rock Circus	Chapter 11: Piccadilly and Saint James	☎ (020) 7734-7203	A ❹ C ❸ F ❻
WOW Shakespeare's Globe Theatre	Chapter 17: Southwark, Bankside, and the London Bridge Area	☎ (020) 7902-1500	Tours A ❸ C ❷ F ❺
WOW Stonehenge	Chapter 30: Day Trips West	☎ (01980) 625368	A ❷ C ❶
Thames Barrier	Chapter 16: Greenwich	☎ (020) 8854-1373	A ❷ C ❶
WOW Tower Bridge	Chapter 15: The City, Smithfield, and Spitalfields	☎ (020) 7403-3761	A ❸ C ❷ F ❺
Winston Churchill's Britain at War Experience	Chapter 17: Southwark, Bankside, and the London Bridge Area	☎ (020) 7403-3171	A ❸ C ❷ F ❺

Attractions	Chapter	Phone	Admission
Woburn Safari Park	Chapter 28: Day Trips North	☎ (0152) 529-0407	A ❹ C ❸

Museums and Galleries	Chapter	Phone	Admission
Apsley House, No. 1 London (Wellington Museum)	Chapter 11: Picadilly and Saint James	☎ (020) 7499-5676	A ❷ C ❶
WOW Ashmolean Museum of Art and Archaeology	Chapter 31: More Day Trips West	☎ (0186) 527-8000	Donation of ❶ requested
Bank of England Museum	Chapter 15: The City, Smithfield, and Spitalfields	☎ (020) 7601-5545	✿
Bankside Gallery	Chapter 17: Southwark, Bankside, and the London Bridge Area	☎ (020) 7928-7521	A ❷ C ✿
Barbican Art Gallery	Chapter 15: The City, Smithfield, and Spitalfields	☎ (020) 7382-7105	A ❷ C ❶
Bramah Tea & Coffee Museum	Chapter 17: Southwark, Bankside, and the London Bridge Area	☎ (020) 7378-0222	A ❷ C ❶ F ❹
WOW British Library	Chapter 19: Bloomsbury and Fitzrovia	☎ (020) 7412-7332	✿
WOW British Museum	Chapter 19: Bloomsbury and Fitzrovia	☎ (020) 7636-1555	✿
Brunel Engine House	Chapter 17: Southwark, Bankside, and the London Bridge Area	☎ (020) 7231-3840	A ❶ C ❶ F ❷
Carlyle's House	Chapter 22: Chelsea	☎ (020) 7352-7087	A ❷ C ✿

Museums and Galleries	Chapter	Phone	Admission
Clink Prison Museum	Chapter 17: Southwark, Bankside, and the London Bridge Area	☎ (020) 7403-6515	A ❷ C ❶
WOW Courtauld Gallery	Chapter 13: Covent Garden and the Strand	☎ (020) 7848-2526	A ❷ C ✿
Cuming Museum	Chapter 17: Southwark, Bankside, and the London Bridge Area	☎ (020) 7701-1342	✿
The *Cutty Sark*	Chapter 16: Greenwich	☎ (020) 8858-3445	A ❷ C ❶ F ❹
Design Museum	Chapter 17: Southwark, Bankside, and the London Bridge Area	☎ (020) 7378-6055	A ❸ C ❷ F ❺
Dickens' House Museum	Chapter 19: Bloomsbury and Fitzrovia	☎ (020) 7405-2127	A ❸ C ❶ F ❹
Dr. Johnson's House	Chapter 14: Holborn and the Inns of Court	☎ (020) 7353-3745	A ❷ C ❶
WOW Dulwich Picture Gallery	Chapter 17: Southwark, Bankside, and the London Bridge Area	☎ (020) 8693-5254	A ❶ C ✿ F ❺
Duxford Airfield	Chapter 28: Day Trips North	☎ (0122) 383-5000	A ❸ C ❷ F ❻
Fan Museum	Chapter 16: Greenwich	☎ (020) 8858-7879	A ❷ C ❶ F ❹
Faraday Museum	Chapter 11: Picadilly and Saint James	☎ (020) 7409-2992	A ❶ C ❶

Museums and Galleries	Chapter	Phone	Admission
Florence Nightingale Museum	Chapter 18: South Bank	☎ (020) 7620-0374	A ❷ C ❶ F ❸
Freud Museum	Chapter 27: Day Trips	☎ (020) 7435-2002	A ❷ C ✿
The *Golden Hinde*	Chapter 17: Southwark, Bankside, and the London Bridge Area	☎ (020) 7403-0123	A ❶ C ❶
Guards' Museum	Chapter 11: Piccadilly and Saint James	☎ (020) 7930-4466, ext. 3428	A ❶ C ❶ F ❷
🌟WOW Imperial War Museum	Chapter 18: South Bank	☎ (020) 7416-5000	A ❷ C ❶ F ❺
Jewel Tower	Chapter 10: Whitehall and Westminster	☎ (020) 7222-2219	A ❶ C ❶
Jewish Museum	Chapter 20: Regent's Park, Camden	☎ (020) 7284-1997	A ❷ C ❶
Kew Bridge Steam Museum	Chapter 27: Day Trips	☎ (020) 8568-4757	A ❷ C ❶ F ❺
London Butterfly House	Chapter 27: Day Trips	☎ (020) 8560-7272	A ❷ C ❶
London Canal Museum	Chapter 20: Regent's Park, Camden	☎ (020) 7713-0836	A ❶ C ❶
🌟WOW London Dungeon	Chapter 17: Southwark, Bankside, and the London Bridge Area	☎ (020) 7403-7221	A ❹ C ❸
🌟WOW London Transport Museum	Chapter 13: Covent Garden and the Strand	☎ (020) 7379-6344	A ❷ C ❶ F ❺

Museums and Galleries	Chapter	Phone	Admission
Museum of Garden History	Chapter 18: South Bank	☎ (020) 7261-1891	❀
WOW Museum of London	Chapter 15: The City, Smithfield, and Spitalfields	☎ (020) 7600-3699	A ❷ C ❀ F ❹
Museum of the Moving Image (*Closed until 2003*)	Chapter 18: South Bank	☎ (020) 7401-2636	
National Army Museum	Chapter 22: Chelsea	☎ (020) 7730-0717	❀
WOW National Gallery	Chapter 12: Trafalgar Square, Soho, Leicester Square, and the West End	☎ (020) 7839-3321	❀
WOW National Maritime Museum	Chapter 16: Greenwich	☎ (020) 8858-4422	A ❹ C ❀
WOW National Portrait Gallery	Chapter 12: Trafalgar Square, Soho, Leicester Square, and the West End	☎ (020) 7306-0055	❀
National Postal Museum	Chapter 15: The City, Smithfield, and Spitalfields	☎ (020) 7239-5420	❀
WOW Natural History Museum	Chapter 21: South Kensington, Kensington, Knightsbridge, and Notting HIll	☎ (020) 7938-9123	A ❸ C ❷ F ❻
Old Operating Theatre, Museum, and Herb Garret	Chapter 17: Southwark, Bankside, and the London Bridge Area	☎ (020) 7955-4791	A ❶ C ❶ F ❸
WOW Old Royal Observatory	Chapter 16: Greenwich	☎ (020) 8858-4422	A ❸ C ❀

Museums and Galleries	Chapter	Phone	Admission
Old Royal Observatory/ National Maritime Museum/*Cutty Sark* combo ticket	Chapter 16: Greenwich	☎ (020) 8858-4422	A ❺ C ❷ F ❻
Pollock's Toy Museum	Chapter 19: Bloomsbury and Fitzrovia	☎ (020) 7636-3452	A ❶ C ❶
Prince Henry's Room	Chapter 14: Holborn and the Inns of Court	☎ (020) 7936-2710	✿
Queen's Gallery *(Closed until summer 2002)*	Chapter 11: Piccadilly and Saint James	☎ (020) 7839-1377	A ❷ C ❶ F ❺
🌟 Queen's House	Chapter 16: Greenwich	☎ (020) 8858-4422	A ❹ C ❷ F ❻
🌟 Roman Baths Museum	Chapter 30: Day Trips West	☎ (0122) 547-7774	A ❸ C ❷ F ❺
Royal Mews	Chapter 11: Piccadilly and Saint James	☎ (020) 7839-1377	A ❷ C ❶ F ❺
🌟 Royal Pavilion	Chapter 29: Day Trips South	☎ (0127) 329-0900	A ❷ C ❶ F ❺
🌟 Science Museum	Chapter 21: South Kensington, Kensington, Knightsbridge, and Notting Hill	☎ (020) 7938-8080	A ❸ C ❷
Science Museum/Natural History Museum/Victoria and Albert Museum combo ticket	Chapter 21: South Kensington, Kensington, Knightsbridge, and Notting Hill	☎ (020) 7938-8080 ☎ (020) 7938-9123 ☎ (020) 7938-8500	A ❻ C ❺
Sherlock Holmes Museum	Chapter 20: Regent's Park, Camden	☎ (020) 7935-8866	A ❷

Museums and Galleries	Chapter	Phone	Admission
WOW Sir John Soane's Museum	Chapter 14: Holborn and the Inns of Court	☎ (020) 7405-2107	✿
Syon House	Chapter 27: Day Trips	☎ (020) 8560-0881	A ❸ C ❷
WOW Tate Britain	Chapter 10: Whitehall and Westminster	☎ (020) 7887-8000	✿
Theatre Museum	Chapter 13: Covent Garden and the Strand	☎ (020) 7836-7891	A ❷ C ❶ F ❹
WOW Tower of London	Chapter 15: The City, Smithfield, and Spitalfields	☎ (020) 7709-0765	A ❺ C ❹ F ❻
WOW Victoria and Albert Museum	Chapter 21: South Kensington, Kensington, Knightsbridge, and Notting Hill	☎ (020) 7938-8500	A ❷ C ✿
WOW Wallace Collection	Chapter 20: Regent's Park, Camden	☎ (020) 7935-0687	✿
Wimbledon Lawn Tennis Museum	Chapter 27: Day Trips: Greater London	☎ (020) 8946-6131	A ❷ C ❶

Monuments, Government Buildings	Chapter	Phone	Admission
Banqueting House	Chapter 10: Whitehall and Westminster	☎ (020) 7839-8919	A ❷ C ❶
WOW Houses of Parliament	Chapter 10: Whitehall and Westminster	Commons: ☎ (020) 7219-4272 Lords: ☎ (020) 7219-3107	✿ ticket required

Monuments, Government Buildings	Chapter	Phone	Admission
The Monument	Chapter 15: The City, Smithfield, and Spitalfields	☎ (020) 7626-2717	A ❶ C ❶

Palaces	Chapter	Phone	Admission
WOW Buckingham Palace	Chapter 11: Picadilly and Saint James	☎ (020) 7839-1377	A ❺ C ❸ (seasonal)
WOW Hampton Court Palace	Chapter 29: Day Trips South	☎ (020) 8781-9500	A ❺ C ❸ F ❻
WOW Kensington Palace State Apartments	Chapter 21: South Kensington, Kensington, Knightsbridge, and Notting Hill	☎ (020) 7937-9561	A ❹ C ❹ F ❻
Spencer House	Chapter 11: Piccadilly and Saint James	☎ (020) 7514-1958	A ❸ C ❸
WOW Windsor Castle	Chapter 31: More Day Trips West	☎ (0175) 383-1118	A ❺ C ❸ F ❻

Churches	Chapter	Phone	Admission
WOW Saint Paul's Cathedral	Chapter 15: The City, Smithfield, and Spitalfields	☎ (020) 7246-8348	Cathedral and Gallery A ❸ C ❶ F ❻ Cathedral A ❷ C ❷ F ❹
WOW Southwark Cathedral	Chapter 17: Southwark, Bankside, and the London Bridge Area	☎ (020) 7407-3708	A ❶

Churches	Chapter	Phone	Admission
Wesley's House and Chapel	Chapter 15: The City, Smithfield, and Spitalfields	☎ (020) 7253-2262	A ❷ C ❶
WOW Westminster Abbey	Chapter 10: Whitehall and Westminster	☎ (020) 7222-7110	Chapels A ❷ C ❶ Museum only A ❶ C ❶
Westminster Cathedral	Chapter 10: Whitehall and Westminster	☎ (020) 7798-9055	A ❷ C ❶ F ❸

Chapter 9
Royal Ceremonies and Annual Events

Great Britain is the land of pomp and circumstance, and the Brits sure know how to put on a show. There is hardly a day without a changing of the guard, a ceremonial march or musical salute, or a full-blown state celebration.

Royal gun salutes are fired on certain royal anniversaries. The scheduled salutes include:

Accession Day, February 6
Queen's Birthday, April 21
Coronation Day, June 2
Prince Philip's Birthday, June 10
Queen's Official Birthday, June 17
Queen Mother's Birthday, August 4

(If an observance falls on a Sunday, the salute is held for the next day.)

Also honored are the State Opening of Parliament, Trooping the Colour, and state visits.

In London, the guns are usually fired at noon by the King's Troop of the Royal Horse Artillery in Hyde Park or Green Park, or at 1 P.M. at the Tower of London by the Honourable Artillery Company. On the Queen's Official Birthday, the salute takes place at 11 A.M.

The basic royal salute is twenty-one rounds; an extra twenty rounds are added in Hyde Park because it is a royal park. On royal anniversaries, sixty-two rounds are fired at the Tower of London: the basic salute plus an additional twenty because the tower is a royal palace and fortress, and twenty-one more for the city of London.

Ceremonies

Ceremonies include the political, the military, and the royal.

Remembrance Day

On Remembrance Day each year (at 11 A.M. on the Sunday nearest the eleventh day of the eleventh month), the queen lays a wreath on the Cenotaph in Whitehall to honor the fallen of the First and Second World Wars and other military campaigns.

State Opening of Parliament

The queen formally opens the new session of Parliament each year, usually in October or November.

She travels from Buckingham Palace to Westminster in the ornate Irish state coach, adorned in the imperial state crown.

The parliamentary session itself is not open to the public, although it is televised. The queen's speech to both Houses of Parliament is written by the ruling party, outlining the legislation that the government plans to introduce in the coming session.

Trooping the Colour (The Queen's Birthday)

The sovereign's birthday is officially celebrated every June by a ceremony called "Trooping the Colour" near Buckingham Palace on Horse Guards' Parade in Saint James's Park.

(The queen's actual birthday is April 21, but tradition for more than two hundred years has called for a celebration of the monarch's birthday in the summer.)

The ceremony is based on the military practice of teaching soldiers to recognize the *colours* (flags) of their battalion so they could recognize them in the heat of battle; the colours were carried (or "trooped") down the ranks.

Since the time of Edward VII, the sovereign has taken the salute in person, often riding on horseback wearing the uniform of whichever of the five regiments of foot guards was trooping.

A typical schedule: the queen departs Buckingham Palace at 10:40 A.M., proceeding in an open coach down the Mall to a ceremony of the Household Cavalry at Horse Guards' Parade at 11 A.M. The queen returns to the palace at 1 P.M., saluted by a Royal Air Force fly-by over the Mall.

The ceremonies at Horse Guards' Parade require purchase of tickets that are difficult to get; the procession down the Mall is open to all. Information: ☎ (0207) 414-2479.

Changing of the Guard at Buckingham Palace

The forty-five-minute changing of the guard ceremony takes place in the forecourt of Buckingham Palace at 11:30 A.M. every day in summer, and every other day for the remainder of the year. (The ceremony is occasionally canceled because of extremely foul weather.)

The New Guard marches to the Palace from Wellington Barracks on Birdcage Walk accompanied by a guards band, relieving the sentries of the Old Guard, and then a procession marches back to Saint James's Palace.

Ceremony of the Keys at the Tower of London

The ancient ceremony to lock the main gate of the Tower of London began as a security measure and continues as a tourist attraction with a heavy dose of security.

Every evening at just before 10 P.M. the chief yeoman warder, outfitted in full formal regalia, carrying a lantern, and accompanied by four armed soldiers of the garrison, locks the gates of the entrance at the Middle Tower and then the Byward Tower.

To observe the ceremony you'll need to apply in writing at least six weeks in advance for free tickets. You'll need to provide your name, address, and telephone number in London, choice of date and any alternate dates, and the number of tickets requested (up to seven). If you are writing from the United States, allow extra time and enclose an international reply coupon (available at post offices) and a self-addressed envelope.

The Lord Mayor's Show

The high point of the annual Silent Change of Lord Mayors in the City of London is a parade of bands, military units, and floats from Guildhall to the Mansion House and law courts and then back again along the embankment. The ceremony takes place each November.

A Selection of Important Annual Events

January

London Parade. Westminster Abbey to Berkeley Square. New Year's Day. Information: ☎ (020) 8744-1750.

Charles I Commemoration. Whitehall. Underground: Charing Cross. Last Sunday in January, beginning at 11:30 A.M. Charles I was executed at the Banqueting House in 1649; in commemoration of the event, members of the King's Army, dressed in period uniforms, march from Saint James's Palace through Horse Guards' to the Banqueting House and eventually to the statue of Charles in Trafalgar Square; they return by the same route.

Chinese New Year. Soho. Underground: Leicester Square. On a Sunday in late January or early February. Parades, dragon and lion dancers, music, and more. Information: ☎ (0207) 734-5161.

February

Accession Day. Gun salutes at Hyde Park at noon, and at the Tower of London at 1 P.M., February 6. (If the date is a Sunday, the salute is held the next day.)

Covent Garden Pancake Day Races. Covent Garden. Underground: Covent Garden. Shrove Tuesday (last day before Lent). Information: ☎ (0171) 375-0441.

Lincoln's Inn Fields Pancake Day Races. Lincoln's Inn. Underground: Holborn. Shrove Tuesday (last day before Lent) beginning at 11 A.M.

March

Head of the River Race. Mortlake to Putney, River Thames. Underground: Putney Bridge. Last Saturday in March. Some four hundred crews of eight-oar boats. Information: ☎ (020) 8788-9471.

Oxford versus Cambridge University Boat Race. Putney to Mortlake, River Thames. Underground: Putney Bridge. Late March or early April. Information: ☎ (0171) 379-3234.

April

Chaucer Festival. Tower of London, Tower Hill. Underground: Tower Hill. Early April. A procession straight out of Chaucer's *Canterbury Tales* marches from Southwark Cathedral to a medieval fair at the Tower of London. Information: ☎ (0171) 709-0765.

London Marathon. From Greenwich Park in Blackheath to Westminster Bridge, via the Isle of Dogs and Victoria Embankment. Mid-April. Information: ☎ (0171) 620-4117. 🖳 www.london/marathon.co.uk.

Tyburn Walk. From the Old Bailey on Newgate Street to Tyburn Convent. Underground: Saint Paul's. Last Sunday in April at 3 P.M. A silent procession to commemorate Catholic martyrs at Tyburn Gallows in the sixteenth and seventeenth centuries.

May

Canalway Cavalcade. Little Venice. Underground: Warwick Avenue. May Day weekend. A pageant of boats, morris dancers, and other celebrations; a highlight occurs Sunday night with an illuminated parade of boats. Information: ☎ (0171) 874-2787.

Covent Garden Festival of Opera and the Musical Arts. Underground: Covent Garden. Two-week celebration in May including opera, choral, and theatrical performances and other special events.

Brighton International Festival. Brighton. First three weeks in May.

June

Trooping the Colour, The Queen's Official Birthday Parade. Horse Guards' Parade, Whitehall, London. Mid-June. Information: ☎ (0906) 850-5453.

Wimbledon Lawn Tennis Championships. Wimbledon. End of June to early July. Information: ☎ (020) 8946-2244.

July

Henley Royal Regatta. Henley-on-Thames, Oxfordshire. Early July.

Paddington Performance Festival. Paddington Recreation Ground. Underground: Maida Vale. First Sunday in July from noon to 6 P.M. Performing artists of high and low culture, from music to clowns and jugglers. Information: ☎ (0171) 375-0441.

Doggett's Coat and Badge Race. London Bridge to Albert Bridge. Underground: London Bridge. A race against the tide to commemorate the accession of George I to the throne. Information: ☎ (0171) 626-3531.

Farnborough International Air Show. Farnborough, Hampshire. Mid-September. Information: ☎ (0171) 227-1000.

Vintners' Company Procession. Upper Thames Street. Second Wednesday in July. Members of the Vintners' Company, led by wine porters sweeping the road with birch brooms, march from Vintners' Hall to the church or Saint James's in Garlickhythe. Information: ☎ (0171) 236-1863.

August

Notting Hill Carnival. Notting Hill, London. Late August summer bank holiday weekend. A huge outdoor festival with a Caribbean flavor; music, dancing, food, and parades. Information: ☎ (020) 8964-0544.

September

Covent Garden Market Festival of Street Theatre. Covent Garden. Underground: Covent Garden. Two weeks in September.

Horseman's Sunday. Church of Saint John and Saint Michael, Hyde Park Crescent. Underground: Paddington. Third Sunday in September, beginning at 11 A.M. The vicar, on horseback, blesses the horses before a show-jumping event a few hours later in Kensington Gardens. Information: ☎ (020) 7262-1732.

October

Trafalgar Day Parade. Trafalgar Square. Underground: Charing Cross. Sunday nearest October 21, beginning at 11 A.M. A parade of sea cadets and marching bands in commemoration of Lord Nelson's victory in 1805. Information: ☎ (020) 7928-8978.

November

RAC London to Brighton Veteran Car Run. Hyde Park, London to Brighton, East Sussex. First Sunday in November. Information: ☎ (0175) 368-1736.

Lord Mayor's Procession and Show. The City, London. Underground: Bank or Temple. The incoming lord mayor rolls from the Guildhall to the Royal Courts of Justice in an elegant gilded coach, followed by a parade of floats and bands and culminating in an evening fireworks show. Information: ☎ (020) 7414-2357.

Part IV
London by Neighborhood

Chapter 10
Whitehall and Westminster:
The Seat of Power

 Houses of Parliament

 Westminster Abbey

 Tate Britain

 Cabinet War Rooms

Banqueting House

Big Ben

Number 10 Downing Street

Horse Guards' Parade

Cenotaph

Jewel Tower

Parliament Square

Westiminster Cathedral

Saint Margaret's Church

Whitehall and Westminster have been the seat of royal, governmental, and religious power in England for a thousand years, dating back to King Canute, who built a palace on a swampy island at the confluence of the Tyburn and the Thames at the beginning of the eleventh century.

Whitehall was a name applied to festive halls. Alongside was the small church that a few decades later Edward III (revered as Edward the Confessor) expanded to become the grand Westminster Abbey.

Edward also built the Palace of Westminster between the Thames and the abbey; after Edward's death in 1066, William the Conqueror was the first to locate his court there, and the palace served as the home of the royal court for the next four hundred years.

The early parliaments of England were held in the chapter house of Westminster Abbey, moving into Saint Stephen's Chapel of the Palace of Westminster when Henry VIII rebuilt and expanded the old Whitehall Palace, reclaiming it as the royal residence.

The king's landholdings were extended away from the river toward Saint James's Park; improvements included a cockpit for cock fighting, a bear-baiting arena, and a tiltyard for human combat competitions. In another form of royal sport, Henry celebrated there his marriage to Anne Boleyn in 1522 and his marriage to Jane Seymour three years later. He died at Whitehall in 1547.

During the reign of James I from 1603 to 1625, the palace had sprawled to two thousand rooms; even so, famed architect Inigo Jones was asked to design an even larger new palace to replace Whitehall, but only the Banqueting House was ever completed. The next king, Charles I, devoted much of his attention to building a spectacular art collection of more than four hundred paintings, including twenty-eight Titians and nine Raphaels; many were scattered during the Commonwealth era when Oliver Cromwell moved into the palace.

The last great ceremony at the palace was the offer of the crown to William and Mary in 1689; they chose to move the royal residence to Kensington Palace, preferring its park-like setting to the damp air along the river. The palace was damaged in a fire in 1691 and was restored by Christopher Wren. But in 1698 the palace burned to the ground, apparently as the result of an accident by a laundrywoman. All that remained was the Banqueting House.

Meanwhile, the House of Commons met at Saint Stephen's and the House of Lords nearby until a disastrous fire in 1834 leveled most of the palace. The conflagration was caused when government clerks set a fire to destroy a large collection of elmwood sticks that had been used for hundreds of years to record tax receipts. All that survived were the Saint Mary Undercroft, a crypt beneath Saint Stephen's that dates back to about 1292, Westminster Hall, and the Jewel Tower.

Construction of new homes for the House of Lords and House of Commons began in 1837, and they were completed in 1847 and 1851 respectively; the famed Clock Tower was not finished until 1858 because of difficulties installing the massive clockwork for what became known as Big Ben.

Today Whitehall is the home of much of England's official government, including the Houses of Parliament. Off Whitehall is Downing Street, a short cul-de-sac that includes the prime minister's official residence at Number 10 and the chancellor of the exchequer's residence at Number 11.

By the way, you can tell if Parliament is in session by looking for a flag flying from Victoria Tower, the tallest of the Westminster towers; another signal is a light at the top of the Clock Tower that houses Big Ben.

🚩 Houses of Parliament

Westminster, SW1. Underground: Westminster.

Both Houses have small viewing galleries that are open to the public, although security concerns make unplanned access very difficult. Foreign vis-

WHITEHALL AND WESTMINSTER

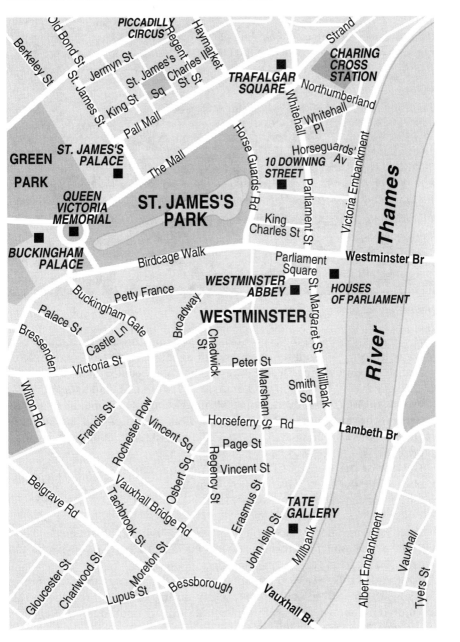

Houses of Parliament

itors can seek scheduled tickets for debates or a tour through their embassy in London; it is very difficult for a nonresident to obtain tickets to Question Time.

House of Commons. Debates are ordinarily scheduled Monday through Wednesday 2:30 P.M. to 10:30 P.M., Thursday 11:30 A.M. to 7:30 P.M., and Friday 9:30 A.M. to 3 P.M. The lively Prime Minister's Question Time, at which the leader of the government faces queries from friendly—and unfriendly—members, is held Wednesday 3 P.M. to 3:30 P.M. ☎ (020) 7219-4272. 🖳 www.par liament.uk.

Gallery of the House of Commons. The Strangers' Gallery is open to the publich while the Commons is sitting—usually 2:30 P.M. to 10 P.M. or later on Monday, Tuesday, and Wednesday; 11:30 A.M. to 7:30 P.M. on Thursday; and 9:30 A.M. to 3 P.M. on Friday.

Question Time takes place every day except Friday 2:30 P.M. to 3:30 P.M., with the prime minister answering questions 3 P.M. to 3:30 P.M. on Wednesday and 11:30 A.M. to 12:30 P.M. on Thursday.

To attend at this time, you can apply to the U.S. Embassy for a card of intro-duction, which will normally permit entry during the early afternoon. They are limited in number, and visitors may find cards are booked for several weeks in advance. The Embassy address is:

Embassy of the United States of America
24 Grosvenor Square
London W1A 1AE
United Kingdom
☎ (020) 7499-9000

Alternatively, visitors may join the public line outside Saint Stephen's entrance, but a wait of one or two hours is usual in the afternoons.

Generally speaking, after ticket holders have left the gallery and the afternoon line has been cleared, there is not, except during controversial debates, too much pressure on places in the gallery for evening sessions. Visitors who wish to minimize waiting times should arrive at 6 P.M. or later. The Commons sits until at least 10 P.M. and the gallery remains open during this time. The Public Information Office (PIO) can advise what is to be debated.

On Friday the Commons sits from 9:30 A.M. to about 3 P.M., and it is usually fairly easy to get into the gallery on Friday. Later in the day a line tends to develop and some delay is inevitable. The same system applies to the day immediately before a recess, whether or not it is a Friday.

House of Lords. Debate times vary. If you don't have a ticket, you can join the lines that build outside the Saint Stephen's entrance; in general, your best chance may be to wait until after 5 P.M. Call ☎ (020) 7219-3107 for daily information. 🖥 www.publications.parliament.uk/pa/ld/ldhome.htm.

Debates are scheduled to begin at 2:30 P.M. Monday to Wednesday and at 3 P.M. on Thursday; there occasionally are debates on Friday, beginning at 11 A.M. The House of Lords Question Time is held Monday to Wednesday 2:35 P.M. to 3:05 P.M. and on Thursday from 3:05 P.M. to 3:35 P.M.

The interior of the building includes some important works of art, installed with the encouragement of Prince Albert. Treasures include five large frescoes that tell the legend of Arthur, located in the Robing Room, which is used by the monarch to accept the Imperial Crown and parliamentary robes for the state opening of Parliament each year.

If you take a tour you'll be able to catch a glimpse of Westminster Hall, little changed from the eleventh century. It was at first used as a banqueting hall. An impressive ninety-two-foot-high oak hammer-beam roof was added in the fourteenth century. At one time it was used for the Law Court, the nation's high court. Guy Fawkes was sentenced to death here for his part in the Gunpowder Plot of 1605, a conspiracy to destroy Parliament. Earlier, Queen Anne Boleyn was condemned in 1536. Charles I was also sent to his death from this room in 1649; in 1661 Charles II, restored to the throne, had Oliver Cromwell's head exhumed and then impaled on the roof spire where it remained for more than twenty years.

During World War II, the Houses of Parliament were hit eleven times by German air raids, including an incendiary-bomb assault by five hundred aircraft in May 1941. The House of Commons was destroyed and serious damage was sustained throughout the old palace. Reconstruction was completed in 1950.

Gallery of the House of Lords. The Strangers' Gallery is open when the House of Lords sits on Monday, Tuesday, and Wednesday from 2:30 P.M., on Thursday from 3 P.M., and occasionally on Friday at 11 A.M. The House of Lords does not usually sit during August, September, and early October; during the two or three weeks before and after Christmas; and for a week or so at Easter and at the Spring Bank Holiday.

To gain entry to the Gallery of the House of Lords, join the queue at Saint Stephen's Entrance to the Houses of Parliament.

Tours. Overseas visitors can obtain a permit to tour the Houses of Parliament by applying to the PIO. When the House of Commons is sitting, the PIO can issue a permit that will enable up to sixteen people to tour the Palace of Westminster between 3:30 P.M. and 5:30 P.M. on Friday afternoon, provided the Commons has concluded its business for the week.

During recesses the days and timing of tours may vary but, as a rule, take place in the morning from 9:30 A.M. to noon on the following days: Christmas recess, Easter recess, spring bank holiday recess, and summer recess in part of July and August. The Houses of Parliament are closed on weekends, bank holidays, and between Christmas and New Year's.

At any time, should either house be sitting unexpectedly, whether during a recess or beyond the usual hour of adjournment on a Friday, tours may have to be canceled, possibly without notice.

Overseas visitors should apply in writing to the PIO as far in advance as possible and, if appropriate, provide an address in Britain where they may be contacted in addition to their U.S. home address.

The Public Information Office address contact information is:
House of Commons
1 Derby Gate
London SW1A 2DG
United Kingdom
☎ (020) 7219-4272, ☎ (020) 7219-4272, or ☎ (020) 7219-5532.

📁 Westminster Abbey

Broad Sanctuary, SW1. Underground: Saint James's Park and Westminster.

Nave, cloisters, and royal chapels are open Monday to Friday 9 A.M. to 4:45 P.M. (last admission 4 P.M.), Saturday 9 A.M. to 2:45 P.M. (last admission 2 P.M.) and 3:45 P.M. to 5:45 P.M. (last admission 5 P.M.). Closed Sunday. Admission to royal chapels and Poets' Corner: adult, ❷; child (younger than 16), ❶; full-time student, ❶; senior, ❶. Admission to nave and cloisters is free. (An audio tour on tape is available for rental for about £6.) ☎ (020) 7222-7110. 🖳 www.westminster-abbey.org.

Supertours of the abbey, conducted by the abbey's *vergers* (church sextons), include the nave, the choir, the high altar, Statesmen's Aisle, Poets' Corner, and the royal chapels including the Coronation Chair; they are conducted daily except Sunday, several times a day. Admission: ❸. Call ☎ (020) 7222-7110 for hours.

Price Bands
❶ £1–£3
❷ £3–£5
❸ £5–£7
❹ £7–£10
❺ £10–£15
❻ £15 and up

Walk in the steps of nearly every English monarch, from Edward the Confessor, who established a church on the site in 1065, to Henry III, who rebuilt the abbey in 1269, to Elizabeth II.

Since 1066 every sovereign except Edward V and

Edward VIII has been crowned here, and it has also been the burial place of kings, queens, and princes. The most recent coronation was Elizabeth II's in 1953; as with every ceremony conducted since 1269, she was seated on the **Coronation Chair**, which contains within it the Stone of Scone, upon which Scottish kings were said to have been crowned for hundreds of years before. The stone now resides in Scotland once more, safeguarded at Edinburgh Castle.

Edward the Confessor's Norman Abbey was finished in 1065 near his palace on Thorney Island; he died soon after its consecration and was buried near the high altar. Henry III honored his predecessor by rebuilding the abbey, creating a new apse, transepts, and choir area in 1269. The magnificent abbey you see today has been in place since then, with additions and reconstruction over the

Westminster Abbey

years. Rebuilding of the nave began in 1376 and was not finished until 150 years later.

The massive flying buttresses on the exterior support the 101-foot-high roof of the **nave**. The stained-glass window at the west end dates to 1735 and depicts Abraham, Isaac, and Jacob, and fourteen prophets; the lowest row of windows includes the coats of arms of Elizabeth I, George II, and church officials.

Also in the west end of the nave is the grave of the Unknown Warrior, anointed by George V and Queen Mary in 1920 to remember the unidentified fallen of World War I. On a pillar nearby is a Congressional Medal of Honor, the highest medal conferred by the government of the United States, given in tribute to the fallen soldiers of Britain.

The **choir** was originally an area used by the monks for worship; the thirteenth-century stalls and furnishings were replaced in the mid-nineteenth century. A choir of about twenty-two male students at the choir school and a group of lay vicars sing daily services there. The organ, whose masters since it was originally built in 1730 have included Orlando Gibbons and Henry Purcell, has its pipes divided on both sides of the choir screen.

The high altar stands in the **sanctuary**. The altar and *reredos* (the ornamental screen above the altar) are a mosaic of the Last Supper, dating from 1867. To the left of the sanctuary is the **north transept**, highlighted by a rose window depicting eleven of the twelve apostles (the traitorous Judas Iscariot is absent). Also in the transept is a collection of monuments to great British statesmen.

In the **south transept** is one of the best-known secular parts of the abbey, **Poets' Corner**. It all started with the entombment of Geoffrey Chaucer, who was buried here in 1400 because he had been clerk of works to the Palace of Westminster; the inscription on his tomb mentioned the fact that he had been a poet and the tradition was born. Today the collection of tombs and memorials includes recognition of William Shakespeare, Lord Byron, William Blake, Charles Dickens, Sir Walter Scott, Emily and Anne Brontë, Henry James, and Jane Austen.

The memorials are not just limited to authors: composer and musician George Frederick Handel is buried here, as are several noted actors. American poet Henry Wadsworth Longfellow, who was very popular in England, is honored with a bust.

And the march of martyrs goes on: in July of 1998 statues of ten modern-day Christian martyrs were put in place in niches above the west door of the abbey; the spaces had been empty since they were built in medieval times.

The martyrs, chosen by a committee, include those of many religious denominations from around the world, such as Dr. Martin Luther King Jr., of the United States; Grand Duchess Elizabeth of Russia; Manche Masmeole of South Africa; Lucian Tapiedi of New Guinea; Maximilian Kolbe of Poland; Dietrich Bonhoeffer of Germany; Esther John of Pakistan; Wang Zhiming of China; Archbishop Janani Luwum of Uganda; and Archbishop Oscar Romero of El Salvador.

The **Henry VII Chapel** lies at the top of the cross-shaped main building. Henry VII began construction here in 1503 as a burial place for his unlucky predecessor Henry VI, who was crowned king in 1422 at the age of nine months and suffered an unstable personal and royal life until he was deposed in 1461; he regained the throne nine years later and was believed murdered in 1471. As it turned out, it was Henry VII himself who was buried here in an elaborate tomb, along with his wife, Elizabeth of York, daughter of Edward IV.

Near Henry VII's final resting place is the tomb of James I (also known as James VI of Scotland) and the elaborate shared tomb of Mary I and her half sister Elizabeth I. Across the aisle is the tomb of Mary Queen of Scots.

The **Westminster Abbey Museum**, along with the **Pyx Chamber** and the **Chapter House**, is in the vaulted undercroft below the former monks' dormitory in the east cloister; this area dates back almost to the origins of the abbey in 1065. Items on display at the museum include the funeral effigy of Charles II from 1685, replicas of the coronation regalia, and armor. The Pyx Chamber was used for more than four hundred years, from about 1200, as a royal treasury; items on display today include plates from the abbey and Saint Margaret's Church.

Sunday services in the abbey include Holy Communion at 8 A.M., matins at 10 A.M., the abbey Eucharist at 11:15 A.M., evensong at 3 P.M., and a congregational service at 6:30 P.M. An organ recital is conducted at 5:45 P.M. On weekdays, services are at 7:30 A.M., 8 A.M., and 12:30 P.M. On Saturday, Holy Communion is at 8 A.M., matins at 9:20 A.M., and evensong at 3 P.M.

🆆🅾🆆 Tate Britain

Millbank, SW1. Underground: Pimlico. Open daily 10 A.M. to 5:50 P.M., Sunday 2 P.M. to 5:50 P.M. Admission: free. Donations accepted. ☎ (020) 7887-8000. 💻 www.tate.org.uk.

Opened in 1897, the Tate Gallery was paid for mostly by the contributions of sugar refiner Henry Tate, who also gave the nation a collection of sixty-five paintings. Subsequent bequests and gifts have built a world-class collection.

The collection features historic British art from the sixteenth century to the present day, including major works by Hogarth, Gainsborough, Reynolds, Stubbs, Constable, Whistler, and Sargent. Over the years the collection of the museum became so large that only a portion of its holdings could be displayed at any one time.

In 2000 the Tate Gallery split into two impressive pieces with the opening of the **Tate Modern** at Bankside on the south side of the Thames, opposite Saint Paul's Cathedral. The new building is an ambitious, $200 million recycling of the former Bankside Power Station.

The original Millbank site is now the **Tate Britain**, showing British works from 1500 to the present day.

The two principal holdings are the British Collection, by artists from the sixteenth through the early twentieth centuries, and the Modern Collection, by British artists from about 1880 and foreign artists from the age of Impressionism and later.

Another important collection is based around the major bequest by the painter J. M. W. Turner of three hundred paintings and some thirty thousand watercolors, brought together for the first time in the Clore Gallery in 1987.

🆆🅾🆆 Cabinet War Rooms

Clive Steps, King Charles Street, SW1. Underground: Westminster. Open daily 9:30 A.M. to 6 P.M. (last admission 5:15 P.M.). Admission: adult, ❸; child, ❶. ☎ (020) 7930-6961. 💻 www.iwm.org.uk/cabinet/cabinet.htm.

When World War II ended in Europe on August 16, 1945, military aides and bureaucrats who had spent six years directing Great Britain's war efforts turned out the lights and locked the doors on the top-secret fortified bunkers between Parliament and Number 10 Downing Street.

For more than thirty years the warren of rooms was left untouched and unviewed. In 1981 Prime Minister Margaret Thatcher directed that the rooms be preserved and opened to the public.

Down below the Government Office Building, north of Parliament Square, was the hidden nerve center of Winston Churchill's war cabinet. Protected by a layer of concrete about three feet thick, the rooms include living quarters for key ministers and military leaders.

The rooms were in the basement of the Office of Works' building which faced Saint James's Park and Horse Guards' Road on one side and Great George Street on the other. The building was considered the strongest structure of any in Whitehall.

As war clouds gathered in 1938 more than three acres of space was converted and reinforced. The complex included a canteen, hospital, shooting
range, and sleeping quarters; some of the rooms had ceilings so low that occu-
pants could not stand upright in them.

The war rooms are maintained as they were when the war ended, including
maps of military strategy, communications equipment, and other artifacts.
Small pins and flags mark the positions of convoys and warships. Near the map
room was a bedroom used by Churchill on some of the worst nights of the
Blitz and a desk from which he made some of his wartime radio broadcasts.

An audio tour plays snippets of Churchill's voice, air-raid sirens, and first-
hand accounts of wartime life. There is a special version for children, presenting wartime Britain from a child's point of view. Recent additions include all
of Churchill's medals, and the flag that was draped over his coffin. Displays of
Churchill's documents and papers are recirculated every few months.

Visitors can see twenty-one of the original rooms. The entrance is on Horse
Guards' Road overlooking Saint James's Park.

Banqueting House

Whitehall, SW1. Underground: Westminster or Embankment. Open Monday
to Saturday 10 A.M. to 5 P.M. (last admission 4:30 P.M.). Admission: adult, ❷;
child, ❶. ☎ (020) 7839-8919. 🖳 www.hrp.org.uk/bh/indexbh.htm.

A dining hall with a most unusual history, the Banqueting House was
designed by famed architect Inigo Jones in Palladian style and based on his
travels in Italy. Completed in 1622, it is the last surviving building of the
sprawling Whitehall Palace, which was destroyed by fire in 1698.

One of the jewels of the interior is a series of ceiling paintings by Flemish
artist Peter Paul Rubens that exalt James I; they were commissioned by his son,
Charles I, in 1630. That deification did not sit well with Oliver Cromwell and
his followers, and Charles I was executed on a scaffold outside the Banqueting
House in 1649. Twenty years later, Charles II celebrated his restoration to the
throne at the same location.

After Whitehall burned, the Banqueting House was converted by Christopher
Wren into a replacement Chapel Royal; it became a museum in 1890 and in
1963 was restored to its original appearance.

The building is still used from time to time for affairs of state. Musical performances can be seen on special dates throughout the year.

Big Ben

Bridge Street. Underground: Westminster.

Most visitors and many Londoners call Saint Stephen's Tower of the Houses
of Parliament "Big Ben," but the title is actually specifically applied to the
largest of five bells hung within the 320-foot-tall tower that rises over the
Houses of Parliament; it chimes on the hour, while four smaller ones sound on
the quarter hour.

There are two theories about the source of the name Big Ben. One plausible
story is that the name is drawn from Sir Benjamin Hall, commissioner of works at

the time the bell was hung in 1858. Another story says the bell was given its nickname in honor of popular boxer Benjamin Caunt, famous for a sixty-round match in 1857.

The clock is the largest in Britain, with four dials each twenty-four feet in diameter; the minute hands are fourteen feet long. Big Ben is actually the second thirteen-ton bell made for the clock; the first cracked during testing. Within the tower are drive weights weighing more than two tons; until an automatic winding system was put in place 1913, it took two men thirty-two hours to wind the clock.

The clock is lit at night. A second lamp above the face is illuminated when Parliament is in session.

The bell originally sounded an E note, but the tone was changed after a crack developed in 1859 because of a clapper that weighed too much for the design.

Number 10 Downing Street

SW1. Underground: Westminster. 🖳
www.number-10.gov.uk.

Big Ben

One of the most famous addresses in the world, Number 10 Downing Street is the official residence and primary office of the prime minister. Next door at Number 11 is the chancellor of the exchequer's residence. The building is not open to the public, and access to the street is restricted for security reasons. The prime minister's website includes a detailed tour of the public rooms.

A street of houses was built by Sir George Downing in 1680; Downing had a prerevolutionary American connection, spending part of his youth in the colonies and becoming the second graduate of Harvard College in Cambridge, Massachusetts. George II gave Number 10 to the prime minister in 1732, and it has been home to the head of government ever since.

The modest terraced facade gives little clue to the real size and grandeur within. Number 10 in fact consists of two houses. The house that faces Downing Street is a typical late-seventeenth-century town house. Interior connections lead to a second building that was enlarged in the twentieth century.

On duty at Horse Guards' Parade
Photo by Corey Sandler

Horse Guards' Parade

Located on the former tiltyard of Whitehall Palace, where Henry VIII held a great tilting tournament in 1540 that drew knights from all across Europe, Horse Guards' is the headquarters of the Household Division. A guardhouse was erected there in 1758; only members of the royal family are permitted to drive through its central arch.

The guard is changed Monday through Saturday at 11 A.M. and on Sunday at 10 A.M. The parade grounds are closed Saturdays in June. For information, call ☎ (020) 7930-4466.

In a corner of the grounds is the location of a walled tennis court said to have been used by Henry VIII.

Cenotaph

Opposite Downing Street stands a simple memorial to the fallen of both World Wars. It was erected in 1920, bearing the flags of the three military services and the merchant navy. *Cenotaph* comes from the Greek words *kenos* and *taphos*, meaning "empty tomb." On Remembrance Day (at 11 A.M. on the Sunday nearest the eleventh day of the eleventh month), the queen lays a wreath.

Jewel Tower

Abingdon Street, SW1. Underground: Westminster. Open daily 10 A.M. to 6 P.M. April 1 to September 20; 10 A.M. to 5 P.M. in October; and 10 A.M. to 4 P.M. November 1 to March 31. Admission: adult and child, ❶. ☎ (020) 7222-2219.

One of the last remaining pieces of the old Palace of Westminster, the Jewel Tower was built in 1365 to hold the personal treasures of King Edward III. A small museum within holds some relics from the palace and pottery rescued from the moat. The collection also includes designs for the reconstruction of the Houses of Parliament after the fire of 1834, and artifacts from the Office of Weights and Measures, which occupied the building from 1869 to 1938.

Parliament Square

SW1. Underground: Westminster.

At the center of the Houses of Parliament and Whitehall, Parliament Square was designed in the 1840s; it became Britain's first official traffic roundabout in 1926. Circling the lawn are statues of famous statesmen, including Sir Winston Churchill glowering at the House of Commons; Benjamin Disraeli; and Sir Robert Peel. And yes, that is Abraham Lincoln seated in front of the Middlesex Guildhall on the north side of the square.

Saint Margaret's Church

Westminster Abbey, Parliament Square, SW1. Underground: Westminster. Open Monday to Friday 9:30 A.M. to 3:30 P.M., Saturday 9:30 A.M. to 1:30 P.M., and Sunday 1 P.M. to 5:30 P.M. Admission: free. ☎ (020) 7222-5152.

An old church, dating back to 1523 (the third church on the site), Saint Margaret's has been a fashionable place for society and political weddings, including that of Winston Churchill, who was married there in 1908. Sometimes known as the "Parish Church of the House of Commons," its famed stained-glass window depicts the engagement of Catherine of Aragon to Arthur, Henry VIII's eldest brother.

The connection to the House of Commons dates at least as far back as Palm Sunday of 1614, when the entire Commons took communion in the church. A pew has been reserved for the Speaker of the House since 1682. In 1918 David Lloyd George led the House of Commons across the road for a thanksgiving service after the armistice for World War I; in 1945 Winston Churchill did the same for World War II. Today the start of each new Parliament is marked with a special service.

Visitors may wonder why there is a second church almost on top of Westminster Abbey; the answer reaches back to the original establishment of Westminster as a Benedictine abbey. The monks were cloistered from the common folk of the area, and so the original church for the populace was built late in the eleventh century.

The Sung Eucharist is conducted Sunday at 11 A.M.

Westminster Cathedral

Victoria Street, SW1. Underground: Victoria. Admission: free. Bell-tower lift open 9:30 A.M. to 5 P.M. Cathedral hours 7 A.M. to 7 P.M., Monday to Saturday. Admission: general, ❶; family ❸. ☎ (020) 7798-9055. 📖 www.west minstercathedral.org.uk.

The principal Roman Catholic Church of England and Wales was completed in 1903 on the site of a former prison.

The 273-foot-high red-brick tower of the cathedral, of Christian Byzan-

Westminster Cathedral

tine style, once offered superb views from the summit; the gallery is still there but many modern buildings now obscure some of the sights.

The cathedral is constructed of brick with contrasting stripes of Portland stone. The interior is decorated with mosaics and is built with more than one hundred different types of marble from around the world.

Chapter 11
Piccadilly and Saint James: Times Square and the Home of the Royals

 Buckingham Palace

 Piccadilly Circus

Apsley House, No. 1 London (Wellington Museum)

Constitution Arch/Wellington Arch

Faraday Museum

Guards' Museum

The Mall

Pall Mall

Queen's Gallery

Ritz Hotel

Royal Academy of Arts

Royal Mews

Saint James's Palace

Spencer House

London Trocadero

Rock Circus

Piccadilly Circus is one of the world's most famous city landmarks, a London equivalent of New York's Times Square. At its heart, Piccadilly is a celebration of commerce, a riot of mercantilism with huge colorful neon signs, gaudy souvenir stores, beeping and flashing video-game arcades, and a rock-and-roll wax museum.

But only half a mile away is the official seat of the British royalty, the Court of Saint James, and just beyond that is the ultra-refined atmosphere of Buckingham Palace, home to the bluest of bloods of the United Kingdom.

🆆🅾🆆 Buckingham Palace

Buckingham Palace Road, SW1. Underground: Victoria or Green Park. State rooms are open for public tour from early August through the end of September. Admission: adult, ❺; child (younger than 17), ❸; senior (older than 60), ❹. Family tickets for two adults and two children were £27.50 in mid-2001. ☎ (020) 7839-1377. Call ☎ (020) 7799-2331 for a twenty-four-hour information line, or ☎ (020) 7321-2233 for credit card bookings for tours. You can also consult 🖳 www.royal.gov.uk/palaces/bp.htm.

Price Bands
❶ £1–£3
❷ £3–£5
❸ £5–£7
❹ £7–£10
❺ £10–£15
❻ £15 and up

Tickets are available on the day of your visit, except in the busiest periods of the year, or in advance at the ticket office in Green Park, which opens daily at 9 A.M. A booking fee is applied to advance ticket purchases.

The **Royal Muse Gift Shop** is open daily, from 9:30 A.M. to 5 P.M.

The queen's modest pied-à-terre in London has 660 rooms, including nineteen formal state rooms, fifty-two royal and guest bedrooms, 188 staff bedrooms, and ninety-two offices. Quite a nice little art collection, too. For most of its history, the palace has been locked away from mere commoners, but in 1993 a small but spectacular section was opened to paying customers to help raise money for the restoration of the fire-damaged Windsor Castle. The tours have proven so popular (and profitable) that they are expected to continue every summer, although admission is still subject to royal whim.

The official residence of the reigning monarch in London was originally built in 1703 for the Duke of Buckingham. The royal standard flies from the pole on the east front when the queen is in residence. (Until the 1997 death of Diana, the Princess of Wales, that was the only flag permitted to fly there; for a short period of time leading up to Diana's funeral, the Union Jack was hung at half-mast.)

When first built, it was more of a country house on the edge of London, and it still retains some of that feel because of its setting between Saint James's Park and Hyde Park, and the surrounding greenery of the Mall and other grand avenues in the area.

In the Middle Ages, the main residence for the British royalty in London was the palace of Westminster, now rebuilt as the Houses of Parliament. From the reign of Henry VIII to William III, the royal palace was at Whitehall. In the eighteenth century, Saint James's Palace, built by Henry VIII as a hunting lodge, was used as the palace.

Buckingham House, rebuilt in 1705 for John Sheffield, Duke of Buckingham, was purchased by King George III in 1761, and in 1820, King George IV commissioned John Nash to convert it and expand it into a state palace. The shell of Buckingham House is still part of the palace, on the west side of the quadrangle. The expanded palace also included the Marble Arch at the east

PICCADILLY AND SAINT JAMES

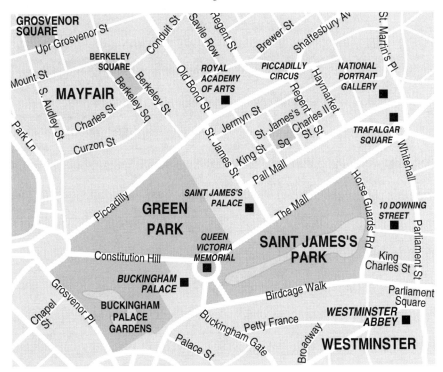

end of the U-shaped structure, which commemorates the victories at Trafalgar and Waterloo.

Both Georges and William IV died before work was completed. Queen Victoria was the first monarch to live at the palace; the nineteen-year-old queen moved in three weeks after her accession in 1837.

Buckingham Palace became too small for Queen Victoria's growing family and inadequate for court balls, and the east front was constructed, joining the wings of Nash's palace and creating a quadrangle and a forecourt. At the same time, the Marble Arch was moved to its present site at the northern end of Hyde Park.

It is the east front, with its formal balcony and the changing of the guard ceremony below, that is the most recognizable feature of the palace today. The façade of the palace was refaced in Portland stone in 1913.

Today the queen and her husband, the Duke of Edinburgh, live in the private apartments on the north side of the palace. There are also apartments for the other members of the royal family, including the Duke of York, on the upper floors of the north and east side.

About three hundred people work at the palace, including officers of the Royal Household for official affairs and a domestic staff; some fifty of the staff have rooms in the palace.

Buckingham Palace

There are seventy-eight bathrooms in the palace, though none is open to the public on tour; there are temporary facilities in the garden for visitors.

The palace is used for numerous events of state, including audiences with the prime minister, foreign and British ambassadors, senior officers of the armed forces, and affairs of the Church of England. Each fall, the queen gives a formal reception in the state rooms for the diplomatic corps. And three times a year there are summer garden parties for notables of public and private life.

State banquets for visiting heads of state are held in the Ballroom. Guests are received in the Music Room and escorted to their tables; a royal procession led by the queen and the visiting head of state enters the room, preceded by the Lord Chamberlain and the Lord Steward, walking backward.

The Buckingham Palace Tour

The palace offers more than 2,500 tickets per day to visitors during the summer opening from early August to early October. You can purchase as many as eight tickets in advance for any day and time or show up at the ticket office and purchase the first available time for the day of your visit. Credit card bookings can also be made by telephone at ☎ (020) 7321-2233.

The ticket booth is in Green Park, across from the main gates of Buckingham Palace; tickets are available after 9 A.M. with the first entry into the palace at 9:30 A.M. and the last at 4:30 P.M. To find the ticket booth, stand with your back to the formal gates at the front of the palace and look across the road on the left side of the Victoria Memorial. A security guard described the appearance of the tent-like structure as "Noah's Ark gone wrong"; you'll understand when you see it.

There's no photography permitted inside the palace, and you'll be asked to check any bags at the security screening room near the entrance; the bags will be transported to the garden exit while you make your tour.

And, yes, there's a gift shop in the garden. The **Buckingham Palace Shop** offers reproduction jewelry, silk scarves and ties; goblets and tumblers with HRH's crown; teas; biscuits; chocolates; and of course, a selection of postcards of some of the treasures of the Royal Collection, the state rooms, and the royal family themselves.

Finally, don't expect to see the queen and her family strolling the halls; they repair to their digs at Balmoral, Scotland, for most of each summer.

Visitors enter through the **Ambassadors' Entrance** in the south wing and into the quadrangle. The **Grand Hall** is decorated with white Carrara marble for the floors and Corinthian columns.

At the south end of the hall is the spectacular **Grand Staircase**, designed by Nash. Skylights above illuminate the gilt bronze balustrade and the white marble steps that circle to the left and right of the formal entrance to the state rooms on the first floor. The portraits around the stairs are those of Queen Victoria's immediate ancestors and relations, as mounted in 1838 after her coronation the year before.

The state rooms open to the public are in the west wing, beginning with the **Guard Room**, the traditional entrance to the rooms of the sovereign. The Guard Room at Buckingham Palace is relatively small, and thus on formal occasions ceremonial guards are in nearby rooms.

Troops include the Yeomen of the Guard; the royal bodyguard begun in by Henry VII in 1485, who dress in Tudor uniform; and the Gentlemen-at-Arms, founded by Henry VIII in 1537, who wear scarlet and gold uniforms deisgned in the nineteenth century.

The next tour stop is the **Green Drawing Room**, where guests and delegations gather before moving to the **Throne Room** or to the **Music Room** to meet the royal hosts. The spectacular domed ceiling is evocative of Middle Eastern mogul tents, a design feature first used by Nash in his design of the Royal Pavilion in Brighton. Among the room's treasures is a Sèvres porcelain potpourri vase from about 1758; it is said to have been owned by Madame de Pompadour, Louis XV's mistress.

The Entrée Stairs at Buckingham Palace

The Picture Gallery at Buckingham Palace
Copyright © Her Majesty Queen Elizabeth II

The formal **Throne Room** includes the throne chairs of Her Majesty the Queen and the Duke of Edinburgh, made for the coronation of Elizabeth II in 1953. Flanking them are the throne chairs of King George VI and Queen Elizabeth from 1937, and the throne chair of Queen Victoria from 1837.

As magnificent as many of the state rooms are, for many visitors it is the fabulous **Royal Collection** of art that is most impressive. The paintings, sculptures, and objects outshine most of the great art museums of the world. In total the Royal Collection is more than three times the size of the collection at the National Gallery.

Past the Throne Room is the spectacular **Picture Gallery**, which runs the length of the state apartments for 155 feet; it is located in what had been the first-floor rooms of the old Buckingham House. Lit from above by skylights, it was designed by Nash to hold George IV's collection of Dutch and Flemish artwork. A set of four marble chimney pieces, designed by Nash, include a circular portrait relief of artists Dürer, Van Dyck, Titian, and da Vinci.

Treasures in the Picture Gallery include on the east wall several works by Rembrandt such as *The Shipbuilder and his Wife* and the ethereal *Agatha Bas* from 1641, Johannes Vermeer's *The Music Lesson* from about 1670, Frans

Hals's *Portrait of a Man*, and Canaletto's *The Piazetta Towards the Torre dell'Orologio*.

On the west wall of the Picture Gallery are Peter Paul Rubens's *Milkmaids with Cattle in a Landscape* from about 1617, Anthony Van Dyck's *Charles I with M. de St. Antonio*, and another notable work by Canaletto, *Piazza S. Marco from a Corner of the Basilica*.

Now picture this: in his relatively more carefree years, Prince Charles celebrated his fortieth birthday with a disco party in the Picture Gallery, the room temporarily reappointed like a harem.

The **East and West Gallery** rooms serve as passageways between the state rooms and the **State Dining Room**. Hung on the West Gallery wall are four late-eighteenth-century tapestries from the Gobelins factory, from a series illustrating the exploits of Don Quixote.

The State Dining Room was originally intended as a Music Room but was converted to its present use for Queen Victoria. It is a room of gilded portraits and plaster with royal red carpeting and wall coverings. The balcony overlooks the gardens.

The adjoining **Blue Drawing Room** is probably the most ornate of the public areas of the palace, divided into bays by large Corinthian columns. Of particular note is Nash's spectacular ceiling, which holds nearly hidden delights in every direction.

The **Music Room**, originally known as the Bow Drawing Room, has a handsome semicircular bow window overlooking the garden below; the vaulted and domed ceiling is gilded. Guests are presented from this room before a dinner or banquet. Queen Elizabeth's three eldest children were baptized in this room in water imported from the River Jordan.

The royal family gathers in the **White Drawing Room** before formally meeting guests waiting in the Music Room.

Visitors descend the **Ministers' Staircase** at the north end of the Picture Gallery to the ground floor and the **Marble Hall**, which lies directly under the gallery. It is used as a sculpture hall, featuring such works as Antonio Canova's *Fountain Nymph with Putto*.

Finally, there is the **Bow Room**, the entranceway to the gardens. It was originally designed to be the library in the private apartments of George IV.

The exit is across the garden where the queen's garden parties are held each summer. You'll exit through **Grosvenor Gate** in Grosvenor Place.

Changing of the Guard

The sovereign and the royal palaces have been guarded since 1660 by the Household Troops. The guard consists of three officers and forty men when the queen is in residence, and three officers and thirty-one men when she is away.

The forty-five-minute changing of the guard ceremony takes place in the forecourt of Buckingham Palace at 11:30 A.M. every day from April through July, and every other day for the remainder of the year. The new guard marches to the palace from Wellington Barracks on Birdcage Walk accompanied by a guards' band and relieves the sentries of the old guard. Then a procession marches back to Saint James's Palace.

The queen's guard usually consists of foot guards in full-dress uniform of red tunics and bearskins; on occasion, other units such as the Brigade of Gurkhas perform the duty.

The Wellington Barracks is the home of five regiments of foot guards, a guards' battalion, and a museum. Birdcage Walk received its name because James I's aviary was formerly located there.

The Guards' Chapel at Wellington Barracks was originally erected in 1877; on June 18, 1944, the chapel was hit by a flying bomb during a Sunday morning service and 121 worshippers were killed. A new chapel was completed in 1963.

WOW! Piccadilly Circus

W1. Underground: Piccadilly Circus.

The Times Square of London, best known for its gaudy advertising signs and lively nighttime activities, the traffic roundabout that is the circus itself features a famous (and surprisingly petite) statue evocative of Eros, the Greek god of love.

The Piccadilly area includes shops, restaurants, and entertainment of various types and intensities, including the **Rock Circus** and the **Trocadero**.

Piccadilly is, along with Oxford Street, one of the two ancient highways that lead to the west from London. The name was given to the area as a joking reference to the source of the fortune of one of the major landlords of the early seventeenth century, the tailor Robert Baker. He was able to buy land to the north of what is now the circus from the sale of *picadils*, stiff collars that were

The statue of Eros in Piccadilly Circus

very popular with the court of the time. Wags named his showy house "Picca-dilly Hall," and the name was eventually applied to the whole area.

The intersection was created in 1819 when Regent Street was first put into place crossing Piccadilly as part of master architect John Nash's plan to connect Marylebone Park (about to be developed as Regent's Park) to the Regent's palace, Carlton House. Marylebone was named after a thirteenth-century parish church in the area that lay alongside Tyburn stream and was known as Saint Mary's by the Bourne, which was later orally abbreviated to Marylebone. It was at first a sprawling private manor and a royal hunting preserve.

At first, the buildings in the area were designed with a concave face to create a circular bowl, but in the 1880s another road, Shaftesbury Avenue, was put through the intersection. In 1893 the **Shaftesbury Memorial Fountain** was erected at the center of the circus. Funds for the statue came from contributions to honor Shaftesbury, a noted philanthropist who had raised funds for the poor; when Shaftesbury Avenue was built, it was routed through some of the most horrible slums of London, the subjects of some of Charles Dickens's writings.

The statue was supposed to represent the Angel of Christian Charity, although that was not how it was seen. By public acclamation it was instead declared to be that of Eros, the Greek god of love. The statue was moved twice—first to Embankment Gardens from 1922 to 1931 while the Underground station at Piccadilly Circus was created, and again during World War II from 1939 to 1948, when it was moved to a safe location out of town.

It was about the time of the erection of the statue that merchants and landlords on the north side of the circus began renting out large electrically illuminated signs on and above their buildings, the most famous of which were the Bovril and Schweppe's signs of about 1910.

Apsley House, No. 1 London (Wellington Museum)

Hyde Park Corner, W1V. Underground: Hyde Park Corner. Open Tuesday to Sunday 11 A.M. to 5 P.M. Closed Monday except bank holidays. Admission: adult, ❷; child (18 and younger), free; senior, ❶. ☎ (020) 7499-5676. 🖳 www.vam.ac.uk/Infodome/associated_museums/apsley_house.

The home of the first Duke of Wellington, Apsley House holds much of the Duke's fabulous collection of paintings, silver, porcelain, sculpture, furniture, orders, medals, and memorabilia that he received as tribute, gathered on his own, or collected as plunder.

One of the finest residences in London, Apsley House was at one time the first home past the tollgate into London from the countryside and was known as "No. 1 London." Today it is considered the last great London townhouse with its collections and family still in residence.

The home was designed by Robert Adam for Henry Bathurst, the Lord Chancellor of the day, and completed in 1778. Wellington purchased the home in 1817 after his military victory over Napoleon at Waterloo. He added Bath stone over the brick and the ninety-foot-long Waterloo Gallery for some of his keepsakes.

Some of the treasures include the *Waterseller of Seville* by Velazquez, a gift from the Spanish Royal Collection to Wellington. Wellington used the house for grand entertainment, and also on display is Wellington's collection of fabulous dinner and dessert services, including the Sèvres Egyptian service commissioned by Napoleon for the Empress Josephine. At the foot of the ornate staircase is Canova's massive nude statue of Napoleon.

The museum is operated as a branch of the Victoria and Albert Museum.

There are more than two hundred paintings in the collection, including a number from the Spanish royalty as well as masterworks by artists such as Goya, Rubens, Correggio, Brueghel, Steen, de Hooch, Wilkie, and Lawrence.

The **Basement Gallery** offers a bit of historical perspective, "Remembering Wellington," which presents the duke as a military figure, politician, and elder statesman through artifacts and personal possessions.

Constitution Arch/Wellington Arch

Hyde Park Corner. Underground: Hyde Park Corner.

The Wellington Arch was built in 1828 and originally included a statue of Wellington. The statue was removed in 1883 when the arch was moved to Constitution Hill, and a new sculpture, the *Quadriga* (a chariot drawn by four horses yoked abreast) was installed in 1912.

Faraday Museum

The Royal Institution, 21 Albemarle Street, W1. Underground: Green Park. Open weekdays 9 A.M. to 6 P.M. Admission: ❶. ☎ (020) 7409-2992. 💻 www.ri.ac. uk/History/MFL&M.html. For information on the Royal Institution, consult 💻 www.ri.ac.uk.

Faraday Museum is a reconstruction of the mid-nineteenth-century laboratory of physicist and chemist Michael Faraday, best known for his discoveries of electromagnetic induction and of the laws of electrolysis.

Faraday was the son of a blacksmith and received little formal education. After he attended a series of lectures given by the British chemist Humphry Davy in 1812, he convinced the renowned scientist to employ him as an assistant in his laboratory at the Royal Institution; in 1833 he succeeded Davy as professor of chemistry.

His most important work took place in electricity and magnetism. In 1821 he plotted the magnetic field around a conductor carrying an electric current; ten years later he discovered the principal of electromagnetic induction. Merging his work in chemistry and electricity, he studied electrolysis.

The Royal Institution was established in 1799 for the study of science. The classical façade to the building, added in 1838, is based on the Temple of Antoninus in Rome.

Guards' Museum

Birdcage Walk, SW1. Underground: Saint James's Park. Open daily except Sunday 10 A.M. to 4 P.M. Closed during ceremonies at Horse Guards'. Admission: ❶. Family pass: ❷. ☎ (020) 7930-4466, extension 3428.

The museum features a display of military weapons, uniforms, and colors, as well as an exploration of the history of the battles undertaken by the guards from the English civil war to the present day.

The Mall

SW1. Underground: Charing Cross, Green Park, Piccadilly Circus.

The 115-foot-wide triumphal formal approach to Buckingham Palace, the Mall was first created about 1660 as a replacement pall-mall alley. After the game declined in favor late in the eighteenth century, it became a gravel walking area near the palace.

After Queen Victoria died, the Mall was rebuilt as a grand processional, from Admiralty Arch to the Queen Victoria Memorial; it is one of the few unbending roads of any length in the capital. The former Mall still exists as a horse path alongside. When foreign heads of state visit London, the flagpoles on both sides of the road fly their flags.

By the way, if you want to sound somewhat like a native, learn to pronounce it as if it rhymed with *pal*.

Pall Mall

SW1. Underground: Charing Cross or Green Park.

One of London's more formal streets, Pall Mall is now occupied by high-tone offices, institutes, shops, and private clubs. It received its name from the Italian or French game of *pallo a maglio* or *palle-maille*, a game that has been described as a cross between golf and croquet. Charles II made the game popular in the park at Saint James's and a royal pall-mall alley was constructed inside the park wall; it later was moved to the area now called the Mall.

By the seventeenth century, the road along the alley became the site of fashionable shops and residences for luminaries, including Nell Gwynne, an accomplished actress and mistress of Charles II; artist Thomas Gainsborough; and Maria Anne Fitzherbert, the somewhat-secret Roman Catholic wife of George IV.

Queen's Gallery *(Closed for Renovations Until Summer 2002)*

Buckingham Palace Road, SW1. Underground: Victoria.

The Queen's Gallery showcases treasures from the queen's fabulous collection. The gallery is located in a former conservatory and chapel on the Buckingham Palace Road side of the palace; the original private chapel at the site was destroyed by a bomb during World War II.

A £10 million, two-year facelift is one of one of the most significant building projects at the Palace since the creation of King George V's familiar Palace front of Portland stone in 1913. The restored gallery is expected to reopen by the summer of 2002.

Ritz Hotel

Piccadilly, W1. Underground: Green Park. ☎ (020) 7493-8181. 🖳 www.theritz hotel.co.uk.

Ritz, as in ritzy, as in hotelier César Ritz—the elegant and oh-so-formal hotel was built in 1906 and features an interior in the style of Louis XVI, with marble floors, crystal chandeliers, and its famed **Palm Court**. Afternoon tea is served (with a dress code enforced).

Royal Academy of Arts

Burlington House, Piccadilly, W1. Underground: Piccadilly Circus. Open daily 10 A.M. to 6 P.M. Admission: charges vary with special exhibits. ☎ (0207) 300-5760. 🏛 www.royalacademy.org.uk.

The oldest fine arts institution in Britain, the Royal Academy was founded in 1768.

The home of the museum since 1868 is **Burlington House**, the last surviving structure of a group of great mansions built in the 1660s on the north side of Piccadilly. The Palladian design has been altered several times in its history. The statues above the windows depict, from left to right, classical Greek sculptor Phidias, Leonardo da Vinci, English sculptor and illustrator John Flaxman, Renaissance painter Raphael, Italian artist Michelangelo, Venetian painter Titian, English portraitist Joshua Reynolds, English architect John Wren, and English prelate and educator William of Wykeham.

Treasures include a marble *tondo* (relief) by Michelangelo, *The Virgin and Child with the Infant St. John.*

Its famous summer exhibition of contemporary art has been held every year since 1769, displaying paintings, engravings, sculptures, and other objects by artists of the day.

Royal Mews

Buckingham Palace Road, SW1. Underground: Victoria. Open all year Monday to Thursday from noon to 4 P.M. From early August to late September also open on Mondays from 10:30 A.M. to 4:30 P.M. Admission: adult, ❷; child, ❶. The Mews is closed on special occasions; call before you visit. ☎ (020) 7839-1377.

The royal garage and stables, the Mews is home to some one hundred gilded and polished state carriages and coaches, including **Her Majesty's Gold State Coach**, first used by George III when he opened Parliament in 1762 and used at every coronation since George IV's in 1821. The four-ton carriage requires eight horses to pull it.

Other vehicles kept here include the **Irish State Coach**, made in Dublin in 1851 and purchased by Queen Victoria; damaged by fire in 1911, it was later restored. The blue and black exterior is decorated with gilt, and the interior is covered in blue damask.

Coaches include the **Glass State Coach**, purchased in 1910 by George V and used for royal weddings, a pair of barouches used by the Queen Mother at the annual Trooping the Colour ceremony, and a set of broughams used daily by official court messengers in London.

Also on display are some of the elaborate harnesses and decorative pieces.

Parked in the royal garage is the **Phantom VI Rolls Royce**, given to the queen in 1978 as a Jubilee present, as well as a 1948 **Phantom IV** and a collection of other vehicles.

The Royal Mews is managed by the Master of the Horse and the Crown Equerry. The stables are home to more than two dozen horses and about that many coachmen and grooms. The building was designed by Nash in 1825.

Saint James's Palace

The Mall, SW1. Underground: Green Park. Not open to the public.

Built by Henry VIII about 1530, Saint James's Palace has been one of the residences of the royalty of England for more than three hundred years.

After fire destroyed Whitehall Palace in 1698, Saint James's became the principal residence in London; Queen Anne and Georges I through IV all spent a great deal of time in the palace. In 1809 much of the palace was destroyed in a fire; it was restored by 1814. By the 1820s, the monarchy moved into the expanded Buckingham Palace.

Today foreign ambassadors to Great Britain are accredited to the Court of Saint James, and some formal events are still held at Saint James's, including the proclamation of a new sovereign and the convening of the Accession Council as part of the process of transfer of power to a new king or queen.

The palace, which includes some lovely carvings and tapestries, is used for offices and residences for some upper-level employees of the Crown, including the lord chamberlain's staff. Prince Charles also set up bachelor digs in the palace after his separation from Princess Diana. It is not open to the public.

Clarence House, on the Mall and attached to Saint James's Palace to the southwest, is the official London residence of the Queen Mother.

Spencer House

27 Saint James Place, SW1. Underground: Green Park. Open Sunday 10:30 A.M. to 5:30 P.M. (last tour 4:45 P.M.). Admission: adult, ❸; child, ❸ (no child younger than 10 admitted). ☎ (020) 7514-1958. 🖳 www.spencerhouse.co.uk.

Spencer House is a private palace completed in 1766 for the first Earl Spencer, an ancestor of Diana, Princess of Wales. After passing through a number of owners, it was restored in 1990, opened as a museum, and made available for receptions and meetings. The Palladian-style palace includes nine state rooms furnished with fine paintings and furniture.

London Trocadero

Piccadilly Circus, W1. Underground: Piccadilly Circus. Open Sunday to Thursday 10 A.M. to midnight, Friday and Saturday 10 A.M. to 1 A.M. Admission: free. ☎ (020) 7439-1791. 🖳 www.troc.co.uk.

Admission is free to the Trocadero with its shops and cafés, but the individual attractions are separately priced from £2 to £7.95. The lead attraction is **Funland**, a futuristic indoor theme park, occupying seven floors and entered by a rocket escalator. The main features are six high-tech rides that combine motion simulation with virtual-reality images. Each floor is uniquely themed, containing a different ride and a host of interactive experiences. Other attractions include the **Rock Circus**, plus outposts of the **Planet Hollywood** and **Rainforest Cafe** chains.

Rock Circus

London Pavilion at Piccadilly Circus. Open daily 11 A.M. to 9 P.M., to 10 P.M. on weekends. Admission: adult, ❹; child, ❸; senior, ❹. ☎ (020) 7734-7203. 🖳 www.rock-circus.com.

A specialized wax museum and part of the Madame Tussaud's group, Rock Circus tells the history of rock and pop with moving wax figures, lasers, and videos.

The London Pavilion was a popular music hall of the late nineteenth century and later an important cinema in the city. The Beatles made their last public appearance there at the 1968 premiere of *Yellow Submarine*.

Chapter 12
Trafalgar Square, Soho, Leicester Square, and the West End

 Trafalgar Square

 National Gallery

WOW National Portrait Gallery

WOW Soho

    Carnaby Street

    Chinatown

    Berwick Street Market

    Liberty and Co. Ltd.

    Hamleys of Regent Street

    Leicester Square

    Saint-Martin-in-the-Fields

In this small area are three of London's liveliest places to eat, shop, protest, celebrate, and be entertained. And there is also a pair of fabulous museums, one for art's sake and the other a view of history as seen through the eyes of artists. (In Chapter 24, you'll find descriptions of the West End theaters, mostly located in "Theatreland" in and around Leicester Square.)

WOW Trafalgar Square

Underground: Charing Cross.

    Trafalgar Square is one of London's central gathering places for most any occasion and famous for annual New Year's Eve celebrations and rallies. It also seems to be the favorite spot in London for the capital city's extensive population of pigeons and pigeon lovers.

    Every Christmas a huge tree is erected here, a gift of the people of Norway

Trafalgar Square

as thanks for Britain's contributions in World War II. Around the square are the National Gallery, church of Saint Martin-in-the-Fields, and Admiralty Arch.

The square is lorded over by a 165-foot-tall Corinthian column topped by a statue of Admiral Nelson, who died in the Battle of Trafalgar against Napoleon's forces. The memorial, at the south side of the square, was installed in 1842.

The National Gallery lies at the north end of the square.

The area was originally known as the King's Mews, a fancy term for stables; the royals kept their horses, hunting hawks, and other animals here, along with their handlers. Chaucer was among those who held the title of Clerk of the Mews. By the end of the eighteenth century, most of the area was used for homes.

In 1840 the buildings were removed and the downsloping land was leveled and paved. At the base of the terrace are placed metal equivalents of the official inch, foot, and yard measures.

In the center of the south side of Trafalgar Square is the famed Nelson Column. At the top is a bronze capital cast from old guns, and above that is a seventeen-foot-tall stone statue of Nelson.

At the base of the column is a set of bas-relief sculptures representing the Battle of Cape Saint Vincent, the Battle of the Nile, the Bombardment of Copenhagen, and finally, the death of Nelson. The sculptures are made from captured cannons. In front of the column on a small traffic island is an equestrian statue of Charles I. A statue of George IV sitting astride a horse is at the northeast corner of the square.

Flanking the column on the north are bronze statues and busts of military commanders who distinguished themselves on Nelson's escapades.

🖿 National Gallery

Trafalgar Square. Underground: Charing Cross, Leicester Square, Piccadilly Circus. Open Monday, Tuesday, and Thursday to Saturday 10 A.M. to 6 P.M., Wednesday 10 A.M. to 9 P.M., Sunday 10 A.M. to 6 P.M. Admission: free. ☎ (020) 7839-3321. 🖳 www.nationalgallery.org.uk.

Listen for the sound of dropping jaws. The National Gallery is one of the richest collections of art on public display, its walls an art textbook presented in chronological order. It's more than can be reasonably absorbed in one day.

Founded in 1824, today the gallery features more than 2,200 works of art, concentrating on European artists from Giotto (about 1267–1337) to Vincent van Gogh (1853–1890). The original collection was that of Russian merchant and banker John Julius Angerstein; it included thirty-eight works by Raphael, Rembrandt, Van Dyck, and others. It was added to in coming years by its directors, who traveled Europe in search of pictures to be acquired. Treasures include Georges Seurat's *Bathers at Asnières*, a famed "cartoon" (a chalk drawing) of the Virgin and Child with Saint Anne and John the Baptist by Leonardo da Vinci, and Titian's *Death of Actaeon*, purchased by a government grant and public subscription in 1972.

The museum has been housed since 1838 in its neoclassical building on Trafalgar Square; several expansions have been undertaken, including the Sainsbury Wing, added in 1991 to house the museum's oldest holdings in the Early Renaissance Collection, and temporary galleries. The modern addition includes the Micro Gallery, a computer database of images and details about the entire collection for students and casual visitors.

The collection is more or less laid out in chronological order, beginning in the Sainsbury Wing with medieval and early Renaissance works from 1260 to 1510. Next in order are the West Wing (the Renaissance era from 1510 to 1600, including Titian, Raphael, Michelangelo, and Holbein), North (principally Dutch works from 1600 to 1700, including Vermeer, Rembrandt, and Van Dyck), and finally the East Wing (featuring English and French art from 1700 to 1900, including Fragonard, Gainsborough, Hogarth, Renoir, Monet, and Cézanne, as well as van Gogh and early Picasso).

The museum is very popular and can be quite crowded on Sunday afternoons and holidays. It has a branch of the popular Pret a Manger sandwich shop in the basement.

🖿 National Portrait Gallery

Saint Martin's Place, Trafalgar Square. Underground: Charing Cross. Open daily from 10 A.M. to 6 P.M., and until 9 P.M. on Thursday and Friday. Admission: free. (Some special exhibitions have an admission charge.) ☎ (020) 7306-0055. 🖳 www.npg.org.uk.

Less celebrated than the National Gallery next door, the National Portrait Gallery concentrates on the history of Britain as presented through art, rather than on great works of art themselves. That's not to say there aren't some won-

National Portrait Gallery

derful pieces by artists such as van Dyck, Gainsborough, and Hans Holbein, including his portraits of Henry VII, Henry VIII, and Thomas More.

Like Britain itself, the museum is at times stiff and proper, and at other times decidedly offbeat and somewhat kinky. And sometimes both at the same time: on one of my visits I spied a formal bust of T. S. Eliot standing next to a modern impressionistic portrait of the poet. In one modern-day gallery, a large four-panel watercolor presents Queen Elizabeth as if she were a pop star.

There are more than nine thousand portraits in the collection, dating back to the late fifteenth century. Among the treasures is the only known portrait of Shakespeare done during his lifetime.

The museum was established in 1859 and moved in 1895 to a new building around the corner from the National Gallery and facing Saint Martin-in-the-Fields; it was expanded in 1937. The Ondattje wing opened in 2000, adding more display areas and The Portrait Restaurant on the roof, offering spectacular views over London. The view extends over Nelson in Trafalgar Square and across Whitehall to the Houses of Parliament, Big Ben, and the London Eye. The restaurant is open daily for lunch and on Thursday and Friday evenings.

🌟 Soho

During the Middle Ages, Soho was farmland, later part of the royal park of Whitehall Palace; its name is believed to come from the hunter's cry, "So-ho!" It went on to become one of London's most fashionable areas when it was first developed in the seventeenth century, later a center of the literary and artistic scene in the nineteenth century, then a declining red-light district through the twen-

SOHO, PICCADILLY CIRCUS, AND TRAFALGAR SQUARE

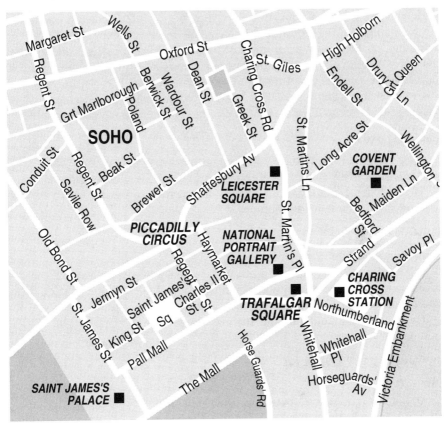

tieth century. Today, Soho is once again mostly a trendy place of galleries, jazz cafés, pubs, and shops with a few peep shows and strip clubs for spice.

The cosmopolitan atmosphere of today's Soho is a vestige of its history as a melting pot for people of many backgrounds, including French Huguenots who settled in the late seventeenth century, and before them Greek Christians; by the middle of the nineteenth century, the population density in the tenements in the area was higher than anywhere else in London. This contributed to the severity of a cholera outbreak in 1854, which hastened the departure of many of the better-off residents. About that time, many theaters and music halls were built, as well as quite a few houses of prostitution.

By the dawn of the twentieth century, the growing West End helped the growth of restaurants catering to the theater crowd. The sex business continued into the 1990s, although a crackdown on striptease clubs and prostitutes has sharply reduced the industry.

The heart of Soho is Old Compton Street with its somewhat funky restaurants and shops.

Carnaby Street

Underground: Oxford Circus. In the last half of the 1960s, this was one of the fashion capitals of the world, the source of the mod style exported around the world by the "British Invasion" of musical groups, including the Beatles. Today, the street is more of a tourist lure, although there are still quite a few unusual clothing stores on the short street and nearby avenues such as Newburgh Street. Inderwick's on Carnaby Street is England's oldest pipe maker, dating to 1797; the meerschaum clay pipe craze of the nineteenth century was born here.

Chinatown

Underground: Leicester Square. 📱 www.chinatown-online.co.uk.

A small but lively collection of restaurants and shops, Chinatown is centered on Gerrard Street in Soho. The Chinese New Year is ushered in with a bang at the end of January or early February.

Berwick Street Market

Underground: Piccadilly Circus.

The market has been at this location since the 1840s, launched with the surprising success of the first imported grapefruits to England. Today it is a lively street market offering fruits, vegetables, and carryout meals.

The Blue Posts public house is the successor to a line of taverns at its location dating back to at least 1739.

Liberty and Co. Ltd.

210–220 Regent Street. Underground: Oxford Circus. 📱 www.liberty.co.uk.

Arthur Liberty's shop opened in 1875, selling imported silk. It became a favorite of the artistic crowd, including painter James Whistler, and many began designing for the store; the products, known as Liberty Prints, were influential style makers through the early twentieth century.

Gilbert and Sullivan used Liberty fabrics for costumes in their comic opera Patience in 1881.

Today the store still sells items from Asia, including silks, home furnishings, and jewelry.

The current building, which dates from 1925, is vaguely Tudor, with a timber façade constructed from the remains of two old naval ships, the HMS Hindustand and HMS *Impregnable*.

Hamleys of Regent Street

188 Regent Street. Open daily, Sunday from noon. ☎ (0270) 494-2000. 📱 www. hamleys.co.uk.

William Hamley opened the Noah's Ark toy shop in London in 1760, selling toys from around the world. The shop, moved from its original location on High Holborn Street, now occupies six floors and sells more than forty thousand different toys and games.

The staff includes demonstrators who fly planes, blow bubbles, and otherwise entice children of all ages to visit and spend.

Leicester Square

Leicester Square

Underground: Leicester Square.

The heart of London's theater district, the land of Leicester Square came into King Henry VIII's hands in 1537; it was acquired by Robert Sidney, the second Earl of Leicester, beginning in 1630. In 1635 the sprawling Leicester House—one of the largest homes of its time in London—was built at its northern edge.

By the eighteenth century, the square was enclosed by fashionable homes, including those of painters William Hogarth and Joshua Reynolds. In the next century, though, the nature of the square changed with the construction nearby of New Coventry Street, bringing hotels, Turkish baths, and shops. The theater district began to grow with the construction of the Alhambra in 1858.

In 1851 the center of the square was occupied by an unusual exhibition named the Great Globe, a sixty-foot-tall globe-shaped rotunda with its interior detailed as a model of the earth. Visitors climbed a four-story gallery within to examine the exhibition. It was taken down in 1862 and the central garden was allowed to fall into disrepair. In 1874 it was purchased by a wealthy member of Parliament and redesigned in keeping with its previous role as a public square. New features included installation of a marble fountain with statues of Shakespeare, former residents Hogarth, Reynolds, and well-known surgeon John Hunter, as well as scientist Isaac Newton, who lived nearby.

The area was so popular as an entertainment district that with the outbreak of the First World War, departing soldiers sang "Farewell, Leicester Square" as a part of the popular song, "It's a Long Way to Tipperary." Briton Charlie Chaplin was honored with a statue in 1981.

The central garden of the square today includes a booth at its western edge selling same-day theater tickets at half price (plus a service charge). The square is also surrounded by ticket agencies that sell tickets at prices ranging from a discount to full price to full price plus a markup. (*See Chapter 24 for some suggestions on how to buy tickets.*)

Saint Martin-in-the-Fields

Trafalgar Square. Underground: Charing Cross. Open daily 8 A.M. to 6 P.M. ☎ (020) 7930-1862. 🖳 www.stmartin-in-the-fields.org.

There was a small church on the site of the London Brass Rubbing Centre as far back as the twelfth century, perhaps for the use of monks from Westminster Abbey who traveled to work in the convent garden. The little church was rebuilt in the mid-sixteenth century, and once again from 1722 to 1726 in the form it now shows.

The classic design of a colonnaded front topped by a tall and narrow spire was copied by many early churches in Colonial America. The ceiling of the chancel is gilded, with a central sunburst presenting the tetragrammaton, the four Hebrew characters representing the unspoken sacred name of God.

The Royal Box at the church is reserved for the royal family and occasionally used; Queen Mary was a regular attendee.

Among those laid to rest here were Charles II's mistress Nell Gwynne, the painters William Hogarth and Joshua Reynolds, and famed furniture maker Thomas Chippendale.

From 1914 to 1927 the church's crypt was used as a shelter for the homeless, and during World War II as an air-raid shelter. Today it is once again a center for the homeless and a soup kitchen; a café nearby caters to tourists.

Just inside the entrance is the national memorial to the victims of injustice of the apartheid era in South Africa; the bronze sculpture was dedicated by Archbishop Desmond Tutu in 1994, the year of the first democratic elections in that country. Along the north wall is a memorial to the Far Eastern prisoners in World War II, many of whom worked on the notorious Railway of Death in Thailand; two pieces of the railway's cars are in a glass case there.

The church has a long history of use for musical performances, including concerts by Handel; today it is often used for concerts and performances by the Academy of Saint Martin-in-the-Fields and by visiting choral and orchestral groups; many well-known classical recordings have been made here. A world-class organ, with 3,637 pipes, was installed in the church in 1990.

Free lunchtime concerts are given several times each week, generally Monday, Tuesday, and Friday; a donation of £2 is requested. A regular series of evening concerts, including performances by candlelight, is also offered. For tickest , call ☎ (020) 7839-8362 or consult 🖳 www. stmartin-in-the-fields.org.

London Brass Rubbing Centre

Open Monday to Saturday 10 A.M. to 6 P.M., Sunday noon to 6 P.M. ☎ (020) 7930-9306.

The London Brass Rubbing Centre is in the basement of Saint Martin-in-the-Fields. It sells finished items and allows paying visitors to create their own brass rubbings.

Chapter 13
Covent Garden and the Strand

 Covent Garden

 London Transport Museum

 Courtauld Gallery

Theatre Museum

Royal Opera House

Seven Dials

Neal Street and Neal's Yard

Cleopatra's Needle

Charing Cross

Roman Bath

Covent Garden is the lively outdoor heart of this district, a collection of shops, restaurants, and street performers that spills out into the surrounding neighborhood. It's also the home of several important museums and the impressive Royal Opera House.

🎀 Covent Garden

Underground: Covent Garden. 💻 www.cgma.gov.uk.

Covent Garden once really was a garden (a convent garden supporting nearby Westminster Abbey) and now is one of the world's oldest urban malls.

First laid out in the 1630s by Inigo Jones, it was London's first planned square in the style of an Italian piazza by way of the design used in the Place des Vosges in Paris.

The public square designed by Jones also included **Saint Paul's Church**; the altar was originally at the west end, with the church's grand portico facing east into the piazza of Covent Garden. Church officials did not like the arrangement and moved the altar to the other end, leaving the east portico as a false door that

115

A busker entertains at Covent Garden
Photo by Corey Sandler

has been happily adopted by street performers as a stage.

Because of its proximity to the **West End**, Saint Paul's has long been known as the Actor's Church.

For more than three centuries, the area was used as the city's fruit, vegetable, and flower market. In the mid-1970s, urban renewal arrived on the scene and Covent Garden was transformed from wholesale to retail with a collection of stylish shops, cafés, and restaurants.

The area is also home to a number of notable theaters, including the **Royal Opera House**, the **Adelphi Theatre**, the **Theatre Royal**, and the **London Coliseum**.

⟦WOW⟧ London Transport Musem

Covent Garden Piazza. Underground: Covent Garden or Leicester Square. Open daily 10 A.M. to 6 P.M., Friday 11 A.M. to 6 P.M. Admission: adult, ❸; child (2–15), ❶; family, ❺. ☎ (020) 7379-6344 or ☎ (020) 7836-8557. ▣ www.ltmuseum.co.uk.

For many visitors, young and old, among the most interesting elements of London are Underground trains and the red double-deck buses of London Transport. Here's your chance to drive away on tours of fancy in a well-stocked touch-and-feel museum.

The museum tells the story of transport and the capital from 1800 to the present day with hands-on exhibits, working models, and high-tech videos and touch-screen displays. Visitors can even put themselves in the driving seat of a bus or a Tube train in a simulator. Actors bring to life some of the characters who have kept London moving for the last two hundred years, working on the buses and digging the Tube tunnels beneath the city.

Located in the heart of Covent Garden in the original Victorian flower market, the Transport Museum has been opened up with upper levels and a glass walkway that offers a unique perspective of the historic buses, trams, and trains.

Price Bands
❶ £1–£3
❷ £3–£5
❸ £5–£7
❹ £7–£10
❺ £10–£15
❻ £15 and up

Complementing the display of vehicles are galleries housing originals of the famous Underground map and posters from the museum's extensive collection.

In nineteenth-century London the horse reigned supreme, and many of the museum's exhibits reflect this, including a replica of London's first horse-drawn omnibus of 1829 and a restored double-deck horse tram dating back to

COVENT GARDEN

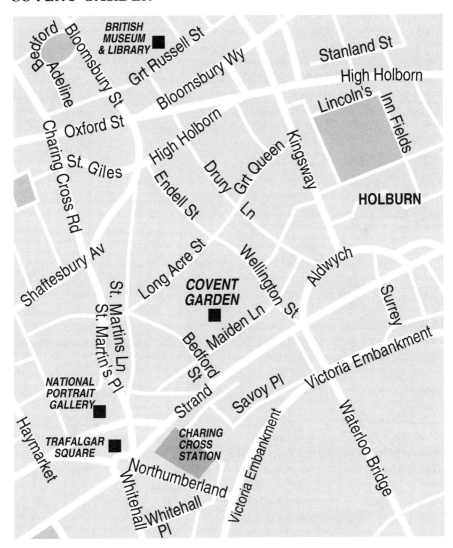

1882. Here's a piece of trivia not for the dinner conversation: by the end of the nineteenth century, horses deposited one thousand tons of horse dung on city streets each day. No wonder, then, that the first motorized vehicles, electrified trams, and the world's first underground system were so happily embraced.

On display at the museum is one of the first mass-produced motor buses in the world, the B type of 1910, which also served as a troop transport during the First World War.

The first underground railways relied on steam locomotives, and on display is Metropolitan Railway locomotive Number 23, built in 1866, which moved trains on the Metropolitan and Circle lines for forty years. Another exhibit is the "padded cell," an 1890 carriage that operated on the City and South

London Railway; it was designed with no windows on the assumption that passengers would be frightened by the sight of the tunnel walls flashing by.

One section of the museum tells the story of the unusual role of the Underground during World War II; much of the system continued running through the Blitz, also serving as a bomb shelter for as many as 130,000 people per night. The deep tunnels were not always a safe haven though; on October 14, 1940, Balham station received a direct hit and sixty-eight people were killed. And on March 3, 1943, a panic at the entrance to a shelter resulted in the deaths of 111 people, mostly women and children.

⬢ Courtauld Gallery

Somerset House, Strand. Underground: Covent Garden, Holborn, or Temple. (Temple station is closed on Sunday.) Open Monday to Saturday 10 A.M. to 6 P.M., Sunday noon to 6 P.M. Admission: adult, ❷; child (younger than 18), free. Free admission after 5 P.M. ☎ (020) 7848-2526. 🖳 www.kcl.ac.uk/inst/courtauld/top.html.

The priceless Courtauld collections feature Old Master, Impressionist, and post-Impressionist art. This relatively small gallery includes works by the greats, including Botticelli, Boudin, Breugel, Cézanne, Degas, Gainsborough, Gaugin, Goya, Manet, Modigliani, Monet, Pissarro, Renoir, Rubens, Seurat, Tintoretto, Toulouse-Lautrec, Van Dyck, van Gogh, and Veronese. Among the stars of the collection are van Gogh's famous *Self-Portrait with Bandaged Ear* and Manet's *Bar at the Folies-Bergère*.

The collection began with the bequest of the personal collection of textile magnate Samuel Courtauld in 1947 and has been added to by other important collectors.

In 2000 the museum opened a permanent exhibition of items from the fabulous State Hermitage Museum of Saint Petersburg in Russia. Five rooms at Somerset House have been turned into miniature replicas of some of the great state rooms at the Winter Palace, home of the Hermitage. Russian craftsmen have made intricate marquetry floors and the rooms are hung with chandeliers. A portion of the proceeds from tickets to the rooms is shared with the cash-strapped Russian museum.

Theatre Museum

Russell Street, Covent Garden. Underground: Covent Garden. Open Tuesday to Sunday 10 A.M. to 6 P.M. Admission: adult, ❷; child, ❶; family, ❹. ☎ (0207) 943-4700. 🖳 theatremuseum.vam.ac.uk.

The museum's permanent collections trace the development of the British stage and its stars from Shakespeare to the present day. Also on display are reconstructions of early theaters, including the 1614 Globe, and memorabilia of great actors such as Garrick, Kean, and Irving. Artifacts include a varied collection of costumes, props, paintings, posters, photographs, models, and other items from British theater, ballet, opera, circus, and rock and pop music.

Begun in 1963, in 1971 its collections merged with those of the Victoria and

Albert Museum, and it was established as a branch of the V&A. In 1987 the museum moved to the old flower market at Covent Garden.

Free guided tours are offered several times daily, and visitors can also observe or take part in theatrical makeup and costume demonstrations and workshops.

Royal Opera House

Covent Garden. Underground: Covent Garden. ☎ (0207) 304-4000. 📖 www.roy alopera.org.

George Bernard Shaw's *Pygmalion* and the musical *My Fair Lady* that came out of it begin their story with the meeting of a rough flower girl and a pretentious gentleman outside a fancy opera house; the scene was Covent Garden and the Royal Opera House.

Covent Garden has been the site of a grand opera house in London since 1732. Between 1735 and 1752, Handel wrote a dozen operas and oratorios for the theater. In 1773 Goldsmith presented the first public performance of his *She Stoops to Conquer*. The original theater, along with many of the original Handel manuscripts, was destroyed by fire in 1808.

The second theater opened in 1809, modeled on the Temple of Minerva in Athens. It, too, was lost to fire; in 1855 it was destroyed in somewhat suspicious circumstances. All that remained was the dramatic frieze of tragedy and comedy over the portico.

The third theater—which has survived as the core of the present building—was designed in 1858, incorporating the old frieze. In 1892 Mahler's *Ring Cycle* had its first performance in English at the theater. Richard Strauss premiered several of his works here, including *Elektra*, *Salome*, and *Der Rosenkavalier*, in the early 1910s.

In late 1999 the theater reopened after an extensive rebuilding project to provide an improved home for the Royal Opera as well as the Royal Ballet.

In addition to improvements in the theater, the renovation added the **Amphiteatre Restaurant** with spectacular views across Covent Garden Piazza; it is open to ticket holders by reservation during performances and to the general public at other times.

Daily backstage tours are offered, although the auditorium may not be open during rehearsals. There are usually three tours a day, daily except Sunday, at 10:30 A.M., 12:30 P.M., and 2:30 P.M. Admission: adult, student, and senior, ❷. Tickets are very difficult to obtain, especially in the summer. For reservations, call ☎ (0207) 304-4000 or visit the box office.

Seven Dials

Monmouth Street at intersection with Mercer and Earlham streets. Underground: Covent Garden.

In the seventeenth century, seven streets fanned out from a central pillar: Great Earl Street, Little Earl Street, Great White Lion Street, Little White Lion Street, Great Saint Andrew's Street, Little Saint Andrew's Street, and Queen Street. The column, with a clock which had six dials, was a convenient rendezvous spot for the criminal element in the rough neighborhood of the time, and it was removed in 1773. (More than a century later, in 1882, it was re-erected in Surrey.)

The area continued as a low-rent district into the nineteenth century, described by Dickens in *Sketches by Boz*. The intersection was later cleared and rebuilt with just four crossing roads. In 1989 a copy of the original monument was installed near its original location.

Neal Street and Neal's Yard

Covent Garden. Underground: Covent Garden.

This former warehouse district has been converted into a lively stretch of artsy shops that sell beads, fragrances, jewelry, books, and more. A side street is Neal's Yard, a health-food mecca.

Cleopatra's Needle

Embankment. Underground: Embankment, Charing Cross.

Older than London itself, Cleopatra's Needle is one of the spoils of the British Empire. The sixty-foot-tall pink granite obelisk was quarried in Aswan in Egypt and erected in Heliopolis about 1475 B.C. Carvings on the obelisk were dedicated to Pharoah Tethmosis III; references to Cleopatra and Ramses II were added later. It was later somehow moved to Alexandria, where it stood for many centuries before it toppled into the sand.

In 1819 it was presented to the British by the Turkish Viceroy of Egypt, but it took nearly six decades before the empire figured out a way to bring the 186-ton booty back home. In 1877 a giant iron pontoon was constructed and the obelisk was towed out to sea; the trip took several months and included a fierce storm off the coasts of France and Spain, in which six seamen drowned and the Needle was nearly lost.

The obelisk was originally to be installed in front of the Houses of Parliament but the ground there was found to be too soft. Instead, it was erected on the embankment of the Thames between the Hungerford and Waterloo bridges. At the dedication in 1878 a time capsule was installed beneath the obelisk; contents included newspapers of the day, several Bibles, a railroad timetable, and photographs of twelve attractive British women.

A twin of the obelisk is in Central Park in New York behind the Metropolitan Museum of Art.

Charing Cross

The area at today's junction of the Strand, Whitehall, and Cockspur Streets. Underground: Charing Cross.

Charing Cross was the location of the last of twelve stone crosses erected by Edward I to mark the resting places for the funeral procession of his wife Eleanor of Castile, as it moved from Nottinghamshire to Westminster Abbey in 1290. A small village known as Charing stood here, at a turn in the road from Bath.

The cross was taken down and broken up in 1647 as the civil war developed. After the Restoration, eight of those accused of the regicide of Charles I were executed and quartered here.

A replica of the cross was installed in 1863 in front of the Charing Cross train station.

All distances from London are measured from the original site of the cross.

Roman Bath

5 Strand Lane. Underground: Temple or Embankment.

The bath is probably not really Roman—archaeologists have yet to find any other evidence of construction of that era in the neighborhood—but it is definitely a Roman-style plunge bath, about six feet wide and fifteen feet long, believed to be fed from an adjacent holy well.

The bath may actually have been part of Arundel House or other palaces that dated from Tudor times to the seventeenth century. It was first mentioned in the late eighteenth century, called an "old Roman bath" but without any historical or scientific foundation for the claim. It was used in the nineteenth century for cold plunges, promoted as a healthy remedy.

There's no formal admission to the site, but visitors can look through a window on Surrey Street to the pool.

(If you're looking for the real thing, be sure to visit the extensive facilities in Bath, one of the day trips you'll learn about in Chapter 30.)

Chapter 14
Holborn and the Inns of Court

 Sir John Soane's Museum

The Inns of Court

Dr. Johnson's House

Prince Henry's Room

Ye Olde Cheshire Cheese

Fleet Street

Holborn is named after the small tributary of the Fleet River that originally was an important feature of the area. It was mentioned as long ago as the tenth century when King Edgar granted lands to Westminster Abbey. The road through the region was first paved in 1417.

The Holborn Bars, first installed about 1130, mark the boundaries of the ancient City of London in Holborn at Gray's Inn Road and at Staple Inn with stone obelisks that are topped with silver griffins. Guards were posted to keep reprobates and lepers out of the city and to collect tolls.

Sir John Soane's Museum

13 Lincoln's Inn Fields. Open Tuesday to Saturday 10 A.M. to 5 P.M., first Tuesday evening of each month 6 P.M. to 9 P.M. ☎ (020) 7405-2107. 📖 www. soane.org.

Like the attic and basement of a wealthy and very eccentric old uncle, this small museum is chockablock with all sorts of fascinating stuff: ancient statues and friezes, intriguing paintings and sketches, buttons, trinkets, and even an old medical skeleton. This place is one of my favorite secrets of London.

John Soan, son of a bricklayer, raised himself up into society through his skills as an architect and marriage to a rich heiress; he changed the spelling of his name to the more lofty-appearing Soane and was appointed architect to the Bank of England in 1788.

He began to use his growing wealth to amass a huge and varied collection of paintings, sculptures, and objects. He began to display his holdings to scholars about 1806 when he was appointed professor of architecture at the Royal Academy. In 1833 Soane negotiated an Act of Parliament to preserve the house and collection for the benefit of "amateurs and students" in architecture, painting, and sculpture.

Among the museum's treasures are the eight canvasses of political satirist William Hogarth's *Rake's Progress* displayed in an unusual parlor in which the walls unfold like a Chinese puzzle to reveal paintings on the fronts and backs of hidden panels. You'll also find the sarcophagus of Seti I, discovered in 1817 and purchased by Soane for £2,000 after the British Museum balked at the price, and a collection of some nine thousand drawings by artist Robert Adam.

At the rear of Number 14 Lincoln's Inn Fields, fourteenth-century arches salvaged by Soane from the ruins of the Palace of Westminster surround the "Monk's Grave," which is actually the tomb of his wife's pet dog Fanny.

The Inns of Court

Underground: Temple or Holborn.

In the Middle Ages, before lawyers took over the world, the Inns of Court were accommodations for barristers who came to London to appear at sessions of the Royal Courts of Justice. They later became training schools for lawyers.

Today four of the inns remain: Gray's Inn, the Middle and Inner Temples, and Lincoln's Inn. Most are used as offices for some of London's most prestigious barristers.

Gray's Inn on Gray's Inn Road was built in the fourteenth century. At least one of Shakespeare's plays, *A Comedy of Errors*, was given its first performance here in 1594. Charles Dickens was employed as a clerk at Gray's Inn from 1827 to 1828. Badly damaged by bombs during World War II, it was rebuilt with

Lincoln's Inn

HOLBORN

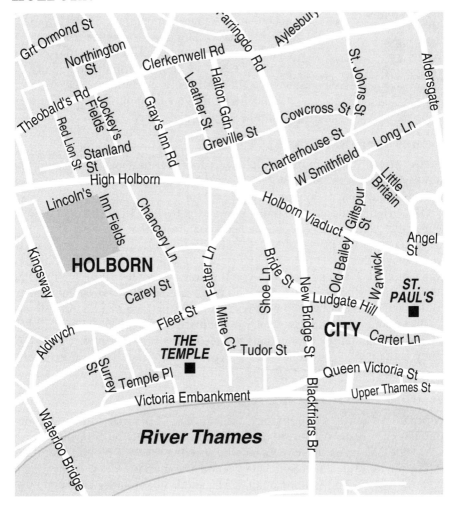

care. The building itself is open for visits by appointment only, although the grounds are open at any time. For information, call ☎ (0207) 458-7800.

The **Inner Temple** on King's Bench Walk and the **Middle Temple Hall** on Middle Temple Lane take their names from the Knights Templar, a chivalrous order devoted to the protection of pilgrims to the Holy Land. The structures were built in the thirteenth century and have survived mostly intact. Shakespeare's *Twelfth Night* was performed at Middle Temple Hall in 1601.

Lincoln's Inn dates back to the late fifteenth century (Christopher Columbus was just heading out to sea) and includes some well-preserved buildings that have hosted luminaries from Shakespeare's contemporary Ben Jonson to insurgent Oliver Cromwell to poet John Donne.

Lincoln's Inn Fields is a protected public space, set aside by developer William Newton in the 1640s to appease the protests of students to an early version of urban renewal. Before then the land was a public execution site.

Dr. Johnson's House

Price Bands
❶ £1–£3
❷ £3–£5
❸ £5–£7
❹ £7–£10
❺ £10–£15
❻ £15 and up

17 Gough Square. Underground: Blackfriars or Temple. Open Monday to Saturday from 11 A.M. to 5 P.M. Admission: adult, ❷; child (10–16), ❶. ☎ (020) 7353-3745. 🖳 www.drjh.dir con.co.uk.

Eighteenth-century scholar Samuel Johnson lived here; in 1755 he published the first substantial English dictionary.

Prince Henry's Room

17 Fleet Street. Underground: Temple or Chancery Lane. Open 11 A.M. to 2 P.M. Monday to Saturday. Admission: free. ☎ (020) 7936-2710. 🖳 www.corpoflon don.gov.uk/history/archiheritage/phroom.htm.

Prince Henry's Room is a former inn, dating back to 1610 and containing a remarkably well-preserved oak-paneled room from that era with the three-feather crest of the Prince of Wales on the ceiling, along with the letters P.H. It is believed this refers to Prince Henry, son of James I, who became Prince of Wales in 1610 but died before becoming king. Over the years, the building also became the home of Mrs. Salmon's Waxworks in 1795 and was later rather crudely covered over before being restored a century ago as a historic place.

The structure now holds a display about diarist Samuel Pepys. Born in 1633, he rose through family connections to a clerkship in the navy office and eventually Parliament. From 1660 to 1669 Pepys kept a diary that included details of the Great Fire of 1666; it was first published in 1825.

Ye Olde Cheshire Cheese

Wine Office Court, 145 Fleet Street. Underground: Blackfriars. Open for lunch and dinner. ☎ (020) 7353-6170. Reservations are strongly recommended.

Ye Olde Cheshire Cheese was a favorite watering hole of Dr. Samuel Johnson, and before him the diarist Samuel Pepys and after him Charles Dickens, Wilkie Collins, Mark Twain, Arthur Conan Doyle, and William Butler Yeats.

The present inn includes elements that date back to 1667 after the Great Fire. Little within has changed in three centuries, although the inn no longer regularly offers the eighty-pound puddings built from ingredients that include steak, kidneys, oysters, and larks; the pies were mentioned in John Galsworthy's *Forsyte Saga*, published in the 1920s.

Fleet Street

Underground: Temple, Blackfriars, Saint Paul's.

Fleet Street was the center of England's newspaper and publishing industry. The country's first printing press was installed here in the late fifteenth century, and the first newspaper, the *Daily Courant*, was produced here in 1702.

London's newspapers moved their presses and later their offices from the crowded downtown area to the Docklands and elsewhere in recent years.

The Fleet River once ran here, but it was long ago channeled underground.

Chapter 15
The City, Smithfield, and Spitalfields

The City

The heart of modern London surrounds the former walled Roman outpost of Londinium, established in A.D. 43 along the River Thames.

The one-mile-square area includes some of the most famous structures of London, such as Saint Paul's Cathedral, the Tower of London, and the Tower Bridge. Once the residential center of London, there are very few homes or apartments left, replaced by the grand churches of Christopher Wren and modern steel-and-glass banks and office buildings. The City was thrice devastated: first by the Great Plague of 1665, followed by the near total destruction of the Great Fire of 1666, and again during bombing raids of World War II.

London's Roman History

When London was established by the Romans in the first century, there apparently already was a thriving trading community along the River Thames.

About the year A.D. 50, the Romans built a bridge across the River Thames linking the two sides of the town of Londinium. The Forum, an open area and marketplace with a basilica, the town hall, and courts, was built about A.D. 70. A series of statues in the area was believed to have included one of the Emperor

THE CITY

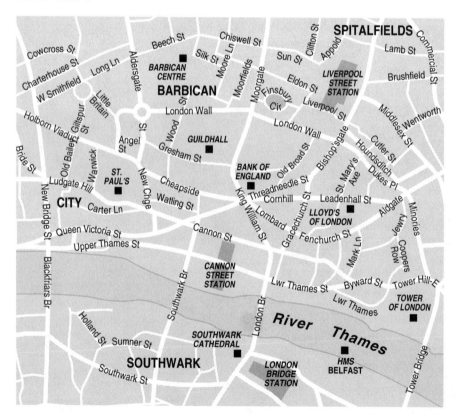

Hadrian; the bronze head of that statue found in the Thames is now on display at the British Museum.

The existence of a Temple of Mithras at today's Queen Victoria Street was first suspected in 1889 when excavations for new construction uncovered sculptures and reliefs. After the area suffered heavy damage from World War II bombing, the foundation of the temple was found; additional archeological digs uncovered new treasures. Many of the pieces and other Roman artifacts and reconstructed rooms are on display in the Museum of London.

The Romans built a three-mile wall around the city, six to nine feet wide and about eighteen feet tall. Stone for the wall was brought up the Thames on barges; at least one of the barges foundered and was located by modern archeologists. Eight main gates led to roads fanning out to other parts of the empire: Aldgate, Aldersgate, Bishopsgate, Cripplegate, Ludgate, Moorgate, Newgate, and Temple Bar, the only survivor.

Much of the original wall still stood through the late eighteenth century when it was taken down as an obstruction to traffic. Segments that were included in later construction exist at Cripplegate and Cooper's Row. A portion of the wall can be seen at the Tower of London, St. Alfege's Churchyard, and a few other places.

London Wall is used as the name of a road running near the former northern boundary of the wall, from Moorgate to the Barbican.

Two centuries after the Romans abandoned their settlement in the year 410, London was occupied by Saxon invaders who brought with them the Christian church. King Ethelbert built the first Saint Paul's Cathedral in 604. When William the Conqueror arrived in 1066, he began the construction of the massive Tower of London just outside the east wall of the City, projecting control within London and power outside. At the same time he began the process that led to some measure of self-government in the city; the rights were expanded in 1215 when King John allowed citizens of London to elect a mayor. During the Middle Ages the electorate was made up of the members of the craft guilds (City Livery Companies) in London. London grew as a trading and commercial center.

The Great Plague of 1665 was spread by Norwegian brown rats, which hitchhiked their way to London aboard trade ships. After several smaller outbreaks in earlier years, plague spread through the crowded houses and businesses, aided by poor sanitation and open sewers. As many as 100,000 residents of London died between Christmas 1664 and early 1666; the conditions were at their worst in the stifling heat of August and September 1665.

Those who could leave moved to the countryside, while the *pesthouses* (rudimentary hospitals) and graveyards were quickly overwhelmed by those who remained. Crews of laborers traveled the streets, calling on families to "Bring out your dead" for burial; they were not often obeyed, for when a home was found to harbor a plague victim, all its residents were locked within for forty days until they had all recovered or died.

The children's nursery rhyme that is innocently recited by children in English-speaking countries is a version of a macabre poem of the time:

Ring around the rosie,
A pocket full of posies.
Ashes, ashes
We all fall down.

The *rosie* refers to the pink rash that was one of the first signs of the plague. Many residents carried a sachet of herbs and spices—a *posie*—to fend off the smell of death and sickness. And "Ashes, ashes" was originally, "Achoo, achoo," after which all fell down.

The plague began to decline with the arrival of cold weather at the end of 1665, and life began to return to normal in the spring of 1666.

On September 2, 1666, another force of nature—aided by human error—led to the near total destruction of the City of London. A fire apparently broke out in Farriner's bakery on Pudding Lane near London Bridge and spread quickly in the force of a strong wind. The blaze continued for four days, destroying two-thirds of the City; thirteen thousand buildings, including eighty-seven churches, Saint Paul's among them, and forty-four livery halls, burned down. Amazingly, only nine lives were lost.

Robert Hubert, a Frenchman, confessed to setting the fire at the bakery and was hanged.

The ill wind that spread the fire did bring some good, for the flames destroyed the population of brown rats and the reconstructed city offered better sanitation and housing conditions; the plague was gone.

A display at the Museum of London tells the story of the disaster through models and paintings.

In the aftermath of the Great Fire, Christopher Wren supervised the rebuilding of churches within the City, including Saint Paul's Cathedral, which was, is, and may forever be one of the dominant features of the London skyline.

Although Wren wanted to redesign the entire layout of the City, it was decided to keep the old street plan to save time; new structures, though, had to be made of brick and stone instead of wood.

Wren rebuilt some fifty-two churches, and added the Monument, a stone pillar that commemorates the Great Fire.

During World War I there were several air raids on London, and several buildings in the City were severely damaged. But it was the Blitz of World War II that was even more devastating than the Great Fire of 1666.

Pool of London

About the year A.D. 50, the Romans built a bridge across the River Thames linking the two sides of the town of Londinium. For nearly all of the succeeding two thousand years there has been a London Bridge near the site, and for much of that time blocking navigation of tall ships farther up the river.

The Port of London developed below the London Bridge in the area that became known as the Pool of London; with the construction of the Tower Bridge in 1894, the section of the river between the Tower Bridge and the London Bridge became known as the Upper Pool. The section immediately downriver is the Lower Pool, as far as the Thames Tunnel from Island Gardens to Greenwich and the Rotherhithe Tunnel.

As commerce grew, the need for deepwater docks for large clipper ships led to the development in the 1820s of Saint Katharine Docks in the Lower Pool on the north side of the river.

By the middle of the twentieth century, the ravages of the Blitz and the arrival of large container ships made the old-fashioned wharves around London obsolete and most of the docks and warehouses fell into disrepair.

Today, though, the Pool of London and the nearby Docklands region are both undergoing a spectacular renaissance for businesses, residences, and entertainment.

In early 1999 Londoners lined up to view the newly discovered coffin of a wealthy Roman woman who was buried 1,600 years ago and lay undisturbed in the heart of the city through most of its history. The last Roman sarcophagus in London was found in 1877.

Workmen located an elaborately decorated lead coffin within a limestone sarcophagus during construction in Spitalfields, an east London district that was outside the city's Roman wall in the fourth century.

The coffin was taken to the Museum of London where archaeologists found a female skeleton, well-preserved ancient leaves, fragments of a gold-thread textile, and a glass vial. According to the museum, the skeleton is that of a young woman, possibly in her early twenties, who came from a very wealthy family in Roman London.

A layer of moist silt at the bottom of the coffin preserved a branch of small leaves, perhaps laurel, bay, or olive.

The coffin was added to the current displays at the museum.

🌟 Tower of London

Tower Hill. Underground: Tower Hill. Open Monday to Saturday 9 A.M. to 6 P.M., Sunday 10 A.M. to 6 P.M. (last admission 5 P.M.). Closes an hour earlier from November to February. Admission: adult, ❺; child, ❹; family, ❻. ☎ (020) 7709-0765. 💻 www.tower-of-london.com.

The fabled Tower of London has been the site of fabulous wealth and awful misery in its nine-hundred-year history. Many of England's early monarchs imprisoned and executed their political opponents here, and more than a few of the sovereigns were themselves held here. It was still used on occasion as a prison through the middle of the twentieth century, housing Hitler's deputy Rudolf Hess for a few days after his capture in 1941.

Among the famed who were imprisoned and condemned here were some of Henry VIII's victims, including Thomas More and Anne Boleyn; Guy Fawkes and some of the other conspirators in the 1605 plot to blow up the Houses of Parliament; and Sir Walter Raleigh in 1617.

Price Bands
❶ £1–£3
❷ £3–£5
❸ £5–£7
❹ £7–£10
❺ £10–£15
❻ £15 and up

Tower of London

The tower is still guarded by flashy-dressing Yeoman Warders, better known as *Beefeaters.*

Begun by William the Conqueror in 1066 as a wooden castle, it was constructed on the ruins of Roman fortifications on the north bank of the Thames. Ten years later, William transformed the fort into a stone palace with walls fifteen feet thick and the area became known as the Tower of London.

Nine hundred years later that original fort is now the White Tower, flanked by four turrets and standing behind two lines of fortifications. Additional buildings, including barracks and a chapel, were added in the fourteenth century. During the centuries, there has been some restoration of the exterior, but the interior is all but unchanged from the Norman era.

The ninety-foot-tall walls around the tower are as much as fifteen feet thick at the bottom to eleven feet at the top. As originally built, there was only one entrance, on the south side through a door fifteen feet above the ground; during times of threat the outside steps were removed.

The cellar level of the keep was used for dungeons, including the infamous Little Ease, a four-foot-square box that bent the prisoner in a space too small to stand or lie down.

Most executions of prisoners took place in public before crowds on Tower Hill outside of the walls. However, seven noted prisoners received a more private send-off at a scaffold erected in front of the Chapel of Saint Peter ad Vincula. Those executed there included Anne Boleyn in 1536 and Catherine Howard in 1542, Henry VIII's second and fifth wives, both convicted of adultery. Also put to death there was Lady Jane Grey, who was queen for just nine days in 1553 after the death of Edward VI before the executioner's blade removed the place to balance her crown. She was executed by her Catholic cousin Mary I, who objected to a Protestant succession.

During the next three centuries, the famed towers within the eighteen-acre walled area were completed. The Tower complex includes:

• **The White Tower.** At ninety feet, the White Tower was the tallest building in London when it was completed in 1097. Around 1240, its walls were white-washed, giving it its name. The interior of the White Tower has been renovated to serve as the home to an expanded exhibition of items from the Royal Armouries, as well as other treasures.

• **The Traitor's Gate.** Prisoners entered the Tower through the Traitor's Gate; not many walked out.

• **Beauchamp Tower.** Some privileged prisoners were held at Beauchamp Tower, sometimes accompanied by servants.

• **The Tower Green.** A few relatively lucky prisoners were accorded the privilege of being executed at Tower Green, away from the madding crowds on Tower Hill.

• **The Bloody Tower.** Built about 1220, the Bloody Tower was named in remembrance of the young sons of Edward IV who were held by their uncle, Richard of Gloucester, after their father died in 1483; neither of the princes— the child king Edward V and his younger brother Richard Plantagenet, the Duke of York—was seen again, and their uncle was crowned king. In 1674 the skeletons of two children were uncovered in the area.

Sir Walter Raleigh spent thirteen years imprisoned at the Bloody Tower but was able to live in relative comfort with his wife and two children. During his stay he even grew tobacco on Tower Green, just outside his apartment. He wrote *The History of the World* (published in 1641) during his imprisonment.

• **The Queen's House.** The black-and-white, timber-framed Queen's House near the Bloody Tower is the home of the Resident Governor of the Tower of London. In years past, it was used to lodge prisoners of high rank, including conspirator Guy Fawkes, in 1605, and Anne Boleyn. Rudolf Hess was the last prisoner held here, in May of 1941. The building is not open to the public.

Fawkes was not executed at the tower. After his confession—reportedly assisted by torture—he was hung, drawn, and quartered in the Old Palace Yard at Westminster.

• **The Martin Tower.** The Martin Tower was the original home of the Crown Jewels for two hundred years, from 1669. The jewels were held on the ground floor while the upper rooms were used as the residence of the Keeper of the Regalia. Until 1815 the public was permitted to reach through the bars and touch and lift the crowns; in that year an apparently deranged visitor pulled apart the State Crown and the custom ended. In 1841, after a fire, the treasures were moved to the Jewel House.

Today, the tower is used for a fascinating exhibition, "Crown and Diamonds: The Making of the Crown Jewels."

Among the items on display here is the coronation crown of George IV. For his coronation in 1821, George IV had constructed a large crown that was the first to use open mounts like a diamond ring; this allowed the diamonds to reflect light much more than previous closed settings. The soon-to-be king, though, did not have on hand the 12,314 diamonds needed to fill it out, and so £65,250 worth of diamonds were rented for the occasion. George IV as king was unable to persuade the government to buy the diamonds; in 1823 they were returned and the crown was never again worn by an English monarch. Today, the denuded crown is shown in a case along with 12,314 real diamonds in a bowl, on loan from the De Beers diamond cartel and worth more than £2 million at current prices.

Also shown is the state crown of George I, the oldest surviving English state crown. It was created in 1715 and used until Queen Victoria's reign. In 1838 the stones were removed and placed in a new crown for Victoria.

• **The Wakefield Tower.** The second largest tower, after the White Tower, the Wakefield Tower was built between 1220 and 1240 and provided royal accommodations for Henry III and his son Edward I. It was later used for storage of records (called for a while the Record Tower) and then the Crown Jewels. The interior has been restored to its appearance at the time of Edward I.

• **The Royal Armories.** The collection in the Royal Armories includes nearly forty thousand items from ancient suits of armor belonging to Henry VIII to crossbows, spears, swords, and early firearms.

• **The Fusiliers' Museum.** This museum features a small collection of artifacts related to the Royal Regiment of Fusiliers, founded in 1685 by James II to protect the royal guns kept within the tower. The Fusiliers were the first regiment to be armed with an improved musket known as a *fusil*. They served in the American War of Independence, the Napoleonic Wars, the Crimean War, the Boer War, the First and Second World Wars, Northern Ireland, and the Gulf War. There is a small additional charge to tour the museum.

• **The Jewel House.** Home of the Crown Jewels, the Jewel House was opened in 1994. The display includes the world's largest uncut diamond. The collection is literally priceless, because many of the pieces are so bound up in the history of the realm.

Most of the Crown Jewels date from 1661, when they were made for the coronation of Charles II; most of the previous collection had been destroyed after the execution of Charles I in 1649, except for a few pieces hidden in Westminster Abbey. The collection was moved to a secret location during the Second World War.

Among the items on display are twelve crowns, including the Imperial State Crown, which is worn by the queen at state events such as the opening of Parliament. This crown was made in 1837 for Queen Victoria's coronation, and includes a sapphire believed to have been part of a ring worn by Edward the Confessor from 1042 to 1066.

The largest precious-cut diamond in the world, the Cullinan (also known as the First Star of Africa), which weighs more than 530 carats, is set in the head of the Sceptre with the Cross. Other notable stones include the Koh-i-noor diamond set in the Crown of Queen Elizabeth the Queen Mother, and the Black Prince's Ruby set in the Imperial State Crown.

In its early days, the tower also accommodated an eclectic royal menagerie that included three leopards given to Henry III in 1235 by the Holy Roman Emperor; on display to the public, their presence is believed to have given rise to the expression "going to see the lions." The king of Norway gave a polar bear in 1252 and the animal was allowed to fish in the Thames at the end of a chain. An elephant arrived in 1255, given by Louis IX.

Among today's residents of the tower is a flock of black ravens; according to legend, if they were ever to depart the tower, the kingdom would fall. There's little chance of that, though: the birds have their wings clipped to prevent flight, and they are looked after by their very own yeoman warder with the title of the Ravenmaster. There's a memorial in the moat in honor of some of the birds who have died at their post.

Every evening at 10 P.M. the ancient Ceremony of the Keys takes place at the tower; the chief yeoman warder, outfitted in full formal regalia, carrying a lantern, and accompanied by four armed soldiers of the garrison, locks the gates of the entrance at the Middle Tower and then the Byward Tower.

The tower is supposed to be the home of a small army of ghosts. The earliest reported sighting was that of Thomas à Becket in the early thirteenth century; he was said to have appeared twice during the building of Beauchamp Tower, reducing the work to rubble on each occasion by striking it with his cross.

The "little princes" (twelve-year-old King Edward V and his nine-year-old brother Richard), who died in suspicious circumstances in 1483, have occasionally been seen as visions dressed in white nightgowns at the Bloody Tower.

Perhaps the grisliest haunting is that of the Countess of Salisbury, the last of the Plantagenets, executed by Henry VIII for political reasons. Refusing to put her head on the block like a common traitor, she ran from the executioner and was pursued by his hacking ax until he cut her down. The haunting is said to include a reenactment of her run across the courtyard as well as the shadow of a great ax, which falls across the place of her death.

And there is the ghost of Queen Anne Boleyn, described by witnesses as a headless figure drifting from Queen's House to the Chapel of Saint Peter ad Vincula and leading a procession of dignitaries down the aisle to the site of her final burial place under the chapel's altar.

The Crown Jewels

The royal collection of expensive baubles and ceremonial weapons, metallic apparel, and shiny headgear that make up the Crown Jewels would be worth millions of dollars if the stones were removed and the settings melted down into gold and silver; they are immeasurably valuable as items of history.

The display includes regalia used at coronations and other crowns donated by sovereigns over the years.

At a coronation ceremony at Westminster Abbey, the sovereign is escorted to the Chair of State by individuals carrying the processional regalia, including two of the royal maces, three swords (Mercy, Spiritual Justice, and Temporal Justice), the Great Sword of State, and Saint Edward's Staff. After the coronation oath, the regent is anointed with the ampulla and spoon. The golden spurs, the jeweled sword, the armills, the orb, the coronation ring, and the sceptres are then presented. Finally, the Archbishop of Canterbury places Saint Edward's Crown on the sovereign's head.

The crowns of England are not allowed to leave the country. Some of the better-known crowns in the Crown Jewels are:

• **Saint Edward's Crown.** The coronation crown of England, Saint Edward's Crown was first used for Charles II's coronation in 1661. Weighing about five pounds, it is made of solid gold and set with 444 semiprecious stones.

• **Imperial State Crown.** Made for Queen Victoria's coronation in 1838, the Imperial State Crown contains the Second Star of Africa (part of the Cullinan Diamond, the largest ever recorded). It weighs about three pounds and is set with over three thousand precious stones. It is intended to be worn by the queen for the return from Westminster Abbey after coronation; it is also worn by the queen for her speech at the annual state opening of Parliament.

• **Crown of Queen Elizabeth the Queen Mother.** Made for Elizabeth when she was crowned queen consort in 1937, the Queen Mother's crown is the only crown mounted in platinum, with more than 2,800 diamonds, including the Koh-i-noor and the Lahore. Many of the stones were taken from a circlet owned by Queen Victoria.

• **Imperial Crown of India.** The Imperial Crown of India was made in 1911 for George V when he was crowned king emperor at Delhi.

• **Small Crown of Queen Victoria.** A lightweight but not quite economy model, weighing only five ounces, the Small Crown was made in 1870. Set in silver and gold, it holds about 1,300 diamonds.

🏆 Tower Bridge

Tower Bridge Road. Underground: Tower Hill, London Bridge. Open daily April to October 10 A.M. to 6:30 P.M., November to March 9:30 A.M. to 6 P.M. (last admission one hour and fifteen minutes before closing). Closed several days around Christmas. Admission: adult, ❸; child, ❷; family, ❻. ☎ (020) 7403-3761. 🖥 www.towerbridge.org.uk.

A masterpiece of Victorian engineering and design completed in 1894, the Tower Bridge is one of the most famous landmarks of London (and often confused by tourists with the departed old London Bridge).

The unusual lifting mechanism was originally powered by huge steam engines that lifted counterbalance weights in the towers that were used to drive gears that lifted each half of the roadway; the design is called a *bascule*, from the French for seesaw. The towers, handsomely faced with stone and capped by decorative pinnacles, support all the winding machinery and the road segments; up high a set of catwalks hold everything upright and allow passage while the bascules are raised.

Visitors can now explore the interior of both towers, including the steam engines, and cross 135 feet above the river on the catwalks (now encased in glass for protection against the elements). One side looks downriver toward Greenwich and the other upriver toward the most famous sites of London. There's an interesting collection of old photos along the walkway and a series of films and demonstrations at various points on the tour.

You'll ride an elevator up the tower on the north side of the river, but there are quite a few sets of stairs as you continue your tour; at the top of the lift you'll find some graffiti from visitors of the 1890s. At the end you descend to the base of the south tower; in the steam engine room you can see the massive accumulators that were raised up the tower to store potential energy for the next lifting. In 1976 the mechanism was converted to electric motors.

Tower Bridge

Today the bridge lifts about five hundred times a year, as many as ten times a day during the summer months. You can call a special Bridge Lift Line at ☎ (020) 7378-7700 to learn details of scheduled bridge lifts for the coming week.

Until near the end of the nineteenth century the only way to cross the River Thames was the London Bridge, which was so overloaded that at times there were queues of several hours. It was decided in 1876 to build a new crossing, but early designs were rejected because they would block tall-masted ships from proceeding farther up the Pool of London.

Another important consideration was that the roads leading to the bridge could not be so steep that they could not be negotiated by horse-drawn vehicles; the solution was a lifting bridge. The Act of Parliament that authorized its building specified a clear width of 200 feet and overhead clearance of 135 feet.

John Wolfe Barry and Sir Horace Jones designed a raising bridge in 1884. After Jones died in 1887, his assistant George Daniel Stevenson took on the project, adding much of the design detail that we see today, including a change from red brick to stone cladding over the steel frame. The bridge was built at a cost of about £1.2 million and ten lives, and was opened on June 30, 1894, by the Prince and Princess of Wales.

🆆🅾🆆 Museum of London

150 London Wall, Barbican. Underground: Saint Paul's, Barbican, Moorgate. Rail: Moorgate. Open Monday to Saturday 10 A.M. to 6 P.M., Sunday noon to 6 P.M. Admission: adult, ❷; child (5–17), ❶; family (two adults and three children), ❹. ☎ (0207) 600-3699. 💻 www.museum-london.org.uk.

A sprawling, modern museum, the Museum of London covers thousands of years in the history of London, from as long ago as 500,000 B.C. through the Roman occupation about A.D. 50 to the Great Fire of 1666 and on to the current day. The nondescript building, which opened in 1976, lies alongside excavations that reveal parts of the old City Wall of London.

One star of the collection is the gilded Lord Mayor's Coach on the lower level. Built in 1757, it leaves its museum space once a year to carry the lord mayor to the inauguration and is also used in royal coronation processions. The coach is decorated with elaborately painted panels. On the front are depictions of Faith, Hope (pointing to the dome of Saint Paul's), and Charity. The rear panel features the Genius of the City greeting Riches and Plenty who pour food and money in her lap; she is receiving ambassadors of Trade and Commerce.

The displays are arranged in chronological order, with twelve galleries starting in Prehistoric London and continuing to the Second World War. The entrance level ends at the Great Fire of 1666, with the story of the city continuing on the lower level. A full visit would take the better part of a day; you might want to make two visits or divide your time with a lunch break at the museum cafe or in a nearby restaurant.

The **Prehistoric Gallery** includes a flint hand ax dated between 350,000 and 120,000 B.C., and an early flat ax of copper from about 2,000 B.C. Other displays tell the story of early rituals and beliefs, the rise of the Celtic tribes, and the development of iron tools and weapons.

In A.D. 43 the Emperor Claudius annexed Britain as a province of the Roman Empire. The settlement of Londinium grew on the north bank of the River Thames, and a smaller village grew on the south side in what is now Southwark. Excavations have revealed public buildings, a forum, a fort, and public baths from about A.D. 100; a city wall was constructed about the year 200. After attacks from other tribes, Rome's commitment to London began to wane, and by A.D. 410 most Roman troops were withdrawn and the city was eventually abandoned.

The **Roman London Gallery** includes a model of the port, a recovered mosaic floor, and other artifacts of the time.

A fascinating collection of objects can be found in the **Medieval London Gallery**, including items from the guildhalls that controlled most of the commerce in the city, the great iron Common Chest that contained the city's seal and records, and a collection of crude lead crosses from the mass burials of the Black Death plague of 1348–49.

In the **Early Stuart London Gallery** visitors will find the Bible and death mask of Oliver Cromwell; the Cheapside Hoard, a display of jewelry and other items from about 1550 to 1640; and a multimedia diorama that tells the story of the Great Fire of 1666.

The **Eighteenth Century London Gallery** includes some of the finery of the aristocratic class as well as the horrors of Newgate Prison.

London thrived in the nineteenth century as its population grew from less than 1 million in 1800 to more than 4.5 million in 1900. The museum's displays include artifacts about the construction of bridges over the River Thames, including the London Bridge of 1831, and the world's first underground railway, running between Paddington and Farringdon Streets in 1863.

The **Imperial Capital Gallery** and the **Early Twentieth Century London Gallery** include displays on the growing importance of the city as a financial and trade center. You'll find re-creations of Victorian and Edwardian bank offices, grocers, barrooms, and other businesses. You'll also find an opulent wooden *lift* (elevator) from Selfridges, an old Woolworth's counter, and a BBC radio studio.

Another gallery shows some of the facts of life of London during the Second World War, including a backyard Anderson bomb shelter, gas masks, ration books, and posters. Recordings of BBC broadcasts and announcements and reminiscences by Londoners of the era are played.

The newest gallery is **London Now**, which includes photographs, paintings, and objects of the 1960s through the current day. You'll see items from the hippies to the punks to the yuppies to the ravers of the 1990s. The "carnival pod" lets visitors try on colorful costumes such as those worn by revelers at the Notting Hill Carnival (held on the weekend of the late-August bank holiday), a recognition of the increasing diversity of today's London.

Visitors who have a special interest in archaeology can also arrange to see the remains of a Roman fort gate still in place in a room under the roadway of London Wall near the museum. The low stone walls and foundations of the northern guardhouse are open to the public on the first Tuesday and the third Friday of each month; contact the museum for details.

〔WOW〕 Saint Paul's Cathedral

Saint Paul's Churchyard. Underground: Saint Paul's. Open Monday to Saturday 8:30 A.M. to 4 P.M. Galleries open 10 A.M. to 4:15 P.M. Visitor shop hours: Monday to Saturday 9 A.M. to 5:30 P.M. and on Sunday 11 A.M. to 5 P.M. Admission to cathedral and crypt: adult, ❷; child, ❶. Admission to galleries: adult, ❷; child, ❶. Combined ticket for cathedral, crypt, and galleries: adult, ❸; child, ❷. Tours available. ☎ (020) 7246-8348. 🖳 www.stpauls.co.uk.

There has been a cathedral at this location since the early seventh century. Archaeologists believe there was an even older Roman temple dedicated to the goddess Diana on the site before then.

The current building, though, is a mere youngster, dating only to the aftermath of the Great Fire of 1666. Christopher Wren rebuilt the cathedral in grand style in 1675, with a 360-foot-high dome that is second only in size to St. Peter's in Rome.

The only monument to survive the Great Fire was that of poet John Donne, who had been dean of Saint Paul's for the last ten years of his life. The remains were taken down with battering rams after an earlier experiment with gunpowder proved unsuccessful.

Wren made several plans for the cathedral; one of the most grand was rejected, but his twenty-foot-long great model for that project is on display in the crypt.

His design used a fabulous dome instead of a steeple. There are actually two domes. From within the cathedral visitors gaze up at a decorative interior dome; a structural brick cone above it supports the lantern at the top of the

Saint Paul's Cathedral

church. Over the cone and the interior dome is the outer dome, which stands sixty feet higher than the ceiling seen from inside.

Resurgam (resurrection) is carved over the pediment on the south door beneath an appropriate sculpture of a phoenix rising from the flames.

The Stone Gallery at the top of the exterior columns is at the base of the outer dome; it offers an unparalleled view over much of London. There are two other galleries above: the Inner Golden Gallery and the Outer Golden Gallery. Above them all is the massive 850-ton lantern, topped with a cross 365 feet above the ground.

On an upper level of the dome is the Whispering Gallery, a place where the acoustics of the rounded room send whispers in an echo around the dome.

The Clock Room in the southwest tower has three bells, including Great Tom, which tolls to note the deaths and funerals of members of the royal family, the lord mayor, and church officials. The bells in the northwest tower are rung for Sunday services and on special occasions.

Wren supervised the construction for thirty-five years until its completion in 1710; he died in 1723 at the age of ninety-one after a return to the completed church. He was one of the first persons to be buried in the crypt, beneath a simple marble slab with a famous epitaph: *Lector, si monumentum requiris, circumspice.* (Reader, if you seek his monument, look around you.)

Even more famous and more flashy are the 1806 crypt of Lord Nelson and the 1852 burial place of Arthur Wellesley, the first Duke of Wellington. Best known for his victory over Napoleon in the Battle of Waterloo, Wellesley also served as British Prime Minister from 1828 to 1830 and again in 1834.

Though its size and fame made it an obvious target during World War II, the cathedral escaped relatively unscathed, in part because of the efforts of volunteers who put out fires and even defused some bombs before they could explode. The former Jesus Chapel behind the high altar, which was damaged by bombs, was restored as the American Chapel in tribute to some twenty-eight thousand Americans based in the United Kingdom who lost their lives in the war.

In this century the cathedral has been used for numerous affairs of state, including the funeral of Sir Winston Churchill in 1965 and the star-crossed wedding of Prince Charles and Diana Spencer in 1981.

Leadenhall Market

Whittington Avenue. Underground: Bank, Monument. Open weekdays 7 A.M. to 5 P.M.

Built on the site of the ancient Roman forum of Londinium, this ornate Victorian food and plant market was built in 1881, replacing one that stood since the Great Fire of 1666, which followed a market dating back to 1377.

Saint Katharine Docks

Saint Katharine's Way. Underground: Tower Hill. 🖳 www.stkaths.co.uk.

Once part of the maritime commercial heart of the city, the docks were constructed from 1825 to 1828 between London Docks and the Tower of London that had before then been a sprawling residential area and the twelfth-century church of Saint Katharine and the site of the former Saint Katharine's Hospital.

The basin off the river was surrounded by yellow brick warehouses used for commodities that included tea, rubber, marble, and live turtles. The design of the docks, though, did not keep up with the growing dimensions of ships and went into a slow decline. By the mid-1960s, the docks were supplanted by larger container-shipping facilities and fell into disuse, finally closing in 1968.

Enter the developers, who have made over the dock area and the old warehouses into offices and a lively collection of shops, restaurants, and bars. The Ivory House, built in 1854 to handle imports of that commodity, was made into some fabulous riverside apartments, with oceangoing yachts down below.

All Hallows by the Tower

Byward Street. Underground: Tower Hill. Open daily 9:30 A.M. to 6 P.M. ☎ (020) 7481-2928. 🖳 www.allhallowsbythetower.org.uk.

There has been a church at this location in the Pool of London area at least as far back as Saxon times, about the year 1000. An arch in the southwest corner of the existing church is believed to be from that period; the remainder of the church has been rebuilt numerous times. Nevertheless, the place claims the title as the oldest church in the City of London.

In 1199 Richard I completed construction of Lady Chapel north of the church, and tradition says that his heart is buried there. The church was damaged in 1650 when a store of gunpowder exploded alongside, destroying more than fifty houses and causing many deaths. The tower was rebuilt in 1659, and famed diarist Samuel Pepys watched the Great Fire of 1666 from the church tower.

William Penn, founder of Pennsylvania, was baptized at the church in 1644. John Quincy Adams, later to be the sixth president of the United States, was married here in 1797.

In 1940 the church was bombed and only the tower, the walls, and some of the furnishings survived. It was rebuilt from 1949 to 1958; the pulpit came from the bombed-out church of Saint Swithin London Stone.

Today visitors can see a portion of Roman pavement, the surviving Saxon crypt, and original parish records. There's also a bookshop and a brass-rubbing center.

Wesley's House and Chapel

47 City Road. Underground: Old Street. Open Monday to Saturday 10 A.M. to 4 P.M., Sunday noon to 2 P.M. Admission: adult, ❷; child, ❶. ☎ (020) 7253-2262.

John Wesley, founder of the Methodist Church, built the chapel in 1778 and preached here until his death in 1791; he is buried behind the chapel. The somewhat austere building has columns made from ships' masts. A museum below explains the history of the church and some of its famous members; former Prime Minister Margaret Thatcher was married in the chapel.

Some of Wesley's personal possessions are on display in his house next door.

The Monument

Monument Street. Underground: Monument. Open Monday to Saturday 9 A.M. to 6 P.M., and Sunday 2 P.M. to 6 P.M. Admission: adult, ❶; child, ❶. ☎ (020) 7626-2717.

The Monument is a 202-foot Doric column designed by Christopher Wren to commemorate the Great Fire of London in 1666, believed to have started just west of the Monument. Built between 1671 and 1677, it is the tallest isolated stone column in the world. Some 311 steps lead to a platform on top that offers superb views of the surrounding city.

An inscription on the north side, in Latin, translates in part as "In the year of Christ 1666, on 2 September, at a distance eastward from this place of 202 feet, which is the height of this column, a fire broke out in the dead of night, which, the wind blowing, devoured even distant buildings and rushed devastating through every quarter with astonishing swiftness and noise." It goes on to grant credit to heaven for finally quenching the fire.

In 1681, in another outbreak of anti-Catholic feeling, another sentence was added: "But Popish frenzy, which wrought such horrors, is not yet quenched." These lines were removed a century and a half later, in 1831.

Other panels record the names of lord mayors of the time and pay homage to Charles II (depicted in one image in Roman toga) and Parliament for their roles in rebuilding the city.

The gallery at the top of the Monument was enclosed with railings in 1842 after a series of suicides from the top of the column.

Bank of England Museum

Bartholomew Lane. Underground: Bank. Open Monday to Friday from 10 A.M.

to 5 P.M. Closed on bank holidays. Admission: free. ☎ (020) 7601-5545. 🖳 www.bankofengland.co.uk/mus_arch.htm.

The museum offers three hundred years of the history of the bank, established in 1694. On display are gold bars, coins and notes, and other instruments of finance, as well as pikes and muskets once used to defend the riches. Documents reveal some of the financial secrets of famed customers, including Horatio Nelson. There's also a high-tech exhibit about today's financial markets.

On display are some of the archaeological finds made during the rebuilding of the bank from 1925 to 1939, including Tudor and Stuart material and four extremely rare Roman gold bars.

Barbican Art Gallery

Barbican Centre. Underground: Barbican. Open Monday and Thursday to Saturday 10 A.M. to 6:45 P.M., Tuesday 10 A.M. to 5:45 P.M., Wednesday 10 A.M. to 8 P.M., Sunday noon to 6:45 P.M. Admission: adult, ❹; child, ❸ (Monday to Friday after 5 P.M. all tickets ❶). ☎ (020) 7382-7105. 🖳 www.barbican.org.uk

The gallery is part of the sprawling arts and conference center at the Barbican, near the old Roman city wall of London. The area was devastated by bombs during World War II and was mostly undeveloped for twenty years afterward. The art gallery is one of the largest in London. There are several cinemas in the complex and a concert hall that is home to the London Symphony Orchestra and the Royal Shakespeare Company.

Mansion House

Walbrook. Underground: Bank, Mansion House.

Mansion House is the official residence of the lord mayor, built in 1753. The City of London is ruled by the Corporation of London and the lord mayor, who, while within the City, outranks everybody but the sovereign. The lord mayor is elected by the City aldermen and the post traditionally rotates to the most senior member who has not already held the post. In addition to the government duties of office, the lord mayor participates in coronation ceremonies as chief butler to the sovereign and also serves as admiral of the Port of London and chancellor of the City University. The lord mayor is also privy to the secret password to the Tower of London.

The chosen lord mayor is the star of two impressive ceremonies on the second Friday of November, beginning with the Silent Change at the Guildhall, when the outgoing holder hands over the symbols of office to the successor. The following day the Lord Mayor's Show includes a procession led by the lord mayor in a spectacular gold state coach, going from the Guildhall past Mansion House to the Law Courts and returning along the Embankment.

Early mayors lived in their own homes and used the Guildhall or one of the livery company halls for entertainment. It was not until 1728, when most of the rebuilding after the Great Fire was completed, that an effort was made to create a residence during the mayor's one-year term.

Construction was begun in 1739, with the grandiose scheme requiring until 1752 for completion. The design features a striking formal Palladian front with six Corinthian columns. The relief sculpture above the pediment shows London trampling on Envy and welcoming Plenty.

Within is the spectacular Egyptian Hall, with interior columns and a clerestory gallery above. In the mid-nineteenth century niches in the walls were filled with marble statues of statesmen and literary figures, including Alexander the Great and Shakespeare.

The building includes a set of eleven holding cells for the magistrate's court, also within; there is a public gallery for the justice courts.

Mansion House was restored in 1931 to its original style, and again after World War II to repair bomb damage.

Most of the ceremonial rooms of the building are not open to the public.

Guildhall

Gresham Street. Underground: Saint Paul's. ☎ (020) 7606-3030. Not open to the public except on special occasions.

Guildhall has been the administrative center of the city of London for more than eight centuries, and there is mention of a meeting hall as early as 1128. Rebuilding of the structure began in 1411 and was finished in 1439. It was one of the largest halls in England in medieval times, after Westminster Hall and the Great Hall of the Archbishop's Palace in Canterbury, and was used for a number of functions, including the trial of one of the conspirators in the Gunpowder Plot.

The building was badly damaged in the Great Fire of 1666, but the exterior walls survived and were used in the reconstruction. In December 1940 the Guildhall caught fire during a bombing raid and the roof collapsed. It was recovered during the war and then rebuilt in 1953.

In the West Gallery are wooden effigies of mythical giants Gog and Magog; from the clerestory windows are hung banners representing the twelve principal city livery companies.

Guildhall Library Clock Museum

Aldermanbury Street. Open Monday to Saturday 9:30 A.M. to 5 P.M. ▣ www.clock makers.org.

Adjoining the Guildhall is the public display of the Clockmakers' Company, featuring more than six hundred watches and clocks from the sixteenth through the nineteenth centuries. The Clockmakers were granted a royal charter in 1631.

Lloyd's of London

1 Lime Street. Underground: Bank, Monument. Organized groups can arrange for a guided tour. ☎ (020) 7327-6210. ▣ www.lloydsoflon don.com.

Founded in the late seventeenth century as an insurance syndicate, Lloyd's takes its name from the coffeehouse where underwriters and ship owners used to meet to agree to contracts.

Unlike most other insurance companies that rely on investments and stockholder equity to pay for losses, Lloyd's members pledge their personal fortunes as collateral for policies. For most of its history, Lloyd's has been a reliable source of income for many well-to-do investors, but in recent years members have suffered some huge losses because of major setbacks.

The present tower, built in 1986, is an unusual stainless steel and glass structure, beautifully floodlit at night; designer Richard Rogers also created the Pompidou Center in Paris.

Hanging above the rostrum of the Underwriting Room is the Lutine Bell. The French frigate *La Lutine* (the goblin) was surrendered to the British at Toulon in 1793; renamed the HMS *Lutine*, it sank in a storm in 1799 with a cargo of gold and silver bullion. There were several salvage missions to the ship, and in addition to bullion worth several hundred thousand pounds, the rudder and bell were retrieved. By tradition, the bell is sounded when there is major news for members—one stroke for bad news and two strokes for the announcement of good news.

Lloyd's of London

Saint Stephen Walbrook

39 Walbrook. Underground: Bank, Cannon Street. Open Monday to Thursday 10 A.M. to 4 P.M., Friday 10 A.M. to 3 P.M. ☎ (020) 7626-8242.

Saint Stephen Walbrook is the lord mayor's parish church, built by Christopher Wren and completed in 1679; it is a lesser-known small gem of the City.

The first church at this site on the bank of the Walbrook was built in the eleventh century and rebuilt in 1439; it was destroyed in the Great Fire of 1666. It was bombed in 1940, but much of its interior furnishings survived.

Wren used the church's coffered dome as a model for the larger Saint Paul's Cathedral.

Modern treasures include a simple white stone altar by sculptor Henry Moore, installed in 1987, and a telephone displayed as a tribute to Rector Chad Varah, who founded the Samaritans, a help line for people in need.

Organ recitals are scheduled on many Fridays.

Saint Mary-le-Bow

Cheapside. Underground: Mansion House. Open Monday and Wednesday from 6:30 A.M. to 6 P.M., Thursday 6:30 A.M. to 7 P.M., and Friday 6:30 A.M. to 4 P.M.

The Bow Church takes its name from the bow arches in the Norman crypt; there has been a church on the site since the eleventh century. By tradition, those born within the sound of the Bow bells can claim to be cockneys. Beginning in 1472, the Bow bells were rung for the 9 P.M. curfew every night.

Rebuilding after the Great Fire, Christopher Wren continued the bow theme on the church's steeple in a design that was modeled after the Basilica of Maxentius in Rome. At its top is a large dragon weathervane.

The church was destroyed again by bombs in 1941 with only the steeple and two outer walls left standing. It was restored in 1962 and new bells were cast.

National Postal Museum

King Edward Building, General Post Office, King Edward Street. Underground: Barbican, Saint Paul's. Open weekdays 9 A.M. to 4:15 P.M. ☎ (020) 7239-5420.

The National Postal Museum features a fabulous collection of British and colonial stamps, including many rarities; also on display is some early post office equipment that includes old letter boxes and franking devices. The original core of the collection concentrated on nineteenth-century British stamps and official documents; the expanded official holdings include the registration or proof sheets of nearly every stamp issued since 1840, as well as the Berne Collection of stamps from member nations of the Universal Postal Union.

The museum is located within the headquarters of the General Post Office, on the site of the former Bull and Mouth Inn, from which mail coaches were dispatched in the eighteenth century. The inn's sign is now part of the collection of the Museum of London.

Legal System

Some of the best drama in London is played out not on the stages but in the courts. Adult visitors are permitted at most trials; cameras, telephones, and food are not permitted, and you can expect bags to be searched.

Central Criminal Court (The Old Bailey)

City of London, EC4. Underground: Saint Paul's. Open weekdays 10:30 A.M. to 1 P.M. and 2 P.M. to 4:30 P.M. A listing of cases is posted outside the building. Entrances are in Newgate Street and in Warwick Passage. ☎ (020) 7248-3277.

The court building opened in 1907 on the site of the notorious Newgate Prison on Old Bailey. By tradition, on certain days of the court calendar judges carry bunches of sweet flowers as a remembrance of the malodorous prison.

A prison stood on Newgate Street as far back as the twelfth century and possibly even earlier. It burned down in the Great Fire of 1666 and was rebuilt six years later. The prison was, quite simply, a horrible place without adequate water and ventilation; regular outbreaks of jail fever—a form of typhoid—spread through the prison. Some wealthier prisoners were able to buy slightly less awful places to stay, while the worst off were cast into wretched places such as the Stone Hold, a dark and dank underground hold. The prison was rebuilt in 1780, and a space was cleared in front for public executions, which were held outside the gates of the prison until 1868.

Across the road from the Old Bailey, the Magpie and Stump pub offered "execution breakfasts" and rented rooms with a view. The current inn was rebuilt in this century on foundations dating back to the eighteenth century.

Newgate was finally demolished in 1902.

There are nineteen courtrooms in the Old Bailey building and an expansion was added in 1972. The courts were damaged severely in World War II and again in 1973 by an IRA bomb.

Royal Courts of Justice

Strand. Underground: Temple. Open weekdays 10 A.M. to 1 P.M. and 2 P.M. to 4 P.M. Check the listing of trials in the main hall. ☎ (020) 7936-6000.

Also known as the Law Courts, the Royal Courts are where the most important civil trials are held.

The massive building was completed in 1882, holding more than three miles of corridors, one thousand rooms, and nineteen courts.

Over the main entrance is a statue of Christ, the western door is guarded by King Solomon, the east door by King Alfred, and the back door by Moses.

London bobbies on duty

Once a year, on the second Saturday in November, the newly elected lord mayor rides in an ornate golden coach from the Guildhall to the courts to be sworn in by the lord chief justice. (The coach is on display at the Museum of London.)

Near the main entrance is a museum of legal dress.

The West Green extension of 1911 added four more courtrooms, and the Queen's Building of 1968 an additional twelve. To relieve pressure at the Old Bailey, some criminal trials are held in the Queen's Building.

Chapter 16
Greenwich

Greenwich is best known as the place from where the world's time and location is measured. Just as important, in parts of Greenwich, time and place have stood still.

Greenwich was the self-declared center of the celebration of the millennium's arrival.

Why did the millennium start in Greenwich? It dates back to an international conference in Washington, D.C., in 1884, where it was decided that the world needed a "Universal Day."

Under the agreement, the day begins at the Prime Meridian of the World (Zero Longitude), also known as the Greenwich Meridian. This imaginary line from North Pole to South Pole runs through the primary transit instrument at the Royal Observatory Greenwich.

Therefore, every day begins in Greenwich.

Getting to Greenwich

One of the benefits of the millennium celebration in London was a set of significant transportation improvements that better link London to Greenwich.

The biggest project was the extension of the Jubilee Underground line south and east from Westminster to link central London with Waterloo, the South Bank, Canary Wharf for Docklands, Greenwich and east London. New stops include North Greenwich. At the same time, the Docklands Light Railway was extended from Island Gardens under the Thames to Cutty Sark in Greenwich and beyond to Elverson Road, Deptford Creek, and Lewisham.

If you're up for an interesting walk under the water, take the Docklands Light Railway from the City of London to Island Gardens and walk through the Greenwich Foot Tunnel.

You can also ride the Connex South Eastern rail from Charing Cross, Waterloo East, Cannon Street, or London Bridge stations to the Greenwich and Maze Hill stations.

And there are numerous river cruises to Greenwich from central London at Westminster Pier; many continue down the river to the Thames Barrier.

🆆🅾🆆 Old Royal Observatory

Greenwich Park. Docklands Light Railway: Cutty Sark. Open daily 10 A.M. to 5 P.M. Admission: adult, ❹; child, free; family (two adults and three children), ❺. Passport ticket, including entry to the Old Royal Observatory, the National Maritime Museum, and the *Cutty Sark*: adult ❻; child, free; junior and senior, ❶. ☎ (020) 8858-4422. 💻 www.rog.nmm.ac.uk.

The Royal Observatory is the most important historical site in the scientific study of time in the world. It is the home of Greenwich mean time, which is based on the mean solar time as it is measured from the Greenwich meridian line (0°0'0" longitude), which passes through the building and out into the courtyard. The meridian passes through the North and South Poles. You will not, of course, be the first person to pose for a picture with your left foot in the Western Hemisphere and the other in the Eastern.

But there is a whole lot more to see in this small museum, including the beautifully restored observatory and the apartments of the astronomer royal. The museum also features one of the world's finest collections of precision clocks and scientific instruments, including many of the original telescopes used by the astronomers royal during the years, as well as a collection of historic astrolabes, globes, sundials, and timepieces large and small.

Price Bands
❶ £1–£3
❷ £3–£5
❸ £5–£7
❹ £7–£10
❺ £10–£15
❻ £15 and up

The museum also displays London's only public *camera obscura*, an old-fashioned entertainment that uses a small opening and lens to project a view of the outside world onto a darkened wall within. Camera obscuras date back at least to the tenth century and were used to observe sunspots and eclipses; later versions were used by artists. There were three camera obscuras maintained at the Royal Observatory in the eighteenth century.

The red ball on top of Flamsteed House still drops at exactly 1 P.M. every day, as it has since 1833, to allow ships on the river below to set their chronometers to Greenwich time before setting out on their voyages.

Founded by King Charles II in 1674, the observatory's original purpose was to be the home of an astronomer royal who would chart the skies "so as to find out the so much desired longitude of places for the perfecting of the art of navigation."

The search for a means to measure longitude became a pressing need as Great Britain and other great maritime nations pushed their explorations around the world. John Flamsteed was named as the first astronomer royal, and the observatory was designed by the noted architect (and former professor of astronomy) Christopher Wren. The observatory was installed atop a small hill in Greenwich Park, which had been mostly a private park of the royals; among its advantages was its relative isolation from the lights of London.

End of the millennium. The Millennium Dome, centerpiece of Britain's countrywide celebration of the change of the calendar, closed with a whimper on December 31, 2000.

The exposition, which cost more than £800 million to put on, attracted just half the expected twelve million visitors in its year of operation.

Several plans for reinventing the structure as an amusement park or a business site fell through in early 2001, and its future is unclear.

Ancient Greek scientists were among the first to find a way to measure distance north and south of the equator (latitude) based on the apparent movement of the sun and the stars. But they found it impossible to calculate east-west coordinates (longitude), because there was no fixed point from which to measure.

The search for a means of measuring longitude became even more pressing after a naval disaster in 1707 when four Royal Navy ships struck underwater ledges off the Isles of Scilly in southwestern England and nearly two thousand sailors died. Parliament offered a prize of £20,000—a substantial sum by today's measure—for a solution.

There were a number of serious and quite a few bizarre suggestions for study, many of which are examined in displays at the museum. One such "solution" involved the use of a mysterious "Powder of Sympathy" and a fleet of seagoing dogs. When the special powder was sprinkled on a weapon that had caused a wound, an injured person was supposed to feel the original pain once more. It was suggested that a group of dogs be stabbed with a knife and then sent out to sea; every day at noon a scientist at Greenwich would stick the same knife into the powder and navigators around the world would be able to know that it was midday in England. This particular experiment was apparently never tested.

The longitude problem was eventually solved by clockmaker John Harrison, who constructed the world's first *chronometer*, an accurate seagoing clock, in

1753. Combined with the publication of the *Nautical Almanac* in 1766, which included the exact angle between the moon and certain fixed stars, navigators were finally able to fix their position at sea. Several of Harrison's clocks are on display at the museum.

The most spectacular room of the astronomer royal's residence—now known as Flamsteed House—is the Great Star Room on its second floor. Popularly known as the Octagon Room because of its eight walls, it was designed by Wren to accommodate the long telescopes of the seventeenth century. Today, it is one of the few surviving interiors by Wren.

Windows afford sky views and impressive views of modern-day London across the river. On one wall is a pair of clocks built for Flamsteed in 1676; the thirteen-foot-long pendulums for each clock move behind the wall above the clock movements. The devices were installed to allow Flamsteed to perform calculations to establish that the earth indeed rotated at an even rate, an important basis for measurement of the stars. (Twentieth-century science has revealed irregularities in our planet's rotation that are taken into account in modern timekeeping and navigation.)

As it turned out, Wren's Octagon Room was not exactly positioned on the prime meridian. Flamsteed performed his studies for the next forty-three years in a small shed at the bottom of the garden, and that shed became the true center of time and space measurement. The meridian line has been adjusted slightly several times, including a repositioning in 1720 by Edmond Halley, and a line drawn in 1884 by George Airy, which has become recognized as the official meridian.

〔WOW〕 Queen's House

On the grounds of the National Maritime Museum, Greenwich. Docklands Light Railway: Cutty Sark. Open daily 10 A.M. to 5 P.M. Admission: adult, ❹; child, ❷; senior, ❸. ☎ (020) 8858-4422.

A sumptuous party house on the former grounds of the Palace of Placentia (Henry VIII's birthplace), the Queen's House was designed in 1616 by famed architect Inigo Jones for Queen Anne of Denmark, wife of James I.

The Queen's House has a mythic feeling to it, a place that seems to ring with the sounds of history; it's one of my favorite places to soak in the feeling of old England. And if the place seems vaguely familiar to Americans, it may be because some believe the White House in Washington was based on Jones's design in Greenwich.

The house is now used for special exhibitions; call for details and hours.

According to court lore, Anne of Denmark accidentally shot James I's favorite hound while hunting in 1614 and the king swore at her in public; afterward he gave her the Manor of Greenwich as an apology. Anne asked Inigo Jones, a painter and designer of scenery and effects for court entertainments and newly appointed surveyor of the king's works, to build a house there. It was his first major assignment as an architect.

Jones, who had been to Italy and elsewhere in Europe, designed a house very different from others in London, introducing classical themes. While the exterior was elegantly simple, the interior was lavishly decorated with wall and ceiling panels, painting and sculptures from the Royal Collection, and fabulous floor and wall treatments.

Work had stopped by the time of Anne's death in 1619; in 1629 the half-finished house was given to Charles I's tempestuous young Queen Henrietta Maria. The interior was mostly unfinished when the civil war broke out in 1642. Anti-Catholic feelings ran high and Henrietta Maria was forced to leave the country for her own safety. It was twenty years before she saw Greenwich again. Her husband was beheaded in 1649 and she lived abroad. Finally, after years of exile, her son was restored to the throne and she returned.

The house was used for grand masquerade balls and banquets. With the accession of William III and Mary in 1689, the house became the official residence of the ranger of Greenwich Park, and the house went into a period of decline. In 1792 the housekeeper and her husband were accused of running a smuggling ring and in general making a "hog stye of the house and a cow-house of the premises."

In 1806 the royal connection with the Queen's House ended when it was purchased from Caroline, Princess of Wales, to provide accommodation for the Naval Asylum, a school for the sons and daughters of seamen. The interior was altered to make staff residences and dormitories for students.

The Queen's House became part of the National Maritime Museum in 1937, housing many priceless maritime artifacts and paintings. One of only three surviving major works by Jones—along with the Banqueting House in Whitehall and the Chapel Royal at Saint James's Palace—the Italianate design is considered England's first classical building. It includes the famed Tulip Staircase, the first example in Britain of a cantilevered round staircase without central support.

Fully restored to the style of the seventeenth century, the house consists of a sequence of interconnected rooms designed for the daily routine of the court: a presence chamber, anteroom, privy chamber, antechamber, and bedchamber. The ultimate honor was to be received in the bedchamber.

The house had no kitchens, guest rooms, or servant rooms; food would have been carried over from the Palace of Placentia or from an outside kitchen.

The Great Hall at the entrance is a perfect forty-foot cube with a black-and-white marble floor, designed by Jones based on Palladio's rules of proportion.

Almost none of the original furnishings of the house still remain, and so the Queen's House has been refitted with replicas or with items from the collection of the National Maritime Museum.

The once magnificent Orazio Gentileschi mural on the ceiling of the Great Hall was removed at the beginning of the eighteenth century and installed at Marlborough House; it was replaced (amid controversy) by a photomural of the original. For some exhibits the mural is hidden behind a screen.

The Royal Apartments are furnished as they may have looked when the house was briefly occupied by the dowager queen Henrietta Maria in the early 1660s. Among the portraits hung on the wall is one of Queen Anne, who is described in contemporary accounts as being large and rather unattractive with a bad complexion and worse eyesight; the painting is much kinder.

🅆🅞🅦 National Maritime Museum

Romney Road, Greenwich. Docklands Light Railway: Cutty Sark. Open daily 10 A.M. to 5 P.M. Admission: adult, ❹; child, free. Ticket also allows admission to Old Royal Observatory. ☎ (020) 8858-4422. 📖 www.nmm.ac.uk.

This extensive museum celebrates Britain's maritime history with models, art, and personal relics. The collection includes 2,500 ship models, four thousand paintings, fifty thousand charts, and 750,000 ship plans.

In 1999 the museum unveiled the Neptune Court, a spectacular new space under a glass roof in a former courtyard. Exhibits in the new space celebrate great ocean liners, merchant shipping, submarines, and more. Among the treasures is Prince Frederick's royal barge, built by King George II's eldest son in 1732. The elaborate carvings are covered in twenty-four-carat gold leaf. The barge was used until 1849 when it went into storage for more than a century.

England's most famous wartime naval officer, Horatio Nelson, is celebrated in a gallery that tells his story with paintings, artifacts, and a multimedia show produced by Jim Henson's Creature Shop. Also on display is the bloodstained uniform Nelson wore at his final engagement at the Battle of Trafalgar.

When the gallery first opened, also exhibited was the musket ball that killed Nelson, removed from his body and preserved in an ornate locket; after three months a representative of Queen Elizabeth II asked for its return, presumably because Her Royal Highness could not bear to live without this particular artifact of history.

The most valuable painting on display is *The Battle of Trafalgar*, a somewhat controversial detailed interpretation by renowned landscape painter Joseph Mallord William Turner. In it, the final word, *duty*, of Nelson's famous battle-flag sequence, "England expects every man to do his duty," still flies. In the water, Nelson's personal motto can be read: *Palmam qui meruit ferat*, which translates from the Latin as "Let he who has earned it bear the palm" or more broadly as "To the victor go the spoils."

Also on display is a nine-foot-high model bust of Nelson based on the figure atop Nelson's Column in London. Relics of Nelson's injuries that resulted in the loss of his right eye and arm include a tourniquet used to staunch the flow of blood during the amputation of his arm, as well as a fragment of the muff made from the beards of oysters to cover the stump of his arm.

A replica of the diamond chelengk worn by Nelson on his admiral's hat is shown. Presented by the sultan of Turkey after his victory at the Nile, the original was stolen from the museum in 1951 and never recovered.

The Nelson exhibit was opened in 1996 and is scheduled to remain on display at least through the end of the "Nelson Decade," which culminates in the two hundredth anniversary of Trafalgar in 2005.

Among artifacts in the museum's collection are personal possessions of famous seamen as well as "lower deck" common sailors. You'll find examples of equipment used on historic voyages including those of Nelson, Cook, and such famous Arctic explorers as Sir John Franklin. There is also a large collection of flags and ships' equipment such as bells, badges, lanterns, and figureheads.

Greenwich Park

Greenwich. Open daily 6 A.M. to dusk.

The former grounds of the royal Greenwich Palace, the park is still owned by the queen but open to the public. The hilltop of the park affords a spectacular view of the Queen's House, the River Thames, and London across the river.

The park was first enclosed in 1433 and was stocked with deer, originally as prizes for royal hunts. Many royal entertainments, including tournaments of various sorts, were held at Greenwich.

According to lore, it was here on May Day of 1536, that Anne Boleyn let drop her handkerchief as a signal to a lover; Anne, her brother, and four others were soon arrested and taken to the Tower of London.

After the Restoration in the seventeenth century, royal landscape gardener André Le Nôtre, the Frenchman who also laid out the gardens at Versailles, was brought to Greenwich to design the park. He installed tree-lined avenues converging on the Queen's House near the Thames.

In 1675 Christopher Wren built the Royal Observatory at the peak of the hill. Near the observatory is a statue of General James Wolfe, the British general who captured Louisbourg and Québec in the French and Indian War in 1758. Wolfe lived on Croom's Hill nearby and is buried in Saint Alfege's Church. There is also a statue of William IV.

At the park's southeast corner is the Ranger's House, built in 1688, used for the Suffolk Collection of seventeenth-century Jacobean and Stuart portraits.

Greenwich Foot Tunnel

The tunnel extends from the Isles of Dogs in the Docklands to Greenwich. Docklands Light Railway: Island Gardens. Rail: Maze Hill, Greenwich. Open twenty-four hours daily; elevators operate 5 A.M. to 9 P.M. daily.

Opened in 1902 to replace a ferry that had run since 1676, the 1,217-foot tunnel was constructed to allow workers in Greenwich to walk to their jobs at the West India docks. In the Docklands area, the entry is a few steps beyond the Island Gardens station of the Docklands Light Railway; in Greenwich the tunnel emerges near the *Cutty Sark* on King William Walk.

The eleven-foot-diameter tunnel runs about fifty feet below the surface of the Thames and is well lit and populated with walkers and joggers and the occasional bicyclist during the course of the day.

There are antique elevators at both ends of the tunnel; the operators can scan television monitors that show goings-on down the length of the tunnel; nevertheless, I wouldn't feel comfortable recommending you make a late-night jaunt through the tunnel.

The *Cutty Sark*

King William Walk, Greenwich. Docklands Light Railway: Cutty Sark. Rail: Charing Cross, Waterlook Cannon Street, or London Bridge to Greenwich. Open daily year-round 10 A.M. to 5 P.M., until 6 P.M. in summer; Sunday from noon. Admission: adult, ❷; child, ❶; family, ❹. ☎ (020) 8858-3445. 🖳 www.cuttysark.org.uk.

The last of the great tea clippers, the *Cutty Sark* was built for a London ship owner in 1869 to be the fastest wind-powered cargo ship in the world. Named after the short shift or dress worn by a character in Robert Burns's *Tam O'Shanter*, the ship was launched in the same year as the opening of the Suez Canal, which marked the arrival of the steamship and the beginning of the end of the clippers. There was a prejudice against carrying tea in all-iron ships at first—it was claimed the metal ruined the taste—but the speed of the steamers won out and the *Cutty Sark* carried its last cargo of tea in 1877.

In 1883 the *Cutty Sark* moved over to the wool trade with Australia, making regular voyages east around the world, outward bound from London around the Cape of Good Hope and returning around Cape Horn.

The clipper was eventually sold to a Portuguese shipping company and re-named *Ferreira*, although it also bore the nickname *A Pequena Camisola*, which roughly translates as "a short shift."

It was still carrying cargo when it was purchased in 1922 and brought back to England and the Thames Nautical Training College. Restored, the clipper sits in permanent dry dock above the River Thames.

Constructed with a wooden hull on an iron frame, the deck and sides of the ship are made of teak. The officers and crew slept in small but tidy cabins on the top deck, with two levels of surprisingly capacious cargo decks below. Today

The Cutty Sark *in Greenwich*
Photo by Corey Sandler

down below you'll find an interesting collection of old figureheads from ships long gone; up top you can walk the decks beneath the 150-foot-tall masts.

From the *Cutty Sark* in dry dock near the River Thames to Greenwich Park is **King William Walk**, formerly known as Tea Pot Row because of an abundance of teahouses.

Nearby is the *Cutty Sark* **Tavern**, built in 1804 and renamed from the Union in 1954 in recognition of its neighbor. There has been an inn on the site for some five hundred years.

Across from the *Cutty Sark* is the tiny, fragile-looking *Gipsy Moth IV*, in which Francis Chichester sailed solo around the world on a 226-day voyage in 1966 and 1967. Chichester was knighted by the queen using the same sword Elizabeth I had used with an earlier English hero of the sea, Sir Francis Drake.

Fan Museum

12 Crooms Hill, Greenwich. Docklands Light Railway: Cutty Sark. Rail: Greenwich. Open Tuesday through Saturday 11 A.M. to 5 P.M. and Sunday from noon to 5 P.M. Admission: adult, ❷; child (7–16), ❶. ☎ (020) 8858-7879. 🖳 www.fanmuseum.org.

The Fan Museum is the only museum in the world devoted to the ancient art and craft of fan making. Housed in a pair of beautifully restored 1721 townhouses in the center of historic Greenwich, the museum is home to a collection of more than three thousand fans from around the world. The backyard offers a peaceful, green garden with a fan-shaped parterre leading off a faithful reproduction of a Georgian–era orangery.

Fans date back at least three thousand years, with the earliest known examples discovered in Egyptian tombs, including the famed Tutankhamun fan with its L-shaped ivory handle and ostrich feathers. A folding form, probably inspired by a Chinese design, appeared in Italy about 1500 and soon thereafter became an essential element of fashion in Europe.

Queen Elizabeth I introduced Britain to fans, and the Worshipful Company of Fanmakers was established in 1709 as a guild for the industry; the organization still exists in London on Fleet Street, with interests expanded to mechanical fans and air-conditioning, as well as fashion items.

The museum's permanent collection occupies the first floor, while changing exhibitions are presented upstairs. You'll see beautifully painted and drawn fans of all manner of design, using materials from paper to tortoise shell, kidskin, and woven ivory. The oldest fan in the museum is a pre-Columbian design made with macaw feathers.

In 1997 the museum presented for the first time ever outside of Russia a collection of fans that had imperial connections, including some that belonged to members of the Russian imperial family. These treasures had been locked away, virtually unseen, in the archives of the Hermitage Museum since the 1917 Russian Revolution.

The heart of the collection was gathered by Hélène Alexander, a leading authority on the subject who had formerly worked at the Victoria and Albert Museum and was founding president of the Fan Circle International. She is regularly at her own small museum; the staff also conducts classes. The small gift shop at the museum includes some unusual items, including a fan that hooks together to form a hat, or is it a hat that can be unhooked to use as a fan? Either way, we walked out with several.

I am partial to an eloquent description of the purpose of a fan, as published in 1760 in London's *Grand Magazine* and quoted in the museum's guidebook: "It exercises the office of the zephyrs, and cools the glowing breast. It saves the blush of modesty by showing all we wish to see, yet hiding all that we desire to conceal."

The museum is a short walk from the *Cutty Sark* or the National Maritime Museum in Greenwich Park.

Trafalgar Tavern

Park Row. ☎ (020) 8858-2437.

A waterside pub built in 1837, the Trafalgar Tavern was originally famous for "whitebait dinners" featuring the tiny fish that once flourished in the Thames. The inn was frequented by government ministers and by literary figures such as Charles Dickens, Wilkie Collins, and William Thackeray. The pub closed in 1915 and served as a home for old merchant seamen and a workingmen's club before it was restored in 1965 and reopened as a restaurant.

Saint Alfege's Church

Greenwich Church Street. Rail: Greenwich. Open 12:30 P.M. to 4:30 P.M. daily. ☎ (020) 8853-2703. 🖳 www.st-alfege.org.

Completed in 1714, the church stands on the site of an even older church that memorialized the martyrdom of Saint Alfege, Archbishop of Canterbury. Alfege was captured by the Danes in 1012; he refused to permit a ransom for his release and was murdered.

Spectacular wooden carvings within were damaged by World War II bombs but have been restored. Other treasures include a reproduction of the baptism certificate of Henry VIII in the original church.

The church holds the tomb of General Wolfe, who died in Québec during the French and Indian War in 1759.

Royal Naval College

Greenwich. Rail: Greenwich. Open Monday to Saturday 10 A.M. to 5 P.M. and on Sunday 12:30 P.M. to 5 P.M. General admission, ❶. ☎ (0800) 389-3341.

A training school for Royal Navy officers and other specialists of the armed forces, the college is within the former Royal Naval Hospital. It was built by Christopher Wren in 1694 on the site of the run-down fifteenth-century royal palace of Henry VIII, Mary I, and Elizabeth I.

Wren's original chapel was destroyed by fire in 1779. The replacement rococo interior includes gilded altar rails and candelabra.

The best-known area is the Painted Hall, decorated in 1708 by artist James Thornhill. The nearby Great Hall features a ceiling painting of William and

Mary handing Liberty and Peace to Europe. In 1805 Admiral Nelson lay in state in the hall.

The chapel and hall of the college are open to the public.

Thames Barrier

Unity Way, Woolwich. Rail: Charlton. Open Monday to Friday 10 A.M. to 5 P.M. (last admission 4 P.M.), Saturday and Sunday 10:30 A.M. to 5:30 P.M. (last admission 4:30 P.M.). Admission: adult, ❷; child, ❶. ☎ (020) 8854-1373. 🖳 www.environ ment-agency.gov.uk/ourservices/flood_a_flood_wi/fld_a_fld_wn_thames_ bar.htm.

The largest movable barrier against floodwaters was put into place across the River Thames just south of Greenwich in 1984.

The Thames has flooded disastrously several times in the history of the city, most recently in 1953. After that tidal surge, a 1,700-foot-wide barrier was put into place with gates that lock into position at a level six feet above the recorded high-water level.

A visitor's center demonstrates the workings of the barrier with the aid of a multimedia show and hands-on exhibits.

Chapter 17
Southwark, Bankside, and the London Bridge Area

 Tate Modern

 Shakespeare's Globe Theatre

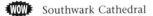 Southwark Cathedral

Dulwich Picture Gallery

London Dungeon

Clink Prison Museum

Winston Churchill's Britain at War Experience

HMS *Belfast*

Old Operating Theatre, Museum, and Herb Garret

Bramah Tea & Coffee Museum

George Inn

Design Museum

Cuming Museum

Bermondsey Antiques Market

Borough Market

Hay's Galleria

The *Golden Hinde*

Brunel Engine House

Saint George the Martyr Church

Bankside Gallery

London Fire Brigade Museum

SOUTHWARK AND LONDON BRIDGE AREA

Blackfriars Br
Upper Thames St
CANNON
STREET
STATION
Southwark Br
Lwr Thames St
Byward St
Tower Hill-E
Coopers Row
Lwr Thames
TOWER
OF LONDON
London Br
River Thames
Hopton St
Holland St
Sumner St
Park St
SOUTHWARK
CATHEDRAL
SOUTHWARK
Southwark St
LONDON
BRIDGE
STATION
St. Thomas St
HMS
BELFAST
Tower Bridge
Grt Suffolk St
Union St
Redcross Way
Borough High St
Newcomen St
Snowsfields
Bermondsey St
BERMONDSEY
Tooley St
Druid St
Blackfriars Rd
Pocock St
Southwark Bridge Rd
Marshalsea
Webber St
Tabard
THE
BOROUGH
Long Ln
Weston St
Leathermkt
Borough Rd
Trinity St
Great Dover St
Manciple St
Tabard St
Harper Rd
Tower Bridge Rd
Abbey St
NEWINGTON
Law St

For many centuries the original London Bridge was the only crossing over the
Thames near the city, and Southwark grew as a staging point at the southern
side of the bridge. At times the wait to cross was several hours long, and the
gates to the city closed at night. And because Southwark was outside of the
jurisdiction of the city, it became an entertainment district with a considerably
looser set of rules. It was a place of pubs and theaters and houses of prostitution and prisons and churches, all of them intertwined in what seems today
like a most unusual fashion.

The Bankside district draws its name from a narrow street that runs along
the Thames at Southwark. It was once most famous for its whorehouses and
bear-baiting pits. The Bishops of Winchester drew up a set of rules to regulate
the brothels in the fifteenth and sixteenth centuries; theaters, including
Shakespeare's Globe on what is now Park Street, the Hope in Bear Gardens, and
the Rose in Rose Lane arrived in the seventeenth century.

🌟 Tate Modern

Bankside, SE1. Underground: Southwark or Blackfriars. Open Sunday to Thursday
10 A.M. to 6 P.M., Friday and Saturday 10 A.M. to 10 P.M. Admission: free, donations
accepted. ☎ (020) 7887-8000. 🖳 www.tate.org.uk/modern/default.htm.

In 2000 the fabulous Tate Gallery near Westminster, which had been burst-
ing at the seams with treasures for decades, crossed the Thames to open the
Tate Modern at Bankside, directly opposite Saint Paul's Cathedral.

The building is an ambitious recycling of the massive Bankside Power Station
that had served the area for decades. The industrial design was updated with a

glass structure running the length of the interior, adding two floors and allowing natural light into the galleries on the top floors.

The east-facing windows of the museum look out across the Thames to the classic lines of Saint Paul's Cathedral. The best views are from galleries on the upper levels.

The impressive entry to seven floors of galleries is through the reworked five-hundred-foot-long turbine room. Still in place on the third floor are some of the station's transformers and switches, pieces of modern art by themselves.

On display is the Tate's contemporary and twentieth-century art. The collection had grown so large that many of its most significant and recognizable pieces had not been shown for years. Must-see treasures include Auguste Rodin's *The Kiss*; Pablo Picasso's *Three Dancers*; and works by Renoir, Pissarro, Degas, Toulouse-Lautrec, and van Gogh. Contemporary artists include David

Saint Paul's Cathedral and the Millennium Bridge, seen from the Tate Modern
Photo by Corey Sandler

Hockney, Roy Lichtenstein, Jackson Pollock, Mark Rothko, and Andy Warhol.

Eventually, the museum will be linked to Saint Paul's Cathedral across the Thames by a pedestrian bridge. The much-anticipated **Millennium Bridge**, the first new crossing of the river since the Tower Bridge in 1894, was meant to be part of the nation's millennium celebrations. When it was opened to the public in June 2000, the slender bridge began to sway and bounce with the load of visitors and less than twenty minutes later police sealed off its entrances.

According to its designer, the bridge was meant to sway gently in the breeze, but most first users were skeptical. The bridge may reopen by the end of 2001 after dampers are installed to absorb the swaying movement.

🅆🅞🅦 Shakespeare's Globe Theatre

New Globe Walk, Bankside. Underground: Mansion House, Blackfriars, or Cannon Street across the river, or London Bridge on the south side of the Thames. ☎ (020) 7902-1500. Box office: ☎ (020) 7344-4444 or ☎ (020) 7401-9919. 🖳 www.shakespeares-globe.org.

Bankside in the fifteenth through the seventeenth centuries was the bawdy side of London, a place of brothels, bear- and bull-baiting pits, and theater of almost every description. The Globe itself is located near Bear Gardens, a name that harkens back to those times.

The Globe was first built in 1599 in North London by actor Richard Burbage in partnership with William Shakespeare and other owners; when the rent was raised, it was taken down and moved to Bankside. The eight-sided exterior walls of the theater enclosed a stage open to the sky; three galleries of seats were arranged around the back and side, with a thatched roof over the top level of seats.

In 1613, during a performance of Shakespeare's *Henry VIII*, a live cannon was discharged and it set fire to the thatched roof and destroyed the theater. The Globe was rebuilt but was taken down by the Puritans in 1644.

When American actor and film director Sam Wanamaker arrived in London for the first time in 1949, he looked for Shakespeare's Globe Theatre in London and was surprised to not find one. He devoted much of his life to raising funds and developing the property close to the original site of the theater in Bankside along the River Thames.

Unfortunately, Wanamaker died in late 1993, four years before completion of the project. The full project, including an education center and rehearsal hall, was completed on September 21, 1999, the four-hundredth anniversary of the first recorded performance at the Globe.

The theater was rebuilt using authentic materials and designs. In addition to the Globe theater building itself, there is an indoor theater based on one designed by Inigo Jones in 1617.

Performances take place in the afternoon and evening using natural lighting, and at times with artificial light replicating daylight.

There are seats for one thousand and standing room for about five hundred, giving the modern Globe about half the capacity of the original.

The cheapest seats are for "groundlings" in the yard; it's standing room only way down front with tickets for most shows priced as low as £5. A fair percentage of seats on the Lower Gallery have limited or restricted views.

Better seats can be found on the Middle and Upper Galleries. But speaking of seats, the gallery seats are authentically hard and backless; you can rent a padded cushion or fashion something of your own to soften the blow for twentieth-century posteriors.

Performance plans call for a mix of Shakespearian classics as well as works by other playwrights of the time, including Thomas Middleton, Francis Beaumont, and John Fletcher. Other events include world music concerts.

The reconstructed theater is the first thatched-roof structure permitted to be built in London since the Great Fire of 1666. (Water sprinklers are hidden within the thatch in a concession to modern safety concerns.)

Shakespeare's Globe Theatre Exhibition

New Globe Walk, Bankside. Underground: London Bridge. Open daily 9 A.M. to 4 P.M. Admission: adult, ❹; child, ❷; family, ❻. ☎ (020) 7902-1500.

The exhibition presents the fascinating story of the reconstruction of

Shakespeare's Globe Theatre, alongside the Tate Modern
Photo by Corey Sandler

Shakespeare's Globe Theatre just east of its original site, using materials, techniques, and craftsmanship of four hundred years ago. A guided tour of the theater is included.

Admission to the exhibit is adult, ❸; child, ❷; and senior, ❸ . A family ticket sells for about the cost of three adult tickets.

Nearby is the site of the **Rose Theatre**, where Shakespeare learned his craft and had his first plays performed. The Rose opened to the public in the spring of 1999 with a sound and light show that tells the story of the area.

The theater, discovered by archaeologists in 1989 at Bankside near the Southwark Bridge, was built in 1587. It was the home of Shakespeare's early works, as well as plays by Marlowe and Ben Jonson.

〖WOW〗 Southwark Cathedral

Montague Close. Underground: London Bridge. Open daily 8 A.M. to 6 P.M. Admission: ❶. ☎ (020) 7407-3708.

The first of four churches on this site was built in the ninth century on the former site of a Roman villa. The first church is credited to Saint Swithun, the bishop of Winchester from 852 to 862; the site is mentioned in the *Domesday Book* of 1086 as a

Price Bands
❶ £1–£3
❷ £3–£5
❸ £5–£7
❹ £7–£10
❺ £10–£15
❻ £15 and up

monestarium. In 1106 Saint Mary Overie (over the river) was built at the site by the Augustinians; they also built a hospital dedicated to Saint Thomas and the Bishop's Palace. The remains of the palace are nearby.

The current structure—the Cathedral Church of Saint Saviour and Saint Mary Overie—includes part of the church begun in 1220 after a fire; it is the earliest Gothic church still standing in London. It was restored again in 1604, and once more in the twentieth century when it was made into a cathedral.

Saint Saviour was the place of worship for many of Shakespeare's contemporaries, with at least five theaters, including the Globe, nearby; today a birthday service in his honor is held annually. His youngest brother, Edmund, is buried at the church.

John Harvard, who founded Harvard College in Cambridge, Massachusetts, was born in Southwark in 1607 and baptized at Saint Saviour; the Harvard Chapel is located off the north transept.

Among the tombs in this church is a wooden effigy of a knight dating from the thirteenth century, one of the oldest such wooden artifacts in Britain.

WOW Dulwich Picture Gallery

College Road. Rail: West Dulwich/North Dulwich. Tuesday to Friday 10 A.M. to 5 P.M., Saturday 11 A.M. to 5 P.M., and Sunday 2 P.M. to 5 P.M. Admission: adult, ❷; child, free. Free admission for all on Friday. ☎ (020) 8693-5254. 🖳 www.dulwichpicturegallery.org.uk.

Britain's oldest public art gallery, the Dulwich Picture Gallery opened in 1817 in Dulwich Village, which has changed little in more than one hundred years. The collection includes works by Rembrandt (*Jacob II de Gheyn*), Van Dyck, Rubens, and Gainsborough. The museum reopened in 2000 after a major renovation.

The original collection was given by Edward Alleyn in 1626, but a major expansion came into the hands of the college in an unusual manner in 1811; much of it was collected by London art dealer Noel Desenfans for Stanislaus II Augustus, king of Poland and lover of Catherine the Great. The king was planning to build a National Gallery in Warsaw, but he was forced to abdicate in 1795, leaving the collection unpaid for.

The Polish king's collection eventually was given to Dulwich College after the Polish government rejected a proposal to establish a national gallery.

The museum building was designed by Sir John Soane and completed in 1813. It was bombed in 1944 and restored.

The museum conducts a series of Saturday morning and evening concerts, lectures, and special events.

Dulwich Village includes Alleyn's College of God's Gift, more commonly known as Dulwich College, and a number of Georgian and older homes. Charles Dickens was a frequent visitor to the Dulwich Club, and it was here he set the retirement place of Mr. Pickwick, who was himself described as a regular browser at the Picture Gallery. Dulwich has been in existence for more than one thousand years, and is one of the most complete of London's surviving villages.

The train from London Bridge to North Dulwich or Victoria to West Dulwich takes about twelve minutes and leaves visitors with about a seven-minute walk to the gallery.

🌟 London Dungeon

28–34 Tooley Street. Underground: London Bridge. Open 10 A.M. to 6:30 P.M. daily. Last admission 5:30 P.M. Admission: adult, ❹; child, ❸. ☎ (020) 7403-7221. 📖 www.thedungeons.com.

Gruesome and gory, the London Dungeon is just the cup of tea for many (but not all) youngsters and adults. The attraction features reenactments of some of the bloodiest events of British history, from a supposed Druid sacrifice at Stonehenge to the Great Plague and most every execution and famous murder in between.

The London Dungeon presents a multimedia celebration of the evil that some men and women do, from religious persecution to torture and execution chambers, as well as the horrors of disease.

You'll meet Vlad Dracule (Dracula to his friends), Henry VIII, and Jack the Ripper, and come face to face with a plague-bearing rat. You'll learn the finer points of legal practices, including the stocks and pillory, judicial drowning, instruments of torture such as the Scold's Bridle for a tart-tongued wife, the rack to assist recalcitrant accused persons in their confession, the guillotine, and the Gibbet Cage where the dead bodies of criminals were hung for display.

Most of the dungeon is set in the appropriately creepy vaults that were built beneath the original London Bridge in Southwark.

You'll meet with a fearsome hanging judge who will happily sentence you (and everyone else in your group) to get to ride on the River of Death, a short water ride to extinction. From there you're dropped off in Whitechapel, where Jack the Ripper was on the loose from August 31 to November 9, 1888.

A signboard midway through the tour lists some of the 222 crimes punishable by death under the medieval "Black Act." They include murder, robbery, sheep stealing, defacing Westminster Bridge, being found upon the King's Highway with a sooty face, and setting fire to your mother's house.

This is a very busy place, with lines building to waits of an hour or more at midday in the summer; among the busiest days of the year for the London Dungeon (and most other tourist venues) is the August bank holiday. Your best bet is to come early or late.

No unaccompanied children are permitted entrance, and the management recommends young visitors be at least nine years old. Plan on at least an hour for the walk-through and rides, although some visitors may choose to linger and absorb all of the simulated blood and gore while others will set their eyes on the exit and proceed there as quickly as possible.

Clink Prison Museum

1 Clink Street. Underground/Rail: London Bridge. Call for hours. Admission: adult, ❷; child, ❶; family, ❹. ☎ (020) 7403-6515 or ☎ (020) 7378-1448. 📖 www.clink.co.uk.

The Clink Prison Museum is an exhibition on the site of the famed prison constructed in the fifteenth century in the bishop of Winchester's park and owned by the various bishops of Winchester until it was destroyed in 1780. When they said someone was "thrown into the Clink," this was the place, and you'll see some evidence of how unpleasant it was.

The area around the Winchester House was under the jurisdiction of the Bishop of Winchester and was called "the Liberty of the Clink." The area included London's red-light district, where the brothels were supervised and licensed by the bishops' men.

Some of the prisoners in the Clink were prostitutes ("Winchester Geese") who somehow ran afoul of the local laws.

The museum includes a display of torture devices and an "adults only" area that has an exhibit about prostitution. There's also a working armory for repairing antique weapons and armor.

Winchester House was the home of the bishops of Winchester for more than five hundred years, beginning in 1109. At the outbreak of civil war, it was converted to a prison for Royalists; with Restoration it reverted to the bishops but it was in such bad shape that it was allowed to fade away and new buildings incorporated parts of the palace or replaced it. In 1814 a fire in a warehouse on Clink Street uncovered a thirteen-foot-wide rose window from the palace.

Winston Churchill's Britain at War Experience

64–66 Tooley Street, London Bridge. Underground: London Bridge. Open daily 10 A.M. to 4:30 P.M. Admission: adult, ❸; child, ❶. ☎ (020) 7403-3171. 🖳 www.britainatwar.co.uk.

A multimedia presentation about wartime Britain and the Blitz, this exhibit features an air-raid shelter plus artifacts that include gas masks, ration books, and more. A cinema presents war news.

You'll enter a London Underground lift and emerge in war-torn London. Take shelter from air raids in a crowded Tube station or a cramped backyard Anderson Shelter. You can listen to speeches by wartime leaders, browse through a 1940s shopping arcade, and visit the Rainbow Corner club. And then you can walk through a smoky bombed street, listening to the cries of the trapped and the rescuers as bombers drone overhead and the sirens sound.

HMS *Belfast*

Morgan's Lane, Tooley Street. Underground: London Bridge. Open 10 A.M. to 6 P.M. daily in summer and until 5 P.M. the remainder of the year. Admission: adult, ❷; child, ❶; family, ❺. ☎ (020) 7940-6300. 🖳 www.iwm.org.uk/belfast/index.htm.

A Royal Navy veteran, the HMS *Belfast* is now preserved as a floating museum on the River Thames near Tower Bridge and offers spectacular views from its decks. The 11,500-ton, 613-foot-long cruiser was built in 1938, served in the difficult Arctic convoy route to North Russia, and later took part in the Normandy landings and in the destruction of the German battle cruiser *Scharnhorst* at

The HMS Belfast *moored in the River Thames*

the Battle of North Cape. It supported United Nations forces in Korea and remained in service with the Royal Navy until 1965.

Under full steam, the ship's boilers developed eighty thousand horsepower, yielding a top speed of thirty-two knots.

A tour of the vessel includes the quarterdeck to the top of the bridge and all the way down through seven decks to the massive boiler and engine rooms below the waterline. Visitors can also explore the heavily armored shell rooms and magazines and get a sense of the life of the crew in the mess decks, officers' cabins, galley, and sick bay. On the open decks are twelve six-inch guns, plus antiaircraft guns. The exhibit is operated as part of the Imperial War Museum.

Old Operating Theatre, Museum, and Herb Garret

Southwark Cathedral Chapter House, 9A Saint Thomas's Street. Underground: London Bridge. Call for hours. Admission: adult, ❶; child, ❶; family, ❸. ☎ (020) 7955-4791. 🖳 www.thegarret.org.uk.

The early–nineteenth-century operating rooms of the former Saint Thomas's Hospital—one for male and the other for female patients—were closed in 1862 when the hospital moved because of the construction of a railway line. Bricked up and abandoned, they were found in 1957 and painstakingly restored.

There are five tiers of viewing platforms over the table and primitive washing basins for the surgeons. Another exhibit explores herbal medicine.

Bramah Tea & Coffee Museum

The Clove Building, 1 Maguire Street. Underground: London Bridge or Tower Hill. Open daily 10 A.M. to 6 P.M. Admission: adult, ❷; child, ❶; family tickets (two adults and up to four children), ❹. ☎ (020) 7378-0222. 💻 www.bramah museum.co.uk.

Edward Bramah knows exactly when the beginning of the end of civilized life began, at least as he defines it: 1956, when the first commercials appeared on British television. "Commercial breaks are too short a period of time to make a proper cup of tea," Bramah says. Before 1956, Britons knew how to brew and enjoy tea; after then came the arrival of tea bags and instant coffee, two products that are, in his judgment, beneath contempt—and not for sale at the museum.

Today, Bramah told me over a pot of the right stuff, over ninety percent of tea is sold in tea bags, a process that uses fast-infusing tea that emphasizes color over flavor. He admits to a passion for tea and coffee, which he called two of the world's most important commodities.

It was the working class that made Britain a nation of tea drinkers, Bramah said, citing examples such as the miners of the north carrying pots of warm tea into their cold workplaces. Ironically, the tea bag was invented in London in 1896 but first caught on in America.

Bramah's career began as a planter on a tea estate in Malawi in 1950. He later became a tea taster for a major British importer, worked with a coffee brokerage company in Kenya and Tanzania, and consulted with China on the redevelopment of the Chinese export tea market. In 1966 he set up his own company and patented a filter-machine design.

The Bramah museum tells the 350-year history of coffee and tea, expressed in ceramics, silver, and prints. Butlers Wharf was chosen for the site of the museum because the area was involved in the coffee and tea trade for more than three hundred years; at its peak the area handled six thousand chests of tea per day. The museum is due to move across the street to a larger location on Butlers Wharf.

The museum is on the south bank of the Thames across from the Tower of London. From the Tower, walk across the Tower Bridge and turn left to Butlers Wharf. It can also be reached by walking along Tooley Street from the London Bridge Tube station. The museum is next door to the Design Museum.

The collection includes one thousand coffeemakers and teapots, including what may be the world's largest, with a twenty-five-gallon capacity and a six-foot circumference. Historical portraits, prints, and maps show the importance played by these commodities in European social and commercial history. A large section of the museum displays unusual teapots, including ones that memorialize figures from history and popular culture from the Mad Hatter to Margaret Thatcher, Ronald Reagan, and Princess Diana, or that bear unusual shapes such as a boot, a "letterbox," and a commode.

Historical perspectives include a look at the Boston Tea Party of 1773 from the other side of the Atlantic Ocean, and the stories of the great China clippers of the mid-1800s.

The Tea and Coffee Room welcomes visitors, and a retail shop sells ground coffee and a range of Bramah teas and related products. You can order a pot of tea and some lovely cakes. The museum has a policy against the use or sale of tea bags, preferring more traditional infusion methods for a superior pot of tea; a similar policy bars instant coffee.

And, for the record, here are Bramah's official instructions on making tea: Milk, about one tablespoon and fully pasteurized, is put into the bottom of the cup first, and tea is added so as to fill the cup to about half an inch from the top. Milk goes into the cup first because, chemically, it is better to add a solvent to an emulsion. In this case milk is the emulsion and tea the solvent. Hot milk or half-filling the cup is not correct.

Buyers in the tea trade put their milk in first to taste tea at its best for buying purposes. The blenders who wish to see how badly the tea could be made deliberately put the milk into the cup after the tea.

George Inn

George Inn Yard, 77 Borough High Street. Underground: Borough, London Bridge. Open during normal bar-license hours.

The last remaining galleried coach inn in London, the George dates back to 1676; before then an inn stood on the spot at least as far back as 1542 and possibly several hundred years before, when the pilgrims of the *Canterbury Tales* spent a night at a nearby inn named the Tabard.

Along the road to London Bridge were a number of inns catering to travelers, among them the George. The original George was damaged by fire in 1670 and then destroyed in 1676 in the Great Fire of Southwark, which took down about six hundred buildings, including the Tabard.

The George was immediately rebuilt, and reached its peak of popularity in the eighteenth century as a station for wagons and then stagecoaches to Kent, Surrey, and Sussex. Stables for coach horses and warehouses for the transfer of freight were built alongside.

The beginning of the end came in the mid-1800s with the opening of the London Bridge railway station. The Tabard was demolished in 1878, and in 1889 the north and east sides of the George were demolished. In 1937 the somewhat decrepit inn was given to the National Trust and was restored.

According to local lore, William Shakespeare was among early patrons of the inn; a tradition of performances of Shakespeare's plays in the open forecourt continues to the present day. Others who bent an elbow at the George included Samuel Johnson, Charles Dickens (who mentioned it in *Little Dorrit*), and Winston Churchill.

Design Museum

Butlers Wharf, SE1, Shad Thames. Underground: Tower Hill. Open Monday to Friday 11:30 A.M. to 6 P.M., Saturday and Sunday 10:30 A.M. to 6 P.M. Admission: adult, ❸; child, ❷; family, ❻. ☎ (020) 7378-6055 or ☎ (020) 7403-6933. 🖳 www.designmuseum.org.

Housed in a converted warehouse in the Docklands, the Design Museum is the first museum to explore the influence of design on everyday life. The Collection Gallery concentrates on the history of design, while the Review Gallery displays international examples of contemporary design. The area's name, Shad Thames, is a corruption of "Saint John's at Thames."

Cuming Museum

155–157 Walworth Road. Underground: Elephant & Castle. Open Tuesday to Saturday 10 A.M. to 5 P.M. Admission: free. ☎ (020) 7701-1342.

The Cuming presents an unusual collection based on the vast private materials of the Cuming family, plus the archaeology of the Southwark area from Roman times to the Industrial Revolution. Another section explores the historical roots of London superstitions, including amulets to ward off lightning, disease, and the all-purpose evil eye.

Richard Cuming began collecting items in 1782 at the age of five when he was given three fossils and an old Indian coin. The collection that he and his son Henry Syer amassed included natural history; ceramics; textiles; archaeology from London, ancient Egypt, Pompeii, and Rome; coins; and a startling array of bizarre and unusual things, such as Bonnie Prince Charlie's hair and the leg of an ancient Egyptian mummy.

Bermondsey Antiques Market

New Caledonia Market, Long Lane and Bermondsey Street. Underground: London Bridge. Open Friday 5 A.M. to about 2 P.M.

Bermondsey is a bustling early-morning antiques market, mostly for the trade but open to the public. When the market itself is closed, there are a number of retail antique shops nearby on Tower Bridge Road.

Bermondsey is the section of Southwark near the London Bridge. The name may have come from "Beormund's eye," a reference to an eye (island) that may have been owned by a Saxon lord of that name. The area once was home to many important wharves and industries, including the now-departed Bermondsey Leather Market and several breweries.

Borough Market

Stoney Street. Underground: London Bridge. Open Monday to Saturday midnight to 10 A.M.

The Borough is a wholesale fruit and vegetable market beneath the railroad tracks; as far back as 1276 the market took place on London Bridge itself, then moved to Borough High Street, and in 1756 to its present location.

Hay's Galleria

Tooley Street. Underground: London Bridge. ☎ (020) 7403-3583. 💻 www.hays galleria.co.uk.

Begun in 1651, Hay's Wharf was the oldest dock in the Port of London, stretching from the London Bridge to the Tower of London on the south side of the river in the Bermondsey area. The wharves were mostly built in 1857. Its warehouses included some of the first cold-storage rooms, dealing in butter and cheese from New Zealand in 1867.

Today the central dock has been covered with a spectacular glass roof on iron columns over market stalls, trendy restaurants, and tony shops.

The *Golden Hinde*

Saint Mary Overie Dock, Cathedral Street. Open daily 10 A.M. to 5 P.M. Admission: adult, ❶; child, ❶. Call in advance to avoid large tour groups. ☎ (020) 7403-0123. 💻 www.goldenhinde.co.uk.

A full-sized replica of Sir Francis Drake's sixteenth-century flagship, the *Golden Hinde* was constructed in Devon and formally launched in San Francisco in 1973 to commemorate Drake's claim of California for Queen Elizabeth I.

Drake set sail in December 1577 on a three-year voyage that circled the globe; his ship was originally known as the *Pelican* but was later renamed the *Golden Hinde* in honor of Sir Christopher Hatton, a sponsor of the voyage, whose family crest included a female deer (*hinde*). The ship repeated Drake's circumnavigation of the globe before going on display in Southwark in 1996.

The relatively small ship carried twenty officers and gentlemen and as many as sixty crew members. It offers an interesting contrast to the huge battleship HMS *Belfast* berthed nearby.

Brunel Engine House

Tunnel Road, Rotherhithe. Underground: London Bridge. Open daily from Easter to the end of September 1 P.M. to 4 P.M.; open first Sunday of every month the remainder of the year. Admission: general, ❶. ☎ (020) 7231-3840. 💻 www.museumweb.freeserve.co.uk/brunel.htm.

The engine rooms were built to hold the steam engines used to drain the world's first underwater tunnel, constructed from Wapping to Rotherhithe from 1805 to 1843. There were numerous delays and problems with the project, and many lives were lost. Engineer Marc Brunel developed a tunneling shield in 1818 that allowed work on a small portion of the face of the tunnel while brickwork was installed at the back of the moving shield.

Intended as a vehicle tunnel, the 1,200-foot-long passage was converted for the East London Railway in the 1860s and is still used for that purpose; trains on the East London Line to Rotherhithe Station pass through the tunnel.

Saint George the Martyr Church

Borough High Street. Open Wednesday noon to 1:30 P.M., Thursday from noon to 2 P.M., and Sunday 10 A.M. to 4 P.M. ☎ (020) 7407-2796.

Dating back at least to 1122, the church was rebuilt in the fourteenth century and again in 1736. A twentieth-century stained glass window includes Charles Dickens's character Little Dorrit, who in the novel of the same name hid in the church when she was locked out of Marshalsea Gaol and was later baptized and married there.

Bankside Gallery

48 Hopton Street. Underground/Rail: Blackfriars. Open Tuesday 10 A.M. to 8 P.M., Wednesday to Friday 10 A.M. to 5 P.M., and Saturday and Sunday 1 P.M. to

5 P.M. Admission: adult, ❶; senior, ❶; child (younger than 16) free. ☎ (020) 7928-7521.

Bankside Gallery is the home of the Royal Watercolour Society and the Royal Society of Painter/Printmakers; the gallery puts on regular exhibitions of work by members.

London Fire Brigade Museum

Winchester House, 94A Southwark Bridge Road. Open by appointment only on weekdays. Admission: ❷. ☎ (020) 7587-2894. 💻 www.london-fire.gov.uk/about/museum1.htm.

The Fire Brigade Museum offers a display of old firefighting equipment and displays about the history of firefighting from 1666, including some equipment from as long ago as 1720. It is located in the former home of Captain Eyre Massey Shaw, superintendent of the London Fire Establishment from 1861 to 1865 and the Metropolitan Fire Brigade from 1866 to 1891. The home was built on part of the former estate of the bishop of Winchester.

The Great Fire of London in 1666 led to the creation of organized fire-fighting companies in London; the first groups were employed by insurance companies. Home and business owners would purchase insurance and attach a plaque on their building with the name of their insurance company. If a fire company arrived at a blaze but found the wrong plaque, they often turned away.

Chapter 18
South Bank

 Imperial War Museum

 London Aquarium

 London Eye

Museum of the Moving Image *(Reopens 2003)*

BFI London Imax Cinema

Florence Nightingale Museum

Museum of Garden History

Lambeth Palace

Royal Festival Hall

The South Bank area, on the Surrey side of the Thames between Waterloo Bridge and Hungerford, had declined into a near wasteland before redevelopment began with the Festival of Britain in 1951. Projects for that event included the Royal Festival Hall.

Fast-forward to the new millennium: a spectacular, if shaky, new pedestrian bridge linking to the foot of Saint Paul's, and the amazing London Eye are the new landmarks, drawing millions of visitors to the area.

Cultural highlights of the area include a world-class aquarium, a celebration of movies and video, and the Imperial War Museum, housed in a remaining portion of Saint Mary of Bethlehem, the insane asylum that gave us the word *bedlam*.

The 450-foot-high London Eye, among the world's tallest Ferris wheels, began turning in early 2000, offering astounding views of the London area.

Sometime by the end of 2001 the Millennium Bridge is expected to reopen, linking the steps of Saint Paul's Cathedral to the new Tate Gallery of Modern Art at Bankside; the elegant structure is the first pedestrians-only bridge to be built across the Thames and the first completely new crossing since the Tower Bridge of 1894. The bridge suffered an embarrassing delay after early users complained

THE SOUTH BANK

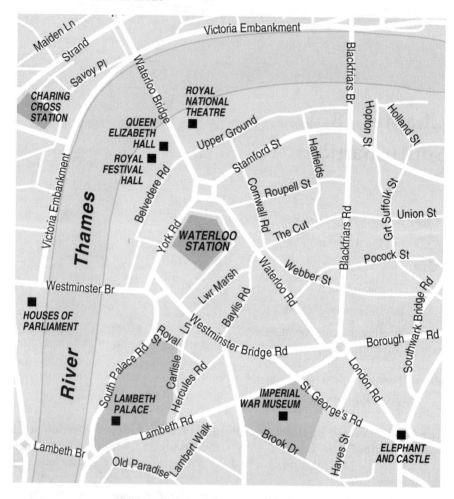

that it swayed enough to induce seasickness. Engineers added bracing to temper the sway that they say had been built into the design.

Footbridges were also added on either side of the existing Hungerford Rail Bridge from Charing Cross to the South Bank, improving the link between the West End and South Bank.

And the latest extension of the Jubilee underground line south and east from Westminster connects central London with Waterloo, the South Bank, Greenwich, and east London.

🔲 Imperial War Museum

Lambeth Road. Underground: Elephant and Castle or Lambeth North. Open daily 10 A.M. to 6 P.M. Admission: adult, ❷; child (5–16), ❶; family (two adults and four children), ❺. ☎ (020) 7416-5000. For recorded information: ☎ (020) 7820-1683. 🖳 www.iwm.org.uk.

The Imperial War Museum owns a staggering collection of the tools of war as well as a demonstration of the tragedies they cause and some of the triumphs of the survivors.

In 2000 the museum opened a major expansion dedicated to a remembrance of the Holocaust. At the entrance is a quote from eighteenth-century philosopher Edmund Burke that sets the tone: "For evil to triumph, it is only necessary for good men to do nothing."

The story of the Nazi persecution of the Jews and others is told through artifacts, photos, movies, and most of all through the recorded voices of dozens of survivors and eyewitnesses. One of the most astounding displays is a huge model of the sprawling Auschwitz death camp.

The main entrance to the museum is home to more than fifty of the museum's most significant exhibits, including a Sopwith Camel airplane from World War I and an American P52 Mustang and a Spitfire from the Battle of Britain in World War II.

Dominating the central space are a German V1 flying bomb and V2 rocket; more than 6,500 V weapons fell on London and the southeast during the war, killing nearly thirty thousand people.

More modern weapons include a Polaris missile, the first submarine-based ballistic missile.

Other items in the main gallery are British, German, Soviet, and American tanks, as well as the fishing boat *Tamzine*, the smallest craft to take part in the Dunkirk evacuation. Nearby is a German one-man Biber submarine.

The lower ground-floor galleries house permanent exhibitions on the First World War, the interwar years, the Second World War, and postwar conflicts. You'll find an amazing collection of some of the major—and touchingly minor—pieces of the past. You'll find air-raid warden uniforms, ration tickets, patriotic posters, and other items that speak volumes about wartime life.

An interesting photo in the museum's collection shows Londoners sleeping on the platform of the Elephant and Castle Underground station during World War II; many of today's visitors to the museum will arrive at that station.

Modern displays include relics of British participation in Korea, Vietnam, the Falklands, and the Gulf War of 1991.

The Blitz Experience takes about twenty persons at a time into a dark, tight shelter where sound, light, and smoke give you a sense of what it must have been like to seek refuge in a bomb shelter. After a few minutes—it seems like more—you'll move on to a re-created section of bombed-out London.

When you emerge from the shelter area you'll see a portion of a real Anderson Shelter, one of more than two million small corrugated-steel structures that were distributed to Britons for installation in their backyards.

Another multimedia gallery gives you a sense of the murderous conditions of a World War I front-line trench on the Somme in the autumn of 1916.

The Imperial War Museum
Courtesy of Imperial War Museum

One recent exhibition disclosed for the first time some of the deepest secrets of Britain's MI5 (domestic) and MI6 (foreign activity) spy agencies. I was fascinated to read about the claimed success of British forces in capturing or killing every known German spy who landed in the United Kingdom during World War II. On display is an Enigma encryption machine, invisible ink used by German World War I spies, and a hidden radio used by MI6 agents during the Cold War.

On the top floor are art treasures, including works by Henry Moore and Paul Nash. The museum's collection of twentieth-century British art is second only to that of the Tate Modern. Archives include millions of feet of film and five million photographs.

The museum also sports a fine bookstore that offers historical volumes and reproductions of posters and paintings.

The museum is housed in the surviving central part of Saint Mary of Bethlehem, the nineteenth-century insane asylum that gave rise to the term *bedlam*. Bedlam dated back to 1247 with the founding of the Priory of Saint Mary of Bethlehem on the site; in the fourteenth century the priory began to specialize in the care of the insane. Until 1770 there were no restrictions on visitors, and the "lunatics," who were often chained or manacled to the walls, were a major public attraction in the area. (Two cells from the old hospital still exist in the basement, although they are off-limits to visitors to the museum.)

The building that now houses the museum was completed in 1815, with the dome added in 1846. The inscription above the main entrance reads *Hen VIII rege fundatum civium largitas perfecit*, which speaks volumes about the role of the taxpayers. It means "Founded by Henry VIII, completed by the bounty of the people."

The hospital moved out in 1930, and six years later, the interior of the main building was converted for use as a museum to house a collection memorializing the First World War. The internal courtyard was covered over with a glass ceiling to form the main display area.

Not long after the museum opened, World War II broke out, and much of the collection was evacuated to storage places outside London; ironically, or perhaps not, the building sustained some damage from bombs during the war.

Also part of the Imperial War Museum are:

- **HMS *Belfast*.** Located at Morgan's Lane, Tooley Street, London. For information, call ☎ (020) 7407-6434 or consult 🖳 www.iwm.org.uk/belfast/in dex.htm.
- **Cabinet War Rooms.** Clive Steps, King Charles Street, London. For information, call ☎ (020) 7930-6961 or consult 🖳 www.iwm.org.uk/cabinet/index.htm.
- **Duxford Airfield.** Duxford. For information, call ☎ (0122) 383-5000 or consult 🖳 www.iwm.org.uk/duxford/index.htm.

🔳 London Aquarium

County Hall, Riverside Building, Westminster Bridge Road. Underground: Waterloo. Open daily 10 A.M. to 6 P.M. Admission: adult, ❹; child, ❸; family, ❺. ☎ (020) 7967-8000. 🖳 www.londonaquarium.co.uk.

London's only aquarium, and one of Europe's largest exhibits of fish and marine life, is located in historic County Hall on the banks of the Thames.

Visitors descend three levels on the dry side of a pair of huge tanks of Atlantic and Pacific marine species. There's a large hands-on Beach Pier tank that features a collection of remarkably friendly stingrays—many of them seem to greatly enjoy the human touch. Another touch tank includes crabs, mussels, and starfish.

The Atlantic tank includes improbably elongated conger eels swimming with turbot, smooth hounds, dogfish, bream, mackerel, and pollock; the Pacific tank is primarily devoted to sharks from around the world.

A recent addition is a twilight tank of caves and coral reefs home to spectacularly luminescent flashlight fish.

The aquarium features more than thirty thousand specimens representing some 350 species of fish, invertebrates, and plant life from around the world. A small tank includes a family of sea horses; a blue-lit environment is the home of an eerie collection of moon jellyfish.

The aquarium is on the South Bank, directly across from the Houses of Parliament and Big Ben. It's an easy walk across Westminster Bridge from the Westminster Tube station, or a quick hop from Trafalgar Square and other central London areas by bus.

All the exhibits are indoors, making the aquarium an appealing destination on a rainy day. The former County Hall also includes a Namco Station video arcade, several restaurants, a 200-room Marriott Hotel, and a 318-room Travel Inn Hotel. And the London Eye now turns alongside.

County Hall was an important modern addition to London when it was officially opened by King George V and Queen Mary as the seat of government of the London County Council.

The site was chosen to improve the South Bank, and its architecture was intended to stand up to the classical design of the Palace of Westminster across the river. Work began on the construction of County Hall in 1909. During excavation, the remains of a Roman "round-bottomed oceangoing" boat were uncovered; the vessel is now on display at the Museum of London.

Much of the South Bank was damaged in bombing raids during World War II, including a direct hit on September 20, 1940, when a bomb made a hole thirty feet deep and wide in the Members' Terrace.

🟥WOW🟥 London Eye

Jubilee Gardens. Underground: Embankment, Waterloo, Charing Cross. Open daily 10 A.M. to 9:30 P.M. Admission: adult, ❹; child, ❸; senior, ❸. ☎ (0870) 500-0600. 🖳 www.british-airways.com/londoneye.

Three times taller than Tower Bridge, four times larger than the dome of Saint Paul's Cathedral, and much more moving: the British Airways London Eye opened in February 2000 as the world's largest Ferris wheel, part of the millennium celebration in London.

Located along the River Thames near Westminster Bridge and Jubilee Gardens, the 450-foot-high wheel offers views of as much as thirty miles.

The thirty-two glass-walled capsules, which hold thirty-five guests each, rotate at a leisurely 1.6 miles per hour, taking fifteen minutes to go from the ground to the top and another fifteen minutes to reach the bottom. Visitors clamber into the slowly moving capsules as the previous guests exit.

You can check out the view from the wheel's website.

At the top of the London Eye above the Houses of Parliament
Photo by Corey Sandler

Museum of the Moving Image *(Reopens in 2003)*

South Bank Centre. *Closed for redevelopment until 2003.* ☎ (020) 7401-2636. ▣ www.bfi.org.uk.

Sometime in 2003 a reconstructed museum dedicated to the history of film and television is due to reopen.

The museum, part of the British Film Institute, originally opened in 1988. The collection includes a *thaumatrope* of the 1820s, a hand-painted disc with an image on each side. When the disc was spun in the hand, the two images merged into one. Another device, the *phenakistoscope*, was a slotted disc with pictures on one side that was rotated and viewed in a mirror to give the illusion of motion. But the breakthrough device was the popular Victorian toy the *zoetrope*, a spinning drum with slots in its side that afforded a view of a sequence of images within.

Cinema treasures include a towering stand-in model of Frankenstein's monster from the 1935 classic *The Bride of Frankenstein*, Marilyn Monroe's shimmy dress from *Some Like It Hot*, and Charlie Chaplin's hat and cane.

During the construction of a new center, many of its treasures are on display at other museums, including the Science Museum in London; some items will also be shown in the foyer of the nearby BFI Imax Cinema.

BFI London Imax Cinema

South Bank Centre. Ticket prices vary by event. ☎ (020) 7902-1234. ▣ www.bfi.org.uk.

Still open is the spectacular BFI London Imax Cinema, which offers the largest screen in Europe and a daily selection of Imax 2D and 3D films, presented from noon to 10 P.M. daily. The powerful sound system includes speakers behind the screen and a sub-bass speaker that is larger than a house.

The five-hundred-seat auditorium, with a seven-story screen, was an especially complex construction project because several railroad and communication tunnels heading beneath the Thames lie just below the surface. The entire building is mounted on resilient bearings, like springs. The circular building features a glass wall wrapped around an interior image wall that has changing pictures.

The Imax Cinema is on the South Bank, next to Waterloo station, a few minutes' walk from the Waterloo Underground station and the Waterloo bus station. There's also pedestrian access from Waterloo or Hungerford Bridge.

Florence Nightingale Museum

2 Lambeth Palace Road. Underground: Waterloo, Westminster. Open Tuesday to Sunday 10 A.M. to 5 P.M. (last admission 4 P.M.) Admission: adult, ❶; children, ❶; family, ❸. ☎ (020) 7620-0374. ▣ www.florence-nightingale.co.uk.

The story of Florence Nightingale, "The Lady of the Lamp," is told through personal possessions, documents, photographs, and multimedia presentations.

Nightingale, born in 1820, studied as a nurse in Europe and Egypt. In 1853 she became Lady Superintendent of the Institution for Sick Governesses on Harley Street in London; in a short period of time she completely revamped the hospital and its level of care. (Its successor hospital in Lisson Grove was named the Florence Nightingale Hospital in 1910, the year of her death.)

In 1854, after the outbreak of the Crimean War between Russia and a coalition of Great Britain, France, the Kingdom of Sardinia, and the Ottoman Empire (now Turkey), Nightingale set off to nurse the wounded at a British hospital in Turkey; she moved on to direct all nursing at the war front.

When the war ended, she returned to London to open the Nightingale School and Home for Nurses at Saint Thomas's Hospital, credited with establishing nursing as a highly trained profession. In 1907 she became the first woman to receive the British Order of Merit.

The current museum is located near Saint Thomas's Hospital on the South Bank.

Museum of Garden History

Lambeth Palace Road. Underground: Lambeth North. Open Monday to Friday 10:30 A.M. to 4 P.M. and Sunday 10:30 A.M. to 5 P.M. Admission: free, but donations accepted. ☎ (020) 7261-1891. 🖳 www.cix.co.uk/~museumgh.

The Museum of Garden History is an exhibition about contemporary and historic gardens of England located in and around the tower of Saint Mary-at-Lambeth, a church that dates its original construction back to 1378; the tower is essentially unchanged in more than six hundred years. The churchyard holds the tomb of John Tradescant, famed as Charles I's gardener, and his son of the same name.

The Tradescants sent expeditions throughout Europe and the Americas in the 1600s in search of interesting plants. They are credited with introducing the pineapple as a decorative motif. Much of the elder's treasure trove, the so-called Tradescant Ark, formed the heart of the original collection of the Ashmolean Museum in Oxford.

Lambeth Palace

Lambeth Palace Road. Underground: Lambeth North, Westminster. Not open to the public.

Lambeth Palace was the London home of the archbishop of Canterbury for more than eight hundred years. The oldest portions of the palace are parts of the chapel and undercroft. The Tudor gatehouse dates from 1485. Other parts of the palace were rebuilt in the early nineteenth century and again after bomb damage was sustained in World War II.

Royal Festival Hall

Belvedere Road, South Bank Centre. Underground: Waterloo. Open 10 A.M. to 10 P.M. daily. ☎ (020) 7960-4242. 🖳 www.royalfestivalhall.org.uk.

One of London's largest concert halls, with as many as 3,100 seats for recitals and a bit fewer for ballet and film presentations, Royal Festival Hall was the only permanent facility built for the 1951 Festival of Britain. Backstage tours are available by appointment when performances are not scheduled.

Chapter 19
Bloomsbury and Fitzrovia

 British Museum

 British Library

Dickens' House Museum

Thomas Coram Foundation Museum

Pollock's Toy Museum

Percival David Foundation of Chinese Art

Fitzroy Tavern

Wellcome Trust Centre for the History of Medicine

Bloomsbury has been, at times, an intellectual center of the universe. Today it's a bit quieter, although the academic world still pays homage at the British Museum, the University of London, and the Dickens' House Museum.

Its name comes from Blemondisberi, the bury or manor of William Blemond, who acquired it in the early thirteenth century. The fourth Earl of Southampton moved to a manor house in the district in the seventeenth century. Later in the century, he laid out a square south of Southampton House for a residential neighborhood, now known as Bloomsbury Square.

Montague House, now part of the British Museum, was built in 1678.

Bloomsbury lies within the square formed by Tottenham Court Road on the west, Euston Road on the north, Gray's Inn Road on the east, and New Oxford Street and Theobald's Road to the south.

The famous Bloomsbury Group of artists and writers of the early twentieth century included novelist E. M. Forster, economist John Maynard Keynes, painters Vanessa Bell and Duncan Grant, and writers Virginia Woolf and Leonard Woolf. A plaque in remembrance of the group hangs in Bloomsbury Square. The name Fitzrovia was coined by writers such as Dylan Thomas and George Orwell, who were among the regular drinkers at the Fitzroy Tavern west of Tottenham Court Road.

BLOOMSBURY

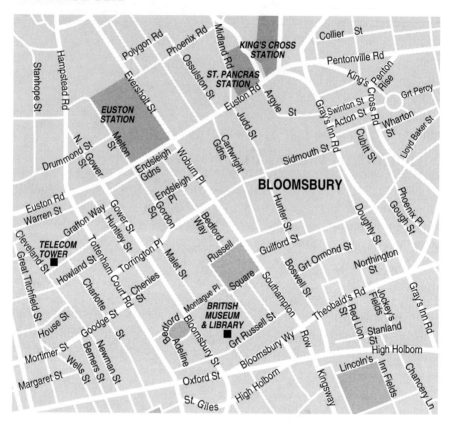

⭐ British Museum

Great Russell Street. Underground: Tottenham Court Road. Open Monday to
Saturday 10 A.M. to 5 P.M., Sunday 2:30 P.M. to 6 P.M. Admission: free, but
donations solicited. ☎ (020) 7636-1555. 💻 www.thebritishmuseum.ac.uk.

One of the world's greatest collections of civilization took a magnificent step
backward in December 2000 with the formal opening of the **Great Court**, a
£100 million millennium project that brought back to life the long-overlooked
inner courtyard.

For more than 140 years the courtyard had been blocked from public view,
occupied by the British Library's immense **Round Reading Room**, added in
1857, and hundreds of book stacks used for storage. Famous readers included
Karl Marx, V. I. Lenin, Mahatma Gandhi, Thomas Hardy, Rudyard Kipling, and
George Bernard Shaw. In 1997 the library began moving its collections to a
new building at Saint Pancras, opening up about 40 percent of the available
museum space.

At the center of the court is the fabulous Round Reading Room, restored to
its blue, cream, and gold decorative scheme. The book stacks are gone, opening
up the courtyard and allowing access to galleries of the museum under a lat-

ticework glass roof. A double staircase curves left and right around the exterior walls of the Reading Room, delivering visitors to the mezzanine floors on the north side of the Great Court. The museum's gift shop, bookstore, and a terrace restaurant occupy the upper level with views of the revitalized courtyard.

From the restaurant level a bridge link takes visitors into the upper galleries of the museum. Beneath the courtyard, in newly excavated space, is the **Centre for Education**, a dedicated schools area and galleries for the African collections.

Founded in 1753, the British Museum is one of the world's greatest institutions, with more than ninety galleries stretching some two and a half miles and extending back to the dawn of human culture in every corner of the globe. Objects on display include the Rosetta Stone, the Elgin Marbles, the Lindow Man, a fabulous collection of Egyptian mummies, the seventh-century Lindisfarne Gospels, two of the four known copies of the Magna Carta, the logbook of Nelson's ship *Victory*, and Shakespeare's first folio of 1623.

The museum was originally based on several significant private collections, including those of physician and naturalist Hans Sloane; the Harleian Collection of statesman Robert Harley, first Earl of Oxford; and the Cottonian Library, gathered by antiquarian Robert Cotton. In 1757 George II added the Royal Library of some 10,500 books collected over time by monarchs from Henry VIII to Charles II.

The Egyptian antiquities department delivers the most oohs and aahs per square foot. You'll find room after room of artifacts, sculptures, sarcophagi, and mummies.

One of my favorite moments at the museum came when I literally bumped into an interesting black stone on a pedestal. It had inscriptions in three ancient languages. I stopped and examined it with interest for a moment before it dawned on me that I was looking at the Rosetta Stone, one of the greatest finds in the history of archaeology.

Later I found myself wandering a blank hallway to a staircase; at the bottom of the stairs I found a portion of the museum's leftover collection of antiquities. There,

The restored Round Reading Room at the British Museum
Photo by Corey Sandler

The British Museum
Copyright © British Museum

stacked on shelves and on the floor, are dozens of spectacular statues, portions of monuments (including huge disembodied feet and hands), and intricate carved stones. Most any other museum in the world could build a major collection around these objects. At the British Museum they're in the basement. (To find them go past the Rosetta Stone to the West Stairs and down to Basement Rooms 77–89.)

Many of the items were brought back to Great Britain as the spoils of war or under the flag of imperialism.

The **Roxie Walker Galleries of Egyptian Funerary Archaeology** presents the museum's unmatched collection of mummies, coffins, funerary statuettes, amulets, and Books of the Dead in a new installation.

Much of the collection of more than eighty thousand objects comes from tombs or contexts associated with the cult of the dead, and it is these pieces—in particular the mummies—that remain among the most eagerly sought exhibits by visitors to the museum. A wide range of material includes animal mummies, canopic jars, funerary statues and shabtis, gilded coffins, amulets, papyri, and tomb fittings, some of which have never before been seen by the public.

In collaboration with several London hospitals, the museum was able to have mummies imaged using a CAT scanner, yielding unprecedented images of "slices" through the body; many of the images are also on display. The installation is located in Rooms 62 and 63.

The Rosetta Stone, a piece of a black basalt stela, was posted as a form of public notice in March of the year 196 B.C. It was discovered in 1799 by French soldiers of Napoleon's army who were digging the foundations of a fort. Its significance was very quickly apparent. It bore a message written in three ancient languages: Greek, a cursive script known as *demotic*, and Egyptian hieroglyphics. Greek scholars were thus able to learn to read hieroglyphics. The stone is a copy of a decree from a council of priests at Memphis on the first anniversary of the coronation of Ptolemy V Epiphanes as king of Egypt.

Another treasure is the Lindow Man, nicknamed by some British wags as "Pete Marsh" after the place of his discovery within a block of peat near Cheshire in August 1984. Scientists have determined that the well-preserved body was that of a man who lived two thousand years ago. Among the findings was that he was in his mid-twenties, about 132 pounds, and 5'6" tall; he had short, darkish hair, a short beard, and a mustache, which an electron microscope showed had been trimmed with shears. They were also able to analyze the remains of his last meal, a mixture of cereals including wheat, rye, oats, and barley that had been ground into a whole-meal flour and baked into a form of griddlecake.

Perhaps most interesting, advanced medical scanners determined that he had been murdered, struck twice on the head, apparently with an axe. A thong around his neck appeared to be a garrote and his neck was broken. One theory is that he was the victim of a ritual killing in the Celtic era. And now the poor guy has been freeze-dried and stored in an environmentally controlled case.

The **Department of Coins and Medals** display of ancient Oriental, Greek, and Roman items was first based on King George IV's collection.

Treasures of the **Department of Greek and Roman Antiquities** include the frieze of the temple of Apollo at Bassae in Greece, and sculptures from the mausoleum at Halicarnassus in Turkey. There's also the infamous Elgin Marbles, a collection of sculptures taken from Athens in 1806 by the earl of Elgin and including a frieze from the Parthenon. The museum has held on to the treasures despite many requests over the years from Greece for their return.)

The museum's collection is too rich to be appreciated on a one-day trip. Instead, I'd suggest make several visits of a few hours, concentrating on particular areas.

One way to avoid crowds, which can be quite large in summer and holiday periods, is to visit on the first Tuesday evening of each month, when the museum is open to the public with an admission charge.

The Rosetta Stone, 196 B.C.
Copyright © British Museum

🟥 British Library

Saint Pancras. Underground: King's Cross/Saint Pancras. ☎ (020) 7412-7332. 📖
www.bl.uk or 📖 www.britishlibrary.net.

The venerated British Library has moved out of its 140-year-old temporary
quarters at the British Museum to a sparkling new building less than a mile
away. The building includes a trio of exhibition galleries displaying some of the
world's greatest literary treasures; a 255-seat auditorium for lectures, films, and
concerts; a bookshop; and a restaurant. And then, of course, there is the
collection: some twelve million volumes, many of them one of a kind.

Some of the library's treasures that will be featured in the galleries include
the Lindisfarne Gospels (A.D. 700); a fourth-century Greek Bible; the Guten-
berg Bible (1455); the unique text of *Beowulf* (A.D. 100); manuscripts by Jane
Austen and Charles Dickens; Leonardo da Vinci's sketchbooks; and one of the
original copies of the Magna Carta (A.D. 1215). Other exhibitions will explore
the history of books and sound recording. Admission is free to the permanent
exhibitions; some special exhibits require the purchase of tickets.

The library's large piazza has an amphitheater for outdoor performances
and is adorned with statues of literary greats, including Shakespeare and Isaac
Newton, as well as busts of some of the founders of the library.

Guided tours of the library, for a charge of about £3, are available. Call the
library for a schedule.

All British Library services are now offered from three sites: Saint Pancras
and Colindale (the Newspaper Library) in London and Boston Spa in West
Yorkshire.

Dickens' House Museum

48 Doughty Street. Underground: Russell Square. Open Monday to Saturday 10
A.M. to 5 P.M. Admission: adult, ❷; child, ❶. ☎ (020) 7405-2127. 📖 www.dickens
museum.com.

The Dickens' House is the only remaining house occupied by Charles Dickens
and his family in London; they lived there from 1837 to 1839, and during that
time he wrote *Oliver Twist, Nicholas Nickleby, Barnaby Rudge*, and portions of
The Pickwick Papers.

The family moved on to a larger home near Regent's Park in 1839; that
house was demolished in 1960.

The museum was begun by the Dickens Fellowship in 1925. Some rooms have
been re-created as they looked during Dickens's time, while elsewhere in the
house is what is said to be the most comprehensive Dickens library in the world,
including first editions of many of his works, as well as portraits, illustrations,
and artifacts of the author and his time.

Thomas Coram Foundation Museum

40 Brunswick Square. Underground: Russell Square. Admission by appointment
only. Admission: ❶. ☎ (020) 7841-3600.

The foundation is the legacy of sea captain Thomas Coram, who was granted a royal charter in 1739 to establish a hospital for the care of deserted young

children. Coram enlisted the aid of some promi-
nent artists, including painter William Hogarth,
as governors and patrons; many gave paintings
in the hope their displays would draw wealthy
benefactors.

The hospital was taken down in 1926, but the
foundation continues with its original purpose in
a building that includes a recreation of the original Governor's Court Room. Among the treasures
of the museum are Hogarth's portrait of Coram, Handel's personal copy of *The
Messiah*, and works by Gainsborough and Reynolds.

Coram Fields, a playground and public garden, is on the former site of the
Foundling Hospital.

Price Bands
❶ £1–£3
❷ £3–£5
❸ £5–£7
❹ £7–£10
❺ £10–£15
❻ £15 and up

Pollock's Toy Museum

1 Scala Street. Underground: Goodge Street. Open 10 A.M. to 5 P.M. Monday to
Saturday. Admission: ❶. ☎ (020) 7636-3452. 🖳 www.tao2000.net/pollocks.

The Toy Museum is a collection of antique toy theaters and other games and
entertainments based on the original collection of Benjamin Pollock. It also
includes puppets, model trains and cars, doll houses, and board games. Novelist Robert Louis Stevenson was a faithful customer of the original store.

The museum is located within a pair of small houses built in 1760. And
there is, of course, a gift shop.

Percival David Foundation of Chinese Art

53 Gordon Square. Underground: Russell Square or Euston Square. Open weekdays 10:30 A.M. to 5 P.M. Admission: free. ☎ (020) 7387-3909. 🖳 www.soas.ac.
uk/PDF/home.html.

This impressive collection of Chinese ceramics from the Sung, Yuan, Ming,
and Qing dynasties of the tenth through the eighteenth centuries was donated
by Percival David to the University of London in 1950. The museum is part of
the School of Oriental and African Studies.

Fitzroy Tavern

16 Charlotte Street. Underground: Goodge Street. Open Monday to Saturday
11 A.M. to 11 P.M. and Sunday noon to 10:30 P.M. ☎ (020) 7580-3714.

The Fitzroy is the pub adopted by a group of illustrious writers including
Dylan Thomas and George Orwell, who declared the area a semi-independent
nation they dubbed *Fitzrovia*. The Fitzroy continues as a restaurant and pub,
complete with a Writers and Artists Bar in the basement, with photographs of
some of its famed customers.

Wellcome Trust Centre for the History of Medicine

24 Eversholt Street. Underground: Euston. Monday to Friday 9 A.M. to 6 P.M. Admission: free. ☎ (020) 7611-7211. 🖳 www.wellcome.ac.uk/en/1/homwtc.html.

The museum and collection are based around the massive library of Henry Wellcome, an early medical and pharmaceutical researcher who died in 1936; there were more than 400,000 books and more than 100,000 prints and drawings in the collection.

The Two10 Gallery houses exhibitions on the theme of science and art. Nearby is the "Science for Life" exhibition at 183 Euston Road, NW1. The exhibition is open Monday to Friday 9:45 A.M. to 5 P.M. and Saturday 9:45 A.M. to 1 P.M. Admission is free.

Chapter 20
Regent's Park, Camden

 London Zoo

 Madame Tussaud's and London Planetarium

 Wallace Collection

The Regent's Canal

London Canal Museum

Regent's Park

Sherlock Holmes Museum

Camden

Jewish Museum

Saint Marylebone Parish Church

Langham Hilton Hotel

BBC Experience

The Regent's Park area is one of the greenest, most interesting sections of London and includes within its boundaries the London Zoo and the throwback Regent's Canal. At its southern edge is the quirky waxen world of Madame Tussaud's and to the east is the bustling neighborhood of Camden.

London Zoo

Regent's Park. Underground: Camden Town, then Bus 274. By waterbus: scheduled service along the Regent's Canal between Camden Lock or Little Venice to the zoo. For waterbus information, call ☎ (020) 7482-2550. Open 10 A.M. to 5:30 P.M. daily, until 4 P.M. in winter. Admission: adult, ❹; child, ❸; family, ❺. ☎ (020) 7722-3333. 🖳 www.zsl.org/londonzoo/index.html.

The London Zoo is one of the world's great zoos, dating back to 1829. There are more than twelve thousand animals on display, and it is renowned for its active conservation program, which has successfully bred species facing extinc-

191

Price Bands
❶ £1–£3
❷ £3–£5
❸ £5–£7
❹ £7–£10
❺ £10–£15
❻ £15 and up

tion. Although it is relatively small and its facilities are old, it is also one of the most attractive, greenest zoos you'll find. Some of the cages allow you to come closer to wild animals than you may be used to; some animals are behind clear-glass barriers allowing a nose-to-nose approach. (Many of the creatures also have "off-show" hideaways where they can remove themselves from display when they feel the need for privacy.)

The **Web of Life**, a glass pavilion celebrating biodiversity on the planet, opened in 1999. The **Mappin Terrace**—billed as London's only mountain—reopened in 1997, after a twelve-year closure for reconstruction, as the home to a pair of the rare sloth bears. Sharing the area are Hanuman langurs (a species of monkey) and Reeve's munjac (a type of deer).

Sloth bears stand only about three feet tall. Their long muzzles and claws are ideal for ripping open termite nests and sucking up the contents. Unique among bears, sloth mothers carry their cubs on their backs when they are little. Loss of habitat and hunting have reduced their numbers to about one thousand in India and just four hundred in Sri Lanka.

Other highlights of the zoo include the **Reptile House, Elephant House, Penguin Pool, Lion Terraces, Invertebrate House, Aquarium, Moonlight World**, and the **Children's Zoo**.

The famed **Snowdon Aviary** allows visitors to walk into a huge cage of exotic birds.

A tunnel that connects the two sides of the zoo is decorated with reproductions of prehistoric cave paintings of Lascaux, France, believed to be about twenty thousand years old. Some of the animals depicted are now extinct.

Special events, including lectures by keepers, are scheduled daily.

The zoo owes its existence to the efforts of Stamford Raffles, who worked his way from a clerkship at the East India Company to various high posts in the British Empire that eventually led to his founding the colony of Singapore. Along the way he acquired a personal collection of animals, including tapirs, clouded leopards, and a Malayan sun bear, which was reared with Raffles's children in the nursery. When he returned to England in 1824 he set about the formation of a collection of animals in London, leading to the creation of the Zoological Society of London. Among the first Fellows of the Zoological Society was Charles Darwin.

Throughout the nineteenth century, most of the animals in the zoo were sent by amateur collectors, including tourists, diplomats, and sailors. The zoo opened the world's first Reptile House in 1849, the world's first public aquarium in 1853, and the first **Insect House** in 1881.

Among famous former residents of the zoo are:

- **Jumbo**. A massive African elephant, Jumbo lived at the zoo for seventeen years until he became too aggressive to give shows. He was sold to P. T. Barnum in 1882 to become the star of the circus; with the proceeds, the zoo built a new reptile house (now used as the birdhouse).

- **Winnie**. This American black bear was left at the London zoo in 1914 by a Canadian soldier at the start of the war; he named the creature Winnie after his hometown of Winnipeg. She was visited by author A. A. Milne and his son Christopher and served as the inspiration for the stories of Winnie the Pooh and Christopher Robin.
- **Guy**. A gentle giant of a gorilla, Guy was one of the zoo's best-loved creatures during his residence from 1947 to 1978. He is honored with a statue.

The zoo itself was an endangered species in the early 1990s, coming close to shutting down because of financial difficulties. Intensive fundraising has brought it back from the brink of extinction.

WOW Madame Tussaud's and London Planetarium

Marylebone Road. Underground: Baker Street. Madame Tussaud's open daily 9 A.M. to 5:30 P.M.; London Planetarium open daily 9:40 A.M. to 5 P.M. Admission for Madame Tussaud's: adult, ❺; child (younger than 16), ❹; senior, ❹. Admission for London Planetarium: adult, ❸; child (younger than 16), ❷; child (younger than 5), free; senior, ❷. Combined ticket for Madame Tussaud's/Planetarium: adult, ❺; child (younger than 16), ❹; senior, ❺. ☎ (020) 7935-6861. 🖳 www.madame-tussauds.com/madam-tussauds/site/london.

Madame Tussaud's is a celebration of celebrity and notoriety. You'll come face-to-waxen-face with some of the most famous characters in world history and some of the best-known faces of television, movies, and politics.

Tussaud was born Marie Grosholtz in Strasbourg, France, in 1761. She was indirectly born into her trade: her mother worked as housekeeper to Philippe Curtius, a doctor and wax modeler. Curtius taught his art to the young Marie and she went on to be appointed art tutor to the sister of King Louis XVI, living at the Palace of Versailles.

With the outbreak of the French Revolution, Grosholtz and her mother were imprisoned and came close to an appointment with "Madame la Guillotine." Instead, she was allowed to prove her loyalty to the new revolutionary order by creating death masks from the severed heads of many of her former employers, including Marie Antoinette and Louis XVI. She also did a study of revolutionary Jean Paul Marat, on display today.

In 1794 Curtius died and Grosholtz inherited his collection; she married engineer François Tussaud the following year. France was still roiled by economic problems, and in 1802 Tussaud decided to leave France (and her husband) and take her exhibition to Great Britain. For the next thirty-three years she took her wax figures from town to town for exhibitions; in 1835 the collection found a permanent home in London on Baker Street, not far from the present building. Tussaud died in 1850, but her sons and then her grandsons kept up the unusual family business. Tussaud's final work was a self-portrait, still on display today.

One of the highlights of the museum was the Separate Room, so-called because it was shielded from the faint of heart by a door and separate admission. Today the collection of murderers and evildoers and some of their victims is featured in the famed **Chamber of Horrors**.

Among the notorious residents of the chamber are Vlad the Impaler (better known as Dracula) and some of the actual death masks modeled by Madame Tussaud during the French Revolution; on display is the guillotine blade used to behead Marie Antoinette. You'll walk through a reconstruction of a London street stalked by Jack the Ripper. And you'll see some relatively obscure murderers, including Dr. Crippen, who was tried and sentenced to death for the murder of his wife in 1910; Tussaud's grandson took photographs during his sensational trial with a camera hidden beneath his bowler hat.

Some children and adults may find the chamber too bloody; there is an escape route for visitors who want to bypass the gore.

The collection has suffered numerous disasters along the way. The first came in 1822 when the traveling collection was shipwrecked en route to Ireland; most of the figures were saved.

In 1925 an electrical fault sparked a major fire that left the floors of the exhibition running with molten wax. Many of the figures and relics, including Napoleon's campaign coach, were destroyed. The Chamber of Horrors was mostly spared, with the irreplaceable death masks of Robespierre, Marat, and Charles Peace among the "survivors."

On September 8, 1940, the first night of the London Blitz, the exhibition was struck by a heavy bomb that damaged or destroyed 352 head molds.

Although the original works were based on death masks, artists at Tussaud's today work mostly from live sittings at a private studio at the exhibition, or on occasion, the sculptor will visit the subject. The sculptor takes precise measurements, including the dimensions of ears and nostrils, and detailed photographs are made. The only part that is modeled from life is the hands.

The original model is done in clay; when it is completed, a plaster "negative" is made and used to cast the wax version. Eyes, makeup, and hairpieces (made from real human hair) are added by experts. Some subjects donate their clothes for use on the likeness. All told, it can take as long as six months and cost up to £20,000 to complete a figure.

The Spirit of London ride takes visitors in and among a constellation of robotic figures, recreating the sights, sounds, and smells of more than four hundred years of London history. Visitors riding in "time taxis" meet Shakespeare at work on a play and Queen Elizabeth in her court, observe the lord mayor of London escaping the Great Fire by boat, experience Britain at war during the Blitz, and then move into modern days with the "Swinging '60s." Today's London is exemplified by a punk rocking the lord mayor's coach.

You'll also see some scenes from the stories of Charles Dickens, including *Oliver Twist*. Dickens was a regular visitor to the exhibition and was said to have based the character of Mrs. Jarley in *The Old Curiosity Shop* on Madame Tussaud.

Lines can build in midday; the best time to visit is early morning or late afternoon. On one visit on a bank holiday the exhibit was packed to the point that it was difficult to see some of the figures. (Camcorders are officially prohibited, although I have seen visitors videotaping everything in sight.)

Planetarium "Planetary Quest"

Open weekdays 12:20 P.M. and every forty minutes until 5 P.M., weekends 10:20 A.M. and every forty minutes until 5 P.M. Children younger than 5 not admitted. Admission: adult, ❸; child (younger than 16), ❷. Combined ticket for Madame Tussaud's/Planetarium: adult, ❺; child, ❸.

The planetarium features an intergalactic journey with a projected sky show on the domed ceiling; you'll also find interactive demonstrations, displays, and scale models.

🤩 Wallace Collection

Hertford House, Manchester Square. Underground: Bond Street. Open Monday to Saturday 10 A.M. to 5 P.M., Sunday noon to 5 P.M. Admission: free; donations accepted. ☎ (020) 7935-0687. 🖳 www.the-wallace-collection.org.uk.

One of the most fabulous private collections of art was bequeathed to the nation in 1897 by the widow of Sir Richard Wallace with the stipulation that nothing ever be added or sold. The art represents the gatherings of four generations of the Hertford family and is presented in the family's beautifully restored home, Hertford House.

The Hertford family served as patrons for a number of great artists. The third marquess of Hertford was a famed member of London society, portrayed as the Marquis de Steyne in Thackeray's book *Vanity Fair*.

The collection includes many pre-Revolution, eighteenth-century French works, purchased at a time when such florid and ornate works were out of fashion in England. The collection was moved across the Channel to London about 1890 during the siege of the Franco-Prussian War; the museum opened in 1900.

As one of the docents explained to me, Sir Richard set forth his collecting strategy as "pleasing pictures, with no bloodbaths, ugly saints, or war scenes." Stars of the collection include *The Laughing Cavalier* by Franz Hals, Rembrandt's *Titus*, and Fragonard's charmingly syrupy *The Swing*. Other artists represented include Gainsborough, Romney, Boucher, Watteau, and Houdon.

You'll also find enough ancient armor to equip a small war, including some of the most intricate and frightening helmets I've ever seen as well as crossbows, halberds, and daggers. There's also a five-hundred-year-old suit of armor for a horse. One room is filled with pages of illuminated manuscripts, protected from the light by individual covers; visitors lift the sheets for a peek and then return the treasures to their dark sleep.

In 2000 four new galleries and a lecture theater were completed, sitting beneath a clear glass roof installed over the museum's inner courtyard.

The Regent's Canal

The Regent's Canal adopted its name because one of its promoters was a friend of the Prince of Wales, later George IV. A company was formed in 1812 to build and operate a canal from Paddington, where a branch of the Grand Union Canal already reached, to Limehouse and the River Thames, in east London.

Construction of the canal turned out to be more difficult than expected, with low water levels that required the damming of the River Brent. The waterway was completed in 1820, but within about twenty years railways were taking away much of the business the canal backers had hoped for.

The Regent's Canal Company was taken over by the larger Grand Union Canal in 1929. There was a brief increase in traffic during World War II. The last horse-drawn boats moved through in 1956, the horses replaced by tractors. By the late 1960s commercial traffic was all but gone.

In recent years the canal has been reborn as a leisure facility, with tour boats and hiking on the towpaths. Boats run from Camden to Little Venice in west London where the canal meets the Grand Union near Paddington. Some boats make stops at the London Zoo in Regent's Park.

Boat Trips on London's Canals

London Waterbus Company. Little Venice–London Zoo–Camden. ☎ (020) 7482-2660. 🖳 www.littlevenicelondon.co.uk/waterbus/londonw.html.

Jenny Wren. Camden–Little Venice. ☎ (020) 7485-4433.

Jason's Canal Boat Trip. Little Venice–Camden. ☎ (020) 7286-3428. 🖳 www.jasons.co.uk.

Willowtree Narrowboat Trips. Yeading–Greenford. ☎ (020) 8841-2100.

Pride of Lee. Limehouse–Old Ford. ☎ (020) 7515-3337.

London Canal Museum

12–13 New Wharf Road, King's Cross. Underground: King's Cross. Open daily except Monday 10 A.M. to 4:30 P.M. Also open bank holidays. Admission: adult, ❶; child, ❶. ☎ (020) 7713-0836. 🖳 www.canalmuseum.org.uk.

The Canal Museum offers an interesting glimpse of nineteenth-century life on the Regent's Canal . . . and one of London's most famous early ice cream factories and ice wells.

The museum includes an exploration of an old narrowboat and the cargoes carried on the canal, which was completed in 1820. About twenty years later, though, the canals were being eclipsed by the growing network of railways.

The museum is located in a former ice warehouse built for ice cream maker Carlo Gatti. In 1850 a huge ice well was dug at the site to store ice imported from Norway by ship and then canal boat. As London grew, availability of local ice—harvested in the winter and stored in wells and sheds through the next summer—was limited and frozen water began to be imported for use by restaurants, stores, and some private residences.

Gatti imported 350 tons of ice from Norway in 1857 and stored it in two thirty-four-foot-diameter ice wells built beneath the building for ice storage. The availability of the ice made the manufacture and sale of ice cream to the public possible for the first time.

The ice wells were used until about 1902; the last import of any ice from Scandinavia was in 1921 when mechanical ice production was well established.

Work is under way on a project to excavate and restore the ice wells and include them in the areas on display.

Regent's Park

Underground: Regent's Park, Baker Street, or Great Portland Street. Open daily 5 A.M. to dusk.

Once part of the huge Forest of Middlesex and then part of Tyburn Manor, Regent's Park was taken by Henry VIII in the sixteenth century. A section of 554 acres was marked in 1539 as a royal hunting park surrounded by a ditch and earthen wall to keep deer within.

It was sold in the aftermath of the civil war in the next century, and thousands of trees were harvested in a short period of time. The property was given back to the Crown at the Restoration, but for nearly 150 years afterward the land was farmed.

When the leases for the farms expired in 1811, a competition was held for the design of a road linking the area to Westminster and for the development of the area. Architect John Nash, an associate of the prince regent, was chosen

REGENT'S PARK

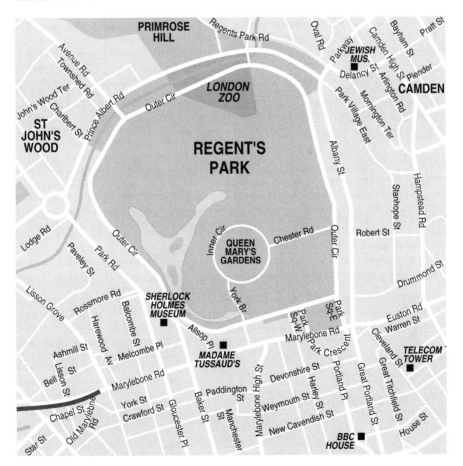

and he created Regent Street, the Regent's Canal, and Regent's Park itself.

The park that Nash planned was to have included a party house for the prince regent, more than fifty villas of classical design, and a series of townhouses in crescents and circuses, trademark designs of the time. The palace was never built.

The **Park Crescent** still exists, a spectacular half circle of homes now converted to offices, near the Regent's Park Underground station at the south end of the park. Eight villas were built, and several remain in or around the park, used as residences for ambassadors and as college facilities.

Nash also planned elaborate terraces; two are now within the London Zoo at the northern edge of the park. **Cumberland Terrace** on Great Portland Street is the most impressive, with a block of Ionic columns.

The boating lake at the center of the park is well stocked with water birds. Nearby is an outdoor bandstand and the 1,200-seat **Open Air Theatre** used for repertory theater, including Shakespeare, in summer months.

Sherlock Holmes Museum

221B Baker Street. Underground: Baker Street. Open daily 9:30 A.M. to 6 P.M. Admission: ❷. ☎ (020) 7935-8866. 🖳 www.sherlock-holmes.co.uk.

A real museum about a fictional detective, the Sherlock Holmes Museum is located in a building between numbers 237 and 239 Baker Street, although the sign out front says 221B, Holmes's fictional address. You may need Sherlock, or perhaps his creator Arthur Conan Doyle, to get to the bottom of it all.

The exhibit includes rooms representative of Holmes's working and living quarters; a shop sells books, deerstalker hats, and pipes.

Camden

Underground: Camden Town.

Architect John Nash's grand scheme for Regent's Park included a canal that ran from the London docks to Paddington, with a passage through the middle of the park. As constructed, the Regent's Canal ended up looping across the northern end of the park.

No longer in commercial use, the canal is now home to leisure and tour boats and a thriving waterside market on High Street and in the Camden Lock building. The place is especially lively on the weekend.

Nearby is the **Stables Antiques Market**, one of the world's largest antique markets set in former Victorian stables and shops on cobbled lanes. You can walk north of Camden Town to the area, or take the Tube one stop farther north to Chalk Farm. The market is open Saturday and Sunday from 10 A.M. to 6:30 P.M. For information, call ☎ (020) 7485-5511.

Jewish Museum

Raymond Burton House, 129–131 Albert Street. Underground: Camden Town. Open Sunday to Thursday 10 A.M. to 4 P.M. ☎ (020) 7284-1997. Closed Friday, Saturday, Jewish holidays, and public holidays. Admission: adult, ❷; child, ❶. 🖳 www.jewmusm.ort.org.

The Jewish Museum features one of the world's best collections of Jewish ceremonial art and a history of Jewish influence in London and Great Britain. The museum dates back to 1932 in its original location. Treasures include a sixteenth-century Torah ark from Italy; an eighth-century, Byzantine-era gold plaque with Jewish symbols; and ceremonial items presented to the lord mayors of London by the Spanish and Portuguese Synagogue, established in 1701.

The Spanish and Portuguese Synagogue is located at Bevis Marks above Bank Street in the heart of London. It was the first such Jewish house of worship in England after Cromwell permitted Jews to return in 1657. Statesman Benjamin Disraeli's father was a member of the congregation, and the boy's birth was recorded there in 1804.

Saint Marylebone Parish Church

Marylebone Road. Underground: Regent's Park. Open Monday 12:30 to 1:30 P.M. ☎ (020) 7935-7315.

The name of the church and the district is drawn from an earlier church named after Tyburn Creek, condensed first to Saint Mary's by the Bourne and later into Marylebone. The first church was built about 1400, restored in 1740, and then rebuilt in 1817. The old, smaller church was maintained as a chapel; it was damaged by bombs in World War II and taken down in 1949.

Poets Robert Browning and Elizabeth Barrett were married here in 1846 after they eloped.

Langham Hilton Hotel

1 Portland Place. Underground: Oxford Circus. ☎ (020) 7636-1000. 🖳 www.hilton.com.

A grand old hotel, the Langham Hilton was born in modern times. Completed in 1865, it was designed as a Florentine palace with six hundred opulent rooms. At its heyday, guests included authors Mark Twain and Oscar Wilde and musicians Antonin Dvorak and Arturo Toscanini. Arthur Conan Doyle used the hotel as settings for scenes in several of his novels. The exiled emperor Napoleon III took up residence for a while; in this century, Emperor Haile Selassie of Ethiopia did the same.

The hotel was severely damaged in 1940 when a German land mine exploded on Portland Place; among its effects was the breaching of a huge rooftop water tank. Restored after the war, in the 1980s it was owned by the British Broadcasting Corporation (BBC), which used it for studios and offices. In 1991 it was restored as the Langham Hilton Hotel.

The marble lobby leads to the Langham's famed **Palm Court**; nearby is the Chukka bar, a celebration of the arcane sport of polo.

BBC Experience

Broadcasting House, Portland Place. Underground: Oxford Circus. Open daily 10 A.M. to 5:30 P.M. and Monday 11 A.M. to 5:30 P.M. Last tour begins at 4:30 P.M. Admission: adult, ❹; child, ❷; family, ❺. ☎ (020) 7765-1109. 🖳 www.bbc.co.uk/experience.

The BBC Experience offers a behind-the-scenes tour of BBC operations, including studios, control rooms, and the history of radio and television.

Located in Broadcasting House, the show employs modern multimedia effects to allow visitors to direct an episode of the popular *Eastenders* television show, produce their own three-minute radio play, and link to live radio broadcasts and the Internet.

Chapter 21
South Kensington, Kensington, Knightsbridge, and Notting Hill

 Natural History Museum

 Science Museum

 Victoria and Albert Museum

 Kensington Palace State Apartments

Kensington Gardens

Albert Memorial

Royal Albert Hall

Hyde Park

Serpentine Gallery

Harrods

Brompton Oratory

Leighton House Museum

Marble Arch

Notting Hill

Portobello Road Market

Queensway

South Kensington and Knightsbridge are among the toniest of London neighborhoods, populated by foreign embassies, fancy galleries, fabulous museums, and high-end shops, including the famed Harrods. Knightsbridge takes its name from an eleventh-century bridge across the Westbourne where two knights were said to have staged a battle to the death.

HYDE PARK

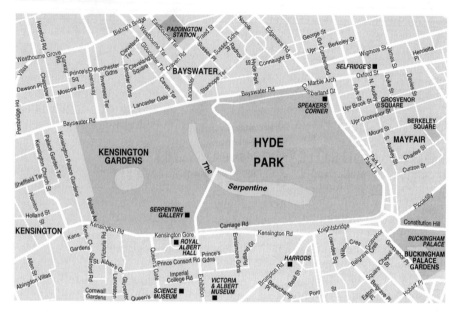

Kensington is just a notch below its southern twin, with a respectable shopping district on Kensington High Street, including an antiques mart at the intersection with Kensington Church Street. On its northern edge is Notting Hill, which in the past few decades has become the center of a thriving Caribbean expatriate community and home to a lively street fair each August.

The three largest museums in South Kensington have joined together to offer a combination ticket; a pass to the Natural History Museum, the Science Museum, and the Victoria and Albert Museum costs ❻ for adults and ❺ for children; the ticket can be purchased at any of the museums.

🟦 Natural History Museum

Cromwell Road. Underground: South Kensington. Open Monday to Saturday 10 A.M. to 5:50 P.M., Sunday 11 A.M. to 5:50 P.M. Closed several days around Christmas. Admission: adult, ❸; child (5–17), ❷; family (two adults and up to four children), ❻. Free admission after 4:30 P.M. weekdays and 5 P.M. weekends. ☎ (020) 7938-9123. 📖 www.nhm.ac.uk.

The Natural History Museum began as a department of the British Museum in Bloomsbury, holding the immense private collection of Sir Hans Sloane, a wealthy physician who died in 1753. During the nineteenth century, the museum was given its own home in South Kensington, opening in 1881 with a spectacular central hall that manages to dwarf even the huge dinosaur skeletons on display below. The hall, like the nave of a cathedral, features a grand staircase that offers views of the displays from above.

Today a million visitors a year explore the collection of sixty-eight million plants, animals, fossils, rocks, and minerals from all over the world. Major exhibitions focus on ecology, geology, human biology, dinosaurs, and creepy crawlies.

Among newer residents is a stinky Tyrannosaurus rex. The robotic re-creation is lifelike in movement, sound, and even smell: every time he opens his mouth the room is filled with eau de swamp. "A strong aroma of rotting flesh would certainly have filled the air," according to a dinosaur expert at the museum. "Its breath would have smelled of the remains of decaying meat, trapped between its huge teeth."

The three-quarter-size robot, standing thirteen feet high and nearly twenty-three feet long, was made by a Japanese company specializing in animatronic creatures.

The **Ecology** exhibition includes a giant video wall following the cycle of water, a walk inside a leaf, and interactive video games about life on earth. In the Mammals section, a spectacular life-sized model of a blue whale has been a London favorite for half a century. Nearby are many other wondrous creatures, from elephants to hippos to camels.

Price Bands
❶ £1–£3
❷ £3–£5
❸ £5–£7
❹ £7–£10
❺ £10–£15
❻ £15 and up

All museums, all the time. Serious museum-goers can save some pounds by purchasing the South Kensington Museums Pass. For as little as £22, you can obtain unlimited entrance for a year to the V&A, the Natural History Museum, and the Science Museum. For information, call ☎ (020) 7938-8538.

The **Human Biology** section includes specimens, models and descriptions about human development, the brain, and physiology.

The **Creepy Crawlies** display includes a gigantic model of a scorpion and a life-sized termite mound. You can stroll through 1 Crawley House for a tour that will forever remove any illusions you may have had about your success in keeping arthropods out of your house.

In **Man's Place in Evolution**, you can come face-to-face with Lucy, the famous missing link australopithecine, found in Ethiopia in 1974.

The museum's **Mineral Gallery** includes spectacular gems, meteorites, and minerals, including a number that date back to the museum's original collection of 1753. The **Earth Gallery** in the former Geological Museum next door, features exploration of the inner core of the earth, including volcanoes and the effects of wind and rain on the surface of our planet.

🦉 Science Museum

Exhibition Road. Underground: South Kensington. Open daily 10 A.M. to 6 P.M. Admission: adult, ❸; child (5–17), ❷. Admission free from 4:30 P.M. to 6 P.M. ☎ (020) 7938-8080. 🖳 www.sciencemuseum.org.uk.

The Science Museum features a spectacular collection of all things scientific and technical. In 2000 the museum opened the **Wellcome Wing**, between the Science Museum, Imperial College, and the Natural History Museum. The addition is devoted to contemporary science, medicine, and technology. Also within is a 450-seat Imax theater.

The Apollo 10 *space capsule on display at the Science Museum*
Photo by Corey Sandler

The largest museum of its kind, the institution includes more than 200,000 items in exhibits spread over seven floors. Famous objects include Alcock & Brown's *Vickers Vimy*, the first aircraft to cross the Atlantic; the model of DNA created by scientists Crick and Watson; and the *Apollo 10* command module, which made the first manned flight around the moon in 1969.

On display is one of the oldest steam engines in the world, dating to 1788, and a massive mill engine, built in 1903 to drive 1,700 looms.

In **Flight Lab**, visitors learn the principles of flight, operate the controls in the cockpit of a small plane, and test a model in a wind tunnel.

There are also several interactive galleries where young guests can find out how things work.

On Air is a fully operational radio station that offers older students the chance to create, produce, and present their own programs, while the Network offers youngsters access to a computer and videotelephony network connected to terminals placed throughout the museum.

A basement area includes the **Secret Life of the Home**, with an astonishing array of historic and current domestic appliances, gadgets, and devices. Other treasures include an actual, gigantic, landing-gear system from an Airbus 330; the Wells cathedral clock dating back to 1392; and Babbage's calculating engine, the world's first computer.

🎇 Victoria and Albert Museum

Cromwell Road. Underground: South Kensington. Open Monday noon to 5:50 P.M., Tuesday to Sunday 10 A.M. to 5:45 P.M. Late view in summer season: Wednesday 6:30 P.M. to 9:30 P.M. Admission: adult, ❸; child (younger than 18), free. ☎ (020) 7938-8500. 🖳 www.vam.ac.uk.

Opened in 1857, the museum contains one of the world's finest collections of decorative arts, with seven miles of galleries and more than 100,000 works of art on display, including sculpture, furniture, fashion and textiles, paintings, silver, glass, ceramics, jewelry, books, prints, and photographs.

The museum is housed in a set of notable Victorian and Edwardian buildings. It was founded as the Museum of Manufactures in 1852, renamed in 1899 by Queen Victoria in honor of her husband Prince Albert when the cornerstone for the present building was laid. Its formal name is still the National Museum of Art and Design.

And if plans come to fruition, sometime in 2004 a new extension named

The Spiral will be added to the V&A, the most dramatic and ambitious project at the museum since the facade was completed in 1909. The walls, rising in inclined planes, will form a self-supporting spiral and create unusual internal gallery space for exhibitions from high design to traditional crafts.

Some of the treasures include the spectacular **Raphael Gallery**, a cathedral-like space that holds seven huge tapestry designs by Raphael, commissioned in 1515 by Pope Leo X for the Sistine Chapel.

The **Islamic Gallery** displays the famed Ardabil Carpet, one of the largest and most magnificent Persian carpets, dated from about 1540.

Other highlights include:

- the world's greatest collection of Constable paintings, and a nearby room-ful of Rodin sculptures
- a dress gallery, spanning four centuries of European fashion to the present day. You'll see a spectacular presentation, from ornate Victorian ball gowns to punk attire of the 1970s and the Wonderbra. Included is a collection of corsets, bustles, and side hoops to support the elaborate dresses of the early eighteenth through the mid-nineteenth centuries
- the **Far East** collection, including ceramics, textiles, lacquerware, furniture, and jade carvings—claimed to be the finest collection of contemporary Chinese and Japanese art outside those countries
- furniture, from Chippendale antiques to contemporary pieces by Frank Lloyd Wright and modern designers
- the **National Collection of Glass** with more than seven thousand objects
- metalwork and jewelry, including medieval, Renaissance, Baroque, and modern pieces made of gold, silver, iron, and copper
- the largest group of Indian art outside India, including sculpture, miniature paintings, elaborate court costumes, jewelry, and weapons
- the **Cast Courts**, with plaster casts of Michelangelo's *David*, the *Portico de la Gloria* from the Cathedral at Santiago de Compostela, and other great works, prepared for Victorian-era art students unable to travel to visit the real works
- the **Sizergh Castle Room**, a dark wood-paneled room created about 1575 for a castle in Westmoreland

One of my favorite stops is the elaborately carved Great Bed of Ware, built about 1590. It was mentioned in Shakespeare's *Twelfth Night* of 1601 when Sir Toby Belch describes a sheet "big enough for the Bed of Ware." The true history of the large bed is not known, but one theory is that it was built as a tourist attraction for an inn at Ware.

A portion of the exterior wall across from the Natural History Museum shows World War II bomb damage; it has been left unrepaired as a memorial.

🟥 Kensington Palace State Apartments

Kensington Gardens. Underground: Queensway or High Street Kensington. Open daily 9:45 A.M. to 5 P.M. (last admission 3:30 P.M.). Admission: adult, ❹; child, ❹; family, ❻. Visits by guided tour only. ☎ (020) 7937-9561. 🖳 www.hrp.org.uk/index2.htm or 🖳 www.royal.gov.uk/palaces/kensingt.htm.

William and Mary bought an old mansion in the country known as Nottingham House, after they took the throne in 1689; they disliked the air at the old Whitehall Palace and moved to Hampton Court while architect Christopher Wren converted Nottingham to a palace. The house includes the traditional separate suite of rooms for the king and queen.

After George II died in his water closet at Kensington Palace in 1760, his grandson George III showed a preference for Buckingham House in London, so Kensington was no longer regularly used as a royal palace.

In 1819 the duke of Kent, remarried to the German Princess Victoria of Saxe-Coburg-Saalfield, returned to Kensington so their child would be born in England. The future Queen Victoria was born there on May 24 of that year. Victoria was living there in 1837 when she was informed of the death of William IV and her accession to the throne. Soon afterward she moved to Buckingham Palace.

The State Apartments were first opened to the public in 1889. From 1912 to 1914 the apartments were used for the London Museum; the museum returned from 1950 to 1975 until the collection was moved to the new Museum of London in the Barbican in 1975.

Half of the palace is still used as royal apartments, most famously as the bachelor digs for Princess Diana after she separated from Prince Charles; after her death, the forecourt was buried beneath floral tributes. Princess Margaret also has a residence there.

The public tour includes the Royal Ceremonial Dress collection in period settings offering a pageant of court attire since 1750.

Kensington Gardens

Underground: High Street Kensington, Queensway, or Lancaster Gate. Open from 5 A.M. to midnight daily.

Once part of the grounds of Kensington Palace, the land was given to the public in 1841 and now connects through to Hyde Park.

Near the west bank of the Serpentine is the famed 1912 statue of Peter Pan, based on J. M. Barrie's fictional character; Peter plays his pipes to the fairies and animals around him. Barrie himself donated the original swings in the children's playground by Black Lion Gate.

The Round Pond, created in 1728, east of Kensington Palace is often used for model boat regattas; in winter it is sometimes open for ice skating.

Albert Memorial

South Carriage Drive, Kensington Gardens. Underground: Knightsbridge.

The elaborate memorial to Queen Victoria's consort was erected in 1876 near the site of the famed Great Exhibition of 1851, a celebration of the dawn of the scientific age that was organized by Albert; the statue shows him with a catalog from the exhibition on his knee. Albert husband died in 1861 of typhoid.

Nearby, nearly two hundred other figures and allegorical symbols represent Engineering, Agriculture, Manufacturing, Commerce, and the continents of Asia, Europe, America, and Africa.

Royal Albert Hall

Kensington Gore. Guided tours available when performances are not under-way. ☎ (020) 7589-3203. 📖 www.royalalberthall.com.

Home of the famous "Proms" classical music concerts as well as many other performances and meetings, the building was originally envisioned as the Hall of Arts and Science, but Queen Victoria unexpectedly added the words "Royal Albert" at the installation of the cornerstone in 1867; it opened in 1871.

The oval-shaped structure is a Victorian elaboration of a Roman amphitheater, with a potential capacity of eight thousand, although modern safety regulations set the limit at about seven thousand.

In 1941 the Promenade Concerts were moved to the Albert Hall after the Queen's Hall was bombed; they have remained there since.

Hyde Park

Underground: Hyde Park Corner, Knightsbridge, Lancaster Gate, or Marble Arch. Open daily 5 A.M. to midnight.

The largest of the royal parks, encompassing more than 340 acres, Hyde Park was originally part of the Manor Hyde, part of the lands of Westminster Abbey seized by Henry VIII in 1536 when the monasteries were dissolved.

First used by the royals for hunting, it was opened to the public in the seventeenth century. As the civil war grew near, forts were built in the park. After the fall of the king the park was sold off; after the Restoration in 1660 Charles II took back the park and enclosed it with a brick wall. The grounds became the wealthy's favored place for parading fancy coaches.

Speakers' Corner at Hyde Park

When William and Mary moved to Kensington Palace in the 1690s, three hundred lamps were hung from branches in the trees along the *route de roi* (King's Road), the first lit road in England. The name *route de roi* gave rise to the nickname Rotten Row, which continues to this day as the name of a road along the south border of the park. The lighting was intended to help cut down on attacks by highwaymen who robbed travelers; bandits continued to work the park well into the eighteenth century, though.

The Serpentine, an artificial lake, was created in 1730 by the damming of the Westbourne River.

The 1851 Exhibition was held in the park in the famed Crystal Palace, which was located near the Prince of Wales Gate between Rotten Row and the Carriage Road. The massive glass building was removed from Hyde Park after the exhibition and re-erected across the river at Sydenham where it was used as an amusement park and concert hall; it caught fire and was destroyed in 1936.

Today Hyde Park is well used for sporting activities, concerts, political demonstrations, and parades. In the middle of the nineteenth century, the park drew large crowds for demonstrations about tax and trading issues; at the time, there was no legal right of assembly and police made arrests. That right was finally recognized by law in 1872, and ever since, the famed **Speakers' Corner** has been a regular gathering place for serious and not-so-serious orators, especially on Sunday mornings. The freedom to speak is accompanied by the freedom to heckle.

Serpentine Gallery

Kensington Gardens. Underground: Lancaster Gate or South Kensington. Open daily 10 A.M. to 6 P.M. ☎ (020) 7402-6075. 🖳 www.serpentinegallery.com.

A one-time teahouse built in the southeast corner of Kensington Gardens in 1912, the Serpentine Gallery is now home to changing exhibitions of contemporary art. Some pieces are displayed outdoors.

Brompton Oratory

Brompton Road. Underground: South Kensington. Open daily 6:30 A.M. to 8 P.M. ☎ (020) 7808-0900.

The spectacular Brompton Oratory, a Catholic church, was completed in 1884 and expanded afterward. Many of the furnishings were brought to England from Europe, including the elaborate Lady Altar and twelve large marble Apostles created in Italy in the seventeenth century.

The idea for an oratory began in Italy in the sixteenth century, gathering communities of secular scholar-priests. Today the Oratory is renowned for its musical concerts.

Leighton House Museum

12 Holland Park Road. Underground: High Street Kensington. Open Monday to Saturday 11 A.M. to 5:30 P.M. Closed Tuesday. Admission: free. ☎ (020) 7602-3316. 🖳 www. rbkc.gov.uk/leightonhousemuseum.

Constructed as a studio for painter Lord Leighton in 1866, the museum's Victorian elegance has changed little over the years; Leighton's paintings and those of his contemporaries are on display in the main area. In 1877 the spectacular Arab Hall was added, showcasing a display of tiles from Cairo, Damascus, Rhodes, and elsewhere, collected by Leighton and others.

Harrods

87–135 Brompton Road, Knightsbridge. Underground: Knightsbridge. Open daily except Sunday from 10 A.M. to 6 P.M. On Wednesday, Thursday, and Friday, open until 7 P.M. ☎ (020) 7730-1234. 💻 www.harrods.com.

Harrods department store

The famed department store Harrods was established in what was then the village of Knightsbridge in 1849. Today, it is one of the world's largest stores, with nearly four thousand on staff.

In 1985 Harrods was purchased by the Al Fayed family, and its windows became a stop on the mourning pilgrimage after the death of Princess Diana and companion Dodi Al Fayed in 1997.

Even if you don't buy anything, the place is worth a trip just to stroll through the incredible food halls. Don't go with an empty stomach and a full wallet.

Marble Arch

Park Lane. Underground: Marble Arch.

A grand work by John Nash, the Marble Arch derived from the Arch of Constantine in Rome. The arch—a bit smaller than many visitors may expect—was first erected outside the main entrance to Buckingham Palace in 1827 and was moved across town in 1851 when the palace was expanded.

Only senior members of the royal family and the royal artillery regiments are permitted to drive under the arch, which today is circled by armies of cabs and buses.

Notting Hill

Underground: Notting Hill Gate. 💻 www.mynottinghill.co.uk.

A district in North Kensington, Notting Hill became a center for immigrants from the Caribbean in the 1950s and 1960s. It's now the home of the largest street carnival in Europe, a Mardi Gras–like celebration held at the end of the summer on a bank holiday weekend. How big? Large enough to virtually paralyze traffic through the area, shut down some Underground stations, and draw between one and two million revelers each year. The two-day carnival includes parades, marching bands, hundreds of food stands, and nightly concerts. Alas, the area also has some of the highest rates of street crime in London.

Portobello Road Market

Portobello Road. Underground: Notting Hill Gate. Antiques market open Friday 9:30 A.M. to 4 P.M. and Saturday 8 A.M. to 5 P.M. Individual shops in the area follow ordinary business hours. 💻 www.portobelloroad.co.uk/welcome.asp.

Home to one of London's most lively markets, Portobello Road Market offers mostly antiques and jewelry but you're likely to find a bit of everything else.

A market since the 1870s, Portobello Road originally sported gypsies selling horses and herbs and later fruits and vegetables. It was originally an unpaved track leading to Porto Bello Farm, named in honor of the capture from the Spaniards of Porto Bello in the Gulf of Mexico in 1739.

Queensway

Underground: Queensway, Bayswater.

A cosmopolitan shopping street, Queensway boasts a varied assortment of restaurants and shops catering to residents and visitors from all around the world. The road was renamed from Black Lion Lane after the accession of Queen Victoria.

Chapter 22
Chelsea

Chelsea has gone in and out of fashion many times, which may be appropriate because of its long history as a trendsetting literary and artistic community. Set along the Thames west of Whitehall and south of Kensington, the area was the home for such famed authors as Jonathan Swift and Thomas Carlyle and American artist James Whistler, who lived in the area for a while.

The area was one of the capitals of hippiedom in the swinging 1960s but has retreated into relative obscurity since.

National Army Museum

Royal Hospital Road, Chelsea, London. Underground: Sloane Square. Rail: Victoria Station. Open daily 10 A.M. to 5:30 P.M. Admission: free. ☎ (020) 7730-0717. 💻 www.national-army-museum.ac.uk.

A paean to the British soldier from the time of Henry VIII to modern days, the National Army Museum offers everything from a sprawling collection of medals and weapons and uniforms to the skeleton of Napoleon's horse. Other treasures include some of Florence Nightingale's jewelry, and battle scenes and portraits by painters such as Gainsborough and Reynolds.

The museum also includes an extensive collection of photographs and film, as well as items related to Commonwealth armies, including the Indian Army from the seventeenth century through India's partition in 1947.

Carlyle's House

24 Cheyne Road. Underground: South Kensington. Open April to October,

211

CHELSEA

Wednesday to Sunday 11 A.M. to 5 P.M. Admission: adult, ❷; child, free. ☎ (020) 7352-7087. 🖳 www.rbkc.gov.uk/ArtsAndMuseums/CarlylesHouse.

Historian Thomas Carlyle wrote many of his most renowned books here in the mid-nineteenth century, including *The French Revolution* and *Frederick the Great*. Charles Darwin, Charles Dickens, John Stuart Mill, Alfred Lord Tennyson, and William Thackeray were regular visitors.

The home itself was built in 1708; it is furnished pretty much as it was when Carlyle died in 1881.

King's Road

Underground: Sloane Square.

The King's Road was originally a private road used by Charles II to travel to Hampton Court, and later by George III to Kew. Others could travel the route only by special pass.

In modern days it is a decidedly public road with a great selection of clothing, antique, and knickknack shops and eateries. The miniskirt, and less appealingly, the punk look, were both born here. A large antiques market, Antiquarius, is located at 135 King's Road. A tony shop at number 120 is located in the former offices of Thomas Crapper, famed water-closet maker.

Royal Hospital

Royal Hospital Road. Underground: Sloane Square. Open Monday to Saturday 10 A.M. to noon and 2 P.M. to 4 P.M., Sunday 2 P.M. to 4 P.M. ☎ (020) 7730-0161.

Designed by Christopher Wren and completed in 1692, the Royal was established by Charles II as a home to veteran soldiers and stands adjacent to the National Army Museum.

Little of the structure has changed in three hundred years. Some of the interior rooms, including the State Room, are lushly appointed; royal portraits dating to Charles I line the halls. A small museum tells the story of the hospital. The Chelsea Flower Show is held on the grounds of the hospital each May.

The more than four hundred residents of the hospital, known as Chelsea Parishioners, wear a daily uniform and a ceremonial outfit of a scarlet longcoat and black tricorner hat.

Chelsea Physic Garden

Swan Walk. Underground: Sloane Square. Open April to October, Sunday 2 P.M. to 6 P.M., Wednesday noon to 5 P.M. Admission: adult, ❷; child and senior, ❶. ☎ (020) 7352-5646. 📖 www.cpgarden. demon.co.uk.

The Chelsea Physic Garden of medicinal and other plants was begun in 1673 by the Society of Apothecaries.

In 1732, a strain of cotton developed in greenhouses here was sent to the Georgia colony in America, helping launch the industry there. The rock garden is the oldest in the country and includes old building stone salvaged from the Tower of London.

Price Bands
❶ £1–£3
❷ £3–£5
❸ £5–£7
❹ £7–£10
❺ £10–£15
❻ £15 and up

Part V
The Royal Family

Chapter 23
The Royal Family

The queen is head of state of the United Kingdom of Great Britain and Northern Ireland, as well as of the Commonwealth. As sovereign, Her Majesty also is head of the navy, army, and air force of Britain.

There's more: she's colonel-in-chief of all Guards regiments and the Corps of Royal Engineers and captain-general of the Royal Regiment of Artillery and the Honourable Artillery Company. She holds similar positions with a number of other units in Britain and elsewhere in the Commonwealth.

Despite the fancy titles, in the modern era the sovereign's powers are quite constrained, limited to certain formal ceremonial activities and actions made with the advice of her ministers.

Although the government, judges, and the armed forces all act in the queen's name, the sovereign is avowedly nonpartisan in political matters. She is kept informed about the government's activities; the prime minister comes to Buckingham Palace when she is in residence for a weekly private audience in which her opinion, if not her advice, is solicited.

She sees all cabinet papers and the records of cabinet and cabinet committee meetings and receives important Foreign Office telegrams and a daily summary of events in Parliament.

The queen also acts as host to the heads of state of the Commonwealth and other countries and notables when they visit Britain.

But most her duties are ceremonial. According to her official biography, the queen has visited nearly every county in Britain to cut ribbons and make speeches. She issues honors to distinguished citizens and a small number of foreigners. She also appears on many public occasions such as the services of the Orders of the Garter and the Thistle, Trooping the Colour, the Remembrance Day ceremony, and national services at Saint Paul's Cathedral and Westminster Abbey.

And she is patron or president of more than seven hundred organizations.

The First Kings of the English

When Rome removed its garrison from Britain in the fifth century, there

The British Royalty

Saxons and Danes

Egbert, King of Wessex	802–839
Ethelwulf	839–855
Ethelbald	855–860
Ethelbert	860–866
Ethelred	866–871
Alfred the Great	871–899
Edward the Elder	899–925
Athelstan	925–939
Edmund 1	939–946
Edred	946–955
Edwy	955–959
Edgar	959–975
Edward II, the Martyr	975–979
Ethelred II, the Unready	979–1013 and 1014–1016
Sweyn	1013–1014
Edmund II, Ironside	1016
Canute the Great	1016–1035
Harold Harefoot/Hardicanute	1035–1037
Harold Harefoot	1037–1040
Hardicanute	1040–1042
Edward III, the Confessor	1042–1066
Harold II	1066

House of Normandy

William the Conqueror	1066–1087
William II, Rufus	1087–1100
Henry I, Beauclerc	1100–1135
Matilda	1135
Stephen	1135–1154

House of Angevin

Henry II, Curtmantle	1154–1189
Richard I, the Lionhearted	1189–1199
John Lackland	1199–1216

House of Plantagenet

Henry III	1216–1272
Edward I, Longshanks	1272–1307
Edward II	1307–1327
Edward III	1327–1377
Richard II	1377–1399

House of Lancaster

Henry IV	1399–1413
Henry V	1413–1422
Henry VI	1422–1461 and 1470–1471

House of York

Edward IV	1461–1470 and 1471–1483
Edward V	1483
Richard III	1483–1485

House of Tudor

Henry VII	1485–1509
Henry VIII	1509–1547
Edward VI	1547–1553
Jane	1553
Mary I	1553–1558
Elizabeth I	1558–1603

House of Stuart

James I	1603–1625
Charles I	1625–1649
Commonwealth	1649–1660

House of Stuart (Restoration)

Charles II	1660–1685
James II	1685–1688
William III and Mary II	1688–1702
Anne	1702–1714

House of Hanover

George I	1714–1727
George II	1727–1760
George III	1760–1820
George IV	1820–1830
William IV	1830–1837
Victoria	1837–1901

House of Saxe-Coburg-Gotha

Edward VII	1901–1910

House of Windsor

George V	1910–1936
Edward VIII	1936
George VI	1936–1952
Elizabeth II	1952–

Succession to the Throne

The Act of Settlement in 1700 laid down that only Protestant descendants of Princess Sophia—the electress of Hanover, granddaughter of James I—are eligible to succeed.

Sons of the sovereign and their descendants have precedence over daughters in succeeding to the throne. Daughters take precedence over the sovereign's brothers. When a daughter succeeds, she becomes queen regnant and has the same powers as a king.

The current order of succession is as follows:

Prince of Wales (Prince Charles)
Prince William of Wales
Prince Henry of Wales
Duke of York (Andrew)
Princess Beatrice of York
Princess Eugenie of York
Prince Edward
Princess Royal (Anne)
Peter Phillips
Zara Phillips

In early 1998, Queen Elizabeth gave her assent to a new plan that would remove male primogeniture from the Act of Settlement. If approved, henceforth the first-born child—male or female—of the regent would be next in line for the throne. Politicians were still debating the plan in 2001; one issue was whether the new act would remove the prohibition against marriage to a Roman Catholic.

Accession to the Throne

There are two stages to installation of a monarch: accession and coronation. The new sovereign succeeds to the throne as soon as his or her predecessor dies or abdicates. The ruler is proclaimed at an Accession Council, which includes members of the Privy Council; members of the House of Lords, the lord mayor and aldermen and other leading citizens of London, and high commissioners of Commonwealth countries are invited to attend.

If the incoming monarch is younger than 18, a regent can be appointed to advise the sovereign.

The formal coronation ceremony takes place once all the pomp and pageantry has been readied. The ceremony itself has changed little in more than a thousand years. Held at Westminster Abbey and conducted by the archbishop of Canterbury, the ceremony demands the monarch take an oath to rule according to law. The monarch is anointed and then crowned; following this, a Holy Communion is celebrated.

followed several hundred years of unrest, including raids by three Germanic tribes: the Angles, the Saxons, and the Jutes. They each established small kingdoms, which eventually came into conflict with each other.

Offa, king of Mercia, established supremacy over many of the other rulers during his reign from 757 to 796 and was the first to be called "king of the English" (a word derived from Angles).

In the last half of the eighth century there were numerous attacks by Vikings from Scandinavia. Northumbria and Mercia were overrun. **Alfred, king of Wessex**, defeated the Danes at the Battle of Edington in 878. Under Alfred's rule, Britain began to come together under a legal code, an economic system, and a series of fortress towns.

Athelstan extended the boundaries of the kingdom, encompassing Scotland and Wales during his reign from 925 to 939.

Under renewed attack by the Vikings in the eleventh century, **Ethelred II** was forced to flee to Normandy. In 1016, Danish leader **Canute** became king of England; later with the additional titles of king of Denmark and Norway, he ruled over a spreading northern empire. He married King Ethelred's widow, Emma of Normandy; his sons, though, were unable to sustain the empire.

In 1042 Ethelred's son **Edward III**, a deeply religious man known as "the Confessor," became king. He built Westminster Abbey; after his canonization in 1161, he was reburied in a shrine there.

Edward died in 1066 without a successor, and the king's council elected his brother-in-law Harold Godwinson as **King Harold II**. In September of that year, Harald of Norway invaded England and was defeated by Harold II at the Battle of Stamford Bridge near York. About the same time, William, duke of Normandy, related to Edward by marriage, landed in Sussex. Harold took his army south and in October of 1066 his army was defeated near Hastings and Harold was killed.

The Norman Kings

William I, known as "the Conqueror," moved to consolidate his hold on power. He built fortified castles, including one on the present site of Windsor Castle, and the White Tower at the Tower of London. William established the feudal system, giving land taken from defeated Saxon nobles to followers who supplied knights to the king.

In 1086 William commissioned the first systematic census of England, known as the *Domesday Book*. It recorded the landed wealth of the nation for taxation purposes; the book has been used by historians ever since and is still occasionally involved in modern-day land disputes.

When William died in 1087 his eldest son Robert was given Normandy and his second son, **William II**, known as "Rufus," was installed in England.

William II and Robert clashed in battle in Normandy, with William winning concessions. He died in 1100 in an unexplained hunting incident in the New Forest in Hampshire. His younger brother, **Henry I**, succeeded to the throne, and in 1106 he captured Normandy from his brother, Robert, who then spent the last twenty-eight years of his life as a prisoner.

Henry I was succeeded by his nephew, **Stephen of Blois**. In 1139, though, Henry's daughter Matilda invaded England claiming the throne; the civil war continued until 1154 when Matilda's son, Henry, count of Anjou, was recognized as heir to the throne.

The Angevins

Henry II extended his reach from England to the continent of Europe, spending only thirteen years of his reign from 1154 to 1189 in Britain and the other twenty-one years ruling in what is now France. He married Eleanor, the heiress of Aquitaine. Henry is credited with strengthening the English legal system, seen by some as the founder of English common law. Disagreements with Thomas à Becket, the archbishop of Canterbury, over church-state relations led to several estrangements. Finally, in 1170, four of the king's men, said to be acting on their own, crossed over from France to Canterbury and murdered the archbishop in his cathedral. Henry's reign ended in chaos; when he died in 1189 he was at war with his sons.

Henry's son **Richard I**, known as "Richard the Lionhearted," left to fight in the Crusades in 1190; on his return from the Holy Land, he was captured in Austria and imprisoned in Germany for a year. While he was off the throne, Philip Augustus, the king of France, invaded Normandy. Richard spent his remaining years, until 1199, fighting successfully to recover his lands.

His brother **John** lost the French lands of Normandy and Anjou in battles that ended in 1205. That was not all that he lost. Unpopular at home because of the loss of France, taxes, and disputes with the church that resulted in his excommunication by the pope in 1209, he was forced to sign a peace treaty with rebellious barons in 1215. That document, known as the Magna Carta, limited royal power and introduced a number of rights, including freedom of the church and legal reforms such as the concept of habeas corpus which requires due process of law before someone is imprisoned.

Though the Magna Carta has endured as the underpinnings of modern law, the king's battles continued and there was civil war at John's death in 1216.

The Plantagenets

John's son, **Henry III**, became king in 1216 at the age of nine, assuming full power in 1227. He came into conflict with the barons again, resulting in the outbreak of war in 1264; fighting ended in 1267 when the king promised to uphold the Magna Carta and subsequent agreements.

Edward I succeeded his father in 1272, extending his empire to Wales by invasion. He consolidated his power by creating a model Parliament in 1295, bringing in the aristocracy and church officials. The next year he invaded Scotland, seizing the king of Scots and the Stone of Scone, upon which Scottish kings were said to have been crowned for hundreds of years before. The stone is now at Edinburgh Castle.

In 1301 Edward I named his oldest son **Edward II** as the first English Prince of Wales, a title now held by Prince Charles, Queen Elizabeth II's son.

A guerrilla war led by Scottish leader William Wallace commenced, resulting in a defeat of the English at Stirling Bridge. Wallace was finally captured and executed in 1305. Edward died in 1307 as he was about to launch another campaign against the Scots. Robert the Bruce, who had become king of Scots in 1306, defeated the English in 1314 at the Battle of Bannockburn.

Edward II had a rocky reign from 1307 to 1327, in part because of debts and the defeat at Bannockburn. In 1326 Edward's wife, Isabelle of France, led an invasion against her husband. In 1327 he was forced to renounce the throne in favor of his son, Edward III, and was later murdered at Berkeley Castle.

Edward III was fourteen when he was crowned in 1327 and assumed power three years later, reigning until 1377. At the beginning of the Hundred Years War, Edward III invaded France in 1338, at first unsuccessfully; in 1346 he landed in Normandy defeating the French king, Philip IV, at the Battle of Crecy. By 1360 Edward controlled more than a fourth of France; by 1374, the French king Charles V had pushed back the English in most quarters. In 1376 the "Good Parliament," which elected the first Speaker to represent the Commons, was highly critical of the king, who withdrew to Windsor for the remaining year of his life. One lasting contribution of Edward was the founding of the Order of the Garter in 1348.

The king's grandson, **Richard II**, became king in 1377 at the age of ten. He crushed the Peasants Revolt of 1381 but fell out of favor because of alleged favoritism to members of his court; in 1388 the "Merciless Parliament" sentenced many of the king's favorites to death. The king struck back in 1397, arresting or banishing many of his opponents, including his cousin, Henry of Bolingbroke. In 1399 Henry returned and, supported by some barons, he captured and deposed Richard and was crowned **King Henry IV**. Richard died in Pontefract Castle in 1400, perhaps the victim of murder.

The Lancastrians

Most of Henry IV's reign was occupied with battles against the Welsh and from within England. In 1403 Henry defeated the Welsh and the Percys of Northumberland at the Battle of Shrewsbury. By 1408 Henry had regained power, but he took ill and died in 1413.

His son, **Henry V**, looked back across the Channel to France, capturing Harfleur and defeating the French at the Battle of Agincourt in 1415 and moving on to Normandy. In the Treaty of Troyes of 1420 he was recognized as heir to the French throne. He died of dysentery in 1422, though, and his nine-month-old son Henry was his heir.

Henry VI was crowned king of England in 1422 and took the title of king of France in 1431. Uprisings—including Joan of Arc's—and Henry's own weaknesses and mental illness led to the loss of Normandy and much of France by 1449. He became incapacitated in 1453, and the Duke of York was named Protector; Henry recovered in 1455 and sought to retake his place on the throne but a civil war broke out between the houses of York and Lancaster, known as the War of the Roses.

In 1460 the Duke of York was killed at the Battle of Wakefield, and in 1461 his son **Edward IV** was crowned king; Henry fled to Scotland but was captured and imprisoned in the Tower of London in 1465. Henry was restored to the throne in 1470; in 1471 Edward IV regained power after the Battle of Tewkesbury and Henry was put to death in the tower.

The Yorkists

Edward IV thus sat on the throne for two periods, from 1461 to 1470 and again from 1471 to 1483; during his reign he made peace with France.

After Edward IV's death, he was succeeded in April 1483 by his twelve-year-old son **Edward V** under the supposed protectorship of his uncle Richard. There immediately ensued a struggle for power between Richard and the Woodvilles, relatives of the Queen Mother. Parliament sided with Richard and declared him the rightful king on the grounds that Edward IV's marriage to Elizabeth Woodville was a breach of promise to another woman.

Richard III imprisoned Edward and his younger brother Richard in the Tower of London in June 1483 and they were never seen again, presumably murdered. In 1674 the skeletons of two children were uncovered in the area, now known as the Bloody Tower.

In 1485 Henry Tudor (a descendant of John of Gaunt, one of Edward III's younger sons) claimed the throne as Henry VII, defeating Richard at the Battle of Bosworth.

The Tudors

Henry VII consolidated some of his power among the houses of Lancaster and York by marrying Elizabeth of York, eldest daughter of Edward IV and thus ending the War of the Roses, and by strengthening his military power; he created the Yeomen of the Guards as his loyal bodyguards in 1485, the oldest military corps still in existence.

Henry also used marriage as a diplomatic tool when it came to his daughters, marrying one daughter to James IV of Scotland (producing the line that led to Mary Queen of Scots), and his other daughter to Louis XII of France.

Henry VIII took the throne at age seventeen, marrying his brother's widow Catherine of Aragon, who produced a daughter, Mary, but not a male heir. Unhappy with that situation and seeking instead the young and beautiful Anne Boleyn, a lady-in-waiting to the queen, Henry VIII divorced Catherine, a step that required he break with the Roman Catholic Church. He ultimately declared himself supreme head of the Church of England.

Anne Boleyn's only surviving child was once again a girl, Elizabeth, born in 1533. In 1536, Henry VIII dispatched Anne Boleyn; charged with incest and adultery, Henry had her executed. A few days later, Henry married Jane Seymour, who died in 1537 after successfully bearing Henry's only legitimate son, Edward.

An arranged marriage in 1540 with Anne of Cleves was intended to forge a tie between England and the Protestant princes of Germany. After a few months, though, Henry found neither Anne nor the diplomatic liaison to his liking, and he divorced her. A few months later he married Catherine Howard; she was executed in 1542 for allegedly having been unchaste prior to marriage and having committed adultery afterward.

In 1543 Henry took his sixth wife, Catherine Parr, who managed to survive him. When Henry died in 1547, his sickly, ten-year-old son ascended to the throne as **Edward VI**. Edward Seymour, Duke of Somerset, the new king's uncle, became protector.

During Edward's reign, the Church of England moved further away from the Roman Catholic Church toward Protestant beliefs. In 1550 the Duke of Northumberland overthrew and later executed Edward Seymour.

Northumberland hurriedly married his son to Lady Jane Grey, one of Henry VIII's nieces and a claimant to the throne. Edward accepted Jane as his heir, and after his death in 1553 from tuberculosis, Jane assumed the throne. However, popular support was with Mary, Catherine of Aragon's daughter and a devout Roman Catholic. Jane was removed from the throne after only nine days, and she and her husband were executed in 1554.

Mary I restored papal supremacy in England during her five-year reign. In 1554 Mary married Philip, king of Spain; the marriage was childless. The connection to Spain, though, brought England into war with France once again, resulting in the loss of Calais in 1558; thus ended England's possessions in Europe. At home, Mary pursued a campaign of religious conversion, including burning Protestants for heresy. When Mary died in 1558, the crown went to her half sister Elizabeth I, daughter of Henry VIII and Anne Boleyn.

Elizabeth I returned England to Protestantism in her reign from 1558 to 1603. She refused to marry or to name a successor, seeking to avoid foreign entanglements and domestic factionalism.

The rightful heir was her cousin, Mary, Queen of Scots, descendant of one of Henry VIII's daughters. Escaping from rebellion in Scotland, she fled to England. Imprisoned by Elizabeth in 1567, Mary plotted with English Roman Catholics and with Spain, France, and the pope.

Elizabeth perceived this as a threat to the English throne, and Mary was executed in 1587; the result was war with Spain. In 1588 Philip of Spain's invasion Armada fleet was defeated; Elizabeth also had to fight off two other Armadas in the 1590s and an Irish revolt from 1595 to 1601 that received some assistance from Spain.

Elizabeth died in 1603, still refusing to name her successor.

The Stuarts

James I, son of Mary, Queen of Scots, had been king of Scotland for thirty-six years when he became king of England as well. Renowned for his creation of a new translation of the Bible, still known as the King James Version, James was relatively tolerant in religious matters, but the attempt by Guy Fawkes and other Roman Catholic conspirators to blow up the Houses of Parliament in 1605 was met by the reimposition of strict penalties on Roman Catholics.

James employed the architect Inigo Jones to build the Banqueting House in Whitehall, which still exists.

The outbreak of the Thirty Years War in 1618 increased financial pressures and widened the conflict between the king and Parliament over foreign policy. When James died in 1625, England was on the edge of war with Spain.

Charles I, James I's successor, ran into difficulties raising funds to pay for wars against France and Spain; Parliament was refusing new taxes. Because they rebelled against his demands he dissolved Parliament and governed for eleven years without it. In 1640 he was forced to call Parliament to pay for a war against the Scots brought about when he tried to impose an Anglican prayer book. An attempt to arrest leaders of the House of Commons and a Roman Catholic rebellion in Ireland caused the outbreak of civil war in 1642.

The English revolution was led by Oliver Cromwell. Charles's army was eventually defeated, and in 1649 he was put on trial for waging war against his own people; condemned to death, he was executed at Whitehall in London.

The Commonwealth/The Interregnum

Cromwell's military successes forced Charles I's son, Charles, into foreign exile. In the period from 1649 to 1660, England was a republic, a time known as the Interregnum ("between reigns") by Royalists, and as the Commonwealth by others.

Cromwell and Parliament clashed over the wording of a constitution and the balance of power between the ruler and legislature as well as religious issues. In 1653 Parliament was dissolved and Cromwell became lord protector, although he later refused the offer of the throne and squabbles continued.

After Cromwell's death in 1658, the army invited Charles I's son, Charles, to become king.

Charles II punished the signers of Charles I's death warrant but otherwise introduced some measure of political tolerance. Religious differences continued, including attempts to exclude Roman Catholics from government and an effort to block James, Charles's Roman Catholic brother and heir, from the throne.

Charles encouraged the building of the Greenwich Observatory, and he was a patron of Sir Christopher Wren in the design and building of Saint Paul's Cathedral and other London buildings.

Charles died in 1685, becoming a Roman Catholic on his deathbed.

James II reigned uneasily for just three years, fighting off an uprising by Charles's illegitimate son, the Duke of Monmouth, in 1685. He attempted to give civic equality to Roman Catholic and Protestant dissenters, which brought him into conflict with Parliament. When his second wife, Mary of Modena, a Roman Catholic, gave birth to a son to be later known as James Stuart, it seemed that a Catholic dynasty would be established.

However, William of Orange, Protestant husband of James's elder daughter, Mary by his first wife, Anne Hyde, a Protestant, was welcomed when he invaded in 1688. The army and navy backed William, and James fled to France.

In 1689 Parliament declared that James had abdicated by deserting the kingdom. **William and Mary** were offered the throne as joint monarchs. Parliament drew up a Declaration of Rights, which limited the sovereign's power and reaffirmed Parliament's control over taxation and legislation. Roman Catholics were excluded from the throne, and the sovereign was required in the coronation oath to swear to maintain the Protestant religion. Parliament tightened controls over spending and use of the armed forces by the sovereign. And many personal and political freedoms were put in place for the first time.

The Bill of Rights had established the order of succession as the heirs of Mary II, Anne, and then William III. But by 1700 Mary had died childless, the last of Anne's seventeen children had died, and William was dying.

The Act of Settlement of 1701 was intended to assure Protestant succession to the throne as well as strengthen the parliamentary system of government. No Roman Catholic or anyone married to a Roman Catholic could sit on the throne. The sovereign now had to swear to maintain the Church of England and, after 1707, the Church of Scotland. The Act declared that the heir to the throne was Princess Sophia, James I's granddaughter, and her Protestant heirs of the House of Hanover.

When William died in 1702, his sister-in-law **Anne** ascended to the throne as the last British sovereign of the house of Stuart. She was the second daughter of King James II; in 1683 she was married to Prince George of Denmark. Soon after she was crowned, the War of the Spanish Succession began.

During her reign the importance of party politics grew, with the Whigs supporting limited monarchy and religious tolerance, and Tories favoring a strong monarchy and the religious power of the Church of England.

Anne continued William's efforts to unite the kingdoms of England and Scotland. In 1707 the Act of Union led to the dissolution of the English and Scottish

Parliaments, replaced by a unified body, with a common flag and coinage; many Scottish legal and religious institutions were preserved.

The Hanoverians

Sophia died two months before Queen Anne in 1714, and under the Act of Settlement, her oldest son **George I** inherited the throne despite the claims of several dozen Roman Catholics closer to the throne.

George I spoke German and French and a little English and regularly visited Hanover. Family infighting, including the imprisonment of his wife by the king in 1694, led to an estrangement with his son George. Unfamiliar with the customs of his own country, the king relied heavily on his ministers. He died in 1727 on a visit to Hanover.

George II ruled from 1727 to 1760, and like his father seemed to prefer Germany to Britain as his home, losing popular support as a result. He committed British troops on behalf of German interests in the War of the Austrian Succession from 1740 to 1748, becoming in 1743 at the age of sixty the last British sovereign to fight alongside his soldiers against the French at the Battle of Dettingen in Germany. During his reign, British power was consolidated in India and Canada. His son Frederick died in 1751, and George's grandson inherited the throne in 1760.

George III, the first British sovereign of the Hanoverian house to be born and educated as an Englishman, is perhaps best known as the king in power when the American colonies rose in successful revolution. He dissolved into insanity beginning in 1788.

George IV took the crown on his father's death in 1820. Already a controversial figure, he did not sit easily on the throne. In 1783 he had secretly married a Roman Catholic widow, Mrs. Maria Anne Fitzherbert, in violation of the law regarding the royal family. Faced with mounting debts, he allowed Parliament to declare the marriage illegal two years later; in 1795, again to help pay debts, he married his cousin, Caroline of Brunswick, but separated after the birth of their daughter, Princess Charlotte, in 1796. When he tried to divorce Caroline on charges of adultery, her trial had to be abandoned in the face of public protests.

George IV acquired many important works of art now part of the Royal Collection, built the Royal Pavilion at Brighton, and made major enhancements to Windsor Castle and Buckingham Palace.

George was succeeded by his brother, **William IV**, in 1830. During his seven-year reign, William signed reforms to the parliamentary system that ended some electoral abuses. His children with Princess Adelaide of Saxe-Meiningen died in infancy.

William's niece, **Victoria**, took the throne in 1837 at the age of eighteen, beginning the longest reign in British history, lasting until 1901. Women were not allowed to hold the Hanoverian throne, though, and the German and English monarchies separated at that time.

She had nine children with her husband Prince Albert of Saxe-Coburg and Gotha; many of the children were married into other European royal families.

Albert was an enthusiastic supporter of arts and industry, organizing the Great Exhibition of 1851, which led to the Victoria and Albert Museum, the Natural History Museum, the Imperial College, and the Albert Hall in London. In 1861 Albert died of typhoid and Victoria retreated into seclusion for many years.

Saxe-Coburg-Gotha

Victoria's son, **Edward VII**, had to wait until the age of fifty-nine to become king, the longest period as heir apparent in British history. He devoted much of his efforts to diplomacy in Europe, a task made somewhat easier by the fact that he was related to nearly every sovereign on the Continent. He died in 1910, and was succeeded by his son George V.

The Windsors

George V's early years were overshadowed by the First World War; he made hundreds of visits to troops and hospitals and pressed for proper treatment of prisoners of war. In 1917, in the face of anti-German sentiment, he changed the family name from Saxe-Coburg-Gotha to Windsor, after the name of the family castle. He died in 1936.

The king's son **Edward VIII** succeeded to the throne in January 1936 for a reign that lasted less than a year. Popular for his war record and social causes at home, he abdicated the throne in December because of his love affair with a twice-divorced American, Wallis Simpson, a liaison which was unacceptable to the Church of England and the government. He died in 1972 in Paris.

Edward VIII's brother Albert had grown up not expecting to be king. In 1923 he had married Lady Elizabeth Bowes-Lyon, and they produced two daughters, Elizabeth and Margaret. When Albert ascended to the throne, he took the name **George VI**.

In 1939 he became the first British sovereign to visit the United States. During the war, he and his wife visited bombed areas in London and around the country, spending most of the time living at Buckingham Palace, which was itself bombed nine times. He died in 1952.

Queen Elizabeth II

Elizabeth Alexandra Mary was born in London on April 21, 1926, the first child of the Duke and Duchess of York, who were later to become King George VI and Queen Elizabeth.

Her early years were spent at 145 Piccadilly, the London house taken by her parents shortly after her birth. She also spent time at White Lodge in Richmond Park and at the country homes of her grandparents, King George V and Queen Mary, and the earl and countess of Strathmore. When she was six years old, her parents took over Royal Lodge in Windsor Great Park as their own country home.

Princess Elizabeth was educated at home with Princess Margaret, her younger sister. According to her official biography, she studied constitutional history and law, art, and music. Her other interests included horses, amateur theatricals, and swimming. Elizabeth's exposure to the public grew during the war years. In 1942 she was appointed colonel of the Grenadier Guards, and on her sixteenth birthday carried out her first public engagement, an inspection of the regiment. She also began to accompany the king and queen on many of their tours within Britain.

When she reached her eighteenth birthday, Princess Elizabeth was appointed a counsellor of state and carried out some of the duties of head of state during the king's absence. Her first official overseas tour took place in 1947 when she accompanied her parents to South Africa. Shortly after the royal family returned from the trip, it was announced that princess was engaged to Lieutenant Philip Mountbatten, the son of Prince Andrew of Greece and a great-great-grandson of Queen Victoria. They were married in Westminster Abbey in November 1947.

In 1952 illness forced King George VI to cancel his plans to visit Africa, Australia, and New Zealand. Princess Elizabeth took his place accompanied by Prince Philip. On February 6, in Kenya, she received the news of her father's death and her own accession to the throne. Elizabeth's formal coronation took place in Westminster Abbey June 2, 1953.

Prince Charles, now the Prince of Wales, heir apparent to the throne, was born in 1948. His sister, Princess Anne, now the Princess Royal, arrived two years later. The queen's third child, Prince Andrew, was born in 1960, and Prince Edward in 1964. Charles married Lady Diana Spencer in 1981; their son, Prince William of Wales, was born in 1982 and is second in line for the throne after Charles.

The queen's private interests include horses and dogs. As an owner and breeder of thoroughbreds, she occasionally visits race meetings and other equestrian events to watch her horses run. In 1984, 1986, and 1991, she made brief private visits to the United States to see stud farms in Kentucky. She usually attends the Derby at Epsom and the Summer Race Meeting at Ascot, which has been a royal occasion since 1911.

The first royal Corgi was Dookie, acquired by King George VI in 1933. The king added a second dog, Jane, in 1938 and two of her puppies were kept in the family. For her eighteenth birthday, Princess Elizabeth was given a Corgi named Susan; the queen's current Corgis are directly descended from Susan. She also owns four "dorgis," a breed mixing Corgis and Dachshunds. According to the palace, the queen looks after her dogs as much as possible. They live in her private apartments and move from house to house with her.

The Royal Collection

The Royal Collection is one of the world's greatest gatherings of art, including some nine thousand paintings, thousands of drawings, watercolors, and prints, as well as many thousands of books, items of furniture, sculpture, glass, porcelain, arms and armor, textiles, and jewelry (including the Crown Jewels).

Most of the collection held by Charles I was dispersed by Oliver Cromwell during the Reformation; today's Royal Collection is mostly made up of items gathered by the royal family after the Restoration in 1660.

The treasures are held by the queen in trust for her successors and for the nation and are not owned by her as a private individual. The administration of

Price Bands
❶ £1–£3
❷ £3–£5
❸ £5–£7
❹ £7–£10
❺ £10–£15
❻ £15 and up

the Royal Collection is funded by visitor admissions to Windsor Castle, the Queen's Gallery, the Royal Mews at Buckingham Palace, the Palace of Holyroodhouse in Edinburgh, and the shops at these locations.

Most of the collection is on display at locations including Buckingham Palace, Kensington Palace, Hampton Court Palace, Saint James's Palace, the Tower of London, Kew Palace and Cottage, Windsor Castle, Frogmore House, Sandringham House, Balmoral Castle, the Palace of Holyroodhouse, and Osborne House. A large portion of the collection is on loan to national institutions, including the British Museum, National Gallery, Museum of London, Victoria and Albert Museum, National Museum of Wales, National Gallery of Scotland, and Brighton Pavilion.

You'll find details about visits to the Buckingham Palace state rooms and the Royal Mews in Chapter 11. For information about tours of Windsor Castle and Frogmore House and Mausoleum, see Chapter 31.

The Palace of Holyroodhouse

Edinburgh, about four hundred miles north of London. Open daily, April 1 through end of October 9:30 A.M. to 5:15 P.M., November 1 through end of March 9:30 A.M. to 3:45 P.M. Admission: adult, ❸; child, ❶; family ❺; senior, ❷. ☎ (0131) 556-1096.

The palace, founded as a monastery in 1128, is the Queen's official residence in Scotland. It is the setting for royal events, including an annual garden party for several thousand guests.

The Queen's Holyrood week usually runs from the end of June to the beginning of July; during her stay she carries out official engagements in Scotland.

Sandringham House

About one hundred miles due north of London, near the ancient port of King's Lynn. Palladian mansion, museum, and seven-thousand-acre grounds open late March to late July and mid-August to early October. Admission: adult, ❸; child ❶; family ❺; senior, ❷. ☎ (0148) 576-2234.

Sandringham was purchased by Queen Victoria in 1861 for her son, later to be Edward VII.

Balmoral Castle

Another of Queen Victoria's homes, Balmoral is located in northeastern Scotland in Braemar. The estate grounds, gardens, and exhibitions are open to visitors from mid-April through the end of July. Admission: ❻. For information, contact the Balmoral Estates office at ☎ (0133) 974-2334. You can also obtain information from the Scottish Tourist Board in Edinburgh by calling ☎ (0131) 332-2433 or consulting 🖳 www.holiday.scotland.net/main.

Part VI
Theater and Shopping

Chapter 24
The West End Theater District

London's theater district—referred to by most as the "West End" even though its boundaries now reach outside that small section of the central city—is one of the most vibrant entertainment scenes in the world, rivaling and in some ways surpassing, New York's Broadway.

The West End stages, in and around Covent Garden and Leicester Square, are relatively intimate and often redolent of theater history.

Theater Tickets

Prices range from about £12 to £50 for most shows. Musicals and productions with big-name stars usually command top dollar—top pound, actually—while dramas, revivals and productions by small companies cost less.

In slower seasons such as winter and early spring, it is common to see special offers such as two-fer coupons for many shows. If you qualify, you can also look for lower-priced senior or student tickets.

If your heart is set on seeing a particular play or musical, or a particular show on a specific day, you may have to pay premium rates to a ticket broker.

For those who want to plan way ahead, you can purchase tickets to many shows through agencies in the United States such as Applause at ☎ (800) 451-9930; Edwards & Edwards at ☎ (800) 223-6108; or London Theatre & More at ☎ (800) 683-0799. Expect to pay list price for tickets, plus a service charge.

There are also numerous ticket agencies in London that generally have blocks of seats for most shows, again at premium rates.

For discounted tickets, the best bet in town for many visitors is the **Same-Day Ticket Window at Leicester Square.** Here you can buy tickets for half price plus a £2 service charge for many current shows. Theaters release unsold tickets a few hours before matinees and evening performances. The booth sells the best available seats at half price; get there early for the best selection.

Not all shows participate in the program, though, and don't count on front-row-center seats to the hottest show in town—although stranger things have happened.

The half-price booth opens daily at noon, and lines begin to form about

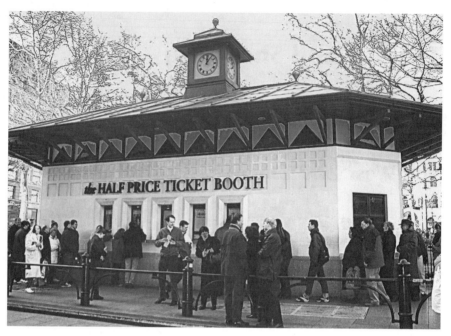

The ticket booth in Leicester Square
Photo by Corey Sandler

thirty minutes ahead of then. One queue is for matinee tickets (generally Wednesday, Thursday, and Saturday, with a few Sunday shows) and the other is for evening productions. The ticket booth closes at 6:30 P.M. Monday to Saturday, and at 3:30 P.M. on Sunday.

One more thing about the Leicester Square booth: it's cash only. No credit cards, no checks, and no traveler's checks. Consider that you'll have to come to the counter with a wallet full of pounds, a fact that is not overlooked by pickpockets and other unsavory folk. There are several ATMs at banks near the square. Foreign exchange bureaus will also issue cash for traveler's checks or credit card advances, although most will add a hefty service fee. In any case, take precautions with money and tickets you carry through the area.

There are also several unofficial theater discount booths in and around Leicester Square that sometimes offer tickets at reduced rates through direct arrangement with some theaters. Be sure to examine your tickets before handing over your money. (Use a credit card if possible, to add a layer of protection to your transaction. In fact, use a credit card anywhere you can for protection and to save on foreign exchange costs.)

If you are truly desperate, you may consider buying seats from a ticket tout cruising Leicester Square or in front of one of the theaters. Be very careful: examine the tickets closely for date and list price and beware of counterfeits.

Note that not all London theaters are air-conditioned; look in the listings that follow for "AC" for summer relief.

London Theaters

Adelphi. Strand. Underground: Charing Cross. AC. Tickets: ☎ (020) 7344-0055. In mid-2001 *Chicago*, a bold, brassy, and cynical transplant from Broadway was in its third year. ▣ www.chicagothemusical.com.

A theater has stood at this location since 1806 when the Sans Pareil was built by John Scott, a local tradesman, to push the career of his daughter as an actress. It was sold and renamed as the Adelphi in 1819. From about 1837 to 1845, many of Charles Dickens's novels were performed as plays here. The first of several rebuildings took place in 1858 when the theater was refashioned in the style of the Opera Comique of Paris. The most recent rebuilding took place in 1930. Seating capacity is 1,500.

Albery. Saint Martin's Lane. Underground: Leicester Square. AC. Tickets: ☎ (020) 7369-1730.

One of the great drama houses of London, the Albery dates back to 1903 when it opened as the New Theatre. Noel Coward's first play, *I'll Leave It to You*, opened here in 1920, and the first London production of George Bernard Shaw's *St. Joan* was presented in 1924. Among those who trod its boards were Edith Evans, John Gielgud, Laurence Olivier, Michael Redgrave, and Ralph Richardson. The theater was renamed in 1973 in honor of Sir Bronson Albery, the longtime theater director. Seating capacity is 879.

Aldwych. Aldwych. Underground: Holborn/Covent Garden. AC. Tickets: ☎ (020) 7416-6009. Opened in 1905, the Aldwych served from 1960 to 1982 as the home of the Royal Shakespeare Company. Seating capacity is 1,092.

Apollo. Shaftesbury Avenue. Underground: Piccadilly Circus. AC. Tickets: ☎ (020) 7494-5070. Designed for musical theater, the Apollo opened in 1901.

Apollo Victoria. 17 Wilton Road. Underground: Victoria. AC. Tickets: ☎ (020) 7416-6054. ▣ www.reallyuseful.com.

Built as the New Victoria Cinema, the Apollo Victoria was converted for musicals in 1979 and converted again as a special-purpose theater in 1984 for Andrew Lloyd Webber's musical on wheels, *Starlight Express*. It is the second-longest-running show in the West End, after Lloyd Webber's *Cats*. The full seating capacity is a gargantuan 2,572, but there are only about 1,500 seats in the *Starlight* configuration.

Cambridge. Earlham Street. Underground: Covent Garden. AC. Tickets: ☎ (020) 7494-5083. In 2001 Andrew Lloyd Webber's *The Beautiful Game* was running. ▣ www.reallyuseful.com.

Opened in 1930, this was the home from 1946 to 1948 of the New London Opera Company. It reopened in 1987 after being shut several years.

Coliseum. Saint Martin's Lane. Underground: Charing Cross. Tickets: ☎ (020) 7632-8300. Home of the Sadler's Wells Opera Company.

Opened in 1904 as a variety house, the Coliseum featured an ornate Edwardian interior. Among early artists in variety shows were Edith Evans, Lillie Langtry, and Sarah Bernhardt. It was converted to use as a cinema in 1961 and went back to live production in 1968 when it became the home of the opera company. It has the largest capacity of active theaters, with 2,358 seats.

Comedy. Panton Street. Underground: Piccadilly Circus. Tickets: ☎ (020) 7369-1731. Opened in 1881 for comic operas, the Comedy was rebuilt most recently in the 1950s. There are 820 seats.

Criterion. Piccadilly Circus. Underground: Piccadilly Circus. AC. Tickets: ☎ (020) 7369-1737. 🖳 www.reducedshakespeare.com. Home to the ongoing comic reviews of the Reduced Shakespeare Company for several years.

Originally built in 1874, the Criterion was one of the first underground theaters in London. During World War II it was used as a BBC studio. There are 605 seats.

Dominion. Tottenham Court Road. Underground: Tottenham Court Road. Tickets: ☎ (020) 7656-1888. 🖳 www.notredameonline.com. In 2001 the French musical *Notre-Dame de Paris* was in its second year.

Built in 1929, the Dominion was converted to a cinema in 1932, before going back to live theater and concerts in the 1980s. The capacity is 2,007.

Donmar Warehouse. Thomas Neal's, Earlham Street. Underground: Covent Garden. AC. Tickets: ☎ (020) 7369-1732.

The Donmar Warehouse is an alternative theater with an unusual history; it was originally the vat room of a brewery converted for use as an early cinema in 1920 and then converted to use as a banana warehouse. It was changed back to a theater in 1960; after renovations in 1977, it was used as a studio theater by the Royal Shakespeare Company and more recently as an intimate home for a wide range of drama.

Drury Lane/Theatre Royal. Catherine Street. Underground: Covent Garden. AC. Tickets: ☎ (020) 7344-4444.

One of the most storied theaters in London, the Theater Royal was first built in 1663. Closed in 1665 and 1666 because of the Great Plague and then the Great Fire, it burned down in 1672 but was rebuilt that same year. Sheridan's *School for Scandal* was first produced here in 1777. The theater was destroyed by fire again in 1809 and rebuilt in 1812 in the form you'll find it now. In recent years it has been home to many well-loved musicals, including *My Fair Lady* in 1958. There are 2,188 seats.

Duchess. Cathering Street. Underground: Covent Garden. AC. Tickets: ☎ (020) 7494-5075. The Duchess is a smaller theater built in 1929. It's longest engagement was for *Oh! Calcutta*, which ran from 1974 through 1979. There are 487 seats.

Fortune. Russell Street. Underground: Covent Garden. AC. Tickets: ☎ (020) 7836-2238. Opened in 1924, the Fortune was home from 1961 through 1964 for the beloved *Beyond the Fringe* revue by Alan Bennett, Peter Cook, Jonathan Miller, and Dudley Moore. There are 432 seats.

Garrick. Charing Cross Road. Underground: Charing Cross. Tickets: ☎ (020) 7494-5085. Opened in 1889, the Garrick has 636 seats.

Gielgud. Shaftesbury Avenue. Underground: Piccadilly Circus. AC. Tickets: ☎ (020) 7494-5066. The Gielgud opened as the Hicks Theatre in 1906; it was renamed in honor of actor Sir John Gielgud in 1990. There are 897 seats. The theater is used for drama and comedy. In 2001 a production of *The Graduate* settled in.

Globe. New Globe Walk. Underground: Mansion House/London Bridge. Tickets: ☎ (020) 7401-9919. See Chapter 17 for details on the Globe Theatre.

Haymarket. Theatre Royal, Haymarket. Underground: Piccadilly Circus. AC. Tickets: ☎ (020) 7930-8800. The Theatre Royal was opened in 1720; it was rebuilt in 1821 just to the south. There are about 880 seats.

Her Majesty's. Haymarket. Underground: Piccadilly Circus. AC. Tickets: ☎ (020) 7494-5400. Andrew Lloyd Webber's *The Phantom of the Opera* opened here in 1986 and was still running in mid-2001. 🖳 www.thephantomofthe opera.com.

One of the great opera houses of England at various points in its life, a theater opened here in 1705 under the management of dramatist William Congreve. In 1711 Handel's *Rinaldo* was performed, and for the next forty years many of the composer's works were performed. The theater was destroyed by fire in 1789 and rebuilt, only to burn down again in 1867, be rebuilt again, and then demolished in 1891. The present structure was erected in 1897.

London Apollo. Queen Caroline Street, Hammersmith. Underground: Hammersmith. Tickets: ☎ (020) 7416-6083.

London Palladium. Argyll Street. Underground: Oxford Circus. AC. Tickets: ☎ (020) 7494-5020. Originally the site of a permanent circus, in 1910 an opulent music hall that featured telephones connecting the luxury boxes was constructed here. There are 2,317 seats.

Lyceum. Wellington Street. Underground: Covent Garden/Charing Cross. AC. Tickets: ☎ (020) 7656-1800. 🖳 www.disney.co.uk. Disney's *The Lion King* roared into town in 1999 and was still playing in mid-2001.

Theatre Royal Haymarket

The first Lyceum was built in 1771 as a concert and exhibition space. In 1802 it was the site of Madame Tussaud's first waxworks exhibition in London. Destroyed by fire in 1830, it was rebuilt nearby several years later. The interior was demolished in 1903 and was rebuilt in 1904 as a music hall before being converted for theatrical productions; after World War II it was once again used as a dance hall before going back to use as a theater.

Lyric. Shaftesbury Avenue. Underground: Piccadilly Circus. Tickets: ☎ (020) 7494-5045. Constructed in 1888 for comic operas, the Lyric has 961 seats.

New London. Drury Lane. Underground: Holborn. AC. Tickets: ☎ (020) 7405-0072. ▇ www.reallyuseful.com. *Cats* has been running here seemingly forever—but actually only since 1981. The show is the longest-running West End musical ever.

Opened in 1973 on the site of the Winter Garden Theatre, this has been the location of theatrical enterprises dating back to Elizabethan times. The unusual stadium-like configuration seats 1,102 guests.

The Old Vic. Waterloo Road. Underground: Waterloo. AC. Tickets: ☎ (020) 7928-7616.

Located in South Bank across the Thames from the West End, the Old Vic was built in 1818 as the Royal Coburg Theatre, with parts of its foundation taken from the thirteenth-century Savoy Palace. Its name was changed in 1833 to the Royal Victoria in honor of the young princess and became a very popular music hall presenting a vaudeville mix. It was renamed again as the New Victoria after reconstruction of the interior in 1871, later taking as its name the Old Vic. It was damaged during World War II. There are 1,067 seats.

Open Air. Inner Circle, Regent's Park. Underground: Baker Street. Tickets: ☎ (020) 7486-2431. ▇ www.open-air-theatre.org.uk.

In summer months, the Open Air is an outdoor repertory theater, which includes productions of Shakespeare. There have been outdoor performances in Regent's Park since 1900. The amphitheater was reconstructed in 1975 and has 1,200 seats.

Palace. Shaftesbury Avenue. Underground: Leicester Square. Tickets: ☎ (020) 7434-0909. *Les Misérables* has occupied the barricades since 1986. ▇ www. lesmis.com.

Built in 1891 as the Royal English Opera House, the Palace opened with Arthur Sullivan's grand opera *Ivanhoe*. In later years it served as a music and variety hall and as a cinema, going back to musicals in the 1920s. Rodgers and Hammerstein's *Sound of Music* ran here from 1961 to 1967, and Andrew Lloyd Webber's *Jesus Christ Superstar* from 1972 to 1980. There are 1,400 seats.

Phoenix. Charing Cross Road. Underground: Tottenham Court Road. Tickets: ☎ (020) 8369-1733. *Blood Brothers* opened in 1991 and was still offered in mid-2001. ▇ www.act-arts.co.uk.

Built in 1930, the Phoenix opened with Noël Coward's *Private Lives*, starring Coward, Gertrude Lawrence, and Laurence Olivier. There are 1,012 seats.

Piccadilly. Denman Street. Underground: Piccadilly Circus. AC. Tickets: ☎ (020) 7369-1734. Built in 1928 and reconstructed in 1960, the Piccadilly briefly served as a cinema in the 1960s. There are 1,132 seats.

The Playhouse. Northumberland Avenue. Underground: Embankment. AC. Tickets: ☎ (020) 7839-4401.

Built in 1882, the Playhouse put forth the first production of George Bernard Shaw's *Arms and the Man* in 1894. It was rebuilt in 1907 after part of the nearby Charing Cross station collapsed onto the structure. From 1951 to 1975 it was a BBC studio, home of the beloved *Goon Show*.

Prince Edward. Old Compton Street. Underground: Leicester Square. AC. Tickets: ☎ (020) 7447-5400. Opened in 1930, the Prince Edward has also served as a cinema and cabaret. There are 1,666 seats.

Prince of Wales. Coventry Street. Underground: Piccadilly Circus. AC. Tickets: ☎ (020) 7839-5987. Built in 1884, the Prince of Wales has 1,133 seats.

Queen's. Shaftesbury Avenue. Underground: Piccadilly Circus. AC. Tickets: ☎ (020) 7494-5040. Opened in 1907, the Queen's has 979 seats.

Royal Court Downstairs. Duke of York's, Saint Martin's Lane. Underground: Leicester Square. Tickets: ☎ (020) 7565-5000.

Many of George Bernard Shaw's plays were first produced at the Royal Court Downstairs, which was built in 1888. Converted to a movie house in 1934, it was heavily damaged by bombing in 1940 and was rebuilt in 1952 to host live productions once again. There are 395 seats.

A second theater, the Theatre Upstairs, uses the former rehearsal room of the Royal Court for experimental productions.

Royal National Theatre. South Bank Centre. Underground: Waterloo. AC. Tickets: ☎ (020) 7928-2252.

A national center for Shakespearian and classic English drama and new works, the National Theatre Company moved from a temporary home under the directorship of Laurence Olivier at the Old Vic across the Thames to the South Bank. The largest of the stages is the **Olivier**, with 1,160 seats, followed by the **Lyttleton** with 890, and the experimental venue of the **Cottesloe** with about four hundred.

Saint Martin's. West Street, Cambridge Circus. Underground: Leicester Square. AC. Tickets: ☎ (020) 7836-1443. 📖 www.vpsmvaud sav.co.uk/m_trap/.

Built in 1916, more than half of this theater's life has been snared by Agatha Christie's *Mousetrap*, which opened in 1952 and was still playing in 2001. There are 550 seats.

Savoy. Strand. Underground: Charing Cross/Embankment. Tickets: ☎ (020) 7836-8888.

The Savoy was opened in 1881 by Richard D'Oyly Carte as home to Gilbert and Sullivan's comic operas. In 1890, after *The Gondoliers* opened, Gilbert had a violent disagreement with D'Oyly Carte over a £500 bill for new carpets, and the famed team of Gilbert and Sullivan split apart. The theater was rebuilt in 1929 and seats 1,125.

Shaftesbury. Shaftesbury Avenue. Underground: Tottenham Court/Holborn. Tickets: ☎ (020) 7379-5399.

Built in 1911 as the New Prince's Theatre, the Shaftesbury was home to many of D'Oyly Carte's Gilbert and Sullivan productions from 1919 to 1926. It was reconstructed in the 1960s and seats 1,300.

Strand. Aldwych. Underground: Charing Cross. Tickets: ☎ (020) 7930-8800. *Buddy*, a musical tribute to rocker Buddy Holly, was into its second decade here in 2001. 🖳 www. idm.co.uk/buddy.

Opened in 1905 to present Italian opera, the Strand has 1,069 seats.

Vaudeville. Strand. Underground: Charing Cross. AC. Tickets: ☎ (020) 7836-9987. Opened in 1870 and rebuilt in 1926, the Vaudeville has 694 seats.

Victoria Palace. Victoria Street. Underground: Victoria. AC. Tickets: ☎ (020) 7834-1317. Constructed as a music hall in 1911, the Victoria Palace became home of the *Crazy Gang* variety show from 1947 until 1962, and the *Black and White Minstrels*, which ran until 1970.

Westminster. Palace Street. Underground: Victoria. The former site of the Charlotte Chapel, the Westminster was opened as a movie house in 1924 and converted to stage productions in 1931. There are six hundred seats.

Whitehall. Whitehall. Underground: Charing Cross. Tickets: ☎ (020) 7867-1119. Built in 1930, the Whitehall has 673 seats.

Wyndhams. Charing Cross Road. Underground: Leicester Square. AC. Tickets: ☎ (020) 7369-1736. In mid-2001, the long-running play was *Art*. 🖳 www.dewynters.com/art/. Built in 1899, Wyndhams has 760 seats.

London Ticket Agents

Fenchurch Booking Agency Ltd. ☎ (020) 7928-8585.

First Call. ☎ (020) 7420-0000. 🖳 www.firstcall tickets.com.

Keith Prowse and Company. U.S. ☎ (800) 669-8687. 🖳 www.keith prowse.com.

Lashmars Theatre Tickets. ☎ (020) 7493-4731. 🖳 www.londontheatre. co.uk/lashmars.

Theatre Ticket Company. ☎ (020) 7851-0300. 🖳 www.theatre ticket.com or 🖳 londontheatre bookings. com.

TheatreNet. 🖳 www.theatre net.com.

Ticketmaster. ☎ (020) 7413-1442. 🖳 www.ticket master.co.uk.

Ticketselect. ☎ (020) 7494-5494. 🖳 www.ticket select.co.uk.

Hot Lines

For an up-to-date listing of West End theater performances with links to websites of some of the shows or theaters themselves, check out the **U.K. Theatre Web** page at 🖳 www. uktw.co.uk, or the **Society of London Theatre**, at 🖳 www.OfficialLon donTheatre.co.uk.

London's West End

Artsline. Information on access by the disabled to theater, films, museums, and other arts. ☎ (020) 7388-2227. 🖳 www.artsline.org.uk.

Kidsline. Information for families. ☎ (020) 7222-8070.

Playlink. Information on adventure playgrounds. ☎ (020) 7820-3800.

Sportsline. Information on sports facilities. ☎ (020) 7222-8000.

Theatreline. Recorded information, charged at premium rates:
- Musicals. ☎ (0891) 559900.
- Plays. ☎ (0891) 559901.
- Comedy. ☎ (0891) 559902.
- Thrillers. ☎ (0891) 559903.
- Opera/ballet/dance. ☎ (0891) 559904.
- Children's shows. ☎ (0891) 559905.

Movie Theaters

The heart of London's movie district is also in and around the West End, and it is there you will find the largest screens and most impressive sound systems . . . and the highest prices. On the weekend, adult ticket prices in Leicester Square can be as high as £7.50. Prices drop by a pound or two for midweek screenings, and most theaters offer reduced-price showings on Monday.

Many of the larger cinemas allow advance telephone bookings using a credit card, charging a service fee for the privilege.

A handful of larger houses sell advanced reservations for assigned seats.

Movie schedules are published in the Sunday newspapers and in entertainment magazines such as *Time Out*.

The king of the West End. Andrew Lloyd Webber is the undisputed king of the West End, if not the rest of the theater world. *Cats* has been on the prowl in London since 1981, and *The Phantom of the Opera*, has occupied a theater in the West End since 1986. He is also the composer of *The Beautiful Game, Jesus Christ Superstar, Starlight Express, Evita*, and other shows.

The Phantom alone has grossed more than $3.2 billion in worldwide ticket sales; that doesn't even include T-shirts, CDs, and books.

In 2000 Andrew Lloyd Webber and a partner paid more than $150 million to buy the Stoll Moss group, adding ten more London theaters to the three he already owned.

His properties include the London Palladium and the Theatre Royal Drury Lane, two of the largest and best showplaces in the West

Chapter 25
Markets and Shops

Among the true delights of London are the shops. In a time when most American cities have lost many of their smaller retail outlets and much of their downtown character to suburban malls and superstores, London's many neighborhoods still offer small shops that sell just about anything.

My daughter succumbed to the city's charms when we stumbled across a bead store that sprawled across two floors of a Soho shop. When she wasn't browsing for beads, she was trawling for trinkets at one of the ubiquitous Accessorize shops. My son could (and did) spend hours cruising the music and bookstores, exiting from one to enter the next.

Markets

Bermondsey (New Caledonian). Bermondsey Square. Underground: Borough/London Bridge. Open Friday 6 A.M. to 2 P.M. Paintings, silver, furniture, and other objects.

Berwick Street. Berwick and Rupert Streets. Underground: Piccadilly Circus or Leicester Square. Open Monday to Saturday 9 A.M. to 6 P.M. Fruits, vegetables, and trinkets.

Brick Lane. Brick Lane and surrounding streets. Underground: Aldgate East or Shoreditch. Open Sunday 5 A.M. to 2 P.M. A bit of everything, from used furniture, clothing, books, CDs, to funky modern rags.

Brixton Market. Electric Avenue, Pope's Road, and Brixton Station Road. Also within Granville and Market Row indoor arcades. Underground: Brixton. Open Monday through Saturday from 8:30 A.M. to 5:30 P.M.; closes at 1 P.M. on Wednesday. The smells, tastes, and styles of the Caribbean transplanted to London and thriving in a lively section of stalls.

Camden. Camden High Street, Camden Lock, and the surrounding area. Underground: Camden Town. Camden Lock is open 9:30 A.M. to 5:30 P.M. daily; street stalls open Saturday and Sunday 10 A.M. to 6 P.M. Clothing new and used, arts and crafts, antiques and furniture, and food.

Columbia Road. Columbia Road. Underground: Shoreditch/Old Street. Open Sunday 8 A.M. to 12:30 P.M. Flowers and plants.

Covent Garden. Underground: Covent Garden. 🖳 www.cgma.gov.uk. The former wholesale market has been transformed into a lively collection of shops, stalls, and eateries worth a visit any day and at most any time. And the nearby Neal Street area offers some classic hippie shops selling beads, funky clothing, and music.

Greenwich. Market Square, College Approach, Stockweel Street, and surrounding area. Rail: Greenwich. Open Saturday and Sunday 9 A.M. to 5 P.M. Used books, music, jewelry, crafts, and clothing.

Portobello Road. Portobello Road. Underground: Ladbroke Grove or Notting Hill Gate. 🖳 www.portobelloroad.co.uk/index.asp. Antiques market open Saturday 7 A.M. to 5 P.M. General market open Monday to Saturday from 9 A.M. to 5 P.M., until 1 P.M. Thursday. The premier antiques market of London. Surrounding stores sell used (not necessarily antique) furniture, clothing, jewelry, household objects, and presumably fresher fruits and vegetables.

Department Stores

Fortnum and Mason. 181 Piccadilly. Underground: Piccadilly Circus. Open 9:30 A.M. to 6 P.M. daily except Sunday. ☎ (020) 7734-8040. 🖳 www.fortnum andmason.co.uk. Home of some of the best-dressed food, provisions, conservative fashion, and sales clerks.

Harrods. 87–135 Brompton Road. Underground: Knightsbridge. Open Monday, Tuesday, and Saturday 10 A.M. to 6 P.M., Wednesday through Friday 10 A.M. to 7 P.M. ☎ (020) 7730-1234. 🖳 www.harrods.com. Very, very British, with exquisite appointments and attentive service. You can buy just about anything to wear or eat or just spend a day wandering the dozens of halls within.

John Lewis. 278–306 Oxford Street. Underground: Oxford Circus. Open Monday to Wednesday and Friday 9:30 A.M. to 6 P.M., Thursday 10 A.M. to 8 P.M., and Saturday 9 A.M. to 6 P.M. ☎ (020) 7629-7711. Fine haberdashery and old-line household goods.

Liberty. 210–20 Regent Street. Underground: Oxford Circus. Open Monday to Wednesday 10 A.M. to 6:30 P.M., Friday and Saturday 10 A.M. to 7 P.M., and until 8 P.M. Thursday. Open Sunday noon to 6 P.M. ☎ (020) 7734-1234. 🖳 www. liberty.co.uk. A wide range of home goods and fashion accessories, including its trademark silk items.

Marks & Spencer. There is a large outpost of the chain at 458 Oxford Street near Oxford Circus. Underground: Bond Street or Marble Arch. Open Monday to Friday 9 A.M. to 8 P.M., Saturday 9 A.M. to 7 P.M., and Sunday noon to 6 P.M. ☎ (020) 7935-7954. 🖳 www.marksandspencer.com. You'll also find branches of Marks & Spencer just about everywhere in the United Kingdom; the store is famous for its underwear and high-tone foodstuffs.

Selfridges. 400 Oxford Street. Underground: Bond Street or Marble Arch. Monday to Wednesday 10 A.M. to 7 P.M., Thursday and Friday until 8 P.M., Saturday 9:30 A.M. to 7 P.M., and Sunday noon to 6 P.M. ☎ (020) 7629-1234. 🖳 www.selfridges.co.uk. Another mega fashion and household department store. In recent years it has gone through a massive, lavish update. The spectacular Food Hall is not to be missed; take care not to browse on an empty stomach.

Fashion

Agnes B. 35–36 Floral Street. Underground: Covent Garden. ☎ (020) 7379-1992. High-tone Ts.

Burberry. 18–22 Haymarket. Underground: Piccadilly Circus. ☎ (020) 7930-3343. 🖳 www.burberry.com. The London outpost of the famed clothing store.

Comme des Garçons. 59 Brook Street. Underground: Bond Street. ☎ (020) 7493-1258. Vive la différence.

DKNY. 27 Old Bond Street. Underground: Bond Street. ☎ (020) 7499-8089. 🖳 www.dkny.com. London outpost of New York fave.

Dolce & Gabbana. 175 Sloane Street. Underground: Sloane Square. ☎ (020) 7235-0335. 🖳 www.dolcegabbanaonline.com. Italian chic.

Emporio Armani. 187–191 Brompton Road. Underground: Knightsbridge. ☎ (020) 7823-8818. 🖳 www.emporioarmani.com. Armani suits and knitwear.

Issey Miyake. 270 Brompton Road. Underground: South Kensington. ☎ (020) 7581-3760. Japanese high fashion.

Laura Ashley. 256–258 Regent Street. Underground: Oxford Circus. ☎ (020) 7437-9760. 🖳 www.laura-ashley.com. Home base for the global women's wear and home furnishings outlet.

Arts and Crafts

Atlantis. 146 Brick Lane. Underground: Aldgate East. ☎ (020) 7377-8855. It lays claim as the country's largest art supply store.

The Bead Shop. 43 Neal Street. Underground: Covent Garden. ☎ (020) 7240-0931. A bustling bazaar of beads on two floors.

Beatties. 202 High Holborn. Underground: Holborn. ☎ (020) 7405-6285. Trains and model kits; branches throughout the city.

L. Cornelissen & Son. 105 Great Russell Street. Underground: Tottenham Court Road. ☎ (020) 7636-1045. Rare, unusual, and ordinary art supplies.

Creative Quilting. 3 Bridge Road., Hampton Court, East Molesey, Surrey. Rail: Hampton Court. ☎ (020) 8941-7075. All things quilting.

Creativity. 45 New Oxford Street. Underground: Holborn or Tottenham Court Road. ☎ (020) 7240-2945. All things needlepoint, knitting, tapestry, and embroidery.

Falkiner Fine Papers. 76 Southampton Row. Underground: Holborn. ☎ (020) 7831-1151. Exquisite and rare writing and art papers.

Russell & Chapple. 23 Monmouth Street. Underground: Leicester Square. ☎ (020) 7836-7521. Specializing in art canvas and other materials.

Spink & Son. 5 King Street. Underground: Green Park. ☎ (020) 7930-7888. Attention numismatists. (Coin collectors, don't you know?)

Stanley Gibbons International. 399 Strand. Underground: Covent Garden or Charing Cross. ☎ (020) 7836-8444. Stamp collectors worship here.

Bookstores

Blackwells. 100 Charing Cross Road. Underground: Tottenham Court Road. ☎ (020) 7292-5100. Branches throughout the city, too.

Books etc. 120 Charing Cross Road. Underground: Tottenham Court Road. ☎ (020) 7379-6838. Books and a café. Branches throughout the city.

Dillons the Bookstore. 82 Gower Street. Underground: Goodge Street. ☎ (020) 7636-1577. Home base for the large chain.

Foyles. 113–119 Charing Cross Road. Underground: Tottenham Court Road. ☎ (020) 7437-5660. About as different from the nearby chain stores as possible.

Waterstone's. 121–125 Charing Cross Road. Underground: Tottenham Court Road. ☎ (020) 7434-4291. Another well-lit, well-stocked chain, with branches everywhere.

Chapter 26
Museum Shops and Galleries

Museum Shops

British Museum Bookshop. Bloomsbury. Underground: Holborn/Tottenham Court Road. ☎ (020) 7323-8587. 🖳 www.thebritishmuseum.ac.uk. Children's shop, bookshop, and giftshop.

    Kenwood House. Hampstead Lane. Underground: Archway/Golders Green. ☎ (020) 8348-1286. Books, gifts, and honey from Kenwood's gardens.

    London Transport Museum. Covent Garden. Underground: Covent Garden. ☎ (020) 7379-6344. 🖳 www.ltmuseum.co.uk. Books, maps, and a collection of posters of Underground art.

    Museum of London. London Wall. Underground: St. Paul's. ☎ (020) 7600-3699. 🖳 www.museum-london.org.uk.

    Museum of the Moving Image. South Bank. Underground: Waterloo. ☎ (020) 7401-2636. *Closed for renovation until 2003.*

    Museum Store. Covent Garden. Underground: Covent Garden. ☎ (020) 7240-5760. Books and gifts from museums and galleries around the world.

    National Gallery. Trafalgar Square. Underground: Charing Cross/Leicester Square. ☎ (020) 7747-2885. 🖳 www.nationalgallery.org.uk.

    National Portrait Gallery. Saint Martin's Place. Underground: Leicester Square/ Charing Cross. ☎ (020) 7306-0055. 🖳 www.npg.org.uk. Art books and art reproductions.

    Natural History Museum. Cromwell Road. Underground: South Kensington. ☎ (020) 7938-9123. 🖳 www.nhm.ac.uk. Books, models, minerals, and more.

    Pollock's Toy Museum. Scala Street. Underground: Goodge Street. ☎ (020) 7636-3452. 🖳 www.tao2000.net/pollocks.

    Royal Academy of Arts. Piccadilly. Underground: Green Park/Piccadilly Circus. ☎ (020) 7300-5760. 🖳 www.royalacademy.org.uk. Books and reproductions.

    Science Museum. Exhibition Road. Underground: South Kensington. ☎ (020) 7938-8000. 🖳 www.nmsi.ac.uk.

    Tate Britain. Millbank. Underground: Pimlico. ☎ (020) 7887-8869. 🖳 www. tate.org.uk. Books, reproductions, and gifts.

Victoria and Albert Museum. Cromwell Road. Underground: South Kensington. ☎ (020) 7938-8434. 🖳 www.vam.ac.uk. Books, reproductions, and gifts.

Galleries

Call for information on current exhibitions, hours, and admission charges.

Barbican Art Gallery. Barbican Centre, EC2. Underground/Rail: Barbican/Moorgate. ☎ (020) 7638-4141. 🖳 www.barbican.org.uk. International exhibitions.

Institute of Contemporary Art. The Mall, SW1. Underground/Rail: Piccadilly/Charing Cross. ☎ (020) 7930-3647. 🖳 www.ica.org.uk.

The Mall Galleries. The Mall, SW1. Underground/Rail: Leicester Square/Charing Cross. ☎ (020) 7930-6844.

Royal Institute of British Architects (RIBA). Portland Place, W1. Underground: Oxford Circus/Regent's Park. ☎ (020) 7580-5533. 🖳 www.architecture.com.

Saatchi Gallery. Boundary Road, NW8. Underground: Saint John's Wood. ☎ (020) 7624-8299. 🖳 www.saatchigallery.org.uk. Contemporary art.

Serpentine Gallery. Kensington Gardens, W2. Underground: South Kensington/Lancaster Gate. ☎ (020) 7402-6075. 🖳 www.serpentinegallery.org. Outdoor displays of contemporary sculptures.

Whitechapel Art Gallery. Whitechapel High Street, E1. Underground: Aldgate East. ☎ (020) 7522-7888. 🖳 www.whitechapel.org. Contemporary art.

Part VII
Greater London Day Trips

Chapter 27
Day Trips: Greater London

North of London

Freud Museum

Kenwood House

South of London

Horniman Museum and Gardens

William Morris Gallery

Wimbledon Lawn Tennis Museum

West of London

Gunnersbury Park Museum

Hogarth's House

Kew Bridge Steam Museum

Royal Botanic Gardens

Southall Railway Centre

Syon House

East of London

Bethnal Green Museum of Childhood

Geffrye Museum

North of London
Freud Museum

20 Maresfield Gardens, Hampstead, London. Underground: Finchley Road.
Open Wednesday to Sunday, noon to 5 P.M. Admission: adult, ❷; student, ❶. ☎
(020) 7435-2002. 🖳 www.freud.org.uk.

Price Bands
❶ £1–£3
❷ £3–£5
❸ £5–£7
❹ £7–£10
❺ £10–£15
❻ £15 and up

The museum is in the former home of famed psychoanalyst Sigmund Freud and his family after Nazi persecution forced them to flee Vienna in 1938; Freud spent the last year of his life in the home.

Preserved by his family as a museum, the heart of the house is the study and consulting room, where Freud essentially reconstructed his antiquities collection and library from Vienna. The walls of the room are lined with glass shelves of books on the subjects you might expect such as neurology, psychology, and psychoanalysis, as well as other interests such as archaeology, ancient history, and anthropology. Also on display are bronze, ceramic, glass, and stone objects from ancient Egyptian, Greek, Roman, and Oriental cultures. Visitors can see two videos, including one with seldom-seen personal films from Vienna and London.

Anna Freud, youngest of his six children and a renowned child psychoanalyst, lived in the house and maintained a practice there for more than forty years until her death in 1982. The museum opened in 1986.

Kenwood House

Hampstead Lane, NW3. Underground: Archway/Golders Green. Open 10 A.M. to 6 P.M. daily, until 4 P.M. in winter. Admission: free. ☎ (020) 8348-1286.

An exquisite gem inside and out, the spectacular neoclassical mansion on Hampstead Heath was most recently remodeled in 1764 by Robert Adam for William Murray who went on to become the first earl of Mansfield and lord chief justice.

Based on a structure that dates from 1616, it is home of the spectacular Iveagh Bequest, a fabulous private collection given to the nation that includes works by Rembrandt, Van Dyck, Hals, and Reynolds. Perhaps the most striking room is the Adam Library, which includes a dramatic painted curved ceiling.

In 1924 the land became a public property and in that year Edward Cecil Guiness, the first earl of Iveagh, bought the house and installed his personal art collection; he gave it to the nation in 1927.

The art includes a self-portrait by Rembrandt as well as works by Van Dyck, Gainsborough, Turner, and others.

Outside the doors is Hampstead Heath, a historic landscaped park open daily 8 A.M. until dusk.

South of London

Horniman Museum and Gardens

100 London Road. Forest Hill. Rail: Forest Hill. Monday to Saturday 10:30 A.M. to 5:30 P.M. and Sunday 2 P.M. to 5:30 P.M. Admission: free. ☎ (020) 8699-1872. 🖳 www.horniman.ac.uk.

The Horniman features an eclectic collection based on objects gathered by Frederick Horniman, founder of a tea importing company. A museum was constructed in 1901 to hold the collection, and it and a fourteen-acre park were presented to the city of London; today visitors can also explore a reconstructed Victorian conservatory.

William Morris Gallery

Lloyd Park, Forest Road, Walthamstow, London. Underground/Rail: Walthamstow Central. Open Tuesday to Saturday and first Sunday of each month from 10 A.M. to 1 P.M., and 2 P.M. to 5 P.M. Admission: free. ☎ (0181) 527-3782. ▣ www.lbwf.gov.uk/wmg.

The William Morris Gallery, celebrating one of England's best-known and most versatile designers, is located at Walthamstow in what was Morris's family home from 1848 to 1856. The former Water House, a substantial Georgian dwelling built about 1750, is set in its own extensive grounds, now Lloyd Park.

The collection includes printed, woven, and embroidered fabrics, rugs, wallpapers, carpets, furniture, stained glass, and painted tiles designed by Morris and by members of his company.

Treasures include Morris's medieval-style helmet and sword, made as props for the pre-Raphaelite murals at the Oxford Union and the original design for Trellis, the earliest of Morris's many wallpapers.

There is also an exploration of Morris's history as a socialist politician.

The nearest Underground and rail station is Walthamstow Central, about a fifteen-minute walk from the gallery. Buses from the station (stop C at the terminus) go to Bell Corner, about 150 meters from the gallery.

Wimbledon Lawn Tennis Museum

Church Road, Wimbledon. Underground: Southfields. Open Tuesday to Saturday 10:30 A.M. to 5 P.M., Sunday 2 P.M. to 5 P.M. Admission: adult, ❷; child, ❶. ☎ (0180) 946-6131. ▣ www.wimbledon.org.

The museum tells the story of lawn tennis from its origins in the 1860s to the present day, with historic equipment, clothing, and videos. Some of the items come from the private collection of noted tennis historian Tom Todd. There's also the chance to grab a glimpse at Wimbledon's Centre Court from the viewing gallery of the museum.

West of London
Gunnersbury Park Museum

Gunnersbury Park, Popes Lane, London. Underground: Acton Town. ☎ (018) 1992-1612. ▣ www.cip.org.uk/parks/gp/museum.htm.

A small museum with an eclectic collection about the heritage of Ealing and Hounslow, Gunnersbury Park includes costumes and clothing, toys, and memorabilia from the Great West Road built in the early twentieth century. The road included a section known as the "Golden Mile" because of the successful factories in the area, including Firestone, Gillette, and Pyrene; many of the factories had impressive Art Deco designs.

The museum is located in a restored neoclassical mansion owned by the Rothschild family from 1835 to 1925; two Rothschild carriages are on display. Other treasures include the Stanhope printing press of 1804, the earliest surviving example of its type. Also in the collection are artifacts from the Ealing Film Studios. A "handling" collection includes replica costumes and clothing from the Victorian era to recent times.

Gunnersbury is said to have gained its name from King Canute's niece, Gunhilda.

Hogarth's House

Great West Road, Hogarth Lane. Underground: Turnham Green. Open April to September 1 P.M. to 5 P.M. Monday to Friday, 1 P.M. to 6 P.M. Saturday and Sunday. Closes at 4 P.M. from October to March. Closed January. ☎ (020) 8994-6757.

Although today it is surrounded by traffic and flown over by jet planes coming in and out of Heathrow Airport, when painter William Hogarth lived here from 1749 until just before his death in 1764, it was his house in the country. He painted pastoral scenes from its windows.

The small museum contains mostly engraved prints of some his most famous works of art; the originals, such as *The Rake's Progress*, can be seen in more major collections in England and elsewhere.

Kew Bridge Steam Museum

Green Dragon Lane, Brentford. Underground: Gunnersbury or Kew Gardens. Rail: Kew Bridge from Waterloo. Open daily 11 A.M. to 5 P.M.; engines under steam on weekends and bank holidays. Weekend admission: adult, ❷; child, ❶; family, ❹. Weekday admission: adult, ❶; child, ❶; family, ❷. ☎ (020) 8568-4757. 🖳 www.kbsm.org.uk.

The museum is within a nineteenth-century pumping station near the north side of Kew Bridge and includes five huge Cornish Beam Engines that were used to pump West London's water supply from the River Thames for more than a century. The Grand Junction 90 is the world's largest working beam engine. On occasion, two of the engines are operated under steam.

In surrounding buildings are four more large engines that demonstrate more modern steam pumps as well as diesel and water-powered systems. The waterworks also had its own short-line railway with a small steam locomotive.

Cornish engines perform work by a falling load that has been lifted by the engine; on the lifting stroke, power is produced by injecting steam above the piston and creating a vacuum below the piston by condensing the steam there.

The Maudslay engine, built in 1838, was the first engine on the site and worked hard continuously until 1944. The Boulton and Watt engine pump was built in 1820 and moved to Kew from Chelsea Waterworks in 1840; it operated until 1943.

The largest engines in the museum—the largest single-cylinder engines in the world—are the ninety- and one-hundred-inch engines that were linked to stroke alternately.

At the end of 1997 a new gallery named Water for Life opened, telling the story of water from the time of the Roman occupation of London through the cholera epidemics of the nineteenth century to the growth of public sanitation and private lavatories, and eventually, to the modern London system.

Royal Botanic Gardens

Kew, Richmond, Surrey. Underground: Kew Gardens. Daily 9:30 A.M. to dusk. Admission: adult, ❷; child, ❶; family, ❺. ☎ (020) 8940-1171. 🖳 www.rbgkew.org.uk.

Considered the most fabulous public garden in the world, Kew Gardens was established by naturalist Sir Joseph Banks in the late eighteenth century; in 1841 the formal royal gardens were given to the public. Today there are displays of more than forty thousand specimens of plants and trees.

The sprawling grounds include **Kew Palace**, built in 1631 and used as a royal palace by George III; the gabled building (sometimes referred to as the Dutch House for that reason) is open to the public from April to October.

The **Palm House** is a Victorian-style greenhouse from 1840; nearby is the **Temperate House**, another indoor display for plants not native to the area. Marianne North, an artist known for her paintings of flowers, gave her works and the **Marianne North Gallery** to Kew in 1882. Among the oldest structures is the **Pagoda**, built in 1762.

Southall Railway Centre

Off Merrick Road/Park Avenue, Southall. Rail: Southall. Open Saturday and Sunday from 11 A.M. to 5 P.M. Admission: adult, ❶; child, ❶. Higher charges for special events). ☎ (079) 7060-3748.

The center features London's largest collection of preserved steam and diesel locomotives at a working museum.

Syon House

Syon Park, Brenford, Middlesex. Underground: Gunnersbury to Bus 237 or 267 to Brent Lea. Open March to October, Wednesday, Thursday, Sunday, and bank holidays 11 A.M. to 5 P.M. Call on Sunday. Gardens are open 10 A.M. to 5:30 P.M. (or until dusk in the winter). Admission to house and gardens: adult, ❸; child, ❷. ☎ (020) 8560-0881. 🖳 www.butterflies.org.uk/lbh_home/syonpark.htm.

The city home of the earls and dukes of Northumberland for more than four hundred years, Syon House includes a collection of art and period furniture set within a spectacular interior designed by Robert Adam. Also on the property is a collection of more than one hundred antique motorcars.

On the grounds of Syon Park is the **London Butterfly House**, open daily 10 A.M. to 5 P.M. spring through fall, and until 3:30 P.M. the rest of the year. Admission: adult, ❷; child, ❶; family, ❹. ☎ (020) 8560-7272. 🖳 www.butterflies.org.uk.

Here humans enter a world of free-flying butterflies in a jungle setting; there's also an aquarium and insect gallery. This is the home of creatures that include the giant atlas moth; the Gallery of Exotica includes the largest spider in the world, along with a collection of iguanas.

East of London

Bethnal Green Museum of Childhood

Cambridge Heath Road, E2. Underground: Bethnal Green. Open Monday to Thursday and Saturday 10 A.M. to 5:50 P.M., Sunday 2:30 P.M. to 5:50 P.M. ☎ (020) 8980-3204. 🖳 www.museumofchildhood.org.uk.

A branch of the Victoria and Albert Museum, the Bethnal Green Museum began as a toy collection and has been expanded to explore the social history of childhood. Children of all ages will enjoy the toys, games, and model trains; some will head for the lavish dollhouses and dolls, including some from royal collections.

The exhibition is housed in an iron structure originally erected as a temporary building at the V&A in 1856. It was moved to its present site in 1872 and encased in brickwork.

The original collection specialized in food and animal products and later an exhibit of art from the collection of Sir Richard Wallace, which later became a museum of its own. The specialization on childhood implements began in 1974.

Geffrye Museum

Kingsland Road, E2. Underground/Rail: Liverpool Street/Old Street. Open Tuesday through Saturday 10 A.M. to 5 P.M., and Sunday, Monday, and bank holidays 2 to 5 P.M. Admission: free. ☎ (020) 7739-9893. ▦ www.geffrye-museum.org.uk.

The Geffrye Museum is a pastiche of old England, from Elizabethan times through the Art Nouveau style of the 1950s, preserved in a group of old almshouses built in 1715 for ironmongers and their widows. The property was bequeathed by Sir Robert Geffrye, lord mayor of London in the seventeenth century, who made his fortune in the slave trade and other commerce. The buildings became a museum in 1914.

Many of the rooms are fully furnished with period pieces, paneling, and portraits from old London homes. A visit is a walk through time, from seventeenth-century rooms with oak furniture and paneling through the refined splendor of the Georgian period, the high style of the Victorians, twentieth-century Art Deco, and postwar utility.

The museum also displays decorative art, paintings, personal possessions, and other materials related to English domestic interiors.

Alongside the museum is an acclaimed herb garden, planted with culinary, household, aromatic, and medicinal plants.

Part VIII
Day Trips Outside of London

Chapter 28
Day Trips North: Cambridge and Environs

Cambridge

The River Cam flows slowly through town, wending its way along the "Backs"—the rears of the storied old colleges of Cambridge. It's worth a trip from busy, busy London to rent a punt and take a floating tour on a summer's afternoon.

Cambridge dates at least as far back as the 1200s when a group of scholars from Oxford fled there to avoid violent unpleasantries between town and gown. A rivalry between the two college towns has continued ever since, made official by the annual boat race on the River Thames between Oxford and Cambridge.

The first college was founded in Cambridge in 1271. By the sixteenth century, the town was an important center in the Protestant reform movement. Its reputation and popularity, though, fell into decline after the civil war. In the nineteenth century Cambridge came into its own as its college expanded beyond religious bases to more secular sciences.

The first women's colleges were established about 1870, but it wasn't until after World War II that women were officially awarded degrees from a Cambridge college.

The most famous of the schools are King's College, Trinity, Saint John's, Magdalene, and Jesus. Most of the colleges are open for tours except during exam periods in May; some assess modest charges for the privilege of entry.

King's College was founded in 1441 by Henry VI, and some of the original buildings continue in use as offices. King's College Chapel on the campus is one of the most famous structures in England, memorialized by William Wordsworth in three sonnets and recorded in paintings by Joseph Turner and Canaletto.

Trinity College is the largest of the colleges, with its impressive Great Court that features a fifteenth-century clock tower (which was a central figure in the film *Chariots of Fire*). Illustrious alumni include Isaac Newton; Lord Byron; Alfred, Lord Tennyson; Vladimir Nabokov; and Bertrand Russell. On the royal side, graduates include Edward VII, George VI, and Prince Charles.

Price Bands
❶ £1–£3
❷ £3–£5
❸ £5–£7
❹ £7–£10
❺ £10–£15
❻ £15 and up

Nearby is **Saint John's College**, which predates Trinity by a few decades; the college is perhaps best known for the Bridge of Sighs, a covered bridge named after a Venetian landmark.

Magdalene College (the name is pronounced as if it were "maudlin") includes the Pepys Building, which contains the library and the famed diaries of Samuel Pepys, donated in 1742.

Across the river is **Jesus College**, founded in 1496 on the site of an ancient Benedictine nunnery.

The best known museum of Cambridge is the **Fitzwilliam Museum** on Trumpington Street. It is open Tuesday through Friday 10 A.M. to 1 P.M., Saturday 10 A.M. to 5 P.M., and Sunday 2:15 P.M. to 5 P.M. Admission: free. ☎ (012) 2333-2993. 🖳 www.fitzmuseum.cam.ac.uk.

The Fitzwilliam was originally established to hold the fabulous collection of antiquities given by Viscount Fitzwilliam in 1816. The Lower Galleries, which open earlier than the Upper Galleries during the week, hold Egyptian sarcophagi and mummies, Greek vases, European porcelain and earthenware, and much more. The Upper Galleries are given over to paintings and sculpture by English and European artists, including Gainsborough, Van Dyck, Titian, Veronese, and Franz Hals.

Duxford Airfield

Duxford, Cambridge. Located eight miles south of Cambridge, about fifty miles from London. Open April through September 10 A.M. to 6 P.M., November to March 10 A.M. to 4 P.M. Admission: adult, ❸; child (5–15), ❷; family (two adults and up to three children), ❻. ☎ (0122) 383-5000. Recorded information line: ☎ (0891) 516816. 🖳 www.iwm.org.uk/duxford.htm.

Duxford Airfield features a collection of more than 140 historic aircraft, from Spitfires to the Concorde, on a former Royal Air Force fighter airfield and U.S. fighter base. The airfield was a major staging base for the Battle of Britain, and the original operations room from that era is open to visitors.

The museum is also the location for several spectacular air shows each year, usually conducted in June, July, September, and October.

Also at the field is the **American Air Museum in Britain**, highlighting the history of American air power and its influence on the twentieth century.

Althorp House: Princess Diana's Final Resting Place

The sleepy town of Althorp, about seventy-eight miles northwest of London in Northamptonshire, jumped into the global forefront in September 1997 when Diana, Princess of Wales, was laid to rest there on an island at the Spencer family estate. Within hours after the burial service, Althorp became the goal of a pilgrimage of tens of thousands of the respectful and the curious.

Beginning in the summer of 1998, the grounds of the home were opened to visitors every day in July and August. (The estate is closed on August 31, the anniversary of Diana's death, for private remembrances.)

Prices in 2001 were adult ❻, child ❸, and senior ❹. The house and grounds are open 9 A.M. to 5 P.M. each day, with tickets sold for morning or afternoon entry. For information or to reserve tickets, call ☎ (0160) 459-2020. Or you can consult ▣ www.althorp-house.co.uk.

Althorp is located five miles west of Northampton, off the A428 heading from Northampton to Rugby. It is about seventy-eight miles from London, and thirty-nine miles from Stratford-upon-Avon.

Silverlink Trains offer service from London Euston to Northampton train station, about seven miles from Althorp. From there a special coach service is offered to bring visitors directly into the grounds. For details, call the Silverlink booking line at ☎ (087) 0512-5240.

The Tour at Althorp

The tour was set up as a private tribute to Diana by the Spencer family; the royal family was informed but not involved, according to press reports.

Visitors are able to walk through the grounds and house and view, from a distance, the island in the Round Oval where Diana is buried. The temple at the edge of the lake has been dedicated to Diana's memory. An avenue of oak trees lines the walk to the house through the Spencer grounds.

A converted stable houses an exhibition about the life and work of Diana. The stable, built in the 1730s in the Palladian style, is considered one of the most notable pieces of architecture at the estate. Items on display include previously unseen childhood personal effects, the Spencer tiara Diana wore at her wedding and many state occasions, family photographs, and movies taken by her father.

Visitor facilities include a restaurant and a shop selling items described by the Spencer family as "inspired by Diana but not cheapening her memory in any way." A complete tour usually takes about two-and-a-half hours.

About the House

The property dates to 1508 when Sir John Spencer, a sheep farmer from Wormleighton, purchased an 8,500-acre estate and home for £800. The home was enlarged in 1573 and decorated with the first of several sumptuous collections of art and furniture.

The first Earl Spencer, member of Parliament for Warwick, was given his title in 1765; he was formerly known as Viscount Althorp. The name was pronounced "Althrup," a form still used by some family members to refer to the home. Althorp House was expanded into a large mansion in 1790, on an estate of fifteen thousand acres.

Diana, who grew up on the queen's estate at Sandringham, moved to Althorp House in 1976.

Woburn Abbey and Woburn Safari Park

About one hour northwest of London and home to the duke of Bedford for four centuries, the Woburn Abbey mansion is called an abbey because it was built on the foundation of an old Cistercian monastery. It holds one of the most important private art collections in the world, including paintings by Van Dyck, Gainsborough, Reynolds, and Velasquez. In the Venetian Room there are twenty-one paintings of Venice by Canaletto.

The abbey is open daily from late March to late September 11 A.M. to 4 P.M., and on weekends only from January to March and October through November. Admission is ❸. For information, call ☎ (0152) 529-0666, or consult 💻 www. woburnabbey.co.uk.

The Woburn Safari Park is an unusual private zoo in which human beings remain in their automobile cages and the animals run free. The best of show includes African white rhinos and Bengal tigers.

The collection includes some unusual creatures, including the world's largest herd of Père David Deer, descended from those originally introduced to the park by the Duke of Bedford in 1894. This species became extinct in its native China until deer from the Woburn herd were reintroduced there in 1985. Other rare and critically endangered animals include the Rothschild Giraffe, of which only forty are believed to exist in the wild; the Vietnamese Sika Deer, which is extinct in the wild; Mountain Bongo, which is rapidly approaching extinction in its native habitat; and the Asian Elephant.

The heart of the park is the **Animal Reserves.** Here visitors drive through a fenced area where the creatures run free. If you don't bring a car, you won't be able to enter this area.

The park is open daily March to October from 10 A.M. to sunset, and from November to February on weekends from 11 A.M. to 3 P.M. Tickets range from ❷ to ❹, depending on the season. ☎ (015) 2529-0407. 💻 www.woburnsafari. co.uk.

To drive to the park from London, follow signs for the M1 and the Midlands heading north to Junction 13 toward Bedford and Woburn. From there follow signs for the park on A4021.

You can also take a train from London to Leighton Buzzard station, about six miles away. Or you can travel from London to the larger station at Milton Keynes and take a public bus from there. Limited service is also available from London's Euston station to Woburn Sands, with connections at Bletchley.

Chapter 29
Day Trips South: Hampton Court, Brighton, and Battle (Hastings)

Head south for two fabulous—and very different—vestiges of old royalty.

In Hampton Court about fifteen miles southwest of London upriver on the River Thames, you'll find the fabulous Tudor palace of Henry VIII and later rulers through Queen Victoria. It's worth a day to wander through the rich apartments of the king and queen, explore the sprawling Great Kitchens, and stroll through the ornate gardens and the famous Great Maze.

Brightons' Royal Pavilion in has been called the most extraordinary palace in Europe, but a better description might be that it is one of the most unusual buildings on the planet, a rich mix of cultures and styles lovingly restored.

WOW Hampton Court Palace

Hampton Court, East Molesey, Surrey. Rail: Hampton Court, about a thirty-minute rail trip from London's Waterloo station. Underground: District Line to Richmond, then the R68 bus from Richmond station direct to the palace. Open in summer, Monday 10:15 A.M. to 6 P.M., Tuesday to Sunday 9:30 A.M. to 6 P.M. In winter the palace closes at 4:30 P.M. Gardens close at 9 P.M. or dusk, whichever comes first. Admission to state apartments and maze: adult, ❺; senior, ❹; child, ❸; family, ❺. Admission to park and grounds: free. Admission to maze only: adult, ❶; child, ❶. Combination tickets with the Tower of London are also available. ☎ (020) 8781-9500. 🖥 www.hrp.org.uk/hcp/indexhcp.htm.

The grandest Tudor residence in England, the royal palace was started in 1514 by Thomas Wolsey, then Archbishop of York and later Cardinal and Lord Chancellor. His private residence had 280 guest rooms and demanded a staff of about five hundred.

Included in the sprawling structure were royal lodgings for Henry VIII and his queen, Catherine of Aragon. Among the best surviving elements of Wolsey's Hampton Court is Base Court, the vast outer courtyard built for his guests.

Price Bands
❶ £1–£3
❷ £3–£5
❸ £5–£7
❹ £7–£10
❺ £10–£15
❻ £15 and up

Wolsey fell from favor by 1528 because he was unable or unwilling to persuade the pope to permit Henry VIII to divorce Catherine of Aragon. Wolsey presented Hampton Court to Henry VIII in hopes of restoring his standing; the king took the palace and land but did not elevate Wolsey.

Henry VIII set about to make the palace his own, installing new buildings and fabulous furnishings, including the Astronomical Clock installed in 1540 over Wolsey's Gate, renamed Anne Boleyn's Gateway. He also installed, at various times, five of his six wives here.

In about a ten-year period, Henry VIII spent £62,000 rebuilding and expanding Hampton Court—the equivalent of about £18 million in today's money. When it was completed about 1540, it included tennis courts, bowling alleys, a hunting park of more than 1,100 acres, and a splendid ornamental garden. The buildings included kitchens covering thirty-six thousand square feet, a royal chapel, the Great Hall communal dining hall, and a huge *garderobe* (lavatory), which could seat twenty-eight people at a time and was known with some pride as the Great House of Easement.

The fabulous Chapel Royal was used by Henry VIII. In 1541 he learned of the supposed infidelity of his fifth wife Catherine Howard while at the chapel; two years later he married his last wife, Catherine Parr, here. The magnificent gilded vaulted ceiling is decorated with the motto of the court, *Dieu et Mon Droit* (God and My Right) with the "n" reversed as was the style in the Tudor era.

Charles I made significant changes during his reign in the first part of the seventeenth century, adding creating ornamental lakes and fountains and an eleven-mile-long channel to supply water. He also brought great works of art to the palace. After the civil war, Charles was held prisoner here for a while by Parliamentarians. After he was executed, Hampton Court was put up for sale, but instead Oliver Cromwell moved in, remaining until his death in 1658.

After the Restoration Charles II had the palace redecorated and installed new gardens reminiscent of the plantings and tree-lined avenues of Europe where he had spent his exile. Some of the privileged escaped the Great Plague in London by coming to Hampton Court in 1665, and a year later Charles II moved some of his priceless pieces of art here to avoid the spreading Great Fire.

In 1688 when William III and Mary II took the throne, the second major rebuilding of the palace began under the direction of Christopher Wren. The original plan called for removing most of the buildings, but fiscal constraints forced a scaling back; only Henry VIII's State Apartments were taken down.

When Whitehall Palace in London was destroyed by fire in 1698, William put his efforts into completing Hampton Court as a palace; he did not live to see the work completed, though, dying as the result of injuries from a fall from his horse in Hampton Court Park in 1702. The King's Apartments, badly damaged by fire in 1986, have been restored to their original glory. More than 1.3 million visitors annually come to the **Hampton Court Palace Gardens**. Visitors young and old enjoy exploring King William III's maze and the ornamental gardens.

There are more than one million bulbs planted in the Wilderness Garden, more than thirty-three thousand box plants, and 100,000 rose bushes. There were once at least three mazes planted in the Wilderness. A staff of forty-one gardeners tends the greenery.

The Home Park across the road from Hampton Court covers an area of 620 acres. It is home to a herd of some three hundred fallow deer, descended from Henry VIII's original group, as well as more than thirty ring-necked parakeets. The oldest tree in the garden is an English oak believed to be more than one thousand years old.

The **Hampton Court Palace Maze** is perhaps the most famous surviving maze in the world. First planted in 1690 for William of Orange, it was the first hedge-planted maze in Great Britain. The hornbeam hedges were replanted with fast-growing yews in the 1960s. About 330,000 visitors enter the maze each year; presumably all of them exit. Shaped like a trapezoid, the maze covers an area of about a third of an acre and encompasses half a mile of paths.

Admission to the maze is included in a ticket to Hampton Court or can be purchased separately. A typical visitor takes about twenty minutes to navigate through.

Also at Hampton Court is the **Great Vine**, supposedly planted by Capability Brown in 1768 during his time as surveyor to George III's gardens and waters at the palace. Now more than 120 feet long, it is the oldest and largest known vine in the world; its roots were planted outside and its branches trained inside the glass house. Carefully tended, it usually blossoms in early May and each September produces a crop of five hundred to seven hundred bunches of sweet black grapes. The fruit, used as dessert grapes, is sold to visitors in the palace shops.

The **Royal Tennis Court** is the oldest one of its kind in use anywhere in the world, one of only two courts in the United Kingdom open to the public to play or view. Henry VIII was an avid tennis player; he built the Royal Tennis Court at Hampton Court about 1532.

Royal, or "real tennis," is a far more ancient game than lawn tennis. The original game, begun in France in the twelfth century, probably derived its name from the French habit of calling out "tenez" before each service.

In the thirteenth century, tennis was actually banned for the lower ranks of society to ensure that their spare time was more productively spent in archery practice.

Anne Boleyn was watching a game of tennis at Whitehall Palace in London at the time of her arrest; she was reported to have complained to her guards that if they had waited to the end of the game she would have won her bet. Legend also says that Henry was playing tennis at Hampton Court when word was brought of Anne's execution.

Real tennis balls were originally made from leather stuffed with human or dog hair. (In Shakespeare's *Much Ado About Nothing*, when Benedick shaves off his beard a character remarks, "the old ornament of his cheek hath already stuff'd tennis balls.") Today the balls are still handmade by the professionals at the court.

The **Tudor Kitchens** at Hampton Court, expanded by Henry VIII in 1529, at one time occupied more than fifty rooms and were staffed by two hundred people providing meals for the eight hundred members of the king's court.

The **Spicery** in the western court was filled with exotic spices imported from the Orient and Europe, as well as English mustard and herbs grown at Hampton Court. In the same courtyard was the **Chandlery**, where wax for candles and tapers was stored, and a **Coal House** for charcoal.

At the eastern end of the court was the **Great Kitchen** with its six great fireplaces, each with spit racks for roasting. In the **Confectionery**, delicate sweet dishes were prepared for the more important members of the court by staff, including the "wife who made the king's puddings"—the only woman known to have been employed in the kitchens.

Meat stock and boiled meat were produced in the **Boiling House** in a great seventy-five-gallon boiling copper. Meat was hung in the **Flesh Larder**, fish was stored in the **Wet Larder**, and seeds and nuts in the **Dry Larder**. Venison, culled from the royal parks, was hung in the Flesh Larder for as long as six weeks before consumption; fresher meat was also supplied from the palace's own pheasant yard and rabbit warren.

Today part of the original complex has been transformed to allow a glimpse of the Tudor kitchens as they appeared when they were in use. The Flesh Larder is stocked with pheasant, rabbits, and wild boar; the Great Kitchens are laid out as if for the Feast of Saint John the Baptist in 1542; and pewter dishes are laden with pies and stuffed carp ready to be carried to the Great Hall.

WOW Brighton

Brighton is a delightfully skewed seaside resort, a wonderful place to spend a summer's day and eve.

The star attraction is the improbable Royal Pavilion, a "believe it or not" of a building. There are also three small but interesting museums, an interesting old shopping district known as the Lanes, and of course, the ocean and beach and the old-time amusement pier that extends out over the water.

The town, fifty miles south of London, is well served by trains from London. Thameslink runs as many as four trains an hour from central London stations, including City Thameslink and London Bridge. Connex South Central runs the Connex Express and other service from London Victoria. Train travel takes a bit less than an hour. For train information, call ☎ (0345) 484950.

National Express buses also connect from London. For information on schedules, call ☎ (0990) 808080.

The seaside is a ten-minute walk from the train station. Like everything else in this town, the beach itself is just a bit different: a narrow strand of polished small stones bracketed by breakwaters and the amusement pier.

A Bohemian Rhapsody

Brighton has offered a Bohemian atmosphere since at least the mid-eighteenth century, a time when George IV, then Prince of Wales, used the home for trysts with his mistress who later became his wife.

The grand Royal Pavilion built by George IV still stands, beautifully restored to its quirky elegance.

Jutting out into the water is the Palace Pier, a wonderfully tacky amusement pier that seems frozen in time. It's a place of carnival games, fish-and-chip and candy stands, and rides. It's worth a visit any day of the year, and especially at sunset and into the evening. The two Victorian-style pavilions on the pier are now filled with video arcades and slot machines where they once had been the home of dance marathons, but there is little else to remove the feeling that you have stepped back into a postwar party.

Also contributing to the party town atmosphere is the fact that Brighton is home to many English-language schools for foreign students. There are also three colleges and a thriving gay community.

Every May the Brighton Festival takes over the town for three weeks, with stage shows, concerts, street performances, and more.

Along the seafront is the overly grand plaster front of the Grand Hotel, where in 1984 the IRA bombed the annual Conservative Party Conference.

For information about Brighton and the Hove region, you can contact:

Brighton & Hove Marketing
P.O. Box 2502
Kings House
Grand Avenue
Hove BN3 2ST
United Kingdom
☎ (0127) 329-2599
💻 www.brighton.co.uk

The Story of Brighton

Mentioned in the *Domesday Book* of 1085 as Bristmestune, the small fishing town on the ocean was later known as Brighthelmstone. It was transformed into the fashionable resort of Brighton in the mid-eighteenth century as the result of the popularity of the supposed therapeutic advantages of seawater, taken as baths and tonics, heated or with milk. Some of the cream of London society came to take the waters.

Among the visitors was the Prince of Wales, later King George IV, who visited his uncle, the Duke of Cumberland, at the seashore in 1783; as a young man of twenty-one, he enjoyed the waters as well as the developing lively theatrical and gambling scene. Three years later he decided to rent a farmhouse there; he also installed Mrs. Maria Anne Fitzherbert, a Roman Catholic widow he had secretly (and illegally) married in 1785, in a villa nearby.

His wife's money helped George pay off some of his debts, and in 1787 he embarked on the construction of a more impressive residence. (That same year he allowed Parliament to declare the marriage null because it was illegal for a sovereign to marry a Roman Catholic.)

The first home, the Marine Pavilion, incorporated the old farmhouse in its left wing, adding a central rotunda with classical columns. The relatively small structure was expanded again in 1802.

George IV became prince regent in 1811 when his father was mentally unable to rule; in 1815 he commissioned architect John Nash to expand and ornament the house.

Nash's vision brought an anglicized version of an Indian palace to Brighton, decorated within as an anglicized version of a Chinese imperial residence. In some places he overlaid a cast-iron framework over the older interiors. He added new rooms, including the Great Kitchen, two new state rooms, the Music Room, and the Banqueting Room.

The work was completed in 1823, three years after George ascended to the throne in 1820 on the death of George III.

Brighton grew most rapidly when rail service was begun in 1841, bringing throngs of Londoners to the waters.

During World War II parts òf the town were severely damaged by bombing attacks by the German air force; bombers unable to reach London or other targets dropped their loads on Brighton before crossing back to their bases on the Continent.

The Royal Pavilion has been almost fully restored to its peak of elegance, a process that included major work in the 1980s and 1990s to repair damage as well as to undo the "improvements" that had been made to the structure over the years. In recent years gardeners have restored the gardens and grounds to the style of the pavilion in its early years.

WOW Royal Pavilion

Brighton. Open daily, October to May, 10 A.M. to 5 P.M., and June to September until 6 P.M. Admission: adult, ❷; child (younger than 16), ❶; family, ❺. A joint ticket including admission to Preston Manor is also sold. ☎ (0127) 329-0900. 🖳 www.brighton-hove.gov.uk/bhc/pavilion.

The Royal Pavilion began as a modest farmhouse rented by George, Prince of Wales, when he first began visiting Brighton in 1783. In 1787, he commissioned the creation of a villa on the site known as the Marine Pavilion; from 1802 the interior was decorated in a vaguely Chinese style.

In 1811 George became Prince Regent, next in line for the throne. Between 1815 and 1822 famed architect John Nash enlarged the villa to its present Indian exterior.

George IV ruled from 1820 to 1830. His brother William IV (1830–1837) shared George's fondness for Brighton, but their niece, Queen Victoria (1837–1901), didn't. Victoria reportedly found the town too crowded; she sold the building to the town in 1850, after she stripped the pavilion of nearly all of its furnishings.

Today Brighton is the only palace in England not in the hands of the royal family. Many original pieces of furniture and decorations have been returned and restored; many items are on loan from the collection of the queen.

The tour begins in the elegantly simple eight-sided **Octagon Hall**. Out front is a small covered porch, a *porte cochere*, built to protect visitors from the elements when they arrived in carriages.

From there, you'll move on to the **Entrance Hall**, an understated room decorated with panels and banners of serpents and dragons against an Oriental green background. In the nineteenth century, the hall led left to the King's

The Royal Pavilion, Brighton
Compliments of Brighton & Hove Tourism and Conferences

Apartments and right to the Red Drawing Room. Modern-day tours, though, proceed through a central door formerly occupied by a hidden staircase used by servants to reach the Long Gallery at the back of the pavilion.

The **Long Gallery** is a rich nineteenth-century interpretation of the Chinese style, decorated in pink, red, and gold with a dramatic painted-glass ceiling. The gallery, which runs down the spine of the building, is flanked by an unusual set of cast-iron staircases detailed and painted to look like bamboo. In wall niches are some interesting colored clay figurines of Chinese court officials loaned to Brighton from the queen's collection. As originally designed, there were mirrors on the backs of the doors at each end; when closed this created an illusion of an endless corridor.

The **Banqueting Room** is dominated by a spectacular central lamp about thirty feet in height and weighing a ton, and held in the claws of a silver dragon. Displayed on the central table and sideboards all around the room is one of the most important collections of Regency silver and silver gilt on public view. The table is set for an ornate dessert course.

At the head of the table is George IV's oversized chair; the king-sized monarch weighed about twenty-three stone (322 pounds) near the end of his life.

Hidden within the ornate canopy, among the dragons and other mythical beasts and heavenly bodies, are some of the symbols of Freemasonry, including the All-Seeing Eye. George, at the time of completion of the Marine Pavilion, was grand master of the Prince of Wales Lodge.

Also worked into the decorations here and elsewhere are some strange combinations of styles, including Oriental bamboo with roses, and bunches of bananas also sprouting rose buds.

Moving through the Banqueting Room you'll enter the **Table Deckers' Room**, where footmen prepared plates for delivery from the kitchen to the table.

The **Great Kitchen** was one of the modern cookeries of its time. Its high ceiling and copper canopies were designed to draw away heat and cooking smells. It also boasted an "automatic spit" and enclosed range, both novelties for the time. The rising draft from the fire turned a metal turbine within the chimney, and a series of gears, pulleys, and chains turned as many as five spits in the fire. Structural cast-iron columns were disguised as palm trees. The collection of copper cooking utensils includes more than five hundred pieces.

George IV reportedly loved the kitchen so much that he included it on tours for his guests and was known to have eaten there with his servants on several occasions.

The **Banqueting Room Gallery** is a remaining piece of the original modest farmhouse. The room was used by guests after dinner for card games and other entertainment. Displayed is a rare suite of Regency giltwood furniture made to commemorate Admiral Nelson and his victories. The next two rooms, the **Saloon** and the **Music Room Gallery**, were also used for entertainment.

The **Music Room**, considered the most spectacular example of the pavilion style, was supposed to have moved George to tears when he first saw it. Grand events included presentations by the king's own band and guests, including the Italian composer Gioacchino Rossini, who performed in 1823.

The decorations of the room, by Frederick Crace, were based in part on books about China published early in the nineteenth century. The red and gold wall paintings were returned to Brighton from Buckingham Palace in the 1860s, but the chimney piece and mirror frame, curtains, and carpeting are contemporary re-creations.

The room has been the scene of two serious disasters. In 1975 an arsonist set a fire in the room and it was severely damaged; however, all but one of the paintings survived. There followed a decade of careful restoration of the spectacular gilt dome and other features; it took seven crafstmen seven months to regild the sixteen thousand cockle shells of the dome. The Axminster carpet was reproduced on a hand loom in India. The restoration had just been completed when an unusual hurricane struck in 1987; one of the large stone balls from the top of the minarets outside was dislodged and crashed through the ceiling and the new carpet. The room has since been fully restored.

The entrance to the **King's Apartments** on the first floor is through hidden doors. The rooms were used by George IV near the end of his life when he was too ill with gout and dropsy—and too overweight—to ascend the stairs to the second floor.

The cast-iron bamboo staircase leads upstairs to the **North Gallery**. This area has been the focus of restoration work in recent years.

At the back of the house are the **Yellow Bow Rooms**, the bedroom suite of two of George's brothers, the Duke of York and the Duke of Clarence; the rooms are restored to their 1821 settings, including a contemporary reproduction of the hand-printed yellow-dragon wallpaper and more than forty Chinese oils and watercolors.

Through the North Gallery is the entrance to **Queen Victoria's Apartments**, including the maid's room and—ready or not—the queen's water closet, a different kind of throne. In the queen's bedroom is a reproduction of a mahogany four-poster bed topped with six mattresses of straw, horsehair, and feathers.

Palace Pier

Marine Parade, Brighton. Open weekdays 10 A.M. to noon, weekends 9 A.M. to noon. Admission: free. ☎ (0127) 360-9361. 🖳 www.brightonpier.co.uk.

You've got your bumper cars, tilt-a-whirl, small but intense roller coaster, fish and chips, and all manner of other wonderfully tacky entertainments installed on an old pier that juts out into the ocean. It's worth a stroll any time, and especially on a warm summer evening. Admission to the pier is free; tickets for rides range from about 50p to £2.

Adorned with filigree arches and a few kiosks, the 1,722-foot-long Brighton Pier opened in grand ceremony in 1899. A concert hall was added a few years later, and the first Ferris wheel was installed in 1932.

There had been two such piers at Brighton, but the West Pier, damaged by storms in the 1970s and 1980s and never repaired, is rusting away.

Other Attractions in Brighton

Volk's Electric Railway

285 Madeira Drive, Brighton. Open weekdays April to September 11 A.M. to 5 P.M. and weekends 10:30 A.M. to 6 P.M. Admission: adult and child, ❶.

Britain's oldest electric railway runs along the top of the beach from near the Palace Pier to near the lively **Brighton Marina Village**. At the marina you'll find the Merchants Quay shopping district, including a factory outlet area.

On the water near the marina is a "clothing optional" beach. Don't get your hopes too high, though; this is not the French Riviera, and some of the visitors demonstrate the reason most of us wear clothes.

Brighton Lanes

As late as 1635, Brighthelmstone was contained entirely within the square known as the Lanes. The narrow cobblestone alleyways are today home to dozens of clothing, jewelry, antique, and gift shops, as well as old inns and contemporary restaurants. Brighton Square is at the heart of the district, which today mostly lies between East Street, North Street, Meeting House Lane, and Prince Albert Street/Bartholomews Avenue. The Lanes are near the beach and Palace Pier.

The **North Lane** area of some 350 more shops extends from the Brighton railway station on Trafalgar Street to the Royal Pavilion.

Brighton Sea Life Centre

Marine Parade, opposite Palace Pier. Open daily 10 A.M. to 5 P.M. Admission: adult, ❸; child, ❷. ☎ (0127) 360-4234.

An acclaimed aquarium and exhibit, the center includes an unusual "Kingdom of the Seahorse" exhibit.

The attraction includes the longest underwater aquarium tunnel in England, which goes through a tank home to sharks, rays, conger eels, and more than sixty other varieties of marine life.

Brighton Museum & Art Gallery

Church Street. Open weekdays except Wednesday from 10 A.M. to 5 P.M., Saturday 10 A.M. to 5 P.M., and Sunday 2 to 5 P.M. Admission: free. ☎ (0127) 360-3005.

The museum features an eclectic collection of paintings, non-Western textiles and masks, and archaeological finds from flint axes to silver coins, displayed in a museum opened in 1873 on the site of Queen Adelaide's stables.

Other displays include clothing from the eighteenth century to the 1980s in the Fashion Gallery; the 20th Century Gallery of Art and Design includes Salvador Dali's famous sofa in the shape of Mae West's lips. My favorite was the strange Willett collection of old household pottery and popular culture items, including some busts of George Washington cast about 1790 after the American colonies had successfully broken away.

The museum has been undergoing renovation; restored galleries are due to reopen by the fall of 2001.

Booth Museum of Natural History

194 Dyke Road, Brighton. Open weekdays except Thursday 10 A.M. to 5 P.M., Saturday 10 A.M. to 5 P.M., and Sunday 2 P.M. to 5 P.M. Admission: free. ☎ (0127) 355-2586.

More than half a million specimens of insects and animals are on display at the Booth Museum. The museum was the creation of the Victorian ornithologist Edward Booth; it was built in 1874 to house his collection of hundreds of stuffed British birds displayed in re-created natural settings. The collection includes dinosaur bones from 140 million years ago and fossil fish a mere 85 million years old. More recent finds include a whale skeleton.

Sussex Toy & Model Museum

52–55 Trafalgar Street, Brighton. Open weekdays from 10 A.M. to 5 P.M., Saturday 11 A.M. to 5 P.M. Open selected Sundays and bank holidays from noon to 4:30 P.M. Admission: adult, ❶; child, ❶. ☎ (0127) 374-9494.

One of the largest and finest collections of toys and models in the world, the Sussex has more than ten thousand items on display, including a spectacular O-Gauge model-train layout, Victorian and modern dolls, military dioramas, and antique figurines.

The museum is located in several abandoned tunnels once used to stable horses beneath the Brighton railway station.

Sussex-Area Attractions

Preston Manor

Preston Drove, Brighton. Open Tuesday through Saturday 10 A.M. to 5 P.M., Sunday 2 P.M. to 5 P.M., and Monday 1 P.M. to 5 P.M. Admission: adult, ❷; child, ❶; family, ❹. ☎ (0127) 329-0900.

Preston Manor is a fully restored Edwardian manor house; visitors can explore more than twenty rooms on four floors in the upstairs realm of the owners and the downstairs of the staff.

The home was originally built about 1250, rebuilt in 1738, and substantially expanded and altered in 1905. The manor was purchased by the Stanford family in 1794 and was the family home for 138 years. It was left to the Brighton Borough Council in 1932. The manor grounds also include an old-fashioned walled garden and a pet cemetery.

Preston Manor is about a ten-minute walk from the Preston Park train station, one stop short of Brighton on the trip from London.

Hove Museum and Art Gallery

19 New Church Road, Hove. Open Tuesday through Saturday 10 A.M. to 5 P.M., and Sunday 2 P.M. to 5 P.M. Admission: free. ☎ (0127) 329-0200.

The Hove Museum has a small but important collection of paintings, ceramics, jewelry, and crafts from the eighteenth through the twentieth centuries. The Hove Gallery shows films of the town made about 1900 by movie pioneers.

Museum of Steam and Mechanical Antiquities

Nevill Road, Hove. Open daily 10 A.M. to 5 P.M. Admission: adult, ❷; child, ❶; family, ❹. ☎ (0127) 355-9583.

A lovingly restored Victorian-era pumping station, today the museum is used as the home of a collection of fire engines and other steam devices as well as the original beam engine water pump. The engines are usually fired up on the first Sunday of the month and on bank holidays.

Barlow Gallery & Museum

Falmer, on the University of Sussex campus four miles east of Brighton. Open Tuesday and Thursday 11:30 A.M. to 2:30 P.M., except August and Christmas and Easter weeks. Admission: free. ☎ (0127) 367-8199.

The Barlow features Chinese and Asian treasures from the twelfth century B.C. to the eighteenth century A.D. The collection includes ancient ritual bronzes, pottery tomb figures, and burial vessels, as well as fine porcelains, carved jades, and celadon wares.

Brighton Fishing Museum

Arch 201 on the beach, below the Old Ship Hotel. Open weekends from Easter to September; call for hours. Admission: free. ☎ (0127) 372-3064.

This museum is a celebration of the fishing history and heritage of Brighton near where today's fishermen sell their catches and mend their nets. The museum is run by local volunteers.

Battle (Hastings)

Above Hastings, about ninety minutes southeast of London, Battle is the eponymously named site for the Battle of Hastings of 1066, one of the most important locations of early British history. The battle took place about six miles north of the coastal town of Hastings.

It was at the Battle of Hastings that William the Conqueror killed King Harold and established Norman Britain. The spot where Harold was killed is marked by a memorial stone. William constructed Battle Abbey in the town center of Hastings to commemorate the event; much of the abbey was destroyed during King Henry VIII's own battles with the church, although some of the pieces still remain.

The abbey and ruins are open daily April to September 10 A.M. to 5 P.M., and October to March 10 A.M. to 4 P.M.; admission is adult ❷, senior ❶, child ❶, family ❹. Train service is available from London's Charing Cross station to Hastings, a sixty-three-mile trip of about ninety minutes. The battle site is served by buses and taxis.

For information about Hastings and the 1066 Country region, contact:
1066 Country Tourism
4–5 Robertson Terrace
Hastings, East Sussex TN34 1JE
United Kingdom
☎ (0142) 478-1111
🖳 www.hastings.gov.uk/tourism/1066.htm

Chessington World of Adventures

Chessington World of Adventures is not to be confused with Disneyland Paris, but it does offer an interesting glimpse into the ordinary life of Londoners. The small, very green place includes basic amusement park fare as well as a small but interesting zoo; it draws more than 1.5 million visitors per year.

The park is located on Leatherhead Road, Chessington, Surrey, and accessible through the Chessington South railway station. It is open daily from mid-March through early November 10 A.M. to 5:15 P.M. It closes at 9 P.M. from mid-July through the end of August, and during "Fright Nights" in late October and early November. Admission is adult, ❺; child, ❺; senior, ❺. For information, call ☎ (0137) 272-7227 or consult 🖳 www.chessington.co.uk.

SWT Stagecoach trains run from London Waterloo to Chessington South station, a trip of about an hour. In recent years, Chessington World of Adventures has offered a discount on presentation of a rail ticket for that day. The train station is an easy fifteen-minute walk from the park. Turn right from the station exit on Garrison Lane and then go left on Leatherhead Road to the park.

Attractions

New in 2001 was the **Trail of the Kings**. From an African-style game lodge, you can check out one of Europe's biggest gorilla families, including silverback Kumba and Shani, who delivered a baby just in time for the season. Also on display are Sumatran tigers, Persian Leopards, and Asian Lions.

Other highlights of the park:

• **Rameses Revenge**. This "entertainment" in the Ancient Forbidden Kingdom was obviously the product of a deranged designer: it's a cross between an over-the-top pirate-ship ride and an egg beater. Riders sit in seats in a set of stadium-like rows. The grandstand moves from right to left, rotating from top to bottom and upside down as it goes. Within seconds, riders are twisting and turning in eighty-foot-high arcs. And then, mercifully, the ride comes to a halt . . . or at least it seems to. We don't want to spoil the surprise, but we can tell you this: it involves the fountain that bubbles innocently at the bottom. We've survived a similar ride, called Hammerhead, at Knott's Berry Farm in Buena Park, California.

• **The Runaway Train**. Just like the name says, this is a runaway trip through California Gold Rush territory in Calamity Canyon.

• **Dragon Falls**. Sail through bamboo jungles, past a giant Buddha, and dive down a rocky crevice into the mouth of a dragon, emerging between a pair of gigantic stone heads.

There are also some entertainments more suitable for younger children and more cautious adults. They include:

• **Professor Burp's Bubbleworks**. Yes, that's really the name. This is a colorful indoor water ride that takes you on a tour of the bubbly Professor Burp's soda pop factory, including an amazing Fruit Juice Fountain Finale.

• **Safari Skyway**. The skyway is an overhead tram ride that offers unique views of many of Chessington's rare and endangered animals and birds.

And for the littlest visitors, there is the **Toytown** area with minirides that include a tiny roller coaster.

Regular entertainment at the park has included the **Big City Circus** with aerial acts, clowns, special effects, and strolling street entertainers.

Winchester

Toward Southampton, about two hours southwest of London, is Winchester, one of the most interesting and important old cities of England. This is also the home of Winchester Cathedral, which became world famous in the 1960s in the words of an insipid pop song.

Winchester was the capital of Saxon England in the years leading up to the Norman conquest in 1066. Parts of the old city walls, and homes and structures from as long ago as the thirteenth century, still survive.

Contemporary Winchester is built over the ruins of the ancient Roman city of Venta Belgarum, home to some six thousand citizens.

The first Christian church in Winchester was erected by King Kenwahl about 648; its outline is marked on the Cathedral Green in town.

King Alfred the Great, the king of Wessex, drove back the Danish invaders and restored the city after the Dark Ages. He made Winchester his capital and was buried there after his death in 899; a statue of Alfred dominates Broadway.

The cathedral was rebuilt soon after the Norman Conquest; it remains as the longest medieval Gothic cathedral in Europe with its 556-foot-long nave. The interior is richly appointed; in addition to formal monuments is a simple stone commemorating author Jane Austen who died in Winchester. The Norman-era crypt includes the tomb of Saint Swithun; the crypt is open only in the summer because of winter floods.

Winchester College is the oldest public school in England. Founded by Bishop William of Wykeham in 1382 to educate poor boys, today most of its students are from very privileged families.

The Winchester train station is served by trains from London Waterloo and by bus service from Victoria coach station.

For information about Winchester you can contact:

Tourist Information Centre
Guildhall, the Broadway
Winchester, Hampshire SO23 9LJ
United Kingdom
☎ (0196) 284-0500
🖳 www.winchester.gov.uk

Chapter 30
Day Trips West: Bath, Stonehenge, Avebury, and Stratford-upon-Avon

Bath

Bath is one of those places where you can feel the tides of history beneath your feet. In fact, that is literally so in this interesting town, where the beautifully preserved Georgian and Victorian buildings in the center stand twenty feet above the remains of the two-thousand-year-old Roman baths that gave the town its name and reason for being.

The town reached another, larger peak during the eighteenth and nineteenth centuries when the cream of British society came to take the waters. Author Jane Austen lived at 4 Sydney Place between 1801 and 1804, and Charles Dickens visited and wrote about the baths.

At the time, though, they didn't really know what was buried below. Today's tourists are much luckier; the baths of Bath are among the world's wonders, and the Victorian-era entertainments built to support the visitors are charming and fascinating in their own way.

The Ancient History of Bath

Imagine the scene two thousand years ago as the Roman invaders found a bubbling pool of hot water and a stream running to the river, the water bright green and the edges of the pool and stream blood red. It seems easy to understand how the Romans treated the place as a direct connection between the world of man and the world of the gods.

Actually, though, the spa had been visited for hundreds of years before by Celtic tribes, including the Dobunni. They believed the spring was a portal through which they could communicate with the underworld and that the gods must be placated with offerings; a number of silver Celtic coins were found in the spring. The Dobunni built a gravel causeway across the mud to the source of the spring.

Within a few years after the Romans invaded Britain in A.D. 43, they had discovered the hot springs and displaced the Dobunni at the spring.

By about A.D. 75 the spa of Aquae Sulis was founded; Sulis was a Celtic deity the invaders equated with their own goddess Minerva.

The first construction involved enclosing the spring in a reservoir wall lined with sheets of lead and supported by oak piles driven into the soft ground. The reservoir helped provide a steady supply of water for the pools and settle out sandy sediment that might have blocked the pipes. Roman engineers even figured out a way to change the direction of flow and use water pressure to clean out the sand deposits when needed.

To the north of the spring the Romans built the temple of Sulis Minerva; to the south they constructed cleansing and curative baths.

Based on architectural finds, including pieces of columns and decorations and surviving Roman temples elsewhere, the temple at Bath is believed to have been a classical design with Corinthian columns and a triangular pediment.

Carved stone pieces of the temple pediment were discovered during the construction of the present Pump Room in 1790; additional excavations between 1981 and 1983 found more pieces and uncovered the fact that some of the fragments of the temple had been used in the Pump Room's foundations.

Within the temple was a simple room known as the *cella*, where the cult statue and sacred objects were kept; outside was a sacrificial altar where religious ceremonies were conducted. During the second century, the Sacred Spring was enclosed in a vaulted chamber. Other archaeological finds suggest there was a circular temple, a *tholos*, in the vicinity; modern theorists say it may have been located beneath the front of the Saxon-era abbey.

The arrangement of the rooms at the baths changed a few times during the Roman years. Visitors went from the *tepidarium* (warm room) to the *caldarium* (hot room) and then finally took a cold plunge into unheated water. In later years a *laconicum* was added, providing a sauna-like dry heat.

The tepidarium and caldarium were heated through the use of hypocausts. Furnaces generated hot air, which was directed below the rooms, heating brick pillars beneath the floor and the floor itself.

The Romans abandoned their empire in Britain in the late fourth century in the face of attacks from the barbarians. After their departure, the temple and baths were allowed to fall into disrepair and collapsed.

But the spring continued to flow and draw reverent visitors. In 675 King Osric of Hwicce in Mercia gave land for the creation of a Convent of Holy Virgins at Bath. Few details are known of the church in the town, although by the year 973 it was significant enough that Edgar was crowned king of England there.

A Medieval Resurrection

The Saxon monastery was torn down and replaced by a new Norman church in the twelfth century. The monastic infirmary was built over the ruins of the Temple Precinct, while the Roman-era walls of the chamber that had once enclosed the spring were used to build a new bath, the King's Bath. Water for the bath passed through the ruins of the Roman reservoir.

In medieval times, bathing in the waters of the spa was seen as a cure or treatment for conditions from colic and gout to paralysis. Modern science speculates that many of these afflictions were related to lead poisoning, perhaps due to lead water pipes dating back to Roman days, as well as the use of lead in alcohol and other foods as a sweetener and fungicide. Ironically, the spa at Bath as well as the water in the Pump Room also used lead plumbing.

During the next few centuries, Bath's appeal as a place of medicinal healing led to the growth of the town. In 1613 and again in 1615 Queen Anne of Denmark, wife of James I, visited Bath, building its status as a social center as well. The move toward high fashion accelerated with the visit of Princess Anne in 1692 and her return as queen in 1702 and 1703.

It was decided to create a more refined approach to the baths where visitors could view the baths and drink the waters in comfort. The first Pump Room was constructed alongside the reservoir in 1706 and enlarged in the 1750s.

In 1727 workmen digging a sewer deep beneath Stall Street discovered a life-sized gilded head of Minerva from the cult statue of the cella of the temple.

In the meantime, though, many contemporary buildings had been installed over the ruins, including a house where famed British artist Thomas Gainsborough lived from 1760 to 1766. In the town the Royal Mineral Water Hospital was built in 1729; it still stands off Union Street.

By the 1780s the popularity of Bath was near its peak and an even grander Pump Room was planned. While the foundations were being built, the steps of the old Roman temple and part of the pediment were discovered.

The Grand Pump Room was opened in 1795, but by that time much of the country had slipped into an economic depression brought about in part by war with France. By custom, today the water is dispensed free to disabled visitors and local residents.

Archaeological Explorations

The full extent of the Roman history of the area was not understood until 1878 when the city surveyor and architect Charles Davis began to explore the area around the King's Bath in search of the source of a leak. He went on to take up the floor of the King's Bath and find the Roman reservoir below.

Archaeological finds in Bath continue to the present day. In 1971 the West Baths were excavated, and from 1979 to 1983 the Roman Sacred Spring and the reservoir were re-excavated and the Temple Precinct beneath the Pump Room was revealed again.

Today the Pump Room stands directly over the Roman Temple Precinct and sacrificial altar. The East Baths extend beneath Kingston Parade. The temple itself lies buried beneath Stall Street.

The buildings at the site, including the Concert Room, now the museum's entrance hall, and the colonnade around the Great Bath, were put into place near the end of the nineteenth century.

The Source of the Waters

The largest of the three hot springs in Bath rises in the Roman Sacred Spring from a depth of about three thousand meters (nearly two miles) below the surface. The water, at a constant temperature of 46.5 degrees Celsius (115 degrees

Fahrenheit), contains forty-three minerals. Calcium and sulphate are the principal dissolved ions, along with sodium and chloride.

Scientists say the 250,000 gallons of water that bubble to the surface in Bath each day fell as rain about ten thousand years ago in the Mendip Hills about twenty miles west. That region is home to noted limestone caves and formations, including the Wookey Hole and the Cheddar Gorge. The water percolates deep into the earth, as much as two and a half miles below the surface, where it picks up heat from the earth's core. The heated water then rises back up, seeking a way out through fissures and faults such as those in Bath.

The water is colorless as it emerges, but picks up a green hue from algae that grows when it is exposed to daylight. The water tasted in the Pump Room is drawn through a borehole sunk below the King's Bath.

🔳 Roman Baths Museum and Pump Room

The Pump Room, Stall Street, Bath. Open daily, April to September, 9 A.M. to 6 P.M.; in August to 9:30 P.M. Open October to March 9:30 A.M. to 5 P.M. Admission: adult, ❸; child, ❸; family, ❻. Combined ticket with Museum of Costume also available. ☎ (012) 2547-7785. 💻 www.romanbaths.co.uk.

The museum includes:

• **The Temple Precinct.** Coins and other offerings to Sulis Minerva were discovered in the spring during the first explorations of 1878 and again in the 1980s when the area beneath the Pump Room was excavated. At that time the paved open-air precinct in front of the temple and the temple steps was found.

• **The Great Bath.** Fed with hot mineral water from the spring, its steps lead down to the flat lead-lined bottom of the five-foot-deep bath.

• **The Sacred Spring.** The spring rises into a reservoir built by the Romans and once covered with a vaulted roof. The roof collapsed into the spring and around 1100 the King's Bath was built over the remains.

The orange tidemark shows the bath's former level from the eighteenth- and nineteenth-century spa; today the water is back down at the Roman level.

Visitors would throw coins or jewelry into the spring, this helped researchers come up with the history of the spa. Also recovered were curses inscribed on a sheet of lead or pewter and committed to the sacred waters in hope of divine intervention. Some curses on display ask for punishment of petty thieves.

• **The Pump Room.** Today, you can take the waters in the simple but elegant Pump Room overlooking the baths; lunch, afternoon tea, and dinner are also served. Among the treasures in the room is the Tompion Clock and Sundial, presented in 1709 to the city by famed clockmaker Thomas Tompion. The clock was designed to be reset based on readings from a sundial outside the window. Above the clock is a marble of Richard "Beau" Nash, Bath's most famous master of ceremonies, placed there in 1752.

Nearby is an eighteenth-century Bath Sedan Chair, complete with a license to allow transport of visitors from their lodgings to the waters.

Price Bands
❶ £1–£3
❷ £3–£5
❸ £5–£7
❹ £7–£10
❺ £10–£15
❻ £15 and up

Bath of the Future

Since 1978 visitors have been unable to bathe in the waters of Bath because of concerns over bacteria. The rejuvenation of the baths will result in the United Kingdom's only working spa.

But Bath is expected to rise again as a spa by the end of 2002 with the opening of a state-of-the-art structure funded by Britain's Millennium Commission.

The glass and stone building, among a very small number of modern structures in the center of Bath, will include immersion pools, water therapy, and treatment rooms. For more details, consult 🖳 www.bathspa.co.uk.

Museum of Costume and Assembly Rooms

Bennett Street, Bath. Open daily 10 A.M. to 5 P.M., Sunday from 11 A.M. Admission: adult, ❸; child, ❶; family ❻. Combined ticket with Roman Baths Museum available. ☎ (012) 2547-7789. 🖳 www.museumofcostume.co.uk.

The **Assembly Rooms** were the heart of the social scene of Bath in the late eighteenth century, a party house presided over by a master of ceremonies.

Richard "Beau" Nash arrived in Bath in 1703 and by 1706 had become the city's master of ceremonies at the age of thirty-two. For the next four decades he devoted himself to making Bath the fashionable place to be, especially during the "season" from October to early June.

By Nash's death in 1761 there were two Assembly Rooms in Bath, but they were apparently inadequate for the party needs of the growing population.

A grand set of Assembly Rooms, at £20,000 the most expensive buildings in eighteenth-century Bath, were completed in 1771 under the design of John Wood the Younger. (Wood's father had designed many of the grand buildings of Bath already, including the Royal Crescent block.)

The formal entrance included a Doric column portico to shelter guests arriving by sedan chairs. The rooms within were simple but elegant, with candlelit crystal chandeliers, formal columns, and marble fireplaces; the high ceilings, decorated with elaborate plasterwork, served to draw off the heat.

The ballroom may seem empty when you visit, but imagine instead the space packed with as many as eight hundred dancers. Around the walls were portable benches for those who preferred to watch.

A gallery above the dance floor held the orchestra. A typical ball would have the hours between 6 P.M. and 8 P.M. devoted to formal minuets, from 8 P.M. to 9 P.M. given to more lively country dances (women had to remove the hoops from their skirts for the country dances), a break to the Tea Room for refreshments at 9 P.M., and then more country dances until 11 P.M. A typical season consisted of about twenty-four dress balls, one a week.

The Octagon Room, a forty-eight-foot-diameter chamber with four marble chimneys, was used for smaller parties and card games and other forms of gambling. It is decorated with a portrait by sometime Bath resident Thomas Gainsborough of Captain William Wade, the master of ceremonies from 1769 to 1777. A separate Card Room was added in 1777 at the back of the building.

Musical concerts also took place regularly. In 1777 they were directed by Italian soprano and composer Venanzio Rauzzini, who brought some of the best-known singers and performers of the day. Mozart had written for Rauzzini, and composer Joseph Haydn visited the Assembly Rooms on one of his visits to the United Kingdom and later wrote a canon in praise of Rauzzini's dog, Turk.

The Assembly Rooms went into decline along with Bath itself in the nineteenth century. The social set had moved on to the seaside resort of Brighton, which was in favor with the court, and to the exotic spas of Europe. There were still events at the rooms, though, including performances by Johann Strauss and Franz Liszt, public readings by Charles Dickens (who described a ball in the Octagon Room in his book *The Pickwick Papers*), and traveling shows of all sorts. And the Assembly Rooms were also forced to compete with the expanded Pump Room and hotels in Bath.

By the early twentieth century, the rooms were in serious financial straits; in 1903 they were forced to sell the Gainsborough portrait to raise funds; it was repurchased in 1988. When World War I broke out, the building was occupied by the Royal Flying Corps, and after the war the ballroom became a cinema.

The rooms might have faded away completely were it not for the Society for the Protection of Ancient Buildings. The group purchased the building in 1931 and gave it to the National Trust, which in turn gave it to the Bath City Council on the condition that the rooms be restored. The Assembly Rooms were reopened in 1938 with a grand eighteenth-century costume ball. Four years later, on April 25, 1942, Bath was heavily damaged by a German bombing raid and the rooms were left as a roofless shell. The Card Room was the only room to escape bomb damage in 1942.

It took until 1956 for the rooms to be restored once again, and subsequent projects were undertaken in the 1970s and a decade later. Today the Assembly Rooms look very much as they did at their peak in the eighteenth century.

The **Museum of Costume** opened in the basement of the Assembly Rooms in 1963, built around the large private collection of Doris Langley Moore.

The museum chronicles the history of fashionable clothes for women, men, and children for more than four hundred years. The displays, which are changed regularly, include more than 150 dressed figures. Each of the more than thirty thousand pieces in the full collection is an original.

The earliest garments date from the reigns of Elizabeth I (1558–1603) and James I (1603–1625), among the few surviving examples of that era. The collection includes dress and undress (informal attire) as well as outlandish court wear, including side hoops too wide to pass through a standard doorway.

More modern selections include items of Edwardian elegance, the development of 1920s style, and modern designs. Every year the museum asks a leading fashion expert to choose a dress or outfit that represents new and influential ideas.

American Museum in Britain

Claverton Manor, Bath. Open daily except Monday 2 P.M. to 5 P.M. from mid-March to early November. On summer bank holiday Sunday and Monday open 11 A.M. to 5 P.M. House and garden admission: adult, ❸; child, ❶. ☎ (0122) 546-0503. 🖳 www.americanmuseum.org.

An unusual museum in an unusual location, the collection concentrates on American life from the seventeenth through the nineteenth centuries, with displays on the New England colonies, Native Americans, the West, the Civil War, and more. Among the treasures of the museum is a collection of quilts.

The Building of Bath Museum

The Countess of Huntingdon's Chapel, the Vineyards, the Paragon, Bath. Open daily except Monday, mid-February to early December 10:30 A.M. to 5 P.M. Admission: adult, ❸; child (10–16), ❶. ☎ (0122) 533-3895. 🖳 www.bath-preserva tion-trust.org.uk/museums/bath.

The story behind the development of the Georgian City is told through artifacts, models, and reconstructions of some of the most important buildings in the history of Bath, focusing on resort life in the time of Beau Nash.

Bath Abbey Heritage Vaults

Bath Abbey, Bath. Open Monday to Saturday 10 A.M. to 4 P.M. ☎ (0122) 542-2462. 🖳 www.bathabbey.org.

The vaults feature a display of artifacts of the ancient Bath abbey dating back to Saxon times, displayed in restored eighteenth-century cellars.

Museum of Bath at Work

Bath Industrial Heritage Centre, Julian Road, Bath. Open Easter to end of October 10 A.M. to 5 P.M., remainder of year weekends only 10 A.M. to 5 P.M. Admission: adult, ❸; child, ❶; family, ❹. ☎ (0122) 531-8348. 🖳 www.bath-at-work.org.uk.

The heart of the museum is a Victorian-era factory frozen in time; Jonathan Burdett Bowler began his business in 1872, making and repairing soda water machinery and bottling his own potions such as Orange Champagne, Cherry Ciderette, and Bath Punch. The business lasted until 1969 when Bowler's grandson retired; when it closed it still had most of its original equipment.

At the Bath Industrial Heritage Centre, the factory has been restored. You'll be able to explore Bowler's carbonating plant, his Dickensian office, and the old machine shops where all manner of equipment was made or repaired. The museum also includes a gift shop, and of course, a sofa fountain.

The factory is about a fifteen-minute walk from the center of the city.

Sally Lunn's

4 North Parade Passage. Open daily from 10 A.M. to 6 P.M., 11 A.M. to 6 P.M. on Sunday. ☎ (0122) 546-1634.

This teahouse is claimed as the oldest house in Bath. Sally Lunn arrived in the 1680s and her baked goods, including the bun named after her, became a favorite of fashionable society. The restaurant serves morning coffees, light meals, and cream teas, plus dinner by candlelight every night except Monday.

The museum in the basement shows some of the Roman and medieval foundations, as well as the original kitchen with its wood-burning oven, Georgian range, and old baking utensils.

Guildhall Market

High Street, Bath. Open daily except Sunday 7:30 A.M. to 5 P.M.

There has been a Guildhall Market in Bath since 1284; today's version includes flower, meat, cheese, fruit, and baked goods stands; a cafe; and small stores selling books and notions.

Royal Crescent

Built by John Wood the Younger between 1767 and 1774 and considered one of the best examples of Palladian design in Bath, this was the first crescent (a half ellipse) of townhouses built in Britain.

Number 1 Royal Crescent

Open mid-February to the end of October 10:30 A.M. to 5 P.M. Tuesday through Sunday, late October to early December until 4 P.M. Closed remainder of the year. Admission: general, ❸; family, ❹. ☎ (0122) 542-8126.

The townhouse has been restored as it would have been furnished near the time of its construction.

Theatre Royal

Barton Street. Box office: ☎ (0122) 544-8844.

The theater is home to traveling productions and local shows, as well as plays and shows on their way to London's West End. The theater was built in 1805 to replace a smaller house in Orchard Street. It has been at the center of Bath's cultural scene ever since.

🎆 Stonehenge

There are few places on this planet more mysteriously attractive than the ancient stone circle at Stonehenge. Stonehenge is located about two miles west of Amesbury in Wiltshire, about ninety miles west of London.

The stones were erected sometime around 1650 B.C.; the site had been in use for more than five hundred years before. Of course, the nature of the "use" of Stonehenge is still unknown.

You can get there by train from London's Waterloo station to Salisbury, about nine miles south of the monument; from Salisbury you'll need to take a public bus (the Number 3 bus runs from the railway station to Stonehenge at least once an hour), tour bus, or taxi to Stonehenge itself.

Several tour-bus companies offer direct trips from London to Stonehenge, about a two-hour drive.

Stonehenge is open daily for visitors mid-March to end of May from 9:30 A.M. to 6 P.M., early June to end of August 9 A.M. to 7 P.M., early September to mid-October 9:30 A.M. to 5 P.M., and mid-October to mid-March 9:30 A.M. to 4 P.M. Admission: adult, ❸; child (5–15), ❶; senior, ❶; family, ❹.

For information you can call ☎ (019) 8062-4715 for a recorded message, or ☎ (019) 8062-5368 during operating hours for personal attention.

The ravages of time and human interference have taken their toll on the stones; it was not all that long ago that visitors were encouraged to chip off a piece to take home as a souvenir. While it used to be possible to get very close to the stones, visitors are now required to keep back behind a low fence. At the summer equinox there is often a standoff between competing groups wishing to use the site, a confrontation that has taken on a political dimension.

Avebury

Stonehenge gets all the press, but the stone circle at Avebury, located at Salisbury Plain about ninety minutes west of London, is larger, more complex, and probably a few hundred years older. There are more than one hundred stones in place, enclosed by massive earthworks and other features; the stones are not nearly as well preserved as those at Stonehenge. Scientists date the construction to about 2500 B.C.—about the same time as the pyramids of Egypt—and have a vague estimation of their purpose: some sort of ritual or religious function.

The inner circle was surrounded by a deep ditch and scientists speculate it once was filled with water to create a shimmering white-stone island.

The small village of Avebury is partly located within the circle and includes the **Alexander Keiller Museum**, which offers background on the area.

The site is open daily April to October from 10 A.M. to 5:30 P.M., and November to mid-December on weekends only 11:30 A.M. to 4 P.M. Admission is free. The museum is open daily in the summer 9:30 A.M. to 6:30 P.M., and in the winter Monday through Saturday 9:30 A.M. to 4 P.M.; admission is ❶.

Silbury Hill, about a mile south of Avebury, is the largest manmade mound in Europe; even after thousands of years of erosion, it stands 130 feet high and covers more than five acres. Archaeologists and researchers estimate the job took thousands of workers several decades to complete.

Avebury is located about twenty miles northwest of Stonehenge. You can take a train from London's Waterloo station to Salisbury and pick up local bus service from there; direct buses and tour coaches are available from London.

🔲 Stratford-upon-Avon

William Shakespeare's hometown, located in central England about two and a half hours northwest of London, has built an industry upon his works.

Stratford, which straddles the Avon River, grew as a center of commerce, and the tradition of weekly markets has continued since the twelfth century. But most visitors come to see the **Shakespeare Centre & Birthplace Museum**, the **World of Shakespeare**, the **Shakespeare Memorial Garden**, and the **Royal Shakespeare Theatre**. A bit outside of town is **Anne Hathaway's Cottage**.

The Birthplace Museum off Henley Street recreates some of the feel of Shakespeare's sixteenth-century life and exhibits artifacts related to the author or the town. The World of Shakespeare is a rather lame audiovisual tableau.

For information, consult 🖥 www.stratford-upon-avon.co.uk.

The best of Shakespeariana is the Royal Shakespeare Theatre, home of the Royal Shakespeare Company. The company presents the Bard's plays on a rotating schedule in the Main House. Works by Shakespeare's contemporaries are presented in the Swan, a theater in the round. The Other Place nearby presents modern and experimental plays. Tickets sell in the range of ❸ to ❻, with decent seats costing about £20. For ticket information, call ☎ (01789) 269191. You can purchase tickets for any of the three theaters by calling ☎ (0178) 929-5623 or consulting 🖳 www.rsc.org.uk.

Stratford-upon-Avon is 120 miles northwest of London. The best train service is offered by Thames Trains from London Paddington; these include trains timed to coincide with theater curtains. Other service is available on InterCity trains to Leamington Spa or Birmingham with connecting service to Stratford-upon-Avon. Bus service goes to Bridge Street in the city center.

Warwick Castle

Warwick Castle is an honest-to-god millennium-old castle, the one-time home of medieval jousts, royal trysts, and perhaps a bit of torture and mayhem over the years. In fact, much of that is still going on . . . in an interesting restoration by the Tussauds Group of London wax museum fame.

The castle was built in the green of Warwickshire in 1068 in the time of William the Conqueror. Visitors meet the various owners of the castle in re-created scenes. In the undercroft are tradesmen including armorers, wheelwrights, blacksmiths, and fletchers (arrowmakers).

The State Dining Room, decorated as it was in 1763, includes a gilded and carved ceiling and an impressive collection of silver and candleholders. Royalty including King George IV, Queen Victoria, Prince Albert, and today's Queen Elizabeth II have dined here.

And then there is the Tussaud centerpiece: the Royal Weekend Party, a recreation in wax of the guests and servants for a simple affair in the summer of 1898. Among the guests was young Winston Churchill.

The grounds were laid out in the 1750s by renowned designer Capability Brown. In peak summer periods, the grounds are home to jousts, falconry, crafts demonstrations, and other education and entertainment activities. On weekends, adults can sit down for a lavish Kingmaker's Feast in the medieval undercroft dining room, served unlimited wine by costumed wenches.

Getting to Warwick

Warwick is about ninety minutes by car northwest of London, about eight miles from Stratford-upon-Avon. Train service is available on the Chiltern Line from Marylebone Station in London.

The castle is open every day except Christmas from 10 A.M. to 6 P.M., with shorter hours in November and December. Admission to the castle is adult ❻, child ❸, senior ❹, and family ❻. You can also purchase a family pass for about the price of three tickets to admit two adults and two children. For information call ☎ (019) 2640-6600 or consult 🖳 www.warwick-castle.co.uk.

Combination tickets with the Chiltern Line train are also available. Call ☎ (099) 016-5165 for information.

Chapter 31
More Day Trips West: Oxford and Windsor

🎇 Oxford

The privileged students at Oxford no longer stroll about town in academic gown and mortarboard except during exam periods and special occasions, not all of the students were born with a silver spoon in their mouths, and there is now a thriving town to go along with the slightly less hidebound gown.

Nevertheless, Oxford offers a fascinating glimpse of old-school England, along with several wondrously eclectic museums and public buildings.

Oxford is about fifty-five miles from London, a ninety-minute rail trip from Paddington station to Oxford's station, about fifteen minutes from downtown. Bus service is also available from London's Victoria coach station to Oxford's Gloucester Green near the town center.

For information about Oxford, you can contact:

Oxford City Council
Clarendon House
52 Cornmarket Street
Oxford OX1 3HD
United Kingdom
📧 www.oxford.gov.uk

The Story of Oxford

Oxford developed as an academic center in the tenth and eleventh centuries because of the scholars at the religious monasteries. By the sixteenth century, a more formalized college system developed, whereby students lived with their tutors in small groups of libraries, chapels, and rooms within courtyards and quadrangles.

Oxford grew as a Saxon trading settlement near the fords where the Thames and Cherwell rivers come together. Oxford was attacked by Danish invaders in the tenth and eleventh centuries. By the thirteenth century it had become a major educational center of Europe. Charles I had Oxford as his capital from 1642 to 1645 during the English revolution.

279

Price Bands
❶ £1–£3
❷ £3–£5
❸ £5–£7
❹ £7–£10
❺ £10–£15
❻ £15 and up

The city of Oxford is best known as the home of the University of Oxford, one of the oldest universities in the world. Many colleges permit visitors except during exam periods in May and June; some offer guided tours led by students.

At the heart of the city is Carfax, where four main streets head out from town. This was the center of the original walled city and is the location of Saint Martin's Tower, the last remaining element of a fourteenth century church; it is open for tours March to October, 10 A.M. to 5:30 P.M., for a charge of ❶.

Museums and Attractions in Oxford

Christ Church College

The largest and perhaps the most traditional of Oxford's colleges is Christ Church on Saint Aldate's. Tours are available Monday through Saturday from 10:30 A.M. to 4:30 P.M. and Sunday 2 P.M. to 4:30 P.M.; tickets are ❶.

The main entrance to Christ Church is beneath the dome of Tom Tower, built in 1681 by Christopher Wren; visitors enter through the adjacent Memorial Garden. Nearby is the college Picture Gallery.

Christ Church Picture Gallery

Christ Church College, Oriel Square. Open Monday to Saturday 10:30 A.M. to 1 P.M. and 2 P.M. to 5:30 P.M., Sunday 2 P.M. to 5:30 P.M.; October to Easter the gallery closes at 4:30 P.M. A guided tour is offered Thursday at 2:15 P.M. Admission: adult, ❶; child (younger than 12), free. ☎ (0186) 527-6172. 🖳 www.chch.ox.ac.uk/gallery.

The gallery, unimpressive for its own slab-like architecture, has a notable collection of Old Master paintings, including works by Tintoretto, Carraci, and Van Dyck, and drawings by artists that include Leonardo da Vinci, Michelangelo, and Rubens.

Three more Oxford colleges lie east: Oriel, Corpus Christi, and Merton, which dates to the thirteenth century with some ancient structures still in use. Behind Merton College, down Deadman's Walk to Rose Lane, is Magdalen College with its fifteenth-century bell tower and Cloister Quad with a full complement of gargoyles.

Saint Mary's Church on High Street offer tours from 9:15 A.M. to 7 P.M. in the summer and until dusk in the winter; a charge of ❶ is made for a visit to the church spire with views of the old city.

Behind the church are some of the most majestic buildings in Oxford, including the Radcliffe Camera, now used as a reading room for the Bodleian Library.

The Sheldonian Theatre is a Christopher Wren design based on the Theatre of Marcellus in Rome; Wren was a professor of astronomy at Oxford at the time. The building, with an observation room in the tower, is open for tours for a few hours in the morning and afternoon for a token admission.

Nearby on New College Lane, Hertford College's buildings are joined by a copy of Venice's Bridge of Sighs. Further down the road is New College itself, founded by William of Wykeham in 1379.

Ashmolean Museum of Art and Archaeology

Beaumont Street. Open Tuesday to Saturday 10 A.M. to 4 P.M., Sunday 2 P.M. to 4 P.M., and bank holidays in summer 2 P.M. to 5 P.M. Closed early September, Christmas, and Easter periods. Admission: free, but a donation of £2 per person is requested. ☎ (0186) 527-8000. 🖳 www.ashmol.ox.ac.uk.

Opened in 1683 the Ashmolean is the oldest public museum in Britain and one of the most interesting and eclectic collections you'll find anywhere. The present building, a neo-Grecian masterpiece, was built in 1845.

Wandering through the halls, I found a roomful of ancient statues, a mummified fish in a coffin, a trio of spectacular maces of the beadles of the University of Oxford from about 1550, and a collection of studies of Rodin's *The Thinker*, prepared by the artist before he completed his masterpiece.

The Ashmolean is not as elegant as the British Museum in London, but it is more of a museum than a temple. It's a great place to sit and surround yourself with thousands of years of history.

In the **Antiquities Hall** near the entrance, many of the statues come from the collection of the earl of Arundel in the seventeenth century. His marriage to the daughter of the earl of Shrewsbury brought him the fortune he needed to collect art. In 1624 he sent William Petty to Asia Minor to collect art; he returned with two hundred statues, reliefs, and inscriptions from Turkish sites in Smyrna (now Izmir); Constantinople (now Istanbul); Pergamum; and the Greek cities of Samos, Ephesus, and Athens.

The **Tradescant Room** displays the remnants of the original collection of the Ashmolean Museum, the gatherings of the Tradescant family. It was begun by John Tradescant the Elder, gardener to Charles I (his actual title was "keeper of His Majesty's gardens, vines, and silkworms"). Some of the items were acquired in the course of his travels of the Continent in search of plants for his boss; others were given him by merchants, sailors, and ambassadors. Tradescant displayed his collection in his house at Lambeth known as "the Ark."

His son, John Tradescant the Younger, inherited the job and his collection on his father's death in 1638. The younger Tradescant made several research trips to Virginia. When he died the collection was given to Elias Ashmole, a government official and scholar. He in turn gave the collection, along with his own materials, to the University of Oxford on the condition that a new building be constructed to display the items. In 1683 the collection went on display at the Ashmolean Museum; that building, on Broad Street, now houses the **Museum of the History of Science**.

The most famous piece of the Tradescant Collection and one of the most important surviving American Indian relics, the so-called Mantle of Powhatan, was collected in 1638 and cataloged as "Powhatan, King of Virginia's habit all embroidered with shells, or Roanoke."

The mantle consists of four deerskins, sewn together with the sinew of the animal. The decoration, made of shell, shows a human figure flanked on one side by a deer and the other by a feline-like animal.

Modern anthropologists now question whether the mantle was actually worn as a garment or was instead used as a formal temple hanging.

Also in the Tradescant Room is the Guy Fawkes Lantern, an ordinary looking sheet-metal construction that has extraordinary meaning to Britons. It was given to the Bodleian Library at Oxford University in 1641 by Robert Haywood, a justice of the peace who had been present at the arrest of Guy Fawkes in the cellars of Parliament House when his rebellious plot was foiled in 1605. It was given to the Ashmolean Museum in 1887 for preservation.

Another important room at the museum is the **Drapers' Gallery**, built in 1939 with funds from the Worshipful Company of Drapers to house objects from the Near East before the Islamic Conquest of about A.D. 650.

Treasures of the gallery include the Jericho Skull, a human skull plastered and decorated with shells from a Neolithic settlement near Jericho, about 7000 B.C. The substitution of bivalve shells for eyes is considered among the earliest attempts at portraiture.

Also on display is a Dead Sea Scrolls jar. About the year 66, threatened by invasion from the Romans, a religious community at Qumran on the northwest shore of the Dead Sea hid their papyrus scrolls in jars for safety. They were found, untouched, after World War II. The oldest of the scrolls include interpretations of the Old Testament in Hebrew.

The Weld-Blundell Prism is one of the oldest known historical texts, dating from the nineteenth century B.C. Written in cuneiform script in what is now southern Iraq, it is considered the finest surviving copy of the list of Sumerian kings.

The collection of fine art includes a set of sculptures by Edgar Degas, also known for his paintings. One of the collection's paintings is a study of a dancer holding her right heel. Degas did a number of quick impressionistic studies of the dancer because he couldn't get models to hold the position very long. The sculptures were found in his studio after his death and were bronzed.

Bodleian Library

Broad Street. Open Monday to Friday 9 A.M. to 6 P.M., Saturday 9 A.M. to 12:30 P.M. Closed Christmas Eve to New Year's Day. Admission: free. ☎ (0186) 527-7000. 🖳 www.bodley.ox.ac.uk.

Guided tours of the Divinity School, Convocation House, and Duke Humfrey's Library are offered April to October several times a day during the week and Saturday mornings, and from November to February on Wednesday at 2:30 P.M. and Saturday at 11 A.M. Tickets are ❶.

The world-renowned research library of the University of Oxford includes the **Divinity School**, built in 1488 and featuring a breathtaking vaulted ceiling. The entrance is through the Old School's Quadrangle, built in 1617 and including the **Tower of the Five Orders**. In Radcliffe Square is the Italianate **Radcliffe Camera** from 1749, the first circular library in Britain, and the Clarendon Building of 1717, built as the home of the Oxford University Press. The **Sheldonian Theatre** was designed by Christopher Wren and completed in 1669; it is still used for university ceremonies.

Museum of the History of Science

Old Ashmolean Building, Broad Street. Open Tuesday to Saturday noon to 4 P.M. Closed Easter and Christmas weeks. Admission: free. ☎ (0186) 527-7280. 🖳 www.mhs.ox.ac.uk.

The museum presents the art and science of astronomical, surveying, navigational, and mathematical instruments, including the largest collection of astrolabes in the world. The former Chemical Laboratory in the basement includes a collection of scary antique surgical and dental instruments, as well as nineteenth-century chemical glassware and physics research instruments.

The museum is housed in the original building constructed for the Ashmolean Museum in 1683.

University Museum and Pitt Rivers Museum

Parks Road and Banbury Road. University Museum open Monday to Saturday noon to 5 P.M.; Pitt Rivers Museum open Monday to Saturday 1 P.M. to 4:30 P.M. Both museums closed some days during Christmas and Easter period. Admission: free. ☎ (0186) 527-0949. University Museum website: 🖳 www.ashmol.ox.ac.uk/oum. Pitt Rivers Museum website: 🖳 units.ox.ac.uk/departments/prm.

These two museums under one roof are both worth visiting.

The University Museum opened in 1860 as the school of natural science; today, the glass-roofed Museum Court holds the extensive collections on that subject. You'll find rare remains of the dodo, extinct since about 1680; dinosaur bones and fossils; and collections on entomology, geology, mineralogy, and zoology. Charles Darwin donated some of his materials to the museum.

In a large storeroom behind is the Pitt Rivers Museum, holding a spectacular anthropological collection from ancient boats, tools, and weapons, to amulets and shrunken heads.

The museum was founded in 1884 when Lieutenant General Pitt Rivers, an influential figure in the development of archaeology and evolutionary anthropology, gave his collection of some eighteen thousand items to the university; the holdings have now grown to half a million pieces.

The museum is mostly organized typologically—grouped by form or purpose rather than by geographical or cultural origin. This is based on Pitt Rivers's theories concerning the evolution of ideas. Also preserved is much of the original Victorian atmosphere, including cluttered cases with small handwritten labels.

The adjoining Balfour Building at 60 Banbury Road holds additional displays on hunter-gatherer societies and ancient and modern musical instruments.

Bate Collection of Musical Instruments

Faculty of Music, Saint Aldates. Open weekdays 2 P.M. to 5 P.M., and Saturday during school terms 10 A.M. to noon. Admission: free. ☎ (0186) 527-6139. 🖳 www.ashmol.ox.ac.uk/BCMIPage.html.

This is a fabulous collection of some 1,500 European woodwind, brass, percussion, and keyboard instruments. Treasures include the Michael Thomas Collection of harpsichords, the William Retford collection of bows and tools, and much more.

Museum of Oxford

Town Hall, Saint Aldates. Open Tuesday to Friday 10 A.M. to 4 P.M., and Saturday 10 A.M. to 5 P.M., and Sunday noon to 4 P.M. Admission: adult and child, ❶. ☎ (0186) 581-5559.

A museum of the story of the city and the university, including reconstructed interiors from the sixteenth century plus a medieval collection.

University of Oxford Botanic Garden

Rose Lane. Open daily 9 A.M. to 4:30 P.M.; greenhouses open daily 10 A.M. to 4 P.M. Admission: ❶ April to August, free other times. ☎ (0186) 527-6920. 🖳 www.ashmol.ox.ac.uk/omc/oxmus242.html.

The oldest botanic garden in Britain has been located on the banks of the River Cherwell in the center of Oxford since the early 1620s. It began as a collection of medicinal herbs for seventeenth-century physicians, and today houses some eight thousand species from almost every botanical family.

Museum of Modern Art

30 Pembroke Street. Open Tuesday to Sunday 11 A.M. to 6 P.M., Sunday 11 A.M. to 6 P.M. On Thursday, the museum is open until 9 P.M. Admission: adult, ❶. ☎ (0186) 572-2733. 🖳 www.moma.org.uk.

The Museum of Modern Art is a small but influential showplace for twentieth-century art, photography, film, and video.

Oxford University Press Museum

Great Clarendon Street. Open during office hours by appointment only. Admission: free. ☎ (0186) 526-7527.

A small museum, the Oxford explores the history, books, and printing equipment of the world-renowned Oxford University Press, which dates back to the fifteenth century.

Oxon & Bucks Light Infantry

T. A. Centre, Slade Park. Open weekdays by appointment. Admission: free. ☎ (0186) 578-0128.

This collection of artifacts of the county regiment of Oxfordshire and Buckinghamshire includes medals, uniforms, badges, and regimental silver.

Rotunda Museum of Antique Doll Houses

Grove House, 44 Iffley Turn. Open May to September on the first Sunday of the month 2:15 P.M. to 5 P.M.; other times by appointment. Admission: adult, ❶. No child younger than 16 admitted.

This is a private collection of more than forty historic doll houses from 1700 to 1900, with period furnishings.

Near Oxford

Cogges Manor Farm Museum

Church Lane, Cogges, Witney. Open mid-March to early November, Tuesday to Friday and on bank holidays 10:30 A.M. to 5:30 P.M., and Saturday and Sunday noon to 5:30 P.M. Admission: adult, ❷; child, ❶.

This working museum includes a historic manor house and original stone farm buildings. The manor house has been restored and includes a Victorian bedroom and nursery and the seventeenth-century study of wool merchant William Blake.

Cooking demonstrations are given each afternoon along with presentations of farm and dairy work and crafts. The twenty-acre farm is stocked with traditional Victorian breeds of farm animals.

Witney is west of Oxford, reachable by a Thames Transit bus.

Banbury Museum

8 Horsefair, Banbury, Oxon. Open April to September, Monday to Saturday 10 A.M. to 5 P.M.; October to March, Tuesday to Saturday 10 A.M. to 4:30 P.M. Admission: free. ☎ (0129) 525-9855.

This small museum tells the story of Banburyshire through old photographs and glass-plate negatives.

Swalcliffe Barn

Shipston Road, Swalcliffe near Banbury, Oxon. Open Sunday and bank holidays, Easter to October, 2 P.M. to 5 P.M. Admission: free. ☎ (0129) 578-8278.

The Tythe Barn was built for the Rectoral Manor of Swalcliffe between 1400 and 1409, and much of its medieval timber half-cruck roof is still intact. It is used to display antique agricultural and trade vehicles.

Abingdon Museum

The County Hall, Market Place, Abingdon. Open Tuesday to Sunday 11 A.M. to 5 P.M., in winter until 4 P.M. Admission: free. ☎ (0123) 552-3703.

A grand seventeenth-century town hall, now used as a museum, the home of the Southern Arts Contemporary Craft Collection.

Didcot Railway Centre

The Station Yard, Didcot. Open daily, late March to late September and at other times and on weekends through the year, 10 A.M. to 5 P.M. Admission: ❷ to ❸, depending on the event. ☎ (0123) 581-7200. 💻 www.didcotrailwaycentre.org.uk.

The Didcot is a recreation of the golden age of the Great Western Railway, including steam locomotives, signals, and relics. Trains run the first and last Sunday of each month, every Sunday in summer, and at other times.

Blenheim Palace

Woodstock, about eight miles north of Oxford. Bus service is available from Oxford. Open for tours daily, mid-March to October, 10:30 A.M. to 5:30 P.M. Admission: ❹. The park is open year-round. Admission: ❷. ☎ (019) 9381-1091. 🖳 www.blenheimpalace.com.

This royally grand structure was built in 1704 as a thank-you gift for John Churchill, the first Duke of Marlborough, after his victory over the French in the Battle of Blenheim. The Italianate structure is the largest private residence in the country and one of the most valuable pieces of real estate anywhere.

Guided tours of the house offer just a glimpse of the palace with its ornate furnishings, including pieces from Versailles, Chippendale chairs, and lots of family portraits of the Marlborough clan.

The most distinguished family member was Sir Winston Churchill, born at Blenheim in 1874 and buried across the way at Bladon Church. An exhibition highlights the Churchill connection.

Outside are elaborate formal gardens designed by Capability Brown, as well as a butterfly house.

〔WOW〕 Windsor

Windsor is a fascinating amalgam, a combination of some of the most hallowed halls of British history, including the storied Windsor Castle, the most hidebound upper-class schools of Eton, beautiful green parks, and lovely city and country lanes. All this comes once you navigate a path past the Burger King, McDonald's, Pizza Hut, wax museum, and other tourist come-ons in the business district.

In this section we'll concentrate on fabulous Windsor Castle, with side trips to other area attractions, including Legoland Windsor, a children's theme park that Queen Elizabeth can likely see in the distance from her royal chambers.

For more information on Windsor, consult 🖳 www.windsor-tourism.co.uk.

Windsor is located about twenty miles west of London, accessible by car by taking the M4 to exit 6. Southwest Trains run from London Waterloo, arriving in about thirty-five minutes at Windsor & Eton Riverside, a four-block walk from Windsor Castle. Thames Trains run from London Paddington with a change of train in Slough, arriving at Windsor & Eton central station, across the road from Windsor Castle. Buses run from London's Victoria coach station. For bus information, call Traveline at ☎ (0181) 668-7261.

On Thames Street in front of the central station is Curfew Yard; a building at the location, now occupied by a fudge shop, was built about 1620 and was supposedly used by Oliver Cromwell in 1648 to sign the death warrant of Charles I. In the basement of the store, a tunnel (now sealed) runs to the dungeons of Curfew Tower at the castle, where criminals were housed and their bodies sometimes hung as warnings to the populace.

You can walk up Thames Street along the walls of the castle to the entrance on Castle Hill.

The Peascod Street pedestrian mall opposite the castle is lined with shops that cater to locals and tourists alike. Mentions of Peascod Street as the home of traders and craftsmen servicing Windsor Castle reach as far back as the thirteenth century. The name comes from a *croft*, or small farm, growing peas.

📵 Windsor Castle

The Royals have called Windsor home for more than nine hundred years. The old place has been through a lot over the centuries, with numerous additions, reconstructions, and repairs, including the cleanup to a disastrous fire in 1992. It endures, though, as the oldest royal residence still in use, and one of the most historically rich places in England, with echoes of kings, queens, and some say, of King Arthur and the Knights of the Round Table.

Windsor Castle is an official residence of Queen Elizabeth, the place where she grew up as a child, and is said to be her favorite place to lay her crown from among all her humble digs. The queen's standard flies from the Round Tower when she is in residence.

Tickets for Windsor are sold at the entrance to the castle and advance reservations are not available. Open daily 9:45 A.M. to 5:15 P.M. Admission to all areas is adult ❺, child ❸, and family ❻. On Sunday, when Saint George's Chapel is closed to tours, charges are ❹, ❸, and ❺ respectively. For all areas, except Queen Mary's Doll House, the charge is adult ❹, child ❷, and family ❻.

Note that because Windsor Castle is an occupied royal palace, it is subject to closure for special events. Reduced-rate tickets are sold when sections are closed. For information, call the twenty-four-hour information line at ☎ (0175) 383-1118 or consult 💻 www.windsor-tourism.co.uk/castle.html.

The castle sprawls over some thirteen acres, including a royal palace, a spectacular collegiate church, and the homes and workplaces of the officials of the castle and church. The old royal hunting forest to the south is now known as Windsor Great Park.

The castle was created by William the Conqueror about 1080 as part of a chain of Norman fortifications around London.

Originally conceived as an entirely defensive position, it is set on a chalk ridge about one hundred feet above the river bank. The central tower or keep— at Windsor the Round Tower—is protected by an outer fenced courtyard or bailey, in the case of Windsor's, by baileys to either side known as the Lower and Upper Wards.

Henry I had domestic quarters in the castle as early as 1110, and Henry II converted the castle into a palace adding two royal apartments, a state residence in the Lower Ward for official occasions, and a smaller private residence on the north side of the Upper Ward.

The oldest existing parts of the castle are in the Round Tower and surrounding curtain wall, which date from the time of Henry II. The half-round towers visible from the High Street were built by Henry III in the 1220s. According to tradition, it was here that King Arthur met with the Knights of the Round Table.

The largest expansion of Windsor took place during the reign of Edward III from 1327 to 1377. The castle took on all the trappings of a medieval palace as the center of his court and the seat of the newly founded Order of the Garter.

Windsor Castle

Saint George's Chapel was begun about 1474 by King Edward IV, and was completed in 1528 by King Henry VIII. The stone vault structure is the burial place of ten British sovereigns. Alongside is Albert Memorial Chapel, originally built by King Henry III in the thirteenth century as a memorial to Edward the Confessor. It was restored and elaborated by Queen Victoria as a memorial to Albert, her prince consort.

Edward IV built the current larger Saint George's Chapel to the west of Henry III's original church. During the English civil war in the mid-seventeenth century, the castle was seized by Parliamentary forces who used a section as a prison for Royalists. King Charles I was buried in the vaults beneath Saint George's Chapel after his execution at Whitehall in 1649.

The Upper Ward and State Apartments were reconstructed after the Restoration of the monarchy in 1660 in the baroque manner, heavily influenced by the French style of Louis XIV. The most spectacular element of the rebuilding was Saint George's Hall, the headquarters of the Order of the Garter.

Many of the rooms featured ceiling paintings by Italian artist Antonio Verrio. They depicted the world through the eyes of the Royalists, including celebrations of the Restoration of the royalty and the Church of England. Most were removed in subsequent remodeling but remain in the Queen's Presence Chamber, the Queen's Audience Chamber, and the King's Dining Room.

The castle's spectacular art collection rivals many of the world's greatest museums, including perhaps the world's finest collection of drawings and notebooks by Leonardo da Vinci.

A major rebuilding took place during the reign of George IV in the 1820s, including an extension of the Round Tower. The Waterloo Chamber was created to celebrate the victory over Napoleon, and the old hall and chapel were joined together and remade as the Gothic-revival Saint George's Hall.

The castle became the favorite residence of Queen Victoria during her reign, and many state occasions were held here. The Grand Staircase was reconstructed during that time, and a new private chapel was built to the east of Saint George's Hall. (It was in or near that chapel that the disastrous fire of 1992 began.)

Queen Elizabeth and her sister Margaret spent most of their childhood at Windsor during the Second World War, and the castle is still much used by the royal family. The court is officially in residence in April, during Ascot week in June when the Garter Day celebrations take place, and during other state occasions, such as visits by world leaders. The queen spends most of her private weekends at the castle through the year.

On November 20, 1992, a fire broke out in the Queen's Private Chapel. The blaze is thought to have been caused by a spotlight igniting a curtain above the altar. The fire spread rapidly at roof level, destroying the ceilings and much of Saint George's Hall and the Grand Reception Room and gutting the Private Chapel, State Dining Room, Crimson Drawing Room, and other lesser rooms. All told, the blaze took fifteen hours to extinguish and one hundred rooms on five floors were destroyed or damaged.

By good fortune, many of the rooms were empty of furnishings at the time because workers were in the process of a rewiring project. Many other items were removed from the castle by firefighters and staff as the fire continued.

The reconstruction project—much of it paid for from funds raised by the opening of Buckingham Palace to tours—extended more than five years.

The damaged rooms, including the ceiling of the Grand Reception Room were reinstated as they were, but the chapel area was redesigned, and a new, more impressive timber ceiling was installed in Saint George's Hall.

The restoration was officially completed in 1997, five years to the day after the fire. As part of the restoration, new areas in what are known as the Semi-State Rooms are open from early October to late March: the Green Drawing Room, the Crimson Drawing Room, the State Dining Room, the Octagon Dining Room, and the China Corridor.

The castle receives about five thousand visitors per day. Insiders say many tour groups make their first stop at Windsor in the morning, resulting in a glut of visitors when the gates open at 10 A.M.; if you are visiting during peak tourism times you may want to arrive an hour or two later.

The last admission to the castle is 4:30 P.M. from March to November and 3:30 P.M. the rest of the year.

The changing of the guard is at 11 A.M. every day in the heart of the summer, and every other day the rest of the year. The new guard marches to the castle about 11 A.M. and the old guard returns about 11:30 A.M.

The tour of the castle begins with an entrance from Castle Hill past the base of the Round Tower. The Round Tower is not open to the public and today is used to house the Royal Archives.

The entrance to the State Apartments leads from the North Terrace.

Stand on the North Terrace and look down into the valley over the River Thames to see the playing fields of Eton, the fifteenth-century college chapel, and in the distance the town of Slough.

Queen Mary's Doll House was created in the 1920s by Edward Lutyens for Queen Mary, consort of George V. A huge project built on a tiny scale of 1:12, the house took three years and thousands of artists and craftsmen to complete. Pictures on the walls were commissioned from notable artists, and many of the hundreds of books in the tiny library were written by authors of the day, some in their own hand; they included Rudyard Kipling, Sir Arthur Conan Doyle, Thomas Hardy, J. M. Barrie, and others.

Working elevators stop at each floor, the electrical system functions, and all five bathrooms have running water.

Nearby is a display of the dolls France and Marianne along with an impressive collection of costumes and possessions, presented to the young princesses Elizabeth and Margaret by the children of France in 1938 following a state visit to France by their parents.

The entrance to the State Apartments is through the **Gallery**, a vaulted room used for a changing exhibition from the Royal Collection. Alongside is the **China Museum**, where cases display treasures from the Crown's china services, some of which are still used for royal banquets and other occasions.

You'll ascend the **Grand Staircase**, a feature added in 1866. The walls are lined with trophies of arms and suits of armor. Overlooking the stairs is the oversized statue of George IV by Francis Chantrey, copied at the king's request from the original bronze at Brighton. Below is Henry VIII's suit of armor from about 1540.

At the top of the stairs is the **Grand Vestibule**, which includes showcases made in 1889 to display some of Queen Victoria's Golden Jubilee presents, some of which are on display. Treasures include an eighteenth-century gold tiger from the throne of Tipu Sultan, king of Mysore, and trophies from the battle of Seringapatam in India in 1799. On display in years past was the lead shot that killed Lord Nelson at Trafalgar in 1805, a valuable which had a short featured role at the National Maritime Museum in Greenwich.

The **Waterloo Chamber** was added at the behest of George IV to commemorate Napoleon's defeat at Waterloo. He commissioned portraits by artist Thomas Lawrence of the sovereigns, statesmen, and military commanders of the campaign; the series includes the first Duke of Wellington, Pope Pius VII, and twenty-eight others. The unusual ceiling of the room has clerestory windows and wood timbers, suggestive of a grand naval ship.

The Waterloo Chamber is still used each June for the luncheon for the Knights of the Garter, and for concerts and balls. The nearby **Garter Throne Room** is the place where the queen invests new knights and ladies of the Garter with the insignia of the order before their formal installation in Saint George's Chapel.

The **King's Bed Chamber** includes a spectacular French gilt-wood "polonaise" bed as decorated in green and purple for the visit of Emperor Napoleon

III in 1855; his initials and those of the Empress Eugénie are displayed on the foot of the bed.

The **King's Dressing Room** and the **King's Closet** hold a king's ransom of fine art, including the 1622 *Portrait of the Artist* by Peter Paul Rubens, Anthony Van Dyck's *Charles I in Three Positions* of 1635, two works by Rembrandt including *The Artist's Mother,* and other masterpieces.

The **Queen's Drawing Room** features a gorgeous carved ebony seventeenth-century cabinet from France.

Perhaps the most opulent of the rooms at Windsor is the **King's Dining Room**, a place of rich wooden paneling and an ethereal ceiling painting by Verrio depicting a banquet of the gods.

When there is a state visit to Windsor, the visiting leader receives the diplomatic corps in the **Queen's Ballroom.**

The small, richly paneled and carved **Queen's Presence Chamber** is used as the Robing Room for the knights of the Garter before the procession to Saint George's Chapel on Garter Day.

One of the most impressive of all the rooms at Windsor is **Saint George's Hall**, a 180-foot-long room that is decorated with the coats of arms of all of the knights of the Garter from the beginning of the order. This was one of the most heavily damaged rooms in the fire of 1992, but it reopened a year after the rest of the castle in 1998 in a restored and improved state. (Most of the artifacts from the room were saved from the fire.)

The Gothic-style architecture was said to have been inspired by the novels of Sir Walter Scott, an author who was a favorite of George IV. The hall is used for banquets on state visits and as part of the Garter Day events.

On the Lower Ward of the castle is Saint George's Chapel, the final resting place of ten British sovereigns. Founded by Edward IV in 1475, it was completed in 1528 by Henry VIII. The chapel is dedicated to the patron saint of the Most Noble Order of the Garter, Britain's highest Order of Chivalry. There are public worship services three times a day.

Alongside is the **Albert Memorial Chapel**, created by Victoria in honor of her husband Albert, a (literally) over-the-top masterpiece of gold, mosaics, and marble. A docent who spends all day there summed up the place with British understatement: "They didn't leave anywhere to rest the eyes," she told me.

When you exit the chapel you'll walk along the enclosed inner courtyard of the Dean's Cloister, built in 1240.

Windsor's Parks

Home Park connects to the castle on the north, east, and south; Windsor Great Park lies south of the boundary of Home Park.

The Great Park of Windsor

The former royal hunting grounds, the Great Park includes some five thousand acres of land connected to Windsor Castle by a three-mile-long, tree-lined avenue known as the Long Walk, first planted by King Charles II in 1685.

The avenue is open to the public. From the castle, turn left onto High Street and continue to Park Street, which leads directly to the northern end of the Great Park.

At the southern end of the park, on Snow Hill, is *Copper Horse*, the equestrian statue of King George III erected in 1831. Beyond Snow Hill are two more royal residences, neither open to the public. The Royal Lodge, once the private retreat of George IV, is the home of Queen Elizabeth the Queen Mother. Past it is Cumberland Lodge, former home of the ranger of the Great Park.

Beyond Cumberland Lodge is Smith's Lawn, where polo matches are played most summer weekends—Prince Charles has been a past participant—and the notable plantings of Valley Gardens and Virginia Water, an artificial lake. The National Carriage-Driving Championships are held in the park each fall.

On the far side of the lake are Roman ruins brought in 1817 from Leptis Magna in Libya for King George IV. The Valley Gardens are open to the public year-round.

During the reign of George IV, a royal menagerie was maintained in the park, including as star resident a Nubian giraffe given to the king by Mehemet Ali, the pasha of Egypt, in 1827. The giraffe was accompanied by a pair of Egyptian cows and two Arab keepers. The animal, alas, did not thrive, and it died two years later.

Frogmore House and Mausoleum

The house, gardens, and mausoleum of Victoria and Albert are open for visits for a limited period in May and August. There are also prebooked guided tours in the summer. For information, inquire at Windsor Castle. All tickets are ❸.

Set within the adjacent Home Park of Windsor Castle, the house dates from the 1680s and was purchased in 1792 for Queen Charlotte. She indulged her interest in botany and gardening with plantings, including rare and unusual species. The house became a favorite of George V and Queen Mary who stayed there for much of the period from 1902 to 1910.

Queen Victoria selected the site for the Royal Mausoleum at Frogmore soon after the death of her husband Prince Albert in 1861; work was completed ten years later. Much of the interior decoration was done in the style of Raphael, Albert's favorite. Victoria joined her husband in the mausoleum in 1901.

Savill Garden in Windsor Great Park

The Great Park, Wick Lane, Englefield Green. November to March 10 A.M. to 4 P.M. Admission: adult, ❷; accompanied child, free; senior, ❷. General information: ☎ (0175) 386-0222; direct line: ☎ (0178) 443-5544.

Some thirty-five acres of English landscaped gardens, Savill Garden includes rose gardens, great lawns, ponds, and streams. Highlights include flowering rhododendrons, camellias, magnolias, spring displays of daffodils, and summer blooms of lilies and hydrangeas. Begun in 1932, the exhibit was expanded in 1995 with the opening of the Queen Elizabeth Temperate House, home to trees, shrubs, and ferns that would not ordinarily thrive in Britain.

Other Windsor Sites

Household Cavalry Museum

Saint Leonard's Road. Open Monday to Friday 10 A.M. to 12:15 P.M. and 2 P.M. to 4:15 P.M. Admission: free. ☎ (0175) 375-5203.

The Windsor home of the Household Cavalry at Combermere Barracks includes a collection of weapons, uniforms, and armor from 1600 to the present day.

Dungeons of Windsor

High Street, opposite Windsor Castle. Open daily 10 A.M. to 5:30 P.M. Admission: adult, ❷; child, ❶.

The dungeons offer an exploration of crime and punishment in and around Windsor from the barbaric thirteenth century to the Victorian era. Highlights include the ducking stool, branding irons, the whipping post, the stocks, and other entertainments strictly for the tourist.

Royal Windsor Race Course

Admission: adult, ❷ to ❻, depending on location; accompanied child (younger than 17), free. ☎ (0175) 386-5234. 💻 www.windsor-racecourse.co.uk.

The course is a fifteen-minute walk from central Windsor or a short water-bus or cab ride. Races are held in the afternoon or evening at this lovely track in the green countryside along the banks of the Thames, the site of races since 1866. The track includes picnic areas, restaurants, and a playground.

River Trips

French Brothers runs boat trips up the Thames with lovely views of Windsor Castle on the bluff and Eton College on the other bank. Tours include thirty-five-minute and two-hour cruises. For information, call ☎ (01753) 851900 or consult 💻 www.boat-trips.co.uk.

The Windsor Festival

If you're lucky enough to be in London at the end of September or early October, head for Windsor to take in the wonderful cultural events of the festival. Typical daily concerts include performances by the English Chamber Orchestra in Saint George's Chapel at Windsor Castle, the Eton Boys' Concert at Eton College Chapel, and an evening of Gilbert and Sullivan in the Waterloo Chamber at the castle. You'll also find piano, violin, and choral recitals at churches and halls all around town as well as lectures and films, including silent horror films with live piano accompaniment at the Dungeon of Windsor.

The festival box office opens July 1. For information and to book by telephone, call ☎ (0175) 362-3400 or consult 💻 www.windsorfestival.com.

Eton College

Eton High Street. Daily tours available March through October. Call for details. ☎ (0175) 367-1177.

Talk about the "old school": Eton was founded half a century before Columbus crossed the Atlantic. Henry VI began the school in 1440 as the "King's
College of Our Lady of Eton Beside Windsor." Most of the other buildings are
a mere one hundred to 150 years old.

A few dozen students, known as *collegers,* live in the college. The rest of the
students, including music scholars and holders of lesser scholarships, are known
as *oppidans* (from the Latin word *oppidanus,* meaning "dwelling in town") and
board with the housemasters in the town. A recent member of the student
body was Prince William; earlier grads included Great Britain's first Prime
Minister, Robert Walpole (1721–1742), and poet Percy Bysshe Shelley.

Eton lies just across the footbridge at the end of Thames Avenue in Windsor.

Legoland Windsor

Legoland is open every day late from March through late September 10 A.M.
to 6 P.M., with summer hours until 8 P.M. mid-July to the end of August. In
the fall it is open weekends in October and the school half-term week at the
end of October. It closes in early November. For information, call ☎ (099) 004-
0404 or consult 🖳 www.lego.com/legoland/windsor.

Prices in 2001 were adult ❻, child ❺, and senior ❺. Round-trip tickets for
the shuttle bus from Windsor, about a fifteen-minute trip, cost adult ❶ and child
❶. The kids are in control at this family theme park, built to celebrate the famed
Lego building blocks—and partially constructed of the very same interlocking
pieces. Kids ages two to fifteen are the primary target, although families of all
ages will enjoy a day strolling through the very green, very clean, and sometimes very crowded park.

Crowds tend to lessen at dinnertime as the youngest visitors head for home.
In the summer the park is open until 8 P.M. The busiest period of the year is
August, and for some reason the park is busier during the week than it is on
weekends.

About those blocks: there are some twenty-five million of the little plastic
thingies at the park. And yes, they are constructed of real Legos and other products of the Lego group, although they are glued together. Most of the models
are built on a 1:20 scale.

A day at Legoland begins, logically enough, at the Beginning, with a lively
"Welcome Show," a Lego-block dinosaur family, and services. From the terrace
at the top of the hill you can see much of the park, and in the distance, Windsor Castle and the Great Park.

You can descend into the park itself on the Hill Train, a funicular that bal-
ances a train at the top against one on the bottom. The train can be a real
logjam, especially at the end of the day; the stairs from the Imagination Centre can be much faster, if a bit tiring.

Legoland attractions include:

• **Imagination Centre.** The star here is the Sky Rider, a pedal-powered highway for youngsters. (If little legs become too tired to complete the trip, the
vehicles are smart enough to take over and bring them on home.)

You'll also find the Space Tower, where children pull themselves to the top to inspect the UFO hovering overhead before "abseiling" to the bottom (we Americans would call it "rappelling"). Alongside is an animated Lego technic dinosaur that puffs smoke and claws the air.

At workshops, children can design buildings to test on earthquake tables, engineer cars to compete on the car speed-test ramp, or control Lego models through computers.

• **Duplo Gardens.** There's a helicopter ride, puppet theater, Fairy Tale Brook boat ride, Duplo train ride, and a wet-and-wild area known as the Waterworks, which is full of fountains, squirt guns, and other watery toys.

• **Lego Traffic.** Do you know any child who doesn't want to drive a car? Here older children are given electric cars to negotiate a course that includes traffic lights, pedestrian crossings, traffic circles, and other cars; successful completion earns a Legoland Driving License. Unlike other kiddie driving areas, here the youngsters are really driving (on the left) on roads without tracks.

There's also a Boating School, where kids can drive mini yachts around an imaginative course that includes fishermen, buoys, rapids, and the rest of the fleet.

• **My Town.** Life-sized buildings are grouped around a harbor and lighthouse, forming the backdrop for a spectacular live-action stunt show presented hourly. Inside the main building is a world of walk-through experiences designed to surprise and delight all ages: shiver in the ice caves, swelter in the tropical jungles, explore the backstage secrets of the Magic Theatre, or practice mechanical skills in the Technic Garage.

Also in the area is Brickafilly's Circus and Fairground where kids don't just watch the clown show—they can take part.

• **Wild Woods.** Here, in the most heavily wooded part of the park, pirates lurk at every turn; you can pan for gold and follow a treasure trail through the Rat Trap, a fearsome labyrinth of treetop walkways, scramble nets, and chutes. Or you can ride the Pirate Falls. You can also explore the three Amazing Mazes, or let off steam on the Muscle Maker and the Bum Shaker.

• **Miniland.** Here you'll find twenty million Lego blocks, used to recreate scenes from Europe, including London, Amsterdam, Edinburgh, and Paris, with some eight hundred model buildings and another seven hundred models of trains, cars, ships, cranes, bridges, fountains, and people. The project took one hundred model makers three years to complete.

There are several snack bars and restaurants; you might also consider bringing a picnic basket or a sack of sandwiches from a restaurant in Windsor.

Legoland is a good place to compare the behavior of American versus British families at a theme park. The Brits are generally a lot more polite; step on their toes and they'll universally say "sorry" to you. They do, though, smoke cigarettes while waiting in line and most everywhere else.

Legoland Windsor is located on the B3022 Bracknell/Ascot Road, about two miles from Windsor town center.

By rail, the Windsor or Eton Riverside stations are each about half an hour from London. Trains run from London Paddington station to Windsor central via Slough, or direct from London's Waterloo station to Windsor & Eton Riverside. A Legoland shuttle bus runs from both Windsor stations to the park.

By coach, Golden Tours offers daily service from major London hotels to the park. Call ☎ (0171) 233-7030 for information. The Green Line operates scheduled service from Victoria; call ☎ (0181) 668-7261 for information.

If you're planning to travel by train to Legoland, consider buying an "all-inclusive" rail and admission package from South West Trains (SWT). Trains depart London Waterloo throughout the day, delivering travelers to Windsor & Eton Riverside station (across the road from Windsor Castle). The special ticket includes transportation on the shuttle bus to Legoland and admission to the park.

In 2001 the tickets were priced at adult ❺, child (5–15) ❺, and slightly less for child (3–4). For information on times and fares, call ☎ (0345) 484950. To purchase tickets in advance by credit card, call Southwest Trains at ☎ (0170) 321-3650.

Chapter 32
Day Trip East: Canterbury

〔WOW〕 Canterbury

The seat of the Church of England, and not coincidentally the home of the spectacular Canterbury Cathedral, Canterbury is about ninety minutes east of London toward Dover.

Archeologists point to evidence of settlements in the area as far back as 3,000 B.C., with the certainty of a fortified site in the area about 700 B.C.

The Romans made their first permanent settlement, named Durovernum Cantiacorum, in A.D. 43. About the year 450, with their empire in collapse, the Romans withdrew; two millennia later, though, the city walls they constructed still stand in much of the city.

The succeeding powers were the Saxons, the Vikings, and then the Normans, who built a major stone castle at the end of what is today named Castle Street; the shell of the building still stands.

There has been a cathedral in Canterbury since about the year 602, when one was first constructed by the Saxons. In 1070 the first Norman archbishop, Lanfranc, had the old structure removed and replaced with a new one. It has since been repaired, expanded, and improved many times. The most notable feature is the Bell Harry Tower, a 235-foot-tall structure completed in 1505.

After Archbishop Thomas à Becket was famously murdered in the Cathedral by agents of Henry II in 1170, followed by reports of miracles at his burial site within, Canterbury became an important pilgrimage stop; some would say this marked the city's debut as a tourist destination. Think back, if you can, to reading Chaucer's *Canterbury Tales* in high school.

If you look carefully at the marble floor near Becket's tomb you can see an indentation made by pilgrims who would work their way across the cathedral to the crypt on their knees.

Also within the cathedral is the tomb of Henry IV and his wife Joan of Navarre. Canterbury Cathedral is open for visitors daily 8:45 A.M. to 7 P.M., with an admission charge of ❶.

By the time Henry VIII dissolved the monasteries in the 1530s in his dispute with the Pope, Canterbury had nearly two dozen parish churches and six friaries and priories.

The city went into decline but was somewhat restored with the arrival of immigrants who fled Europe because of religious persecution there. Among the new arrivals were the Walloons and the Huguenots, who fled the Lowlands and the Northern areas of France. They brought with them a weaving industry and a number of French names and customs that are still present in the area.

Some of those same refugees used Canterbury as the base for a departure to the New World on the *Mayflower*, leaving in 1620 from Southampton to Plymouth, Massachusetts.

Canterbury suffered badly in World War II, more or less by accident. German planes chased away from London often used the Bell Harry Tower of the Canterbury Cathedral as an aiming point to get rid of their load of weapons before heading back over the English Channel to Europe.

And then on May 31, 1942, the Germans targeted Canterbury in reprisal for massive British raids on German cities, including the cathedral city of Cologne. Historians say Canterbury was chosen from a travel book because of its cathedral; the attacks became known as the "Baedeker Raids" after the guide-book's name.

The city itself includes many Tudor homes and sections of the thirteenth- and fourteenth-century walls. The Roman Museum in the Longmarket area exhibits some ancient Roman mosaics and construction. The Canterbury Tales on Saint Margaret's Street memorializes the pilgrims of Chaucer's book.

There are two train stations in town. Canterbury East is the destination for express trains from London Victoria; Canterbury West serves slower trains from London Charing Cross. Both are about a ten-minute walk from the cathedral.

Bus service from London terminates at a station within the city walls at Saint George's Lane.

Bluewater Shopping Mall

Europe's largest indoor shopping mall opened in 1999 in a former chalk quarry near Dartford, nineteen miles east of London.

Bluewater includes more than 320 stores, including John Lewis, Marks & Spencer, and House of Fraser. The mall is expected to attract thirty million visitors a year. At its heart is the Wintergarden, inspired by Kew Gardens; it is the largest greenhouse built in Britain this century. The indoor rainforest includes tropical trees, ponds, and waterfalls.

The center's triangular design incorporates three malls, each designed to appeal to different customers: the high-fashion Guildhall; the family oriented Rose Gallery; and the West End–style Thames Walk.

For relaxation and dining there are nearly forty restaurants, bars and cafes, and a twelve-screen cinema multiplex.

Bluewater is open weekdays until 9 P.M., Saturday until 8 P.M., and Sunday until 5 P.M. It is forty-five minutes by train from London's Charing Cross. For information, call ☎ (0845) 602-1021 or consult 📖 www.bluewater.co.uk.

Chapter 33
Disneyland Paris

With the opening of the Channel tunnel, Paris has become a distant suburb of London. And with that, the ultimate American export, Disneyland Paris, is reachable for a long daytrip or an easy weekend expedition.

The French hate American culture, right? Yeah, sure: tell that to *La Belle au Bois Dormant* (Sleeping Beauty), *Blanche-Neige et les Sept Nains* (Snow White and the Seven Dwarfs), and finally, to Mickey Mouse (no translation needed).

Most of all, tell that to the millions of visitors who head twenty miles east of the City of Lights to Marne la Vallée, home of the City of Mickey.

Disneyland Paris opened in 1992. Though cultural highbrows sniffed haughtily, and bean counters objected to some of the financial underpinnings of the hotels and real estate operations surrounding the attraction, the Magic Kingdom park quickly began drawing tourists.

In 2002 Disney Studios, a second theme park, will open at Disneyland Paris.

Should you go all the way from North America to visit Disneyland Paris? Well, it's one of the most advanced theme parks in the world, decades younger than the Magic Kingdom in Orlando and the even-older Disneyland in Anaheim. But, it is very similar, albeit with a French accent.

For us, the beauty of Disneyland Paris is this: it's a wonderful way to convince the kids to come on a trip to France to see Notre Dame, Versailles, the Champs Elysée, the Louvre, the Pompidou . . . and Mickey and Minnie.

On two of my trips, I chose to make Disneyland Paris my base, venturing west to Paris and Versailles five days in a week, and spending two days in the park. Hotels at the park, although not cheap, are still less expensive than many hotels in downtown Paris. The RER train service to London is easily accessible, or you can rent a car and use the highways.

Although Disneyland Paris is very much an outpost of American culture, as defined by Walt Disney and as refined during a half-century by the moviemaking and theme park empire he created, there is nevertheless a definite French and European gloss to the park. The rides and attractions are narrated in French, but English and other translations are readily available. All park personnel speak multiple languages, and English is very common.

Main Street U.S.A. in Disneyland Paris
Courtesy Disneyland Paris. © Disney

The Magic Kingdom is laid out very much like its cousins in California and Florida. One exception: Tomorrowland is called Discoveryland in France.

Among the highlights of the park:

Phantom Manor. It's got 999 ghoulish French ghosts . . . and this is the highest-tech version of this Disney classic (known as the Haunted Mansion in Florida and California). The story, if you need one, involves a bride who was jilted at the altar. Forever in her wedding dress, she haunts the house and all who visit.

Pirates of the Caribbean. Yo, ho, yo . . . this is one of Disney's very best. A slightly Frenchified version of the classic watery adventure, it's a cruise into the middle of a pirate raid on a Caribbean island town.

Among the highlights are a battle by moonlight as your boat passes beneath the guns of two warring ships; cannonballs land all around in the cool water. Pay attention, too, to the jail scene where a group of pirates tries to entice a mangy dog to bring them the key. The ride includes a wondrous collection of audio-animatronic humans and animals, including robotic chickens and pigs.

***Indiana Jones et le Temple du Peril* (Indiana Jones and the Temple of Doom).** A truly wild roller coaster that careens through the long-buried ruins of the Temple of Peril, right-side up, upside down, and straight at the waters below. Disney turned up the thrills a few notches by reworking the track, mounting the cars backward on the track, and sending guests on a ride that lets them concentrate on where they've been instead of where they're heading. The mine cars back their way through a spiraling inverted 360-degree loop.

Le Château de la Belle au Bois Dormant (Sleeping Beauty's Castle). The centerpiece of the park is Sleeping Beauty's Castle, a very European castle. Located upstairs is *La Galerie de la Belle au Bois Dormant* (Sleeping Beauty's Gallery), which displays the story of Sleeping Beauty through hand-painted storybooks, stained glass windows, and finely woven tapestries. Beneath the castle is *La Tanière du Dragon* (The Dragon's Lair) where a huge animatronic dragon sleeps restlessly

Dumbo the Flying Elephant. A worldwide favorite for youngsters, who wait in line (along with their cranky parents) for the chance to ride on Dumbo in a circular pathway above Fantasyland.

It's a Small World. Every little girl's wildest dream: a world of beautiful dancing dolls from all over the world. There is nothing to get your heart beating here, but even the most cynical—including little boys and adults—will probably find something to smile about in this upbeat boat ride.

Star Tours. The Starspeeder 3000 departs regularly on a short and eventful voyage to outer space in this simulator ride based on the *Star Wars* films of George Lucas.

Le Visionarium. A Cinematronic 360-degree theater presenting a beautifully produced film about French science fiction author Jules Verne, in a spectacular time-travel adventure that soars through Europe. A version of that film was imported to Walt Disney World as *The Timekeeper*.

Space Mountain: *De la Terre à la Lune* (From the Earth to the Moon). Disney's triumph of imagineering, a roller-coaster trip to the moon. This version of the classic goes way beyond the originals at Disneyland and Walt Disney World, beginning with the takeoff: every thirty-six seconds the Cannon Columbiad fires, launching a twenty-four-passenger rocket train through its barrel. Space travelers shoot to the top in a heart-stopping 1.8 seconds, floating through a moment of zero-gravity at the top before descending in the dark through the trip from the earth to the moon with some upside-down spirals, and twists and turns.

Getting to Disneyland Paris from London

By Rail from London. Eurostar services Paris (Gare du Nord station) directly from London Waterloo, with the trip taking about three hours. In the summer and on certain holiday weekends, several trains per day go directly from London to the station at Disneyland Paris.

By Air from London. Most flights from London land at Orly or Roissy–Charles de Gaulle. A four-passenger taxi from either French airport to Disneyland Paris costs in the range of $50 to $75; drivers will levy a surcharge for luggage.

A direct VEA shuttle service links Orly and Roissy–Charles de Gaulle airports to Disneyland Paris. For information, call ☎ (033) 64-30-66-56.

Rental cars are available at both airports; most major companies offer one-way rentals without

Exchange rates. In mid-2001, the U.S. dollar was worth about 7.68 francs, an improvement in buying power for Americans over recent years. At that rate, to convert a price in francs to dollars, multiply by 0.13.

Big Thunder Railroad
Photo courtesy Disneyland Paris. © Disney

drop-off fees, allowing visitors to pick up a car at the airport and leave it at the resort. The least expensive vehicles often are tiny sibcompacts, often with manual transmissions.

By Metro from Paris. The RER Metro line A connects central Paris to the Marne-la-Vallée/Chessy station at Disneyland Paris, a trip that takes between thirty and forty-five minutes. The Metro station is at the entrance to the Disneyland park, and a ten- to fifteen-minute walk to hotels; a complimentary shuttle bus runs between the stations and five of the hotels at the park.

Tickets and Hours

Disneyland Paris splits its year into high seasons and low seasons, with different admission rates and operating hours.

High season includes the period from just before Christmas until January 1, and from about April 1 to early November.

In 2001 ticket rates were:

High Season
>1-day   Adult Fr 236. Child (3–11) Fr 184
>2-day   Adult Fr 459. Child (3–11) Fr 354
>3-day   Adult Fr 636. Child (3–11) Fr 492

Low Season
>1-day   Adult Fr 170. Child (3–11) Fr 140
>2-day   Adult Fr 330. Child (3–11) Fr 270
>3 day   Adult Fr 460. Child (3–11) Fr 380

Operating hours vary by season. Generally, in high-season the park is open from 9 A.M. to 8 P.M., with operations until 11 P.M. on weekends, during the summer and holiday periods. In low-season, the park usually opens at 10 A.M. and closes at 8 P.M. Be sure to check ahead for the operating hours.

Tickets are sold at the park as well as in Disney Stores in Paris, at the Paris Tourism Office, at Paris airports, and at selected Métro and RER stations and offices.

Hotels at Disneyland Paris

Disneyland Hotel. The showplace to stay at the park, a pink-and-burgundy Victorian mansion located at the gates of the park. Packages start at about Fr 1215 per adult.

Hotel New York. A classy bite of the big apple, the four-star hotel includes high-rise towers and brownstone apartments. Amenities include an ice-skating rink out on the plaza in winter. Packages start at about Fr 915 per adult.

Newport Bay Club. An elegant three-star evocation of New England, with a bit of Captain Hook and Mr. Smee thrown in to watch the shoreline. Packages start at about Fr 855 per adult.

Sequoia Lodge. Welcome to one of America's national parks, reborn as a rustic three-star lodge. The lobby includes a massive open log fire. Packages start at about Fr 790 per adult.

Hotel Cheyenne. Wooden sidewalks and dirt roads front the streets of this two-star frontier town. Packages start at Fr 720 per adult.

Hotel Santa Fe. A two-star pueblo of the American Southwest, on the banks of the Rio Grande, complete with an active volcano. Packages start at about Fr 670 per adult.

Davy Crockett Ranch. A community of private log cabins in the woods, a fifteen-minute drive from Disneyland. The cabins include kitchens; amenities include horse rides through the forest and archery. Packages start at about Fr 733 per adult.

Hotels Near Disneyland Paris

In addition to the hotels within the Disneyland park, there are a number of hotels in the surrounding area where you can experience a bit more of a French atmosphere (and escape mouse ears at every turn.)

Some of the hotels offer packages that include theme park admission.

Among neighboring towns are Bussy–Saint Georges, linked to the park by RER line A and motorway A4; there you'll find a Holiday Inn, Sol Inn, and Golf Hotel. In Magny-le-Hongre, about two miles from the park, the Hôtel du Moulin de Paris is alongside Disney's golf courses.

For information and reservations at Disney hotels and participating hotels outside of the park, you can consult a travel agent, or call ☎ (033) 01-60-30-60-53. You can also make reservation on the Internet, at 💻 www.disneyland paris.com.

Disney Village

Just outside the gates to the park is Disney Village, a celebration of American entertainment. Under a starfield made up of tiny lights on wires, you'll find a collection of star-spangled restaurants, clubs, and shops.

And absolutely not to be missed is *Buffalo Bill's Wild West Show*, one of the better dinner theaters I have ever seen. The show is loosely based on an actual touring company brought to France by Buffalo Bill. Ranchers compete in competitions with herds of buffalo, longhorn steer, and dozens of cowboys on horseback. Included is an Old West meal that includes chili, barbecued chicken and beef, and dessert. The show is located next to Festival Disney and there are two performances per night at busy times.

Disney Studios

Disney Studios is due to debut April 12, 2002, the tenth anniversary of the opening of the Magic Kingdom at Disneyland Paris. The new park sits alongside the original park, using the same hotels, train station, and parking lots.

Disney Studios will be a combined theme park and production studio, based on Disney–MGM Studios in Orlando, but with a European spin. Themes include cinema, animation, television, and audiovisual entertainment inspired by the cinema of France, Europe, and Hollywood.

According to plans for the park, the main entrance will open onto a bit of Hollywood at the central plaza. Palm trees—not an ordinary site in central France—dot the boulevard, which is lined with movie set false fronts. Cast members will lie in wait to "discover" visitors for shows.

Among the attractions will be a celebration of Disney animation, including a session with an artist who will demonstrate how cartoons are made. A section of interactive game stations will allow guests to make their own animated sequences and bring them to life.

A tram tour will take visitors on a backstage ride into some of the sets of the park, along with glimpses of the costume department. The tram will also enter Catastrophe Canyon, where visitors will find themselves in the middle of a live action set. Just as the name suggests, disaster strikes when an earthquake tumbles a fuel tanker truck down a hillside right at the tram . . . and, "Cut!"

Among the stage shows will be one in which a volunteer from the audience will be invited to step into a film through a bit of video magic.

Another stage show will demonstrate the world of special effects, including an exploration of some early work by French filmmaker George Mélies, who made the first film of *20,000 Leagues Under the Sea* in 1907.

An open-air amphitheater will be used for a show that pits stunt actors against a group of terrorists in a Mediterranean town, a European version of the Indiana Jones Epic Stunt Spectacular at Disney–MGM Studios in Orlando.

And then there's the Rock 'n Roller Coaster, a serious coaster hidden within a soundstage building. At the original version of the ride in Orlando, the coaster is within Stage 15, the headquarters of G-Force Records. A forty-foot-long Fender guitar hangs over the record company's lobby.

Appendix

Index of London Hotels and Major Booking Agencies

Belgravia

The Berkeley. Wilton Place, Knightsbridge. ☎ (020) 7235-6000. 156 rooms. *Luxury.*
   Diplomat. 2 Chesham Street, Belgravia. ☎ (020) 7235-1544. 27 rooms. *Moderate.*
   Goring Hotel. 15 Beeston Place, Grosvenor Gardens. ☎ (020) 7396-9000. 🖳 www.goringhotel.co.uk. 76 rooms. *Luxury.*
   Halkin. 4 Halkin Street, Belgravia. ☎ (020) 7333-1000. 41 rooms. *Luxury.*
   Holiday Inn Victoria. 2 Bridge Place. ☎ (020) 7630-8888. 🖳 www.holiday-inn. com. 212 rooms. *Luxury.*
   Hotel Inter-Continental London. 1 Hamilton Place, Hyde Park Corner. ☎ (020) 7409-3131. 🖳 www.interconti.com/england/london/hotel_lonic. html. 404 rooms. *Luxury.*
   Lanesborough. Hyde Park Corner. ☎ (020) 7259-5599. 53 rooms. *Luxury.*
   Lowndes Hotel: A Hyatt Hotel. 21 Lowndes Street, Belgravia. ☎ (020) 7823-1234. 🖳 london.hyatt.com/lownd. 78. *Luxury.*
   Royal Westminster Thistle Hotel. 49 Buckingham Palace Road. ☎ (020) 7834-1821. 134 rooms. *Moderate.*
   Rubens at the Palace. 39–41 Buckingham Palace Road. ☎ (020) 7834-6600. 180 rooms. *Luxury.*
   Sheraton Belgravia. 20 Chesham Place. ☎ (020) 7235-6040. 🖳 www.sheraton.com. 89 rooms. *Luxury.*
   Sloane Square Moat House. Sloane Square. ☎ (020) 7896-9988. 🖳 www.moat househotels.com. 105 rooms. *Luxury.*
   Thistle Victoria. 101 Buckingham Palace Road. ☎ (020) 7834-9494. 366 rooms. *Luxury.*
   Windermere Hotel. 142–144 Warwick Way, Victoria. ☎ (020) 7834-5163. 23 rooms. *Moderate.*

Price Bands

Luxury	£90 and up
Moderate	£60 to £89
Budget	£30 to £59
Economy	Less than £29

Bloomsbury

Bedford Hotel. 83 Southampton Row. ☎ (020) 7636-7822. 184 rooms. *Budget.*
   Blooms Hotel. 7 Montague Street. ☎ (020) 7323-1717. 27 rooms. *Luxury.*
   Bloomsbury Park Hotel. 126 Southampton Row. ☎ (020) 7430-0434. 96 rooms. *Luxury.*
   The Bonnington in Bloomsbury. 92 Southampton Row. ☎ (020) 7242-2828. 215 rooms. *Luxury.*

Forte Posthouse Bloomsbury. Coram Street. ☎ (0870) 400-9222. 🖳 www.post house-hotels.co.uk. 287 rooms. *Luxury.*

George Hotel. 58–60 Cartwright Gardens. ☎ (020) 7387-8777. 40 rooms. *Budget.*

Holiday Inn King's Cross. 1 King's Cross Road. ☎ (020) 7833-3900. 🖳 www.holi day-inn.com. 405 rooms. *Luxury.*

Hotel Russell. Russell Square. ☎ (020) 7837-8844. 🖳 www.principalhotels.co.uk/ london_russell/london_russell.html. 329 rooms. *Luxury.*

Imperial Hotel. Russell Square. ☎ (020) 7837-3655. 447 rooms. *Moderate.*

Kingsley Hotel. Bloomsbury Way. ☎ (020) 7242-5881. 137 rooms. *Luxury.*

London Ryan Hotel. Gwynne Place, King's Cross Road. ☎ (020) 7278-2480. 210 rooms. *Luxury.*

Montague on the Garden. 12–20 Montague Street. ☎ (020) 7637-1001. 109 rooms. *Luxury.*

My Hotel. 11–13 Bayley Street. ☎ (020) 7667-6000. 81 rooms. *Luxury.*

President Hotel. Russell Square. ☎ (020) 7837-8844. 447 rooms. 🖳 www.imperial hotels.co.uk/pres.htm. *Budget.*

Radisson Kenilworth Hotel. Great Russell Street. ☎ (020) 7637-3477. 🖳 www.radisson.com. 185 rooms. *Luxury.*

Radisson Marlborough Hotel. Bloomsbury Street. ☎ (020) 7636-5601. 🖳 www.radisson.com. 170 rooms. *Luxury.*

Royal Scot Hotel. 100 King's Cross Road. ☎ (020) 7278-2434. 351 rooms. *Luxury.*

Saint Giles Hotel. Bedford Avenue. ☎ (020) 7300-3000. 🖳 www.stgiles.com. 711 rooms. *Moderate.*

Waverly House Hotel. 130–134 Southampton Row. ☎ (020) 7833-3691. 109 rooms. *Luxury.*

Brompton

Basil Street Hotel. Basil Street, Knightsbridge. ☎ (020) 7581-3311. 91 rooms. *Luxury.*

The Beaufort. 33 Beaufort Gardens. ☎ (020) 7584-5252. 28 rooms. *Luxury.*

Cadogan Hotel. 75 Sloane Street. ☎ (020) 7235-7141. 🖳 www.cadogan.com. 65 rooms. *Luxury.*

Capital. 22–24 Basil Street. ☎ (020) 7589-5171. 40 rooms. *Luxury.*

Egerton House. Egerton Terrace, Knightsbridge. ☎ (020) 7589-2412. 29 rooms. *Luxury.*

Hyatt Carlton Tower. 2 Cadogan Place. ☎ (020) 7235-1234. 🖳 www.hyatt.com. 220 rooms. *Luxury.*

Knightsbridge Green Hotel. 159 Knightsbridge. ☎ (020) 7584-6274. 27 rooms. *Luxury.*

L'Hotel. 20 Basil Street. ☎ (020) 7589-6286. 12 rooms. *Moderate.*

Mandarin Oriental Hyde Park Hotel. 66 Knightsbridge. ☎ (020) 7235-1000. 🖳 www.mandarin-oriental.com/london. 185 rooms. *Luxury.*

Millennium Knightsbridge. 17–25 Sloane Street. ☎ (020) 7235-4377. 224 rooms. *Luxury.*

Rembrandt Sarova. 11 Thurloe Place. ☎ (020) 7589-8100. 🖳 www.sarovahotels. com. 195 rooms. *Luxury.*

Sheraton Park Tower. 101 Knightsbridge. ☎ (020) 7235-8050. 🖳 www.sheraton. com. 287 rooms. *Luxury.*

Charing Cross/Temple

Charing Cross Hotel. Strand. ☎ (020) 7839-7282. 222 rooms. *Moderate.*

Howard Hotel. Temple Place. ☎ (020) 7836-3555. 135 rooms. *Luxury.*

Le Meridien Waldorf. Aldwych. ☎ (0870) 400-8484. 🖳 www.lemeridien-hotels. com. 292 rooms. *Luxury.*

One Whitehall Place. London. ☎ (020) 7839-3344. 280 rooms. *Luxury.*

Royal Horseguards Thistle Hotel. Whitehall Court. ☎ (020) 7839-3400. 280 rooms. *Luxury*.

Savoy. Strand. ☎ (020) 7836-4343. 🖳 www.savoy-group.co.uk/savoy/savoy.html. 215 rooms. *Luxury*.

Strand Palace. Strand. ☎ (020) 7836-8080. 783 rooms. *Moderate*.

Chelsea

Cliveden Town House. 26 Cadogan Gardens. ☎ (020) 7730-6466. 35 rooms. *Luxury*.

Eleven Cadogan Gardens. 11 Cadogan Gardens, Sloan Square. ☎ (020) 7730-3426. 61 rooms. *Luxury*.

Five Sumner Place. 5 Sumner Place. ☎ (020) 7584-7586. 13 rooms. *Moderate*.

London Outpost. 69 Cadogan Gardens. ☎ (020) 7589-7333. 11 rooms. *Luxury*.

Covent Garden

Covent Garden Hotel. 10 Monmouth Street. ☎ (020) 7806-1000. 50 rooms. *Luxury*.

Drury Lane Moat House. 10 Drury Lane. ☎ (020) 7208-9988. 🖳 www.moathouse hotels.com. 63 rooms. *Luxury*.

Radisson Mountbatten Hotel. 20 Monmouth Street, Seven Dials. ☎ (020) 7836-4300. 🖳 www.radisson.com. 127 rooms. *Luxury*.

Euston

Euston Plaza Hotel. 17–18 Upper Woburn Place. ☎ (020) 7383-4105. 🖳 www.euston-plaza-hotel.com. 150 rooms. *Luxury*.

Grafton Hotel. 130 Tottenham Court Road. ☎ (020) 7388-4131. 324 rooms. *Luxury*.

Hotel Ibis Euston. 3 Cardington Street, Euston. ☎ (020) 7388-7777. 300 rooms. *Budget*.

Royal National Hotel. Bedford Way. ☎ (020) 7637-2488. 🖳 www.imperialhotels. co.uk/royal.htm. 1,271 rooms. *Budget*.

Tavistock Hotel. Tavistock Square. ☎ (020) 7636-8383. 🖳 www.imperialhotels.co. uk/tav.htm. 301 rooms. *Budget*.

Thistle Euston. Cardington Street, Euston. ☎ (020) 7387-4400. 360 rooms. *Moderate*.

Hyde Park

The Blakemore Hotel. 30 Leinster Gardens. ☎ (020) 7262-4591. 163 rooms. *Moderate*.

Byron Hotel. 36–38 Queensborough Terrace. ☎ (020) 7243-0987. 42 rooms. *Budget*.

Central Park Hotel. 49 Queensborough Terrace. ☎ (020) 7229-2424. 251 rooms. *Luxury*.

Charles Dickens Hotel. 66 Lancaster Gate, Bayswater Road. ☎ (020) 7262-5090. 193 rooms. *Moderate*.

Comfort Inn Hyde Park. 18–19 Craven Hill Gardens. ☎ (020) 7262-6644. 🖳 www.comfortinn-hydepark.co.uk/hydepark.htm. 60 rooms. *Moderate*.

Commodore Hotel. 50 Lancaster Gate, Hyde Park. ☎ (020) 7402-5291. 90 rooms. *Moderate*.

Hempel. 31/35 Craven Hill Gardens. ☎ (020) 7298-9000. 42 rooms. *Luxury*.

Henry VIII Hotel. 9 Leinster Gardens. ☎ (020) 7262-0117. 107 rooms. *Moderate*.

Mornington Hotel. 12 Lancaster Gate. ☎ (020) 7262-7361. 64 rooms. *Luxury*.

Park Court Hotel. 75–89 Lancaster Gate. ☎ (020) 7402-4272. 390 rooms. *Moderate*.

Plaza on Hyde Park. Lancaster Gate. ☎ (020) 7262-5022. 402 rooms. *Moderate*.

Queens Park Hotel. 48 Queensborough Terrace. ☎ (020) 7229-8080. 86 rooms. *Budget*.

Royal Lancaster Hotel. Lancaster Terrace. ☎ (020) 7262-6737. 🖳 www.royallan caster.co.uk. 418 rooms. *Luxury*.

Stakis Hyde Park. 129 Bayswater Road, Hyde Park. ☎ (020) 7221-2217. 132 rooms. *Luxury.*

Thistle Kensington Gardens. 104 Bayswater Road. ☎ (020) 7262-4461. 175 rooms. *Moderate.*

Whites. 90–92 Lancaster Gate. ☎ (020) 7262-2711. 54 rooms. *Luxury.*

York Hotel. 30–34 Queensborough Terrace. ☎ (020) 7229-9511. 102 rooms. *Moderate.*

Kensington

Blakes Hotel. 33 Roland Gardens. ☎ (020) 7370-6701. 52 rooms. *Luxury.*

Burns Hotel. 18–26 Barkston Gardens. ☎ (020) 7373-3151. 105 rooms. *Moderate.*

Comfort Inn Kensington. 22–32 West Cromwell Road. ☎ (020) 7373-3300. 🖳 www.comfortinn.com. 125 rooms. *Moderate.*

The Copthorne Tara. Scarsdale Place. ☎ (020) 7937-7211. 825 rooms. *Luxury.*

Cranley Gardens Hotel. 8 Cranley Gardens. ☎ (020) 7373-3232. 85 rooms. *Budget.*

Cranley Hotel. 8–12 Bina Gardens. ☎ (020) 7373-0123. 36 rooms. *Luxury.*

De Vere Park Hotel. 60 Hyde Park Gate. ☎ (020) 7584-0051. 92 rooms. *Moderate.*

Eden Park Hotel. 35–39 Inverness Terrace. ☎ (020) 7221-2220. 137 rooms. *Moderate.*

Eden Plaza Hotel. 68–69 Queen's Gate. ☎ (020) 7370-6111. 62 rooms. *Budget.*

Elizabetta Hotel. 162 Cromwell Road. ☎ (020) 7370-4282. 82 rooms. *Moderate.*

Flora Hotel International. 11–13 Penywern Road, Earl's Court. ☎ (020) 7373-6514. 53 rooms. *Budget.*

Forte Posthouse Kensington. Wright's Lane. ☎ (0870) 400-9000. 🖳 www.post house-hotels.co.uk. 544 rooms. *Luxury.*

Forum Hotel London. 97 Cromwell Road. ☎ (020) 7370-5757. 🖳 www.inter conti.com/england/london/hotel_lonfor.html. 910 rooms. *Luxury.*

Gainsborough Hotel. 7–11 Queensberry Place. ☎ (020) 7957-0000. 63 rooms. *Moderate.*

Gallery Hotel. 6–10 Queensberry Place, South. ☎ (020) 7915-0000. 36 rooms. *Moderate.*

Gloucester Hotel. 4–18 Harrington Gardens. ☎ (020) 7373-6030. 601 rooms. *Luxury.*

Gore Hotel. 189 Queen's Gate. ☎ (020) 7584-6601. 54 rooms. *Luxury.*

Harrington Hall. 5–25 Harrington Gardens. ☎ (020) 7396-9696. 200 rooms. *Luxury.*

Henley House Hotel. 30 Barkston Gardens, Earl's Court. ☎ (020) 7370-4111. 20 rooms. *Moderate.*

Hillgate Hotel. 6–14 Pembridge Gardens. ☎ (020) 7221-3433. 70 rooms. *Moderate.*

Hilton National London Olympia. 380 Kensington High Street. ☎ (020) 7603-3333. 🖳 www.hilton.com. 406 rooms. *Moderate.*

Hogarth Hotel. 33 Hogarth Road. ☎ (020) 7370-6831. 85 rooms. *Moderate.*

Holiday Inn Kensington. 100 Cromwell Road. ☎ (020) 7373-2222. 🖳 www.holi day-inn.com. 162 rooms. *Moderate.*

Hotel Number Sixteen. 16 Sumner Place. ☎ (020) 7589-5232. 36 rooms. *Moderate.*

Kensington Hyde Park Towers. 41–51 Inverness Terrace. ☎ (020) 7221-8484. 115 rooms. *Moderate.*

Jarvis Embassy House. 31–33 Queen's Gate. ☎ (020) 7584-7222. 69 rooms. *Moderate.*

Jarvis London Embassy Hotel. 150 Bayswater Road. ☎ (020) 7229-1212. 194 rooms. *Moderate.*

John Howard Hotel. 4 Queen's Gate. ☎ (020) 7581-3011. 40 rooms. *Moderate.*

Jurys Kensington Hotel. 109–113 Queen's Gate South. ☎ (020) 7589-6300. 173 rooms. *Luxury.*

Kensington Edwardian. 40–44 Harrington Gardens. ☎ (020) 7370-0811. 69 rooms. *Moderate.*

Kensington Moat House Hotel. 2–10 Harrington Road. ☎ (020) 7344-9988. 🖳 www.moathousehotels.com. 96 rooms. *Luxury.*

Kensington Park Thistle Hotel. 16–32 De Vere Gardens. ☎ (020) 7937-8080. 352 rooms. *Luxury.*

Kensington Plaza Hotel. 61 Gloucester Road. ☎ (020) 7584-8100. 90 rooms. *Moderate.*

London Kensington Hilton. 179–199 Holland Park Avenue. ☎ (020) 7603-3355. 🖳 www.hilton.com. 603 rooms. *Luxury.*

Milestone Hotel. 1–2 Kensington Court. ☎ (020) 7917-1000. 56 rooms. *Luxury.*

Novotel London Hammersmith. 1 Shortlands, Hammersmith. ☎ (020) 8741-1555. 640 rooms. *Luxury.*

Oki Kensington. 25 Courtfield Gardens. ☎ (020) 7373-9541. 41 rooms. *Luxury.*

Park International Hotel. 117–125 Cromwell Road. ☎ (020) 7370-5711. 🖳 www.parkinternationalhotel.com. 117 rooms. *Moderate.*

Pelham Hotel. 15 Cromwell Place. ☎ (020) 7589-8288. 41 rooms. *Luxury.*

Phoenix Hotel. 1–8 Kensington Gardens Square, Queensway. ☎ (020) 7229-2494. 125 rooms. *Budget.*

Queen's Gate Hotel. 54 Queen's Gate, South Kensington. ☎ (020) 7225-3445. 25 rooms. *Moderate.*

Regency Hotel. 100 Queen's Gate, South Kensington. ☎ (020) 7370-4595. 🖳 www.srs-worldhotels.com/england/london/hotel_lonreg.html. 198 rooms. *Luxury.*

Royal Garden Hotel. Kensington High Street. ☎ (020) 7937-8000. 🖳 www.royal gdn.co.uk. 395 rooms. *Luxury.*

Rushmore Hotel. 11 Trebovir Road. ☎ (020) 7370-3839. 22 rooms. *Budget.*

Stuart Hotel. 110–112 Cromwell Road. ☎ (020) 7373-1004. 58 rooms. *Moderate.*

Swallow International Hotel. Cromwell Street. ☎ (020) 7973-1000. 419 rooms. *Luxury.*

Vanderbilt Hotel. 68–86 Cromwell Road. ☎ (020) 7589-2424. 223 rooms. *Luxury.*

Westbury Hotel. 22–24 Collingham Place. ☎ (020) 7373-0666. 40 rooms. *Moderate.*

Marylebone

The Berkshire. 350 Oxford Street. ☎ (020) 7629-7474. 147 rooms. *Luxury.*

Blandford Hotel. 80 Chiltern Street. ☎ (020) 7486-3103. 33 rooms. *Moderate.*

Bryanston Court Hotel. 50–60 Great Cumberland Place. ☎ (020) 7262-3141. 54 rooms. *Moderate.*

Churchill Inter-Continental London. 30 Portman Square. ☎ (020) 7486-5800. 🖳 www.interconti.com/england/london/hotel_lonchu.html. 408 rooms. *Luxury.*

Clifton Ford Hotel. Welbeck Street. ☎ (020) 7486-6600. 200 rooms. *Luxury.*

Cumberland Hotel. Marble Arch. ☎ (020) 7262-1234. 🖳 www.hotels-of-london.co.uk/cumberland. 890 rooms. *Luxury.*

Holiday Inn Garden Court. 57–59 Welbeck Street. ☎ (020) 7935-4442. 🖳 www.holiday-inn.com. 138 rooms. *Moderate.*

Hotel Concorde. 50 Great Cumberland Place. ☎ (020) 7402-6169. 28 rooms. *Moderate.*

Landmark. 222 Marylebone Road. ☎ (020) 7631-8000. 🖳 www.landmarklondon. co.uk. 303 rooms. *Luxury.*

Langham Hilton. 1C Portland Place, Regent Street. ☎ (020) 7636-1000. 🖳 www.hilton.com. 379 rooms. *Luxury.*

Leonard. 15 Seymour Street. ☎ (020) 7935-2010. 26 rooms. *Luxury.*

London Marriott Hotel–Marble Arch. 134 George Street. ☎ (020) 7723-1277. 🖳 www.marriott.com. 240 rooms. *Luxury.*

Mandeville Hotel. Mandeville Place. ☎ (020) 7935-5599. 165 rooms. *Moderate.*

Montcalm. Great Cumberland Place. ☎ (020) 7402-4288. 106 rooms. *Luxury.*

Mostyn Hotel. 4 Bryanston Street. ☎ (020) 7935-2361. 121 rooms. *Moderate.*

Mount Royal Hotel. Bryanston Street, Marble Arch. ☎ (020) 7629-8040. 689 rooms. *Luxury.*

Radisson Edwardian Savoy Court Hotel. Granville Place. ☎ (020) 7408-0130. 🖳 www.radisson.com. 110 rooms. *Luxury.*

Radisson SAS Portman Hotel. 22 Portman Square. ☎ (020) 7208-6000. 🖳 www.radisson.com. 279 rooms. *Luxury.*

Saint George's Hotel. Langham Place, Regent Street. ☎ (020) 7580-0111. 86 rooms. *Luxury.*

Selfridge Hotel. Orchard Street. ☎ (020) 7408-2080. 294 rooms. *Luxury.*

Sherlock Holmes Hotel. 108 Baker Street. ☎ (020) 7486-6161. 125 rooms. *Moderate.*

Stakis London Harewood Hotel. Harewood Row. ☎ (020) 7262-2707. 92 rooms. *Moderate.*

Stakis London Metropole Hotel. Edgware Road. ☎ (020) 7402-4141. 742 rooms. *Luxury.*

Mayfair

Britannia Hotel. Grosvenor Square. ☎ (020) 7629-9400. 341 rooms. *Luxury.*

Brown's Hotel. Albemarle and Dover Streets. ☎ (020) 7493-6020. 🖳 www.browns hotel.com. 117 rooms. *Luxury.*

Chesterfield Mayfair. 35 Charles Street. ☎ (020) 7491-2622. 110 rooms. *Luxury.*

Claridge's. Brook Street. ☎ (020) 7629-8860. 🖳 www.savoy-group.co.uk/claridges/claridges.html. 133 rooms. *Luxury.*

Connaught Hotel. Carlos Place. ☎ (020) 7499-7070. 90 rooms. *Luxury.*

The Dorchester. Park Lane. ☎ (020) 7629-8888. 244 rooms. 🖳 www.dorchester hotel.com. *Luxury.*

Flemings Hotel Mayfair. 7–12 Half Moon Street. ☎ (020) 7499-2964. 121 rooms. *Luxury.*

47 Park Street. 47 Park Street. ☎ (020) 7491-7282. 52 rooms. *Luxury.*

The Franklin. 28 Egerton Gardens, Knightsbridge. ☎ (020) 7584-5533. 47 rooms. *Luxury.*

Green Park Hilton Hotel. Half Moon Street. ☎ (020) 7629-7522. 🖳 www. hilton.com. 161 rooms. *Luxury.*

Grosvenor House. Park Lane. ☎ (020) 7499-6363. 🖳 www.grosvenor house.co.uk. 437 rooms. *Luxury.*

London Hilton on Park Lane. 22 Park Lane. ☎ (020) 7493-8000. 🖳 www.hilton.com. 447 rooms. *Luxury.*

London Marriott Hotel. Grosvenor Square. ☎ (020) 7493-1232. 🖳 www.marriott.com. 221 rooms. *Luxury.*

London Mews Hilton. Stanhope Row Park Lane. ☎ (020) 7493-7222. 🖳 www.hilton.com. 72 rooms. *Luxury.*

May Fair Inter-Continental London. Stratton Street. ☎ (020) 7629-7777. 🖳 www.interconti.com/england/london/hotel_lonmay.html. 287 rooms. *Luxury.*

Metropolitan. Old Park Lane. ☎ (020) 7447-1000. 155 rooms. *Luxury.*

Sheraton Park Lane Hotel. Piccadilly. ☎ (020) 7499-6321. 🖳 www.sheraton.com. 310 rooms. *Luxury.*

Washington Mayfair. Curzon Street. ☎ (020) 7499-7000. 🖳 www.washington-mayfair.co.uk. 173 rooms. *Luxury.*

Westbury. Bond Street. ☎ (020) 7629-7755. 243 rooms. *Luxury.*

Notting Hill

Bayswater Inn. 8–16 Princess Square. ☎ (020) 7727-8621. 191 rooms. *Moderate.*

Halcyon. 81–82 Holland Park. ☎ (020) 7727-7288. 44 rooms. *Luxury.*

Pembridge Court Hotel. 34 Pembridge Gardens. ☎ (020) 7229-9977. 20 rooms. *Moderate.*

Westminster. 16 Leinster Square. ☎ (020) 7221-9131. 116 rooms. *Luxury.*

Paddington

Delmere Hotel. 128–130 Sussex Gardens, Hyde Park. ☎ (020) 7706-3344. 38 rooms. *Moderate*.

 Great Western Royal Hotel. Praed Street. ☎ (020) 7723-8064. 🖳 www.london-plaza-hotels.com/gwr.html. 238 rooms. *Moderate*.

 Gresham Hotel. 116 Sussex Gardens. ☎ (020) 7402-2920. 40 rooms. *Budget*.

 Hotel Edward. 1A Spring Street. ☎ (020) 7262-2671. 41 rooms. *Budget*.

 Linden House Hotel. 4–6 Sussex Place. ☎ (020) 7723-9853. 30 rooms. *Economy*.

 London Crown Hotel. 144 Praed Street. ☎ (020) 7262-3464. 95 rooms. *Budget*.

 London Hotel. 10 Talbot Square. ☎ (020) 7262-6699. 73 rooms. *Budget*.

 Norfolk Plaza Hotel. 29–33 Norfolk Square. ☎ (020) 7723-0792. 87 rooms. *Moderate*.

 Norfolk Towers Hotel. 34 Norfolk Place. ☎ (020) 7262-3123. 85 rooms. *Moderate*.

 Pavilion Hotel. 34–36 Sussex Gardens. ☎ (020) 7262-0905. 27 rooms. *Moderate*.

 Royal Norfolk Hotel. 25 London Street. ☎ (020) 7402-5221. 59 rooms. *Budget*.

 Royal Sussex Hotel. 78/80 Sussex Gardens. ☎ (020) 7723-7723. 53 rooms. *Budget*.

Regent's Park

Clive Hotel at Hampstead. Primrose Hill Road, Hampstead. ☎ (020) 7586-2233. 102 rooms. *Moderate*.

 Colonnade Hotel. 2 Warrington Crescent. ☎ (020) 7289-2167. 48 rooms. *Moderate*.

 Dorset Square Hotel. 39 Dorset Square. ☎ (020) 7723-7874. 37 rooms. *Moderate*.

 Forte Posthouse Regent's Park. Carburton Street. ☎ (020) 7388-2300. 🖳 www.posthouse-hotels.co.uk. 317 rooms. *Luxury*.

 Langham Court Hotel. 31–35 Langham Street. ☎ (020) 7436-6622. 60 rooms. *Moderate*.

 London Regent's Park Hilton. 18 Lodge Road, Saint John's Wood. ☎ (020) 7722-7722. 🖳 www.hilton.com. 359 rooms. *Luxury*.

 Regent's Park Marriott. 128 King Henry's Road. ☎ (020) 7722-7711. 🖳 www.marriott.com. 303 rooms. *Moderate*.

 Regent's Plaza Hotel & Suites. Plaza Parade, Maida Vale. ☎ (020) 7543-6000. 184 rooms. *Luxury*.

 Swiss Cottage Hotel. 4 Adamson Road. ☎ (020) 7722-2281. 63 rooms. *Moderate*.

 White House. Albany Street, Regent's Park. ☎ (020) 7387-1200. 🖳 www.whitehousehotel.co.uk. 561 rooms. *Luxury*.

Soho

The Berners Hotel. 10 Berners Street. ☎ (020) 7636-1629. 217 rooms. *Luxury*.

 Cavendish Saint James Hotel. 81 Jermyn Street, Saint James. ☎ (020) 7930-2111. 250 rooms. *Luxury*.

 Dukes Hotel. 35 Saint James's Place. ☎ (020) 7491-4840. 65 rooms. *Luxury*.

 Holiday Inn Mayfair. 3 Berkeley Street. ☎ (020) 7493-8282. 🖳 www.holiday-inn.com. 185 rooms. *Luxury*.

 Hospitality Inn Piccadilly. 39 Coventry Street. ☎ (020) 7930-4033. 97 rooms. *Moderate*.

 Le Meridien Piccadilly. 21 Piccadilly. ☎ (020) 7734-8000. 266 rooms. *Luxury*.

 Radisson Edwardian Hampshire. 31–36 Leicester Square. ☎ (020) 7839-9399. 🖳 www.radisson.com. 124 rooms. *Luxury*.

 Radisson Edwardian Pastoria Hotel. 3–6 Saint Martin's Street, Leicester Square. ☎ (020) 7930-8641. 🖳 www.radisson.com. 58 rooms. *Luxury*.

 Rathbone Hotel. Rathbone Street. ☎ (020) 7636-2001. 72 rooms. *Luxury*.

 Regent Palace Hotel. Piccadilly Circus. ☎ (020) 7734-7000. 887 rooms. *Moderate*.

 Ritz Hotel. 150 Piccadilly. ☎ (020) 7493-8181. 🖳 www.theritzhotel.co.uk. 130 rooms. *Luxury*.

Royal Trafalgar Thistle Hotel. Whitcomb Street. ☎ (020) 7930-4477. 108 rooms. *Luxury.*

Shaftesbury Hotel. 65–73 Shaftesbury Avenue. ☎ (020) 7434-4200. 64 rooms. *Moderate.*

Stafford Hotel. 16 Saint James's Place. ☎ (020) 7493-0111. 74 rooms. *Luxury.*

Waterloo

Novotel London Waterloo. 113 Lambeth Road. ☎ (020) 7793-1010. 187 rooms. *Moderate.*

Westminster

Central House Hotel. 37–41 Belgrave Road. ☎ (020) 7834-8036. 50 rooms. *Moderate.*

Corona Hotel. 87–89 Belgrave Road, Victoria. ☎ (020) 7828-9279. 52 rooms. *Budget.*

Dolphin Square Hotel. Dolphin Square. ☎ (020) 7834-3800. 51 rooms. *Luxury.*

Quality Eccleston Hotel. Eccleston Square. ☎ (020) 7834-8042. 115 rooms. *Moderate.*

Rochester Hotel. 69 Vincent Square. ☎ (020) 7828-6611. 80 rooms. *Moderate.*

Saint James Court Hotel. 41–54 Buckingham Gate. ☎ (020) 7834-6655. 389 rooms. *Luxury.*

Sidney Hotel. 76 Belgrave Road. ☎ (020) 7834-2738. 52 rooms. *Budget.*

Stakis London Saint Ermin's Hotel. Caxton Street. ☎ (020) 7222-7888. 283 rooms. *Luxury.*

22 Jermyn Street. 22 Jermyn Street. ☎ (020) 7734-2353. 18 rooms. *Luxury.*

Winchester Hotel. 17 Belgrave Road. ☎ (020) 7828-2972. 18 rooms. *Moderate.*

Major Hotel Booking Agencies

Check these companies for package tours and special assistance on trips to London and the United Kingdom.

Abercrombie & Kent International. Oak Brook, Illinois. ☎ (800) 323-7308. 🖳 www.abercrombiekent.com.

ACFEA Tour Consultants. Edmonds, Washington. ☎ (800) 886-3355. 🖳 www.acfea.com.

Aer Lingus Vacations. New York, New York. ☎ (800) 223-6537. 🖳 www.aerlingus.com/usa00/vacation.html.

AESU. Baltimore, Maryland. ☎ (800) 638-7640. 🖳 www.aesu.com.

All England Car Rentals. Mineola, New York. ☎ (516) 294-6537.

Annemarie Victory Organization. New York, New York. ☎ (212) 486-0353. Luxury tours to Ascot.

Arts & Crafts Tours. New York, New York. ☎ (212) 362-0761, ☎ (800) 742-0730.

Auto Europe. Portland, Maine. ☎ (207) 828-2525, ☎ (800) 223-5555. 🖳 www.autoeurope.com.

AutoVenture. Seattle, Washington. ☎ (206) 624-6033, ☎ (800) 426-7502. 🖳 www.autoventure.com.

Backroads. Berkeley, California. ☎ (510) 527-1555, ☎ (800) 462-2848. 🖳 www.backroads.com.

Barclay International Group. New York, New York. ☎ (800) 845-6636. 🖳 www.barclayweb.com/index.htm.

Batavia Custom Travel. Batavia, Illinois. ☎ (630) 879-2930, ☎ (800) 231-2930. 🖳 www.bataviacustomtravel.com.

BCT Scenic Walking. LaJolla, California. ☎ (760) 431-7306. 🖳 www.bctwalk.com.

Beau Nash International. Thousand Oaks, California. ☎ (805) 375-9957, ☎ (800) 700-6316.

Britain by Choice. Plano, Texas. ☎ (972) 527-8304, ☎ (800) 410-5110.

British Airways. ☎ (800) AIRWAYS. 🖳 www.british-airways.com.

British Airways Tours. ☎ (407) 345-0114, ☎ (800) 359-8722. 💻 www.british-air ways.com/holiday/holiday.shtml.

British Breaks. Middleburg, Virgina. ☎ (540) 687-6971. 💻 www.british breaks.net.

British & European Tours International. Pittsburgh, Pennsylvania. ☎ (412) 650-9495, ☎ (800) 548-5339. 💻 www.beitours.com.

British Midland Airways. ☎ (800) 788-0555. 💻 www.iflybritishmidland.com.

British Network Limited. Upper Carlisle, Pennsylvania. ☎ (800) 274-8583. 💻 www.britishnetworkltd.com.

British Travel International. Elkton, Virginia. ☎ (540) 298-2232, ☎ (800) 327-6097. 💻 www.britishtravel.com.

Caravan Tours. Chicago, Illinois. ☎ (312) 321-9800, ☎ (800) 227-2826. 💻 www.caravantours.com.

Carlson Wagonlit Travel. Minneapolis, Minnesota. 💻 www.carlsontravel.com.

Casterbridge Tours. Staunton, Virginia. ☎ (540) 885-4564, ☎ (800) 522-2398. 💻 www.casterbridgetours.com.

Castles, Cottages & Flats. Boston, Massachusetts. ☎ (617) 742-6030, ☎ (800) 742-6030. 💻 www.castlescottages-flats.com.

CBT Bicycle Tours. Chicago, Illinois. ☎ (800) 736-2453.

Celebration Travel and Tours. Los Angeles, California. ☎ (310) 858-4951.

Celtic International Tours. Albany, New York. ☎ (518) 862-0042, ☎ (800) 833-4373. 💻 www.celtictours.com.

Central Holiday Tours. Jersey City, New Jersey. ☎ (201) 798-5777, ☎ (800) 935-5000. 💻 www.centralh.com.

CIAO! Travel. San Diego, California. ☎ (619) 297-8112, ☎ (800) 942-2426. 💻 www.ciaotravel.com.

Collette Tours. Pawtucket, Rhode Island. ☎ (401) 728-1000, ☎ (800) 832-4656. 💻 www.collettevacations.com.

Concorde Hotels. New York, New York. ☎ (212) 752-3900, ☎ (800) 888-4747. 💻 www.concorde-hotels.com.

Coopersmith's England. Inverness, California. ☎ (415) 669-1914. 💻 www.cooper smiths.com.

Country Cottages. Boca Raton, Florida. ☎ (561) 988-4000. 💻 www.europvacation villas.com.

Country Walkers. Waterbury, Vermont. ☎ (802) 244-1387, ☎ (800) 464-9255. 💻 www.countrywalkers.com.

Cross Country International. Millbrook, New York. ☎ (914) 677-6000, ☎ (800) 828-8768. 💻 www.equestrianvacations.com. Walking and equestrian tours.

Cultural Heritage Alliance. Philadelphia, Pennsylvania. ☎ (215) 923-7060, ☎ (800) 323-4466. 💻 www.cha-tours.com. Organized European tours for teachers and students.

Cunard Lines. New York, New York. ☎ (800) 528-6273. 💻 www.cunardline.com.

Distinctive Journeys International. Chicago, Illinois. ☎ (312) 922-5227. 💻 www.distinctivejourneys.com.

Edwards & Edwards Global Tickets. New York, New York. ☎ (212) 332-2435. West End theater tickets including midweek discount seats.

English Lakeland Ramblers. New York, New York. ☎ (212) 505-1020, ☎ (800) 724-8801. 💻 www.ramblers.com.

Equitour Holidays. Dubois, Wyoming. ☎ (307) 455-3363, ☎ (800) 545-0019. 💻 www.ridingtours.com.

Eurocruises USA. New York, New York. ☎ (212) 691-2099, ☎ (800) 688-3876.

EuroDollar Rent a Car. Los Angeles, California. ☎ (310) 645-9333, ☎ (800) 800-6000.

Europe by Car. New York, New York. ☎ (212) 581-3040, ☎ (800) 223-1516. 💻 www.europebycar.com.

Europe Train Tours. Mamaroneck, New York. ☎ (845) 758-1777, ☎ (800) 551-2085. 💻 www.etttours.com/europe.html.

European Waterways. New York, New York. ☎ (212) 688-9489, ☎ (800) 217-4447. 🖳 www.europeanwaterways.com.

Expo Garden Tours. Redding, Connecticut. ☎ (860) 567-0322, ☎ (800) 448-2685. 🖳 www.expogardentours.com/tours.

Farnum & Christ. Bristol, Tennessee. ☎ (423) 652-2048, ☎ (800) 366-2048. 🖳 www.farnum-christ.com.

Flying Wheels Travel. Owatonna, Minnesota. ☎ (507) 451-5005, ☎ (800) 535-6790. 🖳 www.flyingwheelstravel.com. Tours for wheelchair-bound.

Four Seasons Villas. Marblehead, Massachusetts. ☎ (781) 639-1055, ☎ (800) 338-0474. 🖳 www.fourseasonsvillas.com.

Global Home Network. Herndon, Virginia. ☎ (703) 318-7081, ☎ (800) 528-3549. 🖳 www.globalhomenetwork.com.

Globus & Cosmos. Littleton, Colorado. ☎ (303) 797-2800, ☎ (800) 221-0090. 🖳 www.globusandcosmos.com.

Golden Tulip Hotels International. New York, New York. ☎ (212) 220-6588, ☎ (800) 344-1212. 🖳 www.goldentulip.com.

Golf International, Inc. New York, New York. ☎ (212) 986-9176, ☎ (800) 833-1389. 🖳 www.golfinternational.com.

Golfpac. Altamonte Springs, Florida. ☎ (407) 260-2288, ☎ (800) 523-0007. 🖳 www.golfpactravel.com.

Grand Circle Travel. Boston, Massachusetts. ☎ (617) 350-7500, ☎ (800) 221-2610. 🖳 www.gct.com. Travel for seniors.

Grand Heritage Hotels. Annapolis, Maryland. ☎ (800) 437-4824. 🖳 www.grand heritage.com.

Grande Hotels & Resorts. Sarasota, Florida. ☎ (941) 927-2999, ☎ (800) 468-3750. 🖳 www.grandehotels.com.

Grasshopper Golf Tours. Glen Ellyn, Illinois. ☎ (630) 858-1660, ☎ (800) 654-8712.

Holiday Autos. Upland, California. ☎ (909) 949-1737, ☎ (800) 422-7737. 🖳 www.holidayautos.co.uk.

Holley World Tours. Millbrae, California. ☎ (650) 697-0230, ☎ (800) 652-7847.

Hometours International. Knoxville, Tennessee. ☎ (865) 690-8484, ☎ (800) 367-4668. 🖳 thor.he.net/~hometour/link1.htm.

Hotel London Guide. London. 🖳 www.hotellondon.com.

In Quest of the Classics. Temecula, California. ☎ (909) 302-6488, ☎ (800) 221-5246. 🖳 www.iqotc.com/services.html.

In the English Manner. Atlanta, Georgia. ☎ (404) 231-5837. 🖳 www.english-man ner.co.uk.

In the English Manner. Los Angeles, California. ☎ (213) 629-1811, ☎ (800) 422-0799. 🖳 www.english-manner.co.uk.

Insight International Tours. Boston, Massachusetts. ☎ (617) 482-2000.

International Travel & Resorts. New York, New York. ☎ (212) 476-9463, ☎ (800) 223-9815.

Intropa International/USA. Bellaire, Texas. ☎ (800) 468-7672. 🖳 www.intropa-dmc.at/home.html.

Jetset Tours. Los Angeles, California. ☎ (800) 638-3273. 🖳 www.jetsettours.com.

Jody Lexow Yacht Charters. Newport, Rhode Island. ☎ (401) 849-1112, ☎ (800) 662-2628. 🖳 jodylexowyachtcharters.com.

Josephine Barr. Kenilworth, Illinois. ☎ (847) 251-4110, ☎ (800) 323-5463. 🖳 www.jobarrhotels.com.

Kemwel Holiday Autos. Harrison, New York. ☎ (914) 835-5454, ☎ (800) 678-0678. 🖳 www.kemwel.com.

Kenning Car Rental. Fort Lauderdale, Florida. ☎ (954) 566-7111, ☎ (800) 227-8990. 🖳 www.britishtravel.com/britishtravel/kenning.htm.

Kesher Tours Inc. New York, New York. ☎ (212) 481-3721, ☎ (800) 847-0700. 🖳 www.keshertours.com.

Le Boat. Hackensack, New Jersey. ☎ (201) 236-2333, ☎ (800) 992-0291. 🖳 www.leboat.com.

Legend Tours. San Diego, California. ☎ (619) 293-7040, ☎ (800) 333-6114. 🖳 www.legendtours.com.

Lismore Tours. New York, New York. ☎ (212) 685-0100, ☎ (800) 547-6673.

London Bed & Breakfast. San Diego, California. ☎ (800) 852-2632. 🖳 www.londonbandb.com.

London Bed & Breakfast Agency. London. ☎ (020) 7586-2768. 🖳 www.londonbb.com.

London Guest Suites. Los Angeles, California. ☎ (323) 876-7726, ☎ (800) 664-5663. 🖳 www.londonguestsuites.com.

London Theatre & More. Dallas, Texas. ☎ (214) 328-3844, ☎ (800) 683-0799. 🖳 www.londontheatreandmore.com.

Lord Addison Travel. Peterborough, New Hampshire. ☎ (603) 924-8407, ☎ (800) 326-0170. 🖳 www.lordaddison.com.

Lynott Tours. New York, New York. ☎ (212) 760-0101, ☎ (800) 221-2474. 🖳 www.lynotttours.com.

McFarland Limited. Athens, Georgia. ☎ (706) 543-6737, ☎ (800) 437-2687. 🖳 www.mcfhotels.com.

Maupintour. Lawrence, Kansas. ☎ (785) 843-1211, ☎ (800) 255-4266. 🖳 www.maupintour.com.

MJK Tours. Portland, Oregon. ☎ (503) 224-8001, ☎ (800) 659-9723. 🖳 www.mjktours.com.

Morgantown Travel. Morgantown, West Virginia. ☎ (304) 292-8471, ☎ (800) 637-0782.

Mountain Travel Sobek. El Cerrito, California. ☎ (510) 527-8100, ☎ (800) 227-2384. 🖳 www.mtsobek.com.

National Car Rental/Interrent. Minneapolis, Minnesota. ☎ (612) 830-2121, ☎ (800) 227-7368. 🖳 www.nationalcar.com.

Owenoak International. Darien, Connecticut. ☎ (800) 426-4498. 🖳 www.owenoak.com. Deluxe travel.

Preferred Hotels & Resorts. Chicago, Illinois. ☎ (312) 913-0400, ☎ (800) 323-7500. 🖳 www.preferredhotels.com.

Prestige Villas. Southport, Connecticut. ☎ (203) 254-1302, ☎ (800) 336-0080.

Pride of Britain. Kenilworth, Illinois. ☎ (800) 987-7433. 🖳 www.prideofbritainhotels.com.

Radisson Edwardian Hotels. New York, New York. ☎ (800) 333-3333. 🖳 www.radisson.com.

Rail Europe/BritRail. Harrison, New York. ☎ (914) 682-2999. ☎ (888) 274-8724 in U.S., ☎ (800) 555-2748 in Canada. 🖳 www.raileurope.com.

Relais & Châteaux. New York, New York. ☎ (212) 856-0115, ☎ (800) 735-2478. 🖳 www.relaischateaux.com.

Roamer Tours. Reading, Pennsylvania. ☎ (610) 376-6361, ☎ (800) 422-8540.

The Royal Garden Hotel. Plano, Texas. ☎ (800) 987-9317. 🖳 www.royalgdn.co.uk.

Sarova Hotels. Baltimore, Maryland. ☎ (410) 563-6331, ☎ (800) 424-2862. 🖳 www.sarova.co.uk.

Savoy Group of Hotels. Plano, Texas. ☎ (800) 637-2869. 🖳 www.savoy-group.co.uk/main.html.

Scandinavian Seaways. Fort Lauderdale, Florida. ☎ (954) 491-7909, ☎ (800) 533-3755. 🖳 www.scansea.com.

Scots-American Travel. Harrington Park, New Jersey. ☎ (800) 247-7268. 🖳 www.scotsamerican.com.

Sea Gate Travel Agency. New York, New York. ☎ (212) 404-8800, ☎ (800) 732-2244. 🖳 www.seagatetravel.com.

Showline Tours. New York, New York. ☎ (212) 661-2621.

London Glossary

English	American
ACCOMMODATIONS	
en suite	private bathroom
first floor	second floor
flannel	facecloth or washcloth
ground floor	first floor
half-tester	semi four-poster bed
to let	for hire
singles	twin beds
RESTAURANTS	
afters	dessert
aubergine	eggplant
bangers	sausages
bill	the check
biscuit	cookie or cracker
bucks fizz	mimosa
chips	french fries
courgettes	zucchini
crisps	potato chips
faggots	meatballs
jacket potato	baked potato
jam	jelly
jelly	Jell-O
mash	mashed potatoes

English	*American*
RESTAURANTS (continued)	
my shout	my round
off-licence	liquor store
spotted dick	steamed suet pudding
sweets	candy
TRAVEL	
bonnet	hood
boot	trunk
car park	parking lot
coach	bus
dual carriageway	two-way divided highway
give way	yield
High Street	Main Street
lay-by	road shoulder
lorry	truck
petrol	gas
return	round-trip
roundabout	traffic circle
single	one-way ticket
subway	pedestrian tunnel
tube or *underground*	subway
MISCELLANEOUS	
chemist	drugstore or pharmacy
engaged	busy
jumble sale	yard sale
jumper	sweater
lift	elevator
pants	underwear
plaster	Band-Aid
stalls	orchestra seats
tights	pantyhose
torch	flashlight
trainers	sneakers
trousers	pants
way out	exit

Weights, Measures, and Distance

Linear Measure
One meter is equal to about 39 inches; a meter is divided into millimeters ($\frac{1}{1000}$th of a meter) and centimeters ($\frac{1}{100}$th of a meter).

Millimeters to Inches
Multiply millimeters times .0394 to convert to inches.

1	.039 inch
100	3.94 inches

Inches to Millimeters
Multiply inches times 25.4 to convert to millimeters.

1	25.4 millimeters
12	.304 meter (304 millimeters)

Meters to Feet
Multiply meters times 3.2808 to convert to feet.

1	3.28 feet (39.37 inches)

Feet to Meters
Multiply feet times .3048 to convert to meters.

1	0.3048 meters (304 millimeters)

Meters to Yards
Multiply meters times 1.094 to convert to yards.

1	1.094 yards

Yards to Meters
Multiply yards times .914 to convert to meters.

1	0.914 meters

Distance

Kilometers to Miles
Multiply kilometers times .621 to convert to miles, or divide kilometers by 8 and then multiply the result by 5.

1	0.621
10	6.214
100	62.137

Miles to Kilometers
Multiply the mileage times 1.6 to convert to kilometers.

1	1.609
10	16.039
100	160.934

Capacity

One gallon of liquid is equal to about 4.5 liters. *Liters* is spelled *litres* in England. Here are some conversions:

Liters to U.S. Gallons
Multiply liters times .2642 to convert to gallons.

1	0.22
10	2.2
100	21.998

Quarts to Liters
Multiply liquid quarts times .9463 to convert to liters.

1	0.946

Pints to Liters
Multiply liquid pints times .4732 to convert to liters.

1	0.473

U.S. Gallons to Liters
Multiply gallons times 3.785 to convert to liters.

1	3.785
5	18.925
10	37.85

Weight

Kilograms to Pounds
Multiply kilograms times 2.205 to convert to pounds.

1	2.205
10	22.046
100	220.464

Pounds to Kilograms
Multiply pounds times .454 to convert to kilograms.

1	0.454
10	4.536
100	45.359

Clothing and Shoe Sizes

Women's dresses and skirts are two sizes bigger in the United Kingdom, so an American size 8 would be a 10. Men's suit, shirt, and sock measurements are the same in Britain as in the United States.

Special Offers to *Econoguide* Readers

Look to your left, look to your right. One of you three people on vacation is paying the regular price for airfare, hotels, meals, and shopping. One is paying premium price for a less-than-first-rate package. And one is paying a deeply discounted special rate.

Which one would you rather be?

In this book you've learned about strategies to obtain the lowest prices on airfare, the best times to take a trip, and ideas on how to negotiate just about every element of travel.

And now, we're happy to present a special section of discount coupons for *Econoguide* readers.

All of the offers represent real savings. Be sure to read the coupons carefully, though, because of exclusions during holiday periods and other fine print.

The author and publisher of this book do not endorse any of the businesses whose coupons appear here, and the presence of a coupon in this section does not in any way affect the author's opinions expressed in this book.

Car Rental Certificate

$5	**Off Economy**	**$15 Off Midsize**
$10	**Off Compact**	**$20 Off Full Size**

Valid on any rental at any of the 4,000 locations that we service.
Minimum rental period is seven days. Certificate must be redeemed through Auto Europe in the US.
Prior to departure this certificate cannot be compounded with any other discount and only one discount offer
can be applied per reservation. Offer valid through 12/31/02 and subject to change without notice.

Compliments of **auto⊕europe**®

Contact your travel agent
(800) 223-5555
www.autoeurope.com

Expires 12/31/02

LN02-01

Car Rental Certificate
5% Off Long-Term Leasing

Receive 5% off any long term lease of 30 days or more

Certificate must be redeemed through Auto Europe in the USA. Prior to departure this
certificate cannot be compounded with any other discount and only one discount offer can be
applied per reservation. Offer valid through 12/31/02 and subject to change without notice.

Compliments of **auto⊕europe**®

Contact your travel agent
(800) 223-5555
www.autoeurope.com

Expires 12/31/02

LN02-02

Car Rental Certificate
Free cellular phone rental
with any weekly midsize or larger car rental

Offer applies to rental charges only. Any applicable air charges,
activation fees, or delivery charges are excluded.

Certificate must be redeemed through Auto Europe in the US. Prior to departure this certificate cannot be
compounded with any other discount and only one discount offer can be applied per reservation.
Offer valid through 12/31/02 and subject to change without notice.

Compliments of **auto⊕europe**®

Contact your travel agent
(800) 223-5555
www.autoeurope.com

Expires 12/31/02

LN02-03

Apartments in London
An alternative to high-priced hotels

8% Off

Economy to deluxe • By the night, week, or month • 3-night minimum
• Studio to four-bedroom apartments, all in central London, near Underground •
All have kitchens, color TV, and private bath

Call (800) 664-5663 for information and reservations.
www.londonguestsuites.com
E-mail info@londonguestsuites.com

LONDON GUEST SUITES

Full Service Apartments

LN02-05   Expires 12/31/02

Quick-Find Index to Attractions

(See also the detailed Contents)